D1366577

AN ARTIFICIAL WILDERNESS

An Artificial Wilderness

Essays on 20th-Century Literature

Sven Birkerts

A NONPAREIL BOOK
David R. Godine, Publisher
BOSTON

This is a Nonpareil Book published in 1990 by
DAVID R. GODINE, PUBLISHER, INC.
Horticultural Hall
300 Massachusetts Avenue
Boston, Massachusetts 02115

Grateful acknowledgment is made to the editors of the following magazines, in which these essays first appeared, some under different titles: *The Boston Review*, "Robert Musil," 1979; *The Boston Review*, "Malcolm Lowry," 1979; *The Boston Review*, "Blaise Cendrars," 1980; *The Boston Review*, "V. S. Naipaul and Derek Walcott," 1980; *The Iowa Review*, "Osip Mandelstam," 1981; *The Iowa Review*, "Lars Gustafsson," 1982; *The Nation*, "Robert Walser," © 1982, The Nation Company, Inc.; "Eugenio Montale" reprinted with permission from *The New York Review of Books*, copyright © 1983, Nyrev, Inc.; "Max Frisch" reprinted with permission from *The New Republic*, copyright © 1983, The New Republic, Inc.; "Umberto Eco" reprinted with permission from *The New Republic*, copyright © 1983, The New Republic, Inc.; *The Iowa Review*, "Walter Benjamin," 1983; *The Nation*, "Salman Rushdie," © 1983, The Nation Company, Inc.; *Michigan Quarterly Review*, "Television: The Medium in the Mass Age," 1983; *The Boston Phoenix*, "Peter Schneider," 1984; *The Boston Phoenix*, "Marguerite Yourcenar," 1984; "Thomas Bernhard" reprinted with permission from *The New Republic*, copyright © 1984, The New Republic, Inc.; *The Boston Phoenix*, "Joseph Roth," 1984; *The Boston Phoenix*, "Cyril Connolly," 1984; *The Boston Phoenix*, "Julio Cortázar," 1984; *The Boston Phoenix*, "Rereading," 1985; "Michel Tournier" reprinted with permission from *The New Republic*, copyright © 1985, The New Republic, Inc.; *The Boston Phoenix*, "George Steiner," 1985; *The Boston Phoenix*, "Marguerite Duras" (part 1), 1985; "Yaakov Shabtai" reprinted with permission from *The New Republic*, copyright © 1985, The New Republic, Inc.; *The Boston Phoenix*, "Gregor von Rezzori," 1985; *The Agni Review*, "Notes from a Confession," 1985; *The Threepenny Review*, "Roger Shattuck," 1985; *Pequod*, "Osip Mandelstam's Armenian Journey," 1985; *The Threepenny Review*, "Erich Heller," 1985; "Heinrich Böll" reprinted with permission from *The New Republic*, copyright © 1986, The New Republic, Inc.; *The Chicago Tribune*, "Marguerite Duras" (part 2), 1986; *The Boston Phoenix*, "Primo Levi," 1986; *The Village Voice*, "Joseph Brodsky," 1986; *The Nation*, "Eva Demski," © 1986, The Nation Company, Inc.; "The School of Gordon Lish" reprinted with permission from *The New Republic*, copyright © 1986, The New Republic, Inc.; *The Boston Phoenix*, "Jorge Luis Borges," 1986; *The Boston Phoenix*, "Docu-fiction," 1986; *Ploughshares*, "An Open Invitation to Extraterrestrials," 1986; *The Boston Review*, "The Leaning Umbrella: A Reflection on Flaubert," 1987; *Pequod*, "Some Notes Concerning the Impossibility of Literary Biography," 1987.

Library of Congress Cataloging in Publication Data

Birkerts, Sven.
An artificial wilderness : essays on 20-century literature / Sven Birkerts.
p. cm.
Reprint. Originally published: New York : Morrow, c1987.
Includes bibliographical references.
ISBN 0-87923-807-0 (pbk.)
1. Literature, Modern—20th century—History and criticism.
I. Title.
[PN771.B47 1989] 89-45387
809′.04—dc20 CIP

First Printing
Printed in the United States of America

For my family and for Lynn

Contents

Introduction

Introductions are the most suspicious of documents. Written last, positioned first, their tone so often reminds me of those self-exonerating explanations of behavior that get concocted for the judge and jury. "Your Honor, I had just stepped out for a quiet cup of tea . . ." The writer asks for indulgence, affirms that the contents, however unruly, belong to a single epoch of sensibility, and so on. But justice usually prevails: the reader turns to these preliminaries last, if at all.

I have been worrying the matter for some time now, looking for the one angle of retrospect that would convert seven years of "occasions" into a single balanced entity. I have come up with this short parable.

A traveler finds that he is lost in a densely overgrown terrain—the underbrush has closed up around him. So he begins chopping with his machete. He works entirely by instinct. In order that he not succumb to despair, he refuses to look back over his shoulder. For hours, days, weeks, he addresses himself to the underbrush directly in front of him.

He makes his way very slowly toward a distant rise. Gradually, almost imperceptibly, the incline lifts him. He keeps chopping, until finally he comes to the top of the hill. Then he stops and turns around. And as he surveys the countryside stretching out below him on every side, he has a peculiar realization. He was not cutting a path to *get* anywhere—he was cutting it just to find out where he was. Now as he looks at the trail at his feet, the trail over which he sweated and cursed, it looks familiar, purposeful. It was. Because of it, he no longer feels lost; he has somehow become a part of the country around him. Impulsively, he decides to give the trail a name.

I can translate this into a more concrete narrative. One day, while I was still an undergraduate at the University of Michigan, I walked into a secondhand bookshop in downtown Ann Arbor. It was a dusty, sour-smelling place called The Wooden Spoon. I bother giving the name and location because something decisive happened there: I caught a disease. How else to describe it? Before I stepped in, I was a bookishly inclined college kid; when I came out I was like a convert to a religious sect. Suddenly nothing mattered so much as acquiring books, reading books, being around books. I began to spend all of my free time at bookstores and rummage sales. Every night I returned to my apartment with a knapsack full of new "finds." I had not the slightest idea of where this mania might be leading me.

I passed most of the decade after college working in bookstores: new, used, rare. I even ran a mail-order business, buying and selling literary first editions. And I read. Constantly, obsessively: I chewed my sandwich with an open book in my lap. For this was the substance of the revelation I'd had that afternoon in The Wooden Spoon: that there existed a whole universe of writers and books that my college syllabus did not so much as brush up against. Every book I read sent me out after a dozen others. Henry Miller's *Books in My Life* led me to John Cowper Powys, Jean Giono, Blaise Cendrars; Cendrars led inexorably to Rémy de Gourmont and Rabelais. Then there were contemporary writers of every description. The artistic photomontage covers of Grove Press and New Directions lured me toward the European existentialists. I had scarcely begun to ingest Sartre and Genet when the South American "boom" arrived: García Márquez, Cortázar, Fuentes . . . It was not a restful, satisfying period. I was confused. With every page I turned, I felt that I was losing ground. I longed for calm retrospection, not to read but to *have read.*

I think of my distress in this period as being book related. But there were deeper causes. These were the anxious seventies, and the newspapers that I sold across the counter demanded a very different kind of reading. Headlines told of arms proliferation, rising oil prices, inflation, nuclear meltdown, ecological panic at Love Canal, hostages and assassinations. When friends confided that they were nervous about "the world," I didn't have to ask them what they meant. I was in the same state. I kept looking back to Auden's lines from "September 1, 1939":

> Waves of anger and fear
> Circulate over the bright
> And darkened lands of the earth
> Obsessing our private lives;

and I derived what solace I could from the final stanza:

> Defenceless under the night
> Our world in stupor lies;
> Yet, dotted everywhere,
> Ironic points of light
> Flash out wherever the just
> Exchange their messages. . . .

Those "points of light" gradually became the objects of my search. Literature was worth nothing if it could not help us to make sense of our historical circumstance. It was in this period that my hitherto undisciplined reading began to take a direction.

Though I had grown up on a steady diet of American moderns—Salinger, Heller, Mailer, Bellow, Percy, and others—I found that I was growing more and more dissatisfied with the local product. In this most frightening epoch, American writers seemed to have retreated into a perverse kind of hibernation. Self-consuming metafiction (Coover, Barth, Barthelme), genre subversion (Vonnegut, Doctorow, Vidal), docu-fiction (Mailer, Capote), numb affectlessness (Carver, Beattie)—none of these trends connected me with the larger picture, the world beyond the words.

In my frustration, I began to search out translated works by writers like Czeslaw Milosz, Max Frisch, Milan Kundera, Heinrich Böll, Marguerite Yourcenar, and Michel Tournier. I liked the exotic-sounding names, the aura of obscurity—I won't deny that. But what I discovered when I began to read was a powerful sense of confirmation. Translations or no, here were books that dealt with themes and subjects that mattered. They offered perspectives that allowed me to make some sense of my own disquiet. Maybe because the authors had known more directly the brutalities of history—had suffered—they were able to break that terrible membrane of *self.* Their sentences seemed to lead me out toward things, places, and events. Many—most—were bleak in outlook, but somehow the very fact of their writing assured me that we still moved within the realm of meaning. I realized that the truth, however pessimistic, was more fortifying to the spirit than detached stylistic virtuosity. As Shakespeare wrote: "The worst is not so long as we can say 'This is the worst.'"

Every reader knows how serendipity works—coincidentally encountered allusions open hidden doors, formerly peripheral names become new centers of interest. These various postwar European writers eventually brought me around to the masters of an earlier generation. It was a great shock to find that my own forebodings and preoccupations were inscribed in the prose of Robert Musil, Walter Benjamin, and Osip Mandelstam. I started to understand that the social and political turmoil of our times was not just a coda to the Second World War; the root system extended at least as far as the beginning of the century. The work of these writers bore witness to the collapse of a whole civilization. We were still living among the reverberations. My stray intuitions began to take on a more explanatory shape.

I wrote my first essay on Robert Musil. The urge to explore my thoughts in a more formal manner had been building up for some time. Musil supplied the pretext. I simply could not believe that his novels, especially the three-volume *Man Without Qualities,* were out of print and unknown. What could be more pertinent to our age than his icily ironic dissection of a culture on the brink? I wanted to bring the news to readers.

I had not expected essay writing to be so satisfying. I loved the gathering, sifting, and pondering. What's more, reading with the goal of writing had a galvanizing effect on reading itself. As soon as I finished the Musil essay, I started casting about for other projects. I had a long list of neglected favorites: Malcolm Lowry, Blaise Cendrars, Max Frisch . . . As it had been with books, now it was with essays: every subject created around itself a web of future possibilities. I was the traveler lost in the underbrush. Chopping.

R. P. Blackmur once described criticism as "the formal discourse of an amateur." I like the implicit tension between "formal" and "amateur," as well as the latitude that the definition permits. For these essays are finally the arguments and enthusiasms of a reader. An amateur. They advance no strict program, defend no theoretical fortification. I write about what has moved or affected me as a reader.

This is not to say, however, that I have no interest in the critical heritage or in current debates. On the contrary. My responses have been goaded at every turn by the example of more vigorously polemical or systematic critics. The New Critics have shown me what can be done with close reading, and Marxist critics have convinced me that social and political assumptions underlie even the most fugitive expressions. Structuralists and poststructuralists have stirred me up in other ways, as I will explain. So if I finally hew to no one line, it's not because I can't decide between competing "isms." It's rather that I can't, as a reader, make peace with any discipline that promotes its own interests over those of the text in question. A deconstructionist reading of Rousseau is finally more about deconstruction than about Rousseau. It may be that an insistence on the primacy of the work is what defines the amateur.

Still, I don't want to make my position sound too naïve. I have, for example, deep disagreements with the structuralist and poststructuralist methodologies. Rooted as they are in the premises of Saussurean linguistics, both propose that the correspondence between language and the world is ultimately arbitrary, a matter of convention. Any system of differentiated signs could serve us just as well. This may not seem like much, but the implications turn out to be devastating. For if language is indeterminate at its foundation level, then all linguistic production, literature included, rests upon nothing more substantial than a system of relative distinctions. In the end, this not only permits texts to be exposed, and their falsely privileged "signifiers" to be unmasked, it *encourages* such operations.

Seen in this light, poststructuralism turns out to be the inverse of humanism. Where humanism was, broadly speaking, constructive in its outlook (cultures were felt to progress, wisdom and values could be transmitted from generation to generation), poststructuralism severs its object from historical context in order to take it apart. Maybe cultures get what they deserve. It's hard not to see this professedly neutral practice as a masked expression of rage, an assault upon a credo that was powerless against barbarism and collapse.

One also hears a great deal these days about something called postmodernism. Though it is not a critical theory so much as a rubric for a collective sense of cultural impasse, it shares with poststructuralism a cynical rejection of the humanist assumptions. Postmodernism contends that everything has been done, that all artistic modes and genres have been exhausted. Innovation is no longer seen as possible. Style, therefore, is no longer bound to historical context. The artist (architect, composer, writer) is free to perform exercises in combination. A classical pediment can be set against a rococo facade; a minor or pop-culture genre, like the pulp or the mystery, can be "rewritten" into literary acceptability. Art is to be viewed more as an arena for ingenuity than as an expressive necessity.

If there were nothing but recent American fiction to go by, I would almost have to cede the postmodernists their point. Fortunately, there is more to contemporary literature than is dreamed of in that philosophy. Indeed, I believe that the writers discussed in this book give vigorous lie to the argument from exhaustion. But we have to look beyond our borders. For it is no coincidence that most of the authors are from cultures that feel, or have recently felt, the sharp pressure of history. Combinatory exercises, not to mention "indeterminacies" and "sliding signifiers," can't matter much to the writer who would speak of hunger, terror, or the ongoing incidence of evil.

I see now that my choice of subjects has everything to do with the life we have all been living in the last decades. The essays are a kind of thinking by proxy, a way of testing perspectives. The recurrent questions are simple in the asking, but they are no less daunting for that. How did humanism—the faith in an ongoing human enterprise—fail? What has come in the wake of that failure? What are the grounds for hope, if any?

The reader will find that I sustain a guarded and much-qualified optimism with respect to these ultimate questions. The visions of the individual writers are often grim, but their resourcefulness, their determination to make coherent artistic statements, is heartening. Though they vary tremendously in manner and method—compare Primo Levi's reportorial sanity with the elaborate gnostic symbolism of Michel Tournier—the sum of their expressions makes me believe that the future can still be shaped.

If my experience with Musil is any indication, however, many of these works have yet to break the culture barrier. Despite the efforts of essayists like Susan Sontag, V. S. Pritchett, George Steiner, and John Updike, all of whom bring word of important foreign writers, the names seldom elicit more than a shrug. There is, as yet, no forum here for the reception of serious international writing. When Czeslaw Milosz won the 1980 Nobel Prize for literature, for example, American readers were taken aback. *Czeslaw Milosz?* I was working in a bookstore in Cambridge at the time, and my co-workers and I fielded questions all day long. We had to tell customers that most of Milosz's books were out of print. The same thing happened when Elias Canetti won the prize, and again with Jaroslav Seifert and Claude Simon. Ezra Pound's citing of Kipling (in "Provincialism the Enemy") puts the business concisely: "Transportation is civilization."

Part of the problem, I think, involves the secondary status of translated texts. Writers from other languages are felt to be the property of those who can read them in the original. That is, of native speakers and academics. This is absurd, of course. If we confined ourselves to our area of linguistic competence, none of us would see past our noses. But the taboo persists. Department scholars publish articles in professional journals while the lay reader remains unaware. The better magazines and book supplements try to keep up with the more visible new releases. But without a more sustained follow-up attention, the writer (often blessed with an unpronounceable name) disappears in the cataract of printed matter. Not everyone can be rescued by the Nobel Prize.

Transportation *is* civilization. And some transportation is taking place. For one thing, writers themselves are learning from the translated works of other cultures. As García Márquez once apprenticed himself to versions of Faulkner, so young American writers are now learning tricks from Gregory Rabassa's renderings of García Márquez. The nutrients trickle into the bloodstream. Reading Milan Kundera in English is, arguably, as useful to the aspiring stylist as a study of Hemingway, Carver, or Pynchon. The eventual internationalization of literature seems inevitable, but the process could be much accelerated.

I am encouraged by the willingness of American publishers to keep taking risks on literary imports. The hope, of course, is to come up with another *Tin Drum, A Hundred Years of Solitude, The Name of the Rose, The Lover* . . . The consequence for the reader is a vastly expanded field of choices. In the last few years alone, we have seen the issue of nearly all of Tournier, Bernhard, Duras, Yourcenar, Frisch, and Levi, to name just a few. Transportation is civilization. Every exchange across cultures between writer and reader betters our chances; the barriers of political rhetoric are rendered that much less absolute.

In the opening stanza of "The Shield of Achilles," Auden has Thetis inspecting the shield that Hephaestos has wrought for her warrior son:

She looked over his shoulder
    For vines and olive trees,
Marble well-governed cities,

And ships upon untamed seas,
But there on the shining metal
His hands had put instead
An artificial wilderness
And a sky like lead.

The hope of these essays is that the smithy's vision can be undone.

AN
ARTIFICIAL
WILDERNESS

PART I

German-Language Fiction

Robert Musil
(1880–1942)

Robert Walser
(1878–1956)

Joseph Roth
(1894–1939)

Max Frisch
(1911—)

Gregor von Rezzori
(1914—)

Heinrich Böll
(1917–1985)

Thomas Bernhard
(1931–1989)

Peter Schneider
(1940—)

Eva Demski
(1944—)

Though they share German as a literary language, these nine writers are of Austrian, Swiss, central European, and German origins and represent three distinct generations.

Musil, Walser, and Roth had all reached maturity by the time of the outbreak of World War I. Musil and Roth took the self-destruction of the Austro-Hungarian Empire as the core subject of their fiction. Two more-different responses, however, could not be imagined. Musil, aggressively ironic, dubbed the faltering empire "Kakania" (literally, "Shit-land"); his gargantuan novel The Man Without Qualities *satirized preparations for a commemorative "Austrian Year." Roth struck a far more elegiac note in his* Radetzky March, *and near the end of his life he wrote: "I am a conservative and a Catholic, consider Austria my fatherland, and desire the return of my Empire." He drank himself to death in Paris in 1939.*

The writers of the next generation, though all abhorring Nazism and war, contend with their history in diverse ways. Böll, a renegade Catholic, realistically documents the effects of battle and privation upon the lives of ordinary German citizens. Rezzori, often far more expressionistic in his means, vents a harsh invective; his main target is the opportunistic society of postwar Germany. Frisch bypasses the larger historical panorama in order to probe what might be called the moral anatomy of the individual.

Thomas Bernhard is not interested in these subtle ambiguities. His novels, the darkest in all contemporary literature, rehearse the repetitions of an existence that has become unendurable.

Peter Schneider and Eva Demski, both born in Germany in the 1940's, concern themselves with the complexities of political affiliation in a postwar Germany. Schneider focuses upon a divided Berlin and examines the ways that the Wall has become internalized by its inhabitants. Demski's Dead Alive *traces out the implications of terrorist action in 1970's Frankfurt. Both writers show that there are no simple or uncompromised courses of action left.*

Robert Musil

To the memory of Paul Mattick

He hated people who could not live up to Nietzsche's words about "suffering hunger in the spirit for the sake of the truth"—all those who give up half-way, the faint-hearted, the soft, those who comfort their souls with flummery about the soul, who feed it, because the intellect allegedly gives it stones instead of bread, on religious, philosophic and fictitious emotions, which are like buns soaked in milk.

—ULRICH in *The Man Without Qualities*

The career of Robert Musil excelled in disappointments and bitter ironies. Since his death—in exile and poverty—these disappointments and ironies have lived on; only now they are visited upon his readers, or more accurately, his prospective readers. For with the exception of a paperback reissue of *Young Törless* (1955),* Musil's first published book, and the first volume (1953) of his gigantic, albeit unfinished, *The Man Without Qualities,* his works are difficult to find in this country. Volumes II and III of the latter work were published in the late 1950's only to be remaindered and, finally,

*A date in parentheses refers to a work's first publication in the United States, unless otherwise noted.

pulped. For a time it was possible to obtain a volume of his stories, published variously as *Five Women* and *Tonka and Other Stories* (1966), but even a glowing preface by the likes of Frank Kermode was not sufficient to keep the book afloat in the treacherous waters of public demand. (The book was reissued in 1986.) It seems that even now, decades after his death, the curse of obscurity still clings to Robert Musil.

If this were not indignity enough, there is still the fact that much of what Musil wrote waits to be translated. Two plays, *Die Schwärmer* and *Vinzenz oder Die Freundlin Bedeutender Männer,* and a prose collection, *Nachlass zu Lebzeiten,* lie undisturbed in their native language. The English title of this last might be: *The Posthumous Papers of a Living Author,* and is Musil's comment upon his own obscurity. He was himself bitter and incredulous, and he deeply resented the reputations achieved by writers like Thomas Mann and Hermann Broch. Musil could only assume that history would vindicate him and that he would be discovered by readers in the future. His assumption was not entirely in vain. Musil can claim more dedicated readers today than he could in his lifetime. But even so, the numbers are small. To the extent that this is owing to the neglect of the publishing industry, there is just no excuse. Such neglect is hardly excusable where lesser authors are concerned. But Musil is not a lesser author. He is one of the few great moderns, one of the handful who ventured to confront the issues that shape and define our time. To use a modern metaphor: he has a range and a striking capacity every bit as great as that of Mann, Joyce, or Beckett. The time is right for getting the whole of Musil translated and into print and for starting in on the work of clarifying his particular importance.

We must linger a moment longer on the subject of ironies and disappointments. Columbia University Press has issued Frederick G. Peters's *Robert Musil, Master of the Hovering Life* (1978). The book is subtitled *A Study of the Major Fiction,* and as such it fulfills its claims competently, if not always imaginatively: Peters goes through the works one by one, moving at all times with a narrowly adjusted focus and a professorial gait. Appropriate analogies from Kierkegaard, Nietzsche, and the psychoanalytic thinkers (especially Jung) are supplied, and they help us to understand the range of Musil's concerns. But we do not get any closer to the man, and we come away with little sense of what his struggle for vision involved. The impression one has is that the same tactics could have been applied to any other modern writer, with only a requisite adjustment of relevant theories and textual data. Occasionally, though, Peters will quote from Musil himself. It is at these moments that we glimpse the disparity between the writer's and the critic's enterprises.

Peters discusses, in order, *Young Törless,* the five stories, and *The Man Without Qualities.* Surprisingly, he does not disclose any information about the two plays or *Nachlass zu Lebzeiten.* He dissects Musil's various attempts at reconciling the rational and the mystical. This is a sound approach, perhaps the soundest, and Peters can be credited with the fact that he never takes off into improbable speculation. He is at all times close to his texts. What is interesting, however, at least to the contentious reader, is his final appraisal of *The Man Without Qualities.* While admitting that we cannot know for certain what Musil planned, Peters makes the conjecture (substantiated in part by Musil's own notes) that the quest for reconciliation is doomed. He theorizes further that Musil could not finish the novel for that reason. The opposite view is highly arguable: that Musil *would not* finish so long as he could not find a truthful synthesis. That he was still working on the day he died suggests that he had not given up hope.

What is unfortunate is that the publication of this book will not promote a revival of interest in Musil. This should have been the occasion for a preliminary redress of balances, such as can be effected by a major biographical/critical study. But who can plan a literary revival? Had Peters felt that such a responsibility lay partially in his hands, he might have approached his task differently. He might have attempted the difficult kind of criticism: that which results from deep imaginative penetration into the thought and substance of his subject. But even the opening chapter—which attempts a survey of Musil's life and career—supplies no information that is not already available in one of the few other skeletal accounts of the man. (The most interesting of these is by John Simon and appears as an afterword to the paperback reissue of *Young Törless.*) So, unless we come to the book with a thorough acquaintance with the bulk of Musil's output, we stand to gain very little. The situation is not unlike that of being handed a fancy menu at a restaurant, only to be told that the kitchen is closed.

To what do we owe this state of affairs? Why are we not in the midst of a revision of reputations comparable to that which has recently resulted in the canonization of Walter Benjamin? Musil is difficult, true, but he is no more difficult than any other major writer. The prevailing view is that Musil is the property of a small, self-flattering elite. And such a view, especially when the current of anti-intellectualism is running high, is enough to keep a writer at the margins of demand. Another reason that might be advanced is that his masterwork, *The Man Without Qualities,* is unfinished. But this is not the obstacle it seems. Musil himself acknowledged in a diary entry: "What the story that makes up this novel amounts to is that the story that was supposed to be told in it is not told." The plot is, as it were, a coatrack, a pretext for the play of ideas. We don't read Musil for the story—we read him for his mental ferocity, his humor, and his uncanny grasp of the contradictions of the modern age.

Musil is a philosopher, an aphorist, an essayist. Appropriately enough, Nietzsche is the one figure to whom he repeatedly doffs his hat. We find in both the same impatience, the same determination to stay in motion, and the understanding that the truth is itself a process, its seeker forever embattled. We turn to Musil because he never lies to us and because he never hides from the unsightly implications of a particular thought. The only explanation for our continued neglect is that we are still not ready. His attempted synthesis of rational thought and mysticism is unfamiliar. We are used to an either/or. Musil looks for a way of saying: both.

It is not easy to come to terms with the vastness and refracted density of Musil's work. Its most striking single quality is that any number of contradictory conclusions may be correct, none of them exclusively. Robert Musil was, at various times, a scientist, an engineer, a student of psychology, a logician, and was at all times, in the fiber of his being, a mystic, a moralist, and most significantly, a man who yearned to live beyond the pale of good and evil. His intellectual repertoire is vast; within it, his specific interests and areas of expertise are like so many radii. At the hub is a single obsession: to fathom and depict the psyche in its myriad forms and movements. To understand the meaning of Musil, it is necessary to proceed with generosity and openness of mind. To do so is to be rewarded in a very special way. When one experiences thought in the way that Musil experienced it, one is liable to undergo a revaluation of values. This possibility at once removes the discussion from a strictly literary realm. For Musil was a philosopher in the ancient sense of the word: he was a lover of truth.

In his life, too, Musil defies the customary literary approach. He cannot be pinpointed on the grid of trends, schools, or influences. To begin with, he did not come to literature via literature. He was an emissary from the practical, technical world. He was first a military man, then an engineer and inventor (with a patented chronometer to his credit). Later he sought an academic career, turning his attentions to advanced problems in logic and experimental psychology. His Ph.D. thesis was on the epistemology of Ernst Mach. (Mach's theories on sense impressions were highly influential in Vienna in Musil's time.) Upon completion of his degree, despite a number of offers of university appointments, Musil turned away from academia. He had decided upon writing.

It was not an unambiguous choice. Peters cites the following from Musil:

> A man who is after the truth sets out to be a man of learning; a man who wants to give free play to his subjectivity sets out, perhaps, to be a writer. But what is the man to do who is after something that lies between?

His own answer was to become what he saw as a "master of the hovering life," to navigate freely between the two, ideally embracing both.

Early in the first volume of *The Man Without Qualities,* Ulrich, the central character (and clearly Musil's mouthpiece), reflects upon his reasons for leaving the engineering profession. He says of engineers:

> They revealed themselves to be men who were firmly attached to their drawing boards, who loved the profession and were admi-

rably efficient in it; but to the suggestion that they should apply the audacity of their ideas not to their machines but to themselves they would have reacted much as though they had been asked to use a hammer for the unnatural purpose of murder.

Musil did not become a professional writer without some encouragement. Between the years 1902 and 1906, during the time he was studying at the University of Berlin, he wrote *Young Törless.* The book was published in 1906 and met with some critical acclaim—as well as a certain not undesirable public outrage, this on account of his treatment of adolescent homosexuality. One wonders what Musil would have decided had the silence that faced him in later years greeted him then.

In *Young Törless* we see Musil in his first attempts at the depiction of psychic reality, here as it is manifested in the growth process of a young man at an Austrian military school. Musil himself had attended several such academies; the second, Weisskirchen, in Moravia, was the same academy Rilke had attended several years earlier. He attempts the difficult, for his subject matter is confusion and uncertainty and calls for extreme delicacy. Joyce attempted the same thing in his *Portrait of the Artist as a Young Man.* It is an index of their difference that Joyce should choose a religious crisis as the pivotal event, while Musil should turn his scrutiny upon the psychosexual crisis.

Musil's treatment of homosexuality and sexual debasement, while not explicit in the current sense of the word, was nevertheless characterized by an unapologetic directness. Musil is rarely given the credit he deserves with respect to his boldness and originality in sexual matters. The borderline experience—anything, in fact, that savored of the taboo—attracted him. This fascination is evident in various permutations in the stories and finds its apotheosis in the incest obsessions of the third volume of *The Man Without Qualities.*

Musil pointed out to the critics of *Young Törless* that the intimated homosexuality was actually incidental to the novel; Basani, the victim of the various debasements, could just as well have been a woman and the bisexuality could have been replaced by another "perversion." The important thing was, of course, the presentation of psychic turmoil in the experience of Törless. What is striking about the novel is that the narrative is mainly internal, that its concern is unrelentingly particular, and that it nevertheless succeeds in sustaining the high degree of tension that keeps these features from becoming obstacles. The shifts and tropisms that carry Törless from his first confusion through a series of initiation rites, and finally bring him to his first maturity, are catalogued with perfect economy and accuracy. The result is a convincing portrait, all the more so for having been modeled from within.

We have very few firsthand accounts of Musil. The descriptions and anecdotes available indicate that he was a severe, reserved man, punctilious in manner and painstaking in details of dress. Peters observes that Musil was one of those individuals who have no real biographies, that the major thrust of all energies is directed inward. It is difficult to disagree, especially in the absence of all but the most unsatisfying scraps of information. We know, for example, something of his likes and dislikes, but we know next to nothing of the reasons. Musil liked: Balzac, Dostoevsky, Kafka, Rilke, and, in movies, Chaplin and Astaire. He disliked: Joyce, Kraus, and Mann. It would be of great interest to learn why he disliked Karl Kraus. The opinion he held of Mann was revised somewhat in later years; Musil was deeply moved to learn that Mann had written letters on his behalf to the Bollingen Foundation. But he would never let go of the idea that Mann was a popularizer, a species of intellectual that he could not abide. He had nothing but contempt for the likes of Stefan Zweig. Critic Hans Mayer relates how he once suggested to Musil that he emigrate to South America. Musil simply shook his head: "Stefan Zweig is in South America."

Musil worked slowly and patiently at his craft. The will to perfection was dominant. He had the conviction, too, that he would live into his eighties. (To this end he exercised regularly; to other ends he smoked cigarettes with gusto.) There is not a trace of haste or rashness in anything he produced. During the twenty years after the publication of *Young Törless,* Musil published only two plays and five stories. But each of the stories is a model of compression and ripened insight. In their economy and control they recall the Flaubert of *Trois Contes.*

The first two stories, "The Perfecting of a Love" and "The Temptation of Quiet Veronica," appeared together in 1911 under the title *Unions.* They were written during the period following Musil's courtship of Martha Marcovaldi, whom he married in 1910. Both are strange, obsessive pieces, treating of jealousy, personal destiny, the psychology of love and sexuality, and the quest for mystical union. They are difficult to summarize, for the plot lines are minimal. Taken together they supply us with a dramatic representation of the extent to which Musil absorbed and transformed personal experience.

Both stories, interestingly enough, are written from the point of view of the female psyche, and both move along a path of almost total inwardness. One wonders how much Musil knew of Rilke at this stage, for there are many points of resonance between the two. The surface events are sketched only dimly; their function seems to be that of giving contour. The reader is drawn through an element of almost unbearable density—it is within this deep, shadowed place that the characters' struggle for self-recognition and fulfillment is waged. In each story the moment of resolution brings a tremendous liberation. It is unfortunate that none of the stories is currently available, for one of the strong points of Peters's study is the careful analysis he supplies.

Stylistically and otherwise, *Unions* presents a striking contrast to *The Man Without Qualities.* The stories represent, perhaps, the serious and inward counterpart to the brilliant, satiric pictures of love that Musil gives us in the later work. It is interesting to learn that Musil admitted in later years that he valued "The Perfecting of a Love" above all his other writings.

The collection *Three Women* did not appear until 1924. In the interval between the two collections, Musil was variously occupied, first as a librarian at the Technical University of Vienna, a job he despised because it consumed his optimum writing hours, and then, after moving back to Berlin, as one of the editors of *Neue Rundschau,* and still later, after 1914, as an officer with the Austro-Hungarian Army. When *Three Women* finally appeared, it revealed a significant departure from *Unions.* The external world had come back into view, and the narrative was no longer strictly interior. It appeared that Musil had found a way to modulate his vision. The focus, highly magnified as ever, could now move freely between objective and subjective poles. Furthermore, the emphasis was shifted from the female to the male psyche. The preoccupations, though, are much the same: all three stories are concerned with unfolding destinies. Romantic love is, in each case, the wondrous or terrifying event, the ordeal by which the men are brought face to face with themselves.

Both collections of stories (as well as the plays, which are not dealt with here) were, according to Musil, gateways or approaches for readers to *The Man Without Qualities.* But there is nothing in the prose that will prepare us for the leap, the sudden widening of scope. From the narrow focus, the obsessive rendering of the individual psyche, we move to a panorama that contains a whole society: Vienna on the eve of the collapse of the Hapsburg monarchy. The style is now cool and detached; its object is nothing less than an evaluation of the whole modern epoch.

> But if there is such a thing as a sense of reality—and no one will doubt that it has its raison d'etre—then there must also be something that one can call a sense of possibility. . . . The sense of possibility might be defined outright as the capacity to think how everything could "just as easily" be, and to attach no more importance to what is than to what is not. It will be seen that the consequences of such a creative disposition are remarkable, and unfortunately they not infrequently make the things that other people admire appear wrong and the things that other people prohibit permissible, or even make both a matter of indifference. Such possibilitarians live, it is said, within a finer web, a web of haze, imaginings, fantasy and the subjunctive mood.
>
> —*The Man Without Qualities*

Musil worked on *The Man Without Qualities* for nearly twenty years. It is natural, especially in a work so animated by intellectual concern, to expect that it should change and grow, much as the man who wrote it changed and grew. According to one of the disciples of Heraclitus, you cannot step even once into the same river. Indeed, this is one of the fascinating things about the novel. The terrain we cross in moving from Volume I to Volume III changes significantly. The scientific, speculative level that is at first so dominant begins to yield to a renewed preoccupation with the things of the spirit, specifically with mystical awakening. (Musil had studied the mystics carefully; he transcribed important features of their reports into a notebook he entitled *Borderline Experiences.*) It was Musil's intention to bring about a wedding of the polar strains in his being. From all indications, he could not find a suitable solution. We are left with an unresolved tension, a suggestion that the two parallels are moving toward their intersection in infinity. As things stand—and it is a matter for regret—we cannot survey the book from all sides. Part of it will remain consigned to the realm of the possible.

There is no point in this short account in attempting a detailed synopsis of the various personages and incidents that pull the narrative along. Suffice it to say that the surface action describes the fantastic and highly involved preparations for an "Austrian Year," an event to end all events, which is to commemorate the seventy-year reign of the emperor Francis Joseph. The year is 1913, and it was part of Musil's plan to have the end of the book coincide with the outbreak of the war. History would supply the epilogue, for after World War I the Austro-Hungarian Empire vanished. The presentation of incident is calculated in such a way that we are able to watch the whole mechanism of society in operation. The bureaucrat, financier, socialite, military man, artist, and criminal are brought together into close quarters. As the complications intensify, we feel as though we are watching a mad dance of death, a waltz at the very brink of an abyss. At the center of it all, implicated against his better judgment, is the figure of Ulrich, "the man without qualities."

Ulrich is a thinker of rare caliber, a possibilitarian. His analytic tendency has carried him to his own brink. He simply cannot make up his mind to do anything; one thing looks as good as the next. Ulrich has, therefore, decided to take a year off from all occupation in order to figure things out once and for all. His past, as it is presented to us, bears distinct resemblances to Musil's. Each of Ulrich's careers has proven insufficient. His concern is with ultimates. But what is a man bent upon ultimates to do in society?

The phrase "man without qualities" is somewhat misleading, for Ulrich does, in fact, possess a full complement of qualities. What Musil wants us to understand is that Ulrich lives among the possible far more than among the actual and that he has come to understand the interchangeability of truths. His problem is that while he is able to grasp this multiplicity intellectually, his being nevertheless hungers after the one, the *summa* of truths. As a result, he sees anything short of the ultimate as a matter for indifference. Events, for Ulrich, are unaccented. Each thing is accorded an equal nod. This reorganization of character passes in the eyes of the world as something highly suspect, as a lack of qualities.

One of the maddening things about this book is that Ulrich is never delivered from his situation. He remains in suspenseful poise until the narrative breaks off. This, paradoxically, is to be attributed to the high sincerity of Musil's effort. He was not willing to finish in any way but the true way, the way that would be fully consonant with his own resolution of the same problems. To that extent, the life of the novel and the life of the man were one and the same. Exploring Ulrich, we explore the mind of his creator.

The form of the novel is not revolutionary; it upsets no established canons. Musil had little patience with formal experiments. He was interested in ideas. It is on this level that his contribution is original and subversive.

In their preface to the first volume, the translators, Eithne Wilkins and Ernst Kaiser, state: "He was the writer above all others who summed up and finished off the classical novel of tradition." Such words come as a surprise, particularly since the two lived with the work for such a long time. It would seem that the precise opposite is true, that *The Man Without Qualities* is the negation of the whole system of values that produced that kind of novel. Behind its mannered facade, it is a wide-open farce, a cosmic joke. The whole structure of the novel, the webwork of bureaucratic and social intrigue, is but a pretext for the radical thrust of Ulrich's observations. These, if we look carefully, reveal themselves to be the antithesis of every thesis, the very inverse of the certified views that sustain a society. (Or, in the case of the Austro-Hungarian Empire, *fail* to sustain a society.)

To the shallow actualities of the day. Ulrich replies with a barrage of speculative possibilities. These, concerned as they are with the nature of technology, the functioning of power, the idiocy of bureaucratic systems, and the erosion of values, place Ulrich in the very vanguard of the modern. He anticipated the cultural applications of relativity, indeterminacy, and the like. A substantial book of epigrams could be culled from the reflections of Ulrich. These, in their sum, would topple any notion of *The Man Without Qualities* as classical novel. The central irony of the book is perhaps this very thing: it is only impersonating a novel.

As a writer and thinker, Robert Musil is clearly a case unto himself. But this is not to say that certain comparisons are inappropriate. The careers of Musil and Hermann Broch (1886–1951), for instance, reveal several important areas of convergence. Both writers came to literature from technical backgrounds; in each case the choice was made after a period of formal studies in psychology and philosophy. Both sought to depict the psyche in relation to what they conceived as ultimates. Still, affinities notwithstanding, there is a significant distance between Musil's work and Broch's culminating effort, *The Death of Virgil.* Broch attempted the wholly interior, wholly mystical answer. Musil could not be so one-sided. He could not dismiss the rational demand.

Musil's mystical strain must not be underestimated, though. In spite of the seeming dominance of the rational in the later writing, the nonrational is always present as counterpoint, either visibly or implicitly. In the stories, as we have seen, it is the central concern, sometimes in combination with the forces of romantic love, sometimes as an undifferentiated yearning. The transition from the interior focus of the stories to the externalized, intellectual scope of *The Man Without Qualities* suggests, at first glance, that Musil had abandoned the nonrational part of the quest. But this is not the case. Rather, what was formerly approached in subjective terms has been transformed; the mystical has been lifted into the light of day.

This shift was not effected without struggle. There is evidence that Musil tried to force himself to reject his mystical inclinations. Early in the first volume of *The Man Without Qualities,* we find a fascinating, somewhat incongruous chapter entitled "The Forgotten Exceedingly

Important Affair with the Major's Wife," in which Ulrich recollects an experience of solitary mystical union.

> It was an utterly changed form of life. Everything about it was shifted out of the focus of ordinary attention and had lost its sharp outlines. Seen in this way, it was all a little scattered and blurred, and yet manifestly there were still other centers filling it again with delicate certainty and clarity. For all life's problems and events took on an incomparable mildness, softness, and serenity, and at the same time an utterly transformed meaning. If, for instance, a beetle, there, ran past the hand of the man sunk in thought, it was not a coming nearer, a passing by and a disappearing, and it was not beetle and man; it was a happening ineffably touching the heart, and yet not even a happening but, although it happened, a state. And, aided by such tranquil experiences, everything that generally goes to make up ordinary life was imbued with transforming significance, wherever Ulrich met with it.

Still, however important the experience has been for Ulrich, as the chapter ends we are made to understand that it has been an anomaly, a one-time state. The implication is that Ulrich has subsequently turned away from such irrational experiences. It is almost as if Musil himself believed that he could indulge in the mystical one last time and then be rid of it. Subsequent chapters bear this out. In fact, it is not until we reach the third volume that we realize that Ulrich (and, by implication, Musil) has only repressed this part of his nature. What we then confront is the return of the repressed.

With the death of Ulrich's father, his long-lost sister Agathe comes to live with him. The new living situation produces an extraordinary tension in Ulrich, at first sexual, later (after Musil decided that an incestuous resolution would be too easy) in terms of a more complex desire, a desire not unlike that explored in the stories. After an excruciating scene in which Ulrich has been watching Agathe dressing to go out, in which she has unveiled before him the hitherto unknown arts and artifices of feminine beautification, he reflects:

> The moment I manage to have no more egocentric and selfish feelings toward Agathe, and no single ugly feeling of indifference either, she draws all the qualities out of me the way the Magnetic Mountain draws the nails out of the ship! Morally I'm atomised into a pure and primal state in which I'm neither myself nor her. I wonder is that what's meant by eternal bliss?

This is as close to surrender as Ulrich ever gets. Musil continues his balancing act, one foot firmly anchored in the rational. Ulrich remains the man of reason with the spirit that yearns for reasons that reason knows nothing of. Successive onslaughts have carried him closer to the answer, perhaps as close as it is possible to get without surrendering language. Musil has guided us to that line that marks off what can be spoken of and what must be passed over in silence; he leaves us nervously inclined forward.

Volume I of *The Man Without Qualities* was published to considerable acclaim. It was only after its publication that the real trials began. The story of Musil in his later years is the well-known story of the tribulations of genius.

After the war, Musil refused to work for a living. He was bent upon devoting his full powers to the realization of his task. Such willfulness, in combination with his material circumstances, could have but one outcome: dire poverty. In 1933 a small group of admirers formed the Musil Gesellschaft ("Musil Society") to help finance his endeavor. It helped, but only partially. As Hitler came to power, Musil emigrated to Switzerland. The Swiss government, nervous that the country might become a haven for writers and other undesirables, suggested repeatedly that he move elsewhere. Musil chose to ignore the suggestions.

Bitterness and frustration prevailed in these last years. Musil could not understand why, after such an auspicious beginning, his sequel efforts were ignored. The prosperity and public success of Mann and Broch obsessed and wounded him. In a wry note, he questioned whether God had intended spirit to perish from the earth. "That," he said, "would explain why he is not treating Robert Musil better."

(Musil would have been amused, perhaps, to learn that his name's anagram in English reads: I, Mr. Troubles.)

Still, there are various kinds of recompense, not all of them readily apparent. Musil was allowed to die an enviable death. To quote from his translators' preface:

> He had spent the morning as usual at his writing table and in the garden, and had gone upstairs to take a bath before luncheon. His widow wrote: "When he was satisfied with the way work was going—which was not often the case—he was cheerful. I have rarely seen him so cheerful as he was five minutes before his death. He had written some sentences that were to stand." He was probably doing his gymnastics when he collapsed. The expression on his face when he was found a short while later was one of mockery and mild astonishment.

Then, of course, there is the matter of reputation. Musil's is growing, and it will continue to grow. The readers of the future that he hoped for are finding him. There is one last reward: the gates that go to the place of the great swing only one way; once you have gained admission, you cannot be asked to leave.

Robert Walser

The Swiss writer Robert Walser meets all of our requirements for ranking as one of literature's darling unfortunates. He was solitary, impoverished, he scribbled in miserable rooms, *and* he spent the last third of his life in an insane asylum. That his quick, febrile prose was admired by Musil, Benjamin, and Kafka and at the same time escaped wide notice is an added cachet. But even so, with all his credentials in order, the canonization might not take place. The problem is that Walser's name has somehow become tangled up with Kafka's; his singularity has been obscured because of a few superficial similarities. A careful reading of Walser's *Selected Stories* (1982) will testify to the difference between them: Walser's buoyant, sportive, manic voice curls itself like an ivy vine around the somber constructions of K.

Walser is one of the most remarkable and fully realized stylists in modern literature. He has the rarest of gifts, the ability to get spirit onto the page at the flick of a pen. Each story, each sentence is as particular and unique as a fingerprint. "I am a little worn out, raddled, squashed, downtrodden, shot full of holes," begins the sketch titled "Nervous." A simple string of words has the reader tensed for perilous descent. In Walser's hands the language plays and suffers, it vibrates exactly to the rhythms of the psyche: delicacies of frequency are disclosed where we least suspect them. It is here that style fulfills its highest aspiration: it merges with content.

I have been talking abstractly, as if these pieces were without subject, a kind of music. Of course this is not true. In each there is an incident or observation or, more likely, a field of incidents. But these are wholly subordinated to Walser's own reactions and to his constant astonishment at the fact that there is a world and that one is allowed to go about in it.

Take the centerpiece story, "The Walk." It is nothing more—or less—than a fifty-page ramble in the company of Robert Walser. (Walser was, it should be mentioned, one of that select order of writer-walkers that includes Nietzsche, Hamsun, Benjamin, and Thoreau, for whom walking was not merely an activity conducive to thought but was a fusion of the physical and mental that made it possible to think with the whole being.) Walser's walk covers a course of several miles and involves a half-dozen encounters, none of them dramatically significant. But what an odyssey! He moves from one thing to the next with antennae bristling. His sensibility dilates from timorousness to brash boldness, zigzags from dispassionate observation to the cry of a soul overwhelmed.

There is no progress in the story except the progress of the walk itself. The encounters are like hallucinations—they are momentarily everything, and then they are left behind and never referred to again. The same is true of observations. At one moment the walker is in fine fettle, looking forward to lunch with a woman friend; in the next he is outraged by the ostentatious gold lettering on a baker's signboard. In a flash he moves from the particular to the universal:

> But loathsome boasting and swaggering began in some corner, in some nook of the world, at some time or other, advanced step by step like a lamentable and disastrous flood, bearing garbage, filth, and foolishness along with them, spreading these throughout the world. . . . To the devil with every miserable desire to seem more than one is.

How different is this tone from that of the little sketch "The Job Application," where Walser exploits the note of obsequiousness to the limit. The speaker is the *commis,* the clerk figure that he uses again and again:

> Assuredly there exists in your extensive institution, which I imagine to be overflowing with main and subsidiary functions and offices, work of the kind that one can do as in a dream?—I am, to put it frankly, a Chinese; that is to say, a person who deems everything small and modest to be beautiful and pleasing, and to whom all that is big and exacting is fearsome and horrid.

Walser loved to mimic, to play with voices—as here he throws the quavering syllables of the underling into sudden contact with the imperious syntax of authority. The rhythms alone unmask the relations of power.

Walser wrote prodigiously. The present selection is a sampler of pieces written between 1907 and 1929, the prime years of Walser's literary career. In this interval Walser modified his style several times. Increasing mastery prompted him to greater daring: the associative leaps became more adventurous, the transitions more oblique. Yet even the slightest sketches bear his special impress. We might think of these stories as many fragments of a broken mirror. One holds sky and a moving cloud, another gives us a face or a blooming rose. There is the sense that if we could have all of Walser's writings together—including the many stories that are yet untranslated—it would be possible to fit them edge to jagged edge and see the world as it has never been seen before.

The fractured mirror is a suggestive image. In 1929, when he was fifty-one, Walser committed himself to a sanitorium. The diagnosis was acute schizophrenia. The qualities that distinguish his prose, the special keenness, the excited fling of his transitions, the sense that the world is being received by a mind miraculously unburdened by categories and concepts, these are in some way inseparable from the pressures of his mental disorder. We cannot say, of course, that the prose was that of a schizophrenic—we do not know the particular history of his illness—nor do we have any way of comparing his writings before and after (as we do with, say, Hölderlin), since he stopped writing in 1933, the year he was forcibly put in an asylum. ("I'm not here to write," he later told a friend, "I'm here to be mad.") Still, a writer does not choose his style: it emerges of its own accord from the complexities of the soul. Thus, it is not insignificant that every adjective descriptive of Walser's work can be prefixed by the modifier "hyper."

Walser certainly understood his situation—he knew that he was doomed. In "Helbling's Story" he writes: "It is just as if one were not of coarse enough cut for this life." He saw clearly how every quantum of exerted will displaces its equivalent in receptive capacity. He chose to be without will, to open himself as much as possible to experience. Or maybe he did not choose. As early as 1908, in his novel *Jacob von Gunten,* he had pondered his nature and his fate:

> Perhaps I shall never put out twigs and branches. One day some fragrance or other will issue from my nature and my originating. My arms and legs will strangely sag, my mind, pride, and character, everything will crack and fade, and I shall be dead, not really dead, only dead in a certain sort of way, and then I shall vegetate and die for perhaps another sixty years.

Self-prophecy? Walser did break down, and he did live on for another twenty-seven years. But if we heed this part of his self-prophecy, we must at least hear out the other part. A few sentences further on he envisions that condition:

45

I don't respect my ego at all, I merely see it, and it leaves me cold. Oh, to come in from the cold! How glorious! I shall be able to come into the warmth, over and over again, for nothing personal or selfish will ever stop me from becoming warm and catching fire and taking part.

Robert Walser

Joseph Roth

The deeper messages of art are usually ignored by the very people who should be paying attention. The news made by economists and scientists is capped with banner headlines, whereas the news that stays news is regarded as a species of leisure. By and large, our historians persist in studying manifestations, tracing the outer contours of circumstance, and searching for political and socioeconomic causes. The twentieth century is viewed as a direct outgrowth of the nineteenth, and so on. The illusion is upheld that it is one vast and complex historical experience *Homo sapiens* is having. A historian who took the arts of our age to heart, however, would have to break with his peers. For if anything emerges from the great explosion of modernism, it's this frightening perception: that our collective existence no longer has an immanent purpose or direction. Historians need to realize that the event experienced as meaningful and the event experienced as arbitrary are two very different events.

Joseph Roth was a little-known Austrian novelist, who, in the decade of the thirties, in poverty and exile, wrote a dozen or so novels. The most popular of these, *The Radetzky March,* was published in Germany in 1932 and translated into English the very next year. It was out of print for decades, until a revised translation appeared in 1974, and was later reissued in paperback by Overlook Press as part of an energetic effort to get Roth's work back into circulation. And Roth's vision of the two channels of history—the meaningful and the meaningless—is more pertinent than ever. Indeed, in artistry and reach it surpasses most current grapplings with the subject; even the novels of as canny a writer as Milan Kundera seem blanched in comparison.

On the surface, *The Radetzky March* is, like *Buddenbrooks,* a chronicle of passing generations. Like Mann's novel, too, it projects the dissolution through time of a family's energy and sense of purpose. But the comparison should not be pressed too far. Whereas *Buddenbrooks* is dense with personality, lore, and pattern, Roth's stage is strangely unpopulated. The principal characters are silent and solitary; they move under an enormous mass of empty sky. At the center of *The Radetzky March* is, finally, not so much family or individuality as the whirring of time in the lives of men (women are almost entirely excluded).

The Trotta family was awarded its honorary "von" after the Battle of Solferino, in the middle years of the nineteenth century. Young Lieutenant Trotta, acting on courageous impulse, saved the emperor Francis Joseph from a bullet. The Trotta name was promptly inscribed on the emperor's list; so long as the Austro-Hungarian Monarchy endured, protection and patronage would never be denied.

The lieutenant, uncomfortable with new rank and title, retires into provincial obscurity, ceding the stage to his son. Franz von Trotta, all rectitude and righteousness, is the first to break with the family's military tradition. He joins the civil service instead and, trading on the luster of his name, advances to the coveted post of district commissioner. The order of his days mirrors the precision of the marching band that plays the "Radetzky March" outside his window each Sunday. The district commissioner will live on like this for long decades. It is Carl Joseph, his son, who becomes the effective center of the novel.

We would have to look far to find a less likely protagonist than Carl Joseph. From childhood on, he is uncertain and vague, a being in whom the current of life flickers at a low voltage. His mother has died; the punctilious district commissioner rules over him, enforcing all manner of barren proprieties ("His father arrived, the boy clicked his heels, the sound reverberating through the quiet old house"). Small wonder, then, that he decides to join the army—only when he is being controlled is he aware that he exists.

Before Carl Joseph enlists, however, life takes a swipe at him. He is to deliver a message to a certain sergeant major. The officer is not at home, but his young wife asks the boy in for a glass of lemonade:

> "What an age since we've seen you, Herr von Trotta," the Sergeant-Major's wife was saying. "You've grown quite big. Are you over fourteen?"
>
> "Oh yes, well over."
>
> He thought he'd get away as soon as he could. He would finish the lemonade in one gulp, bow politely, leave messages for her husband, and go. He stared helplessly at the lemonade; it seemed impossible to finish. Frau Slama filled it up again. She brought cigarettes; he was not allowed to smoke. She lit one and exhaled the smoke, carelessly, with distended nostrils, beating the air with her foot. Suddenly, without a word, she snatched the cap from his knees, and put it on a table. She thrust her cigarette between his lips. . . .

Roth choreographs the rest of the scene perfectly: pious rigidity yielding to the sweet anarchy of desire. Thomas Mann would have seen in that yielding the portents of death; Roth holds off, at least for a time. And when death does come—Frau Slama dies in childbirth after the affair has ended—the sting is all the more bitter.

When Carl Joseph hears the news, he is undone. His narrow ledge of meaning crumbles under him. He is not, of course, the first young man to have lost a love or to have contemplated the grave. But life has given him nothing to hold against dread—nothing, that is, except order. He soon finds that order can do nothing about dread except contain it. The rituals of army life cannot free him, and neither can the drink that he increasingly turns to, or even his drawn-out affair with an older woman. But Carl Joseph is not alone in his despair. The whole of the officer corps is caught up in a desperate debauchery. Garrison life begins with a morning brandy and ends in the gambling dens at night. Clearly something larger than personal torment is at issue: these men, the empire's elite, are not drinking to hide from the present or the past, they are fleeing the future. Chojnicki, a cynical local aristocrat, puts it bluntly: "We are done for." He is not just referring to the fate of the empire, or of Europe; he is echoing Nietzsche's shattering news that God is dead. The meaninglessness Carl Joseph feels has less to do with individual death than with the dry rot at the core of his times. His specific malaise is, it turns out, general.

As readers, of course, we have the advantage of hindsight. We know, as Roth did, that in 1914 the world collapsed in upon itself; we feel behind each formalized gesture the awful pressure of the coming catastrophe. Roth manipulates this tension masterfully. The men at the garrison hear rumors—of strikes, of agitation by nationalist groups, of tensions along the Russian frontier. But daily life is unrelieved by event, and Francis Joseph is in his fifth decade on the throne. It's as if the universe were holding its breath.

Carl Joseph finally comes to crisis. He has accumulated an enormous gambling debt, and now must either pay or be disgraced. Despairing, he writes a letter to his father asking for help. The old district commissioner rallies his resources immediately. When friends and neighbors prove unable to assist him, he decides to carry his plea to Francis Joseph himself. The family name must be saved at any cost.

The district commissioner presses his claim with supreme single-mindedness. At last he is face to face with the emperor:

> Francis Joseph's whiskers were tinged with yellow, especially around the mouth, otherwise they equalled Herr von Trotta's in whiteness. . . . They were like two brothers, one of whom had become an emperor and the other a district commissioner. Very

> human, like all that followed in this audience . . . was Francis Joseph's gesture just at this instant. For he feared there might be a drop at the end of his nose and drew out a handkerchief from his breeches pocket, and passed it lightly across his moustache. Then he glanced down at the memorandum. Aha! Trotta, he thought.

The scene is a tender one. We know that the collapse is almost at hand, but even at this late moment the web of honor and decency still holds: Francis Joseph intercedes to save the wastrel son. It is, at least in the book, the last triumph of the old dispensation.

Shortly after Carl Joseph is reprieved, word comes that the archduke Ferdinand has been assassinated. Troops are quickly mobilized. Carl Joseph is shot in an early skirmish with a Cossack brigade; his end is sudden and matter of fact. War has engulfed everything, the novel included, and the life of one more soldier is of no great consequence. Some time later, the multitudes gather in the courtyard of the imperial residence to hear that the emperor has died. Three days after, severing the final bond between the Trotta family and the empire, the district commissioner dies in his bed.

The sources of Roth's particular power are hard to pin down. Neither plot nor character will account for it. True, the district commissioner emerges as a compelling figure—his fidelity takes on a tragic dimension as the novel progresses; but Carl Joseph is the very reverse. He is a husk, a frightened, self-occupied failure. His decline is inevitable, and we can even take a certain pleasure in watching it. But this is not when the novel achieves its greatness. No, the pity and terror are felt when we realize that Carl Joseph is a transparency, that we are looking right through him at the impersonal rush of history. His emptiness turns out to be a precise emblem of the moral vacuum of the times.

The assumptions of the old order were of a breathtaking simplicity. As the Trottas are bound to the empire through the beneficence, or grace, of Francis Joseph (and, in the case of the district commissioner, by the faith that repays that grace), so is Francis Joseph bound, through the Holy Roman Church, to the eternal order in God. The district commissioner and his generation were born into a world where the secular and the transcendental are closely woven. But even they must feel the chill of what is to come. At one point, while visiting his son at the garrison, the district commissioner meets the nihilistic Chojnicki. They drink and start conversing: "The Fatherland," he says, "has ceased to exist." The district commissioner is agog as Chojnicki explains that the sanctions are gone, that God has abandoned the emperor.

> The District Commissioner walked across the room, the old boards creaked under his feet. He went to the window and saw the narrow strips of the dark-blue night through the gaps in the blinds. Suddenly, all natural occurrences and all the events of daily life were imbued with threatening and incomprehensible significance. Incomprehensible the whispering chorus of grasshoppers, incomprehensible the glitter of the stars. . . .

What the district commissioner sees after a night of drunken conversation is what Carl Joseph has inherited as a child of his time. In the course of a generation, history has lost its connection to the transcendental. The district commissioner never quite loses faith; his son never had it to begin with. It's hard to say which of the Trottas is the more tragic.

Roth ends *The Radetzky March* with the deaths of the emperor and the district commissioner, letting the rest of our bloody century supply the epilogue. Robert Musil planned to do something similar with his never-to-be-finished opus, *The Man Without Qualities.* Another countryman, satirist Karl Kraus, had once called Hapsburg Austria a "proving ground for world destruction," and when the collapse came, it must have seemed in Vienna that history had not only accelerated but changed its very nature. Never before had so massive a structure fallen so swiftly, or left so little behind—a brittle fossil demolished by a hammer blow.

Roth, unlike many gleeful modernists, was not out to celebrate the coming of the new; it was forced on him, as it was on Musil. They responded in different ways: where Musil mustered a cerebral sarcasm, Roth chose an elegiac tone. In response to an editor's query, he once wrote: "I am a conservative and a Catholic, consider Austria my fatherland, and desire the return of my Empire." Although the desire was not to be gratified (Roth reportedly drank himself to death in a Paris garret), it did not distort his art. With the utmost discipline, without any lapses into sentimentality, he registered his nightmare on the page. Overlook Press should be commended: brick by brick it is restoring what looks like a major edifice.

Max Frisch

The precision-minded Swiss have never been famous for grand gesture or passionate utterance. It is as if exposure to the mighty contours of the land has over generations pruned back the national soul and turned its energies inward. Auden, connoisseur of craggy places and intricate inwardness, might have singled Switzerland out as one of his "comfy" places—but then, his idea of "comfy" also included boiled meat and cold potatoes. Freud's cigar certainly glowed more brightly when he considered how much *Geld* was tucked away in the penetralia of the Zurich banks. The Swiss reserve is at once federal and personal.

Out of this mountain fastness comes novelist, dramatist, and perennial Nobel candidate Max Frisch, whose career has been one long assault upon repression, self-satisfaction, and bourgeois right-mindedness. Frisch—the Swiss who would not be Swiss—has done everything in his power to throw off the burden of his heritage. In the forty years since he quit architecture for writing, he has expressed himself with great inventiveness upon a single theme: the near impossibility of living truthfully. He determined early on that the will to self-deception acts on the character as powerfully and almost as inevitably as gravity acts on the body. From his first major novel, *I'm Not Stiller* (1958), right up through the novella *Bluebeard* (1983), he has argued that the self is not a given, that love is anything but the voluptuous surrender in a TV ad, and that it was the imperialistic ego that Blake named as "the invisible worm/That flies in the night."

Frisch does not exempt himself from these grim assessments. Indeed, he learned much of the bad news by reading his own character. He admits in interviews that his temperament is depressive and that his writing is a struggle against great inertia. The works since the mid-1970's—*Montauk, Man in the Holocene, Triptych,* and *Bluebeard*—bear this out. Once abundant, prodigal of invention, Frisch's narratives now look as though they have been carved from a close-grained material. And yet there is no sense of lost amplitude. Like Beckett's, Frisch's reductions draw much of their power from their position; each is the latest evolutionary moment in a complex *oeuvre*. Both writers have mastered the "Giacometti effect": the more skeletal the content, the more resonant the surrounding space.

For all its formal alteration, Frisch's work reveals an underlying consistency. The structural and stylistic shifts mark his maturing, the varying of his concerns, his need for increasingly direct statement. The man grows, but he is the same man. The narrative refinements of *I'm Not Stiller, Homo Faber* (1959), and *Gantenbein* (1966), yield to the rougher approaches, collage and diary techniques, in the later books. The former tend to be more exploratory, conscientiously fictional, more avid for the Truth about our inner experience; the latter show us how little we know and how little we may presume. This is not to say that Frisch has abandoned the noble Socratic pursuit. Rather, he appears to have determined that the larger part of experience is opaque, unknowable, and that this in itself makes up much of its truth. The unknowable becomes more and more important. Eventually it functions as space does in the famished sculptures of Giacometti.

I'm Not Stiller, the first of Frisch's novels to be translated into English, was not his first novel. In fact, it belongs to his second literary career. The first had been aborted in the late 1930's. A young Frisch, set on becoming an architect, carried all his published works—a novel, a novella, several stories—into the woods and burned them. He pursued his new profession with some success. But in the 1940's he started writing again, and by 1943 he had arrived at an existential crossroads. The completion of his first major architectural commission coincided with the publication of his first mature novel. Many years later, *I'm Not Stiller* would have as its central concern the Kierkegaardian question: how does one choose oneself? The epigraph, from *Either/Or,* tells us a great deal about how Frisch worked through his dilemma: "As the passion for freedom awakes in him (and it awakes in the choice, as it is already presupposed in the choice), he chooses himself and fights for this possession as for his happiness, and this is his happiness."

In *I'm Not Stiller,* as in the novels that follow, Frisch works to set out the line that separates true identity from self-deception, and, collaterally, love from egotism. He can stand with Proust as one of the great anatomists of love and obsession. If jealousy is one of the mainsprings of Frisch's narratives, this is because he understands that it is not so much a reflex of love as an eruption of thwarted egotism. Where relationships are founded not by authentic selves but by actors, where they consist not in sacrifice but in the mutual mirroring of fictions, there infidelity will bring the horrifying revelation. Time and again Frisch's "actors" are shocked from their spells by betrayal. When they are undone it is not by the loss of love but by the destruction of illusion.

The conceits of fiction served Frisch well for a time. He could tell stories about men and women who did not exist as selves and who lived by improvising stories with their lives. Subject matter and method dovetailed neatly. Anatol Stiller could insist, against all evidence, that he was not the Stiller who had abandoned his wife. In the absence of a deeper contract with the self, a man is what he tells and what he makes others believe. Truth, then, is just the hardiest fiction. So too, in *Gantenbein,* the narrator takes up mask after mask to tell a story and, as in *Rashomon,* no single version is right or wrong. But Frisch held back from becoming a thorough fabulist. He made use of the fabulist's tricks and told a clever tale, but ultimately *I'm Not Stiller* and *Gantenbein* are anchored to the world. When his wife Julika dies, Stiller has to swallow the hard news that the wages of fiction are facts. In the same way, Gantenbein comes to himself in an empty apartment and realizes that no amount of inventive telling will bring his Lila back to him.

After *Gantenbein,* Frisch's prose changed decisively. Deliberate artifice disappeared, and a new set of concerns came to the fore. It was as if he had said all that he could, or wanted to, about the private sources of despair. The new Frisch was blunter, more public, much less occupied with subjective inwardness. The voice reflected the change. It became flat, unemphatic, ironic. All presumption vanished.

The transitional book is *Sketchbook, 1966–1971.* (Frisch had completed a *Sketchbook, 1946–1949,* in 1950, a much more self-consciously "literary" effort.) Some might argue that a writer's journals do not constitute new work, but Frisch's *Sketchbook* clearly does. Carefully written and carefully arranged, its collage format directly anticipates that of *Montauk.* Cohesiveness comes from the subject matter. There are really only two topics of meditation: what is the place of the individual in a drastically outscaled political reality, and, on a very different plane, how does a person age and face death?

Frisch is disconcertingly frank on both topics. He offers no optimistic catchwords, no consolations, and no program except that of facing the truth. As an observer of the political sphere, he is attentive, sensible, and, naturally, aghast at the abuse of power in the name of ideology. Sympathetic to agitation and protest, he nevertheless can see only the growing irrelevance of the values of the individual. In one section he chronicles his meeting with Henry Kissinger. The two men are together at the White House, chatting about books and writing. Frisch keeps reminding himself that only a few days before, this same man helped set in motion the bombing of Cambodia. He is, by turns, fascinated by the intricate coexistence of power and personality and ashamed at his own inability to state his outrage over the war. He probes his feelings. Is it mere cowardice, a fear of giving offense? The situation, Frisch knows, is more complex. By expressing outrage he would also be creating the illusion that communication between writers and politicians mattered. Or else he would be forcing upon his host and himself the truth that both would prefer to avoid—that in events of this scale the views of individuals count for nothing. And yet, he thinks, maybe this is precisely what must be brought into the open. ". . . I am not a political person," writes Frisch in *Montauk,* "because I *verinnerliche* everything . . . I take everything personally to heart."

This difficult, self-deflating frankness has become a hallmark of Frisch's writing. As he confesses his inadequacy during his visit to the White House, so does he discover every fear and subterfuge of the "doomed," or death-bound, man. *Sketchbook* is an organon of the psychology of aging, and as such it is almost unique in literature.

> The doomed man has already stopped kissing his daughter, or at least he gives his kiss an ironical air. He is equally shy of kissing other young women when the social occasion . . . would permit it. He considers his lips an imposition. If on such occasions a young woman kisses him artlessly along with everyone else, the doomed man betrays himself by feeling disconcerted.

The same cast of mind is carried over into the brief autobiographical novella *Montauk* (1975). Frisch professes to be giving a straightforward description of events, external and internal, of a weekend spent at Montauk on Long Island. The writer, in his sixties, is there with a young woman. They could be said to be having a tryst, except that he admits to feeling "presumptuous" whenever he has a romantic urge. The two pass their time walking, sunning, playing Ping-Pong, once making a try at love. Throughout, Frisch heeds the sharp intrusion of memories. These are given in the first person, while the rest is narrated in the third. "He wishes there did not have to be memories." Memory, for Frisch, is the organ of remorse; it brings him face to face with his failures. The happy moments of the past have already been destroyed by the fact of their passing. What remain vivid are his disintegrated marriages, the unhappy finale of his love affair with the writer Ingeborg Bachmann, betrayals and deaths. And no felicity in the present can temper these visitations. They are the legacy of the way he has lived his life.

Montauk becomes art rather than mere reportage by virtue of Frisch's self-severity, his eye for nuance, and his great skill at collage assembly. Detachment and intimate revelation strike a perfect balance. His jump-cuts carry us from present to past and back until we feel the inward rush of space and time, and experience the private allusiveness that comprises the life of the psyche.

In 1979, Frisch published an even slimmer novella, *Man in the Holocene.* The plot was minimal. An old man is alone in his house in the mountains during a storm; he takes a foolhardy walk; he suffers bouts of memory loss. As he tacks up bits of information from the encyclopedia, we are given—once again in collage form—all manner of facts about the age of the earth, fossils, climate, evolution, geologic transformation. The counterpoint is intentionally obvious. We are to contemplate the various magnitudes of natural process, to grasp that at a certain scale the glories and failings of the race are negligible. Still, in the old man's desperate fight for memory, something glimmers. We could not call it hope—Frisch is not one to feed us hope; more likely it is a remnant of the ancient evolutionary spark.

Man in the Holocene had the feel of a closing statement. Considered alongside *Triptych,* which was published shortly after, and which presented a series of postmortem dialogues, it gave every indication that Frisch was moving into the preserves of silence. Indeed, given the premises he had established, silence was the logical next step.

The appearance of Frisch's *Bluebeard* is for this reason startling. Slim, as exquisitely crafted as any of his other works, it is at once a stride forward and a return to certain former tendencies. Dr. Felix Schaad has been acquitted of the murder of Rosalinde A., a prostitute and one of his seven former wives. The narrative consists of the obsessive replaying of the trial in Schaad's mind. Try as he may, he cannot silence the testimony. He walks, drinks, plays billiards by himself—nothing helps. The voices of former wives, friends, and neighbors come to him as he lines up difficult shots. His billiard game mirrors the cause-and-effect pattern that now has him captive.

It is not clear from the testimony or Schaad's behavior whether he has or has not committed the crime. What does emerge from the various accounts is that he has lived his life as a supremely egotistical creature. As the testimony comes to an end, Schaad quite suddenly breaks. He rushes back to his hometown and makes a confession at the police station. The town is nowhere near the scene of the crime, though, psychologically speaking, it is the very place. ("Why exactly did you drive to Ratzwill?" "It is where I was born.") Having made the confession, Schaad drives his car into a tree in an unsuccessful suicide attempt. While he is in the hospital, news comes that the real murderer has been arrested. But this makes no difference to the now-speechless Schaad. He has discovered his guilt. He did not murder Rosalinde, but he could have. The murder was a specific event, but his guilt is a condition of the soul. Schaad's final utterances—" ," " ," and " "—are the most damning of admissions.

Bluebeard has been executed with the sharp geometrical inevitability of a perfect combination shot. Frisch is not so much returning to earlier themes as he is bringing the preoccupations of a lifetime under a more calculated and intense pressure. Eliot's remark, that each new masterpiece changes our relation to the masterpieces of the past, can be applied to this newest addition to Frisch's *oeuvre*. *Bluebeard* suggests that Frisch's zeal for serious, difficult subjects has not abated, that those of us who prophesied silence were premature. His tidings are no cheerier than usual, but we have never looked to Frisch for cheer. He has always been there to remind us that there is no simple prescription for truthful living, and that happiness is that point in geometry where parallel lines meet.

Gregor von Rezzori

"And yet the chatter of the visionaries is the salt of reality. . . . It is the herring paste without which you people could not eat your frozen potatoes because they would stick in your craw. . . ."

—*The Death of My Brother Abel*

There is something in writers that wants to have the last word. On our shores whole generations have chased after the *fata morgana* of the Great American Novel, the supreme fiction that would express once and for all the complexities and contradictions of our experience. The impulse, in the main, has been affirmative, even awe inspired: to find words for the diversity and velocity of it all. The situation is somewhat different on the other side of the Atlantic. We find the same omnivorousness, but with a reversed incentive. The European writer is driven to put a frame around a catastrophe, to explain the complete collapse of a refined and confident civilization. If no one ever rhapsodizes about the Great European

Novel, it may be because the adjective "great" does not stick easily to a subject matter so emphatically somber. But some sort of epithet is in order. For rank upon rank of novelist—from Musil, Broch, and Mann to, more recently, Grass, Böll, Skvorecky, and Kundera—have tried to get to the heart of the matter. Their efforts have yielded up many of the important works of our century. And the interrogation goes on. Indeed, after forty years the rise of fascism and the war are still the dominant subjects of European fiction. Perhaps an epithet would just trivialize things.

I don't believe that there is a definitive "last word" about the nightmare side of our century, but of those writers who are in a position to speak, few have better credentials than Gregor von Rezzori. Born in 1914 in the east central European region of Bukovina (which became a part of Romania after World War I), educated in Vienna, Rezzori came of age in the volatile years before the *Anschluss.* He crossed and recrossed the battle fronts, lived in many of the great capital cities. His story-cycle, *Memoirs of an Anti-Semite,* published here in 1981, reveals his uncanny ability to pick out the myriad nuances of cultural and racial interaction; his wanderings clearly stood him in good stead. On top of this, he lived for many years in postwar Germany (working in film and radio)—no novelist could wish for a better spatial or temporal coign of vantage. *The Death of My Brother Abel* (1985) is Rezzori's attempt at a visionary *summa.* It is both a failed novel and a document quick to the core with insight and provocation.

The year is 1968. Rezzori's unnamed narrator (born, we learn, in 1919), a highly paid script-writer for the booming German film industry, has taken refuge in a fleabag hotel in Paris. He is there to write his great novel, already many years in the planning; with it he will at once sort out his experience and, no less important, vindicate the hopes placed in him by his recently deceased friend Schwab (the brother Abel figure in his imaginings). The narrator is after nothing less than a complete understanding of the *Zeitgeist.* He believes that as a man both displaced in space and cut loose, "amputated," from time—the meaningfully sequential seasons he knew in his youth—he holds the key to the sufferings of a whole generation. As one conversant with the new syntax of cinema, he also has a procedure:

This can hardly be depicted except as a literary equivalent of looking at rushes, but I admit that this unsteadiness in storytelling is, no doubt, due to many years of watching movie editors at work and witnessing their laudable persistence, the way they scour through the "takes," the way they comb through the wealth of filmed events, forming a new series that is often the opposite of the original outline, until the intended meaning of the whole becomes acutely evident.

What we have, then, is a vast, digressive tour of the cutting-room floor. Vivid images from boyhood and adolescence are interlarded with the more diffuse depictions from later years, and the whole is knit together by lengthy, and occasionally gaseous, meditations on the larger meaning of things. The result is, by turns, enthralling, disconcerting, tiresome, and terrifying. At his worst, Rezzori can sound like Henry Miller in one of his decline-of-the-West tirades; at his best, he has a poetic intensity seldom encountered in contemporary literature. Here is a fragment of his rhapsody on a vanished time:

> Our souls lived in that old world of the faraway times, when Nuremberg was renowned for its *Lebkuchen* and its toy boxes, not for its trials and the subsequent gallows. The times when in such ghastly places as Cologne or Coventry the gingerbread houses crowded in an intricate confusion around the cute dignity of the stepped town-hall gables, shadowed by the heavenward soaring of the cathedrals. . . . When the vast countryside was lovely with its silent lakes and ponds reflecting the cloud castles of the minnesingers and the poetic Wittelsbachs on the mountains. The lead-glistening light of storm-brewing, grain-ripening summer afternoons long ago reflecting the heaviness of our hearts; the murmuring of brooks under alders and hazelnut bushes, from which beautiful Melusina peers out . . . Melusina, mind you, and not the radioactive refuse of the nearest chemical factory. . . .

Quick oscillations of sensibility—in this case between devotion and irony—power much of the novel.

The tale that we assemble from Rezzori's "takes" is compelling but inconclusive. As a boy the narrator moves from vast country estates to Mediterranean watering holes, following his mother's restless jaunts in pursuit of the European *haut monde.* We read about legendary uncles and sumptuous furnishings; every particular is tendered with Nabokovian care. (We learn far more about such an uncle than about the woman he later marries, or his son. . . .) Later, after the death of his mother, comes a grim adolescence in Vienna with his petit bourgeois relatives. Rezzori gives us several close-up shots of the milieu that took so readily to the Führer's solutions. But then, as the actual menace encroaches, fragmentation ensues. The narrator wanders from place to place, alone, or with his lover, a young, rich—and married—Jewess; he is in and out of uniform, in Berlin, in Vienna, on his uncle's estate in Bessarabia. The progressive confusion is reflected in the narrative. We can no longer be sure about our coordinates as images and partial narratives pull us to and fro. Some will reckon this as a viable kind of mimesis; others will long for the security and evenhandedness of a more conventional tale.

The postwar years are even less defined. The narrator spends some time in Nuremberg (possibly to give testimony), meets and marries a German girl, begins associating with a ragtag band of intellectuals—they meet in the ruins of a hut and toast their new ideas with home-brewed schnapps. After a son is born, the marriage begins to founder. And then, all at once—literally overnight—comes the "currency cut." Instant prosperity: new buildings, goods, easy money. Our hero is divorced, working for the movies. With fists full of ready cash, he moves from place to place, taking up with women of all descriptions, including, most memorably, Gaia, a six-foot African princess. It is during this phase that he meets Schwab, the brilliant, alcoholic novelist manqué who insists that he, the narrator, is the only one who can write the "Nobel prize" book about the catastrophe. *The Death of My Brother Abel* wants to be just that.

If this novel has a besetting flaw, it's ambitiousness. The immensity of Rezzori's scope forces the narrative out of shape every few pages; the clean lines of its vignettes and recorded memories invariably blur into the chaos of commentary, not all of which is as focused as it could be. We don't feel, by the end, that we have been guided *to* something.

The recounted life, however fascinating, does not move with the surge of inevitability. And the time-jump sequences, though effectively imitative of the workings of memory, often force us off the track of our attention.

This same ambition, on the other hand, this desire to take on the experience of a whole era, is also the source of much of the novel's power. To the narrator's obsessiveness we owe the many charged passages—the beautiful streams of invective against postwar sterility, the barbed meditations on history and human nature, and the elegiac renderings of the past.

The *Zeitgeist,* for the narrator, is more than just a set of images and moods—it is the force underlying history itself. He sees it as "something breathing, pulsing through the world, making mankind lean alternately in one direction, then the other, like a wheat field in the wind. . . ." A mystical conceit? Perhaps, but Rezzori brings it tellingly to life in these pages. Late in the book, for instance, as he is describing the days just before the *Anschluss,* before Hitler himself arrives in Vienna, the narrator fastens his gaze on an old flower woman. Watching her strange, unconscious movements, he understands how the inchoate energies of an event are expressed long before there can be any understanding of their import:

> She had left her baskets of primrose, violet and narcissus posies, and they stood there tempting any dog's leg, while she ran—no, rolled—in a drunken zigzag across the empty square. Only Raphael Donner's smooth fountain nymphs, so beautiful and motionless in their slender grace, were watching her twirl and whirl and swirl, while she flung up her sleeve stumps with the root ends, as though trying futilely to take wing—and she shrieked, croaked, panted, *"Heil! Siegheil! Siegheil!"* And although Viennese flower women have voices like Anatolian mule-drivers, she sounded very woeful, indeed stifling in the resonance of the huge void, like the lament of a hare drowning in a rain barrel.
>
> Only then did it dawn on me that something extraordinary had occurred: an era had come to an end.

Such a view, that there are irresistible and blindly functioning forces that determine history, can only result in a moral nihilism. Which is precisely what Rezzori comes to in this novel. He ends with a lacerating assessment of the proceedings at Nuremberg: that they were utterly meaningless, that the postwar effort to bring moral and legal standards to bear upon the atrocities was insane. Quite bluntly: "There were no murderers anymore and no victims, because there was no more human reason able to distinguish between good and evil." The eye cannot move idly over these words. Indeed, our fitness for the future can be measured by the degree to which we protest.

Heinrich Böll

There is a distinct, if abstract, satisfaction to be gotten from working complex equations, factoring out extraneous numerals until at last the simple terms greet each other across the equal sign. An analogous pleasure, but more sensory and emotional, awaits the reader of the stories of Heinrich Böll. Here the distraction and clutter are stripped from human commerce and we are brought face to face with our vestigial selves. The aesthetic effect, however, has a bitter cause. For the force of Böll's vision depends most often upon the reductions wrought by fear, confusion, and suffering. That is—to collapse three nouns into one—by war.

Böll needs no introduction. Long before the Nobel Prize consolidated his international reputation in 1972, he had earned the honor of being the spokesman for an entire generation of Europeans, a representative of the times. Böll's youth and young manhood had coincided with the rise of Nazism; he was conscripted in 1939 and spent five years in uniform, at the front and in American POW camps. His first work—which blasted the senselessness of imperialistic conflict—found a ready audience during the shell-shocked years of German reconstruction. He was ever of his time—in recent decades he was an outspoken peace activist—and ever at an angle to it, bearing witness.

Nor did Böll refuse the dais. His fiction, from the first, concerned itself with the common life of the insulted and injured. It gradually widened its reach, in novels such as *Group Portrait with Lady* (1973) and *The Safety Net* (1982), to embrace the whole social order. *The Stories of Heinrich Böll* (1986), weighted to favor the early stories, does not preserve the proportions of the career. Its bulk is for, and about, the voiceless—frightened boys who were handed guns and orders, bereaved mothers and wives, children. We get the cauterized emotions and hunger-sharpened perceptions experienced by the suffering majority, and very little about the yes-men and perpetrators. The cumulation of simple perspectives is genuinely affecting. If many of the settings and situations recur from story to story—railway stations, barracks, bombed-out buildings; arrivals, departures, furtive trysts—this is not because of any artistic shortcoming, but because war levels differences. Smoking rubble and fear are the same everywhere.

The collection is arranged chronologically. Thus, by the time we finish we have moved from the chaos of mortar fire through the monochromatic austerity of reconstruction to the disquieting blandness of prosperity. But the war is always there, if not directly on the page then as an implicit point of historical reference—akin to the painter's vanishing point. The slight satiric vignettes set in the near present would mean nothing without the memory of disaster. Which is to say that Böll is faithful to the way that events become history in the collective memory.

It may be that in death everyone is the same, but at the moment of dying individual uniqueness is most piercingly disclosed. In that instant—or so the writer's imagination would have it—the full path of destiny flashes out, and every act and choice can be viewed under the aspect of inevitability. A string of incidents, however unremarkable, becomes a tale. In two of the novellas included here, *And Where Were You, Adam?* and *The Train Was on Time,* Böll makes use of this revelatory possibility. In *And Where Were You, Adam?* he splices together the complex outer circumstances—the significant encounters, delays, choices—that lead up to the death of the soldier Feinhals. Here the young Böll (this was one of his early publications) indulges his appetite for the dramatic convergence. Feinhals is hit by an artillery shell just when he believes his homeward journey is over—"and he rolled in death onto the threshold of the house. The flagpole had snapped, and the white cloth fell over him." The clumsy and obvious knotting of the narrative belies the skill shown in other passages throughout, where terror, fatigue, and a range of freighted human confrontations have been caught with the eye of a practiced watcher.

The Train Was on Time, likewise an early work, attempts an inward rendition of the destined event. But in this account the strategy is reversed. The young soldier, Andreas, has a vivid premonition of the time and place of his death. The novella takes us through the excruciating days of waiting, building suspense by the minute until the expected finally happens: "Now we must be in Galicia, he thought, quite close to Lvov, since Lvov is the capital of Galicia. Now I must be just about in the center of the net where I'm going to be caught." There is an undeniable power in this kind of procedure—*Oedipus Rex* is the paradigm—but the portentousness gets to be too thick by the end. More memorable, finally, are the sketches drawn along the way, of Andreas's interminable train ride and of his fellow soldiers. Böll did not pull a description like this out of airy nothing:

> It was horrible to have the man leaning over the map with him. Andreas could smell the canned meat on his breath, which was still not quite free of the odor of digested, partially acidulated schnapps. He could smell the sweat and grime and was too wrought up to see anything; then he saw the man's finger, a thick, red, dirty, yet very good-natured finger, and the man said, "That's where I have to go."

A good many of the shorter fictions also turn on the idea of fatedness. In "Stranger, Bear Word to the Spartans We . . ." a dying soldier is carried into an infirmary that he realizes was once his secondary-school classroom; the handwriting that he notices on the blackboard is his own. We don't need to be told that he will die in that room. "Adventures of a Haversack," similarly, traces the bizarre circuit that a dead infantryman's bag must follow in order to end up, long years later, on its original nail.

Böll's penchant for meaningful intersections seems to be at odds with the unblinking naturalism of his treatment of character and place. One may be tempted to dismiss it as an unfortunate artifice. But it is possible, I think, to accept it as his attempt to depict the inexplicable change in the order of things that cataclysm initiates. I have often heard from veterans of the European war that miraculous meetings, deus ex machina escapes, perversely ironic deaths, were all accepted as natural. It is almost as if the exponential increase of the death factor intensifies the play of significance, as if the laws of daily life are abolished when a boiling point is reached. But with Böll we also cannot discount the religious influence.

Böll thought of himself as an unorthodox, even renegade, Catholic. Reared in the faith, drawn by temperament to its moral humanism, he was permanently alienated by Church hypocrisy. As he wrote in his memoir *What's to Become of the Boy?* (1984): "After the seizure of power, the Reichstag fire, and the March election, it was, incredibly, the Vatican that accorded the Nazis their first major international recognition." To the end of his life, Böll could not reconcile the spirituality of the creed with what he saw as the opportunism of its organizational vessel.

Still, a religious sensibility is active in his work. It is evident both in his humane treatment of characters, even the lowliest, and in the narrative developments that tend in every instance to meaningful resolution. Though Böll does not gloss over facts—in his world the evidence of suffering far outweighs evidence of redemption—he does not exclude redemption altogether, which is no small victory for spirit in times as dark as these. The scale, nevertheless, is always modest. One looks in vain for suggestions that some larger struggle between good and evil has been engaged. The flawed and purblind human soul is not viewed as arena enough for the contest, or trophy enough to contend over.

Böll's intimations of higher meaning are there to mitigate suffering—they stand no chance of canceling it. But the possibility remains that death will bring sudden inner reconciliation, if not something even better. In "Reunion on the Avenue," for instance, we read about the death of two trench-mates, who just one minute before had been drinking schnapps and confiding their dreams:

> . . . and while noise sprang to life around me, the frantic barking of the machine gun from Heini's dugout and the sickening impact of the grenade launchers that we called pipe organs, I became quite calm: for mingling with Hecker's darker blood that still covered the bottom of the dugout was a lighter, miraculously light blood that I knew was warm and my own; and I sank down and down until I found myself, smiling happily, at the entrance to that avenue which Hecker hadn't known how to describe, because the trees were bare, solitude and desolation were nesting among wan shadows, and hope died in my heart, while far off, at an immense distance, I could see Hecker's beckoning figure outlined against a soft golden light. . . .

Two thirds of the way through the collection, Böll's tone perceptibly changes. He gives us, first, a handful of tales from the postwar period, and as violence and horror recede, irony and shrewd psychological observation take over. In a story called "Business Is Business," a cynical survivor studies his suddenly prosperous—and just as suddenly amnesiac—black marketeer, and reflects upon the remarkable plasticity of human nature. "Everything was fine," he thinks,

> your medical insurance was still OK, you had yourself de-Nazified a bit—the way you go to a barber to get rid of that tiresome beard—you chatted about decorations, wounds, acts of heroism, and came to the conclusion that you were a pretty fine fellow after all.

Böll seldom gets any more strident. Either you pick up the message or you don't.

Irony gives way to flatter satire as the stories take on life in recent decades. The writing is more detached, the thematic presentation more idiosyncratic—but at the same time the impact (at least for the non-German reader) is diminished. Pieces like "The Thrower-Away," about an efficiency expert working in secret in the basement of a large firm, and "The Staech Affair," which looks at the consequences of monk absenteeism at a highly touristed monastic retreat, make perfect sense. Still, at times they feel like sections of an encoded dialogue that Böll may have been carrying on with his compatriots. For the power of satire derives from a play upon particulars, and here we cannot be sure that we're catching all of the barbs. "Murke's Collected Silences," on the other hand, negotiates more universal terrain: a pompous culture czar insists that all references to God in his archive of radio tapes be replaced by the phrase "that higher Being Whom we revere." The sharp opposition between his bloated self-regard and the sly, puncturing wit of the underling Murke—whose hobby is piecing together bits of taped silence that he has gathered—provides delicious comedy.

Böll's strengths were those of a witness, not those of an inventor. His satiric eye was keen, but he had trouble sustaining plots that could serve as credible vehicles. For this reason, the fiction that deals with the immediate circumstances of war is the most vivid. The directionless momentum of combat, the unrelieved tensions of waiting and watching, supply a natural frame and free the author from the need to contrive situations. True, Böll was sometimes guilty of resolutions that exceeded even the prodigal inventiveness of the three fates, but his palpable rendering of fundamental drives and emotions—his ability to sound the depths of the average heart—more than compensated. He knew that the patina of culture and sensible behavior is easily cracked. This collection, which honors an ample achievement, stands also as a reminder of the real hierarchy of human needs:

> He hastily broke off a hunk of bread: his chin was trembling, and he could feel the muscles of his mouth and jaws twitching. Then he dug his teeth into the soft, uneven surface of the bread

where he had broken it apart. He was eating bread. The bread was stale, must have been a week old, dry rye bread with a red label from some bakery or other. He continued to dig in with his teeth, finishing off even the brown, leathery crust; then he grasped the loaf with both hands and broke off another piece. Eating with his right hand, he clasped the loaf with his left; he went on eating, sat down on the edge of a wooden crate, and, each time he broke off a piece, bit first into the soft center, feeling all around his mouth the touch of the bread like a dry caress, while his teeth went on digging.

Thomas Bernhard

Among Nietzsche's posthumously published notes we find the following: "Let us consider this idea in its most terrifying form: existence as it is, without meaning or goal, but inescapably recurrent, without a finale into nothingness . . . Those who cannot bear the sentence, There is no salvation, *ought* to perish." Serving up that "existence as it is" has long been one of the main activities of modernist literature, especially in Europe, but the sternly enjoined "ought" has proven thorny even to the most fire-hardened pessimists. The organism manifests a striking sort of obstinacy when its own cessation is at issue. What our masters show us, by and large, is man in a state of deadlock, unable to bear the sentence and unwilling to perish. Beckett's "I can't go on, I'll go on" more or less sums it up.

But the Austrian novelist Thomas Bernhard has made it his special program to restore to Nietzsche's proposition its cutting edge. Putting to one side the matter of eternal recurrence, he asks: is an existence without meaning or goal—he does not doubt that this is its true character—bearable or not? If it is, then what is the toll exacted from the psyche? If it is not . . . From the first, Bernhard's novels, *Gargoyles* (1970), *The Lime Works* (1973), *Correction* (1979), and *Concrete* (1984), have explored the options with an unflinching gaze. Konrad in *The Lime Works* endures his hellish life—poverty, paralysis of creative will, a crippled, importuning wife—for as long as he can. When he reaches the end of his tether, when his reserves are gone, he shoots the woman in the head and lapses into catatonia. In *Correction,* Roithamer, the philosopher, struggles to achieve the perfect integration of his life and his thought; at last he concludes that he has done everything that he can, and must, do, and hangs himself in a clearing in the forest. Possibilities of redemption or reclamation are nowhere suggested.

Concrete is very much of a piece with the earlier works. The same thematic elements are present, though in different groupings, and the investigation of the psyche's response to the "impossible" nature of existence proceeds apace. Even the narrator, Rudolph, is instantly recognizable. Obsessed, depressed, loathing himself and others, he is but the latest carrier of Bernhard's acetylene torch. And he takes it from his predecessor with a vertiginous rush:

> From March to December, writes Rudolph, while I was having to take large quantities of prednisolone, a fact which I'm bound to record here, against the third acute onset of my sarcoidosis, I assembled every possible book and article written by or about Mendelssohn-Bartholdy and visited every possible and impossible library in order to acquaint myself thoroughly with my favorite composer and his work, preparing myself with the most passionate seriousness for the task, which I had been dreading throughout the preceding winter, of writing—such was my pretension—a major work of impeccable scholarship.

"Every possible book," "acquaint myself thoroughly," "preparing myself with the most passionate seriousness . . ." The most elementary schooling in Freud will give us the typology: Rudolph is repressed, narcissistic, obsessive-compulsive. We are hardly surprised when we learn in the following pages that he is incapable of putting pen to paper to begin his masterwork. To call him "blocked," however, would be to attach a simplifying epithet to what is, in fact, a total paralysis of soul. Rudolph is not obstructed by some malfunctions in part of his being—his being itself is a knot. And as Bernhard's narrative proceeds, we begin to register the dimensions of his crisis, its self-consuming circularity.

Rudolph is a master at displacing and shifting blame; he is unable to stare his demon in the face. He cannot begin his treatise, he insists, because he lives in dread of his older sister. She preys on his weakness. He has only to decide to begin and she will promptly appear on his doorstep. Her unannounced visits—the very possibility of them—assault his nerves and destroy his composure. And what a sister! Projected through the enlarging mechanism of his neurosis, she is like some horrible two-dimensional cutout—loud, domineering, crass, the very incarnation of bourgeois philistinism. Against such a visitant all of Rudolph's delicacy and refinement must shrink away.

As readers, though, we have an advantage of objectivity. True, she is an irritating, self-important creature; but she is not nearly the harpy that her brother makes her out to be. The contrast between images underlines for us the severity of the malaise. Her negative attributes—which Rudolph conflates with those of his culture—loom larger as his condition worsens:

> My sister spreads it around Vienna that I am a failure, especially in those quarters where the effect is most devastating for me. I'm continually hearing her say to all and sundry *My little brother and his Mendelssohn-Bartholdy.* She's not embarrassed to call me a madman in everybody's hearing. . . . I know she talks like this about me and gets me an exceedingly damaging reputation everywhere. She recoils from nothing in order to get money, that is to do business, and rather than ruin a party she'd call me anything.

But to all of this he nonetheless adds: "On the other hand I've always loved her, with all her dreadful faults—loved her and hated her."

Lacerating relationships supply much of the central tension in Bernhard's work. Invariably his withdrawn, compulsive males are pitted against small-minded, intractable women. Not in a sexual way, though—the men are too disembodied for that; the opposition is, if this is possible, even more primary. Everything in the female psyche exists for the sole purpose of affronting the man. And this state of affairs is as necessary as it is intolerable. Konrad serves and placates his wife even as he reviles her; Roithamer continues to visit his crude, shrewish mother long after it is clear to him that nothing but pain could ever result from their contact. These characters are so far removed from the daily human commerce that they can only feel their reality in the presence of an adversary. As to why it should always be a woman—a mother, wife, sister—Bernhard gives no clue. Nothing in the work suggests the origin or etiology of this primal face-off. It is simply presented as the state of things. As readers, we feel at times unwelcome, as if we have arrived by mistake at the site of some incomprehensible private exorcism.

Meanwhile, Rudolph, riding the swell of his vituperations, realizes that he cannot endure another winter in his village of Peiskam. And his sister urges him on: "If you don't get away soon, you'll go to pieces and die." He tantalizes himself with images of the island of Palma. There, away from everything, free of his sister and his life-sapping culture, he will work. Nothing will prevent him. Making a decision, though, and following it through are two very different things for Rudolph. His character makes it all but impossible to act. Time and again he gets himself to the brink, has his papers and medicines all packed and ready, only to back down. His health cannot sustain the journey, he will die in a strange hotel, he will not be able to work without his books and materials . . . Bernhard is aware of the possibilities for humor in Rudolph's indecisiveness:

> I was caught up once more in my own personal comedy. I'd changed course, and once again it was simply a laughing matter or a crying matter, depending on how I felt, but since I wanted nei-

ther to laugh nor to cry, I got up and checked whether I had packed the right medicaments. I had put them in my red-spotted medicine bag. Had I packed enough prednisolone, spironolactone and potassium chloride? I opened the medicine bag, looked inside, and tipped out the contents on the table by the window.

Bernhard's style, with its peculiar recursive throb, its controlled clause repetitions, is wonderfully suited for recapturing the myriad forms of psychic hypertrophy. In *The Lime Works* the relentless circularity mimes the process of a mind that is no longer in control of its own momentum (". . . his wife had spoken to him about a pair of mittens she was making for Konrad, she had been working on this one pair of mittens for six months, because she unravelled each mitten just before she had finished knitting it . . ."). In *Correction,* on the other hand, the insistent hammering of clauses, not so different from the above, is used to project the extreme difficulty of thought. Roithamer (very much a Wittgenstein figure) and his narrator, who is also a philosopher, proceed by way of repetitions because thought cannot hope to penetrate reality in any other way—truth is not to be caught on the wing. Stylistically conjoined in this way, "genius" and madness look like the heads and tails on a spinning coin.

But Rudolph is neither genius nor madman—quite—and to transmit his particular condition, Bernhard loosens the weave of his prose somewhat. Sentences are shorter and jumpier and are paced to suggest the erratic movements of a psyche bent upon hiding from itself. Phrase repetitions are manipulated in symphonic fashion: they give us the crescendo and diminuendo of uncontrollable nervous activity.

After interminable and, for the reader, infuriating vacillations, Rudolph finally does travel to Palma. He arranges himself in his hotel room, puts his papers in order—and is no more able to work than he was before. Only now, away from his sister, he has removed his main excuse for inactivity. By escaping to freedom he has painted himself still further into a corner. But he cannot see this. For Rudolph the future remains an inexhaustible fund of propitious moments—the miracle is certain to happen.

At this point, Bernhard inserts a curious flashback. Rudolph is in

Palma on a previous visit. Walking in the town one day, Rudolph meets a young German woman named Anna Hardtl who promptly tells him her tragic story: her husband just recently jumped/fell to his death from their hotel window. Rudolph listens intently while she traces for him the events of their life together, and he accompanies her when she goes to look for the grave in the nearby cemetery. The whole circumstance somehow seems to gratify his own morbidity. We steel ourselves for some dark broodings. But no—quite unexpectedly, in the course of a long sentence, we recall that years have passed, that Rudolph is now in Palma a second time. It is a disturbing switch. So little has changed. The unfortunate Anna is a memory, but everything else remains as before: Rudolph is still ailing, his book is still unwritten . . .

Nevertheless, years do not pass without some mark. In the interval since he was last in Palma, Anna's story has worked its way into his system. And as Rudolph walks along the familiar streets, the spell is renewed. One morning he wakes up possessed by her image. "I must go to the cemetery as quickly as possible," he tells himself. In three breathless sentences he is there, standing in front of the stone. He sees that there is a new plaque and that Anna's name has been engraved under her husband's. "Suicido," explains the porter. Rudolph rushes back to the hotel in a taxi—"I drew the curtains in my room," writes Rudolph, "took several sleeping tablets, and woke up twenty-six hours later in a state of extreme anxiety."

Concrete ends with a spasm. We are pitched out into uncertainty. Are we to trust the momentum of the last pages, to assume that Rudolph hurries to throw himself from the window? It would be consonant with Bernhard's belief—that durability is finite in the face of pain. What's more, the logic of events fits well with Camus's insight about suicide, that a single event, a straw, is enough to trigger a person who has been steadily, imperceptibly "undermined" by life.

On the other hand, recalling Nietzsche's formulation, we may also venture the opposite: that Anna's strength of character, the purity of her despair, enabled her to grasp her situation and act upon the imperative, and that it is Rudolph's tragedy to be without that strength. We can imagine without difficulty how he drags himself forward from day to day, as before, pushing his stake to the next square, waiting for the next—redeeming—turn of the roulette wheel. Bernhard has calculatedly left us to our own devices. He has pressed the expected exclamation point down to make a tensely bent question mark.

Reading through Bernhard's novels consecutively, one begins to remark, and later enlarge upon, a problematic paradox. As we have seen, the concerns are dark ones and the conclusions unrelievedly bleak. Madness and suicide dance attendance upon exacerbated consciousness; there is no relief except through self-deception. Whatever our own biases might be, we set them apart while the writer performs. But here is the crux: writing is, by its very nature, an effort at the redemption of pain. So long as it continues, it intimates that redemption is possible. The statements Bernhard makes are, in a sense, contradicted by the fact of their being made. We feel, and respond to, the authorial presence behind the projected voices. But it is difficult to hear the writer keep saying, "I can't go on," without eventually muttering, "But you do." As Shakespeare understood, "The worst is not so long as we can say: This is the worst."

Still, we must concede that Bernhard's is a very real and impassioned despair, and that the novels, even though they move within a confined locus, have emblematic force. Konrad, Roithamer, and Rudolph, in their production or paralysis, represent what Susan Sontag has called "the artist as exemplary sufferer." Their torments are caused, in part, by the conditions of the modern social order, and their invectives are not wholly off the mark. What Rudolph writes on the eve of his departure for Palma could just as well have been set down by Konrad or Roithamer:

> If I go away, I said to myself, sitting in the iron chair, I shall be leaving a country whose utter futility depresses me every single day, whose imbecilities daily threaten to stifle me, and whose idiocies will sooner or later be the end of me, even without my illnesses. Whose political and cultural conditions have of late become so chaotic that they turn my stomach when I wake up every morning, even before I am out of bed. Whose indifference to intellect has long since ceased to cause the likes of me to despair, but if

> I am truthful only to vomit . . . in which everything that once gave pleasure to so-called thinking people, or at least made it possible for them to go on existing, has been expelled, expunged and extinguished, in which only the most primitive instinct for survival prevails and the slightest pretention to thought is stifled at birth.

This is not lament—this is rage. We can only guess at its deeper origins, though the relationships depicted in the novels may give us a clue. Where rage of this intensity is directed outward, we often find the sociopath; where inward, the suicide. Where it breaks out laterally, onto the page, we sometimes find a most unsettling artistic vision.

Peter Schneider

Anyone who presumes to review a book really ought to take a moment to glance at the cover. I say that to castigate myself: I did not notice that Peter Schneider's *The Wall Jumper* (1983) calls itself "a novel" until it was way too late. True, the lettering was inconspicuous, and I was in a hurry to start reading. But the fact is that I got all the way through *The Wall Jumper* without considering even once that I might be reading fiction. What's more, I remarked to myself several times that documentary is gradually establishing itself as *the* prose form for our age. Where does this leave us? On the one hand, it tells you a little bit about my reviewing habits; on the other, and more important, it says something about current notions of genre.

Peter Schneider

The boundaries between literary forms are a good deal more porous than the wall that constitutes the subject of this book.

The Wall Jumper can be called a novel only on the flimsiest, most fashionable grounds: that the narrative "I" is a fiction. I'm sure that there are plenty of grad students in New Haven who could go off on quite an excursus about this, but I prefer to skip over the subtleties. Schneider has written a first-rate piece of personal reportage, one that creates its effects anecdotally, *en passant,* and that succeeds precisely because it avoids the more elaborate illusionism that the novel has always taken as its central imperative. In other words, my misreading was the right reading—somebody just happened to slap the wrong label on. I much prefer discussing the excellence of this little book to pulling it apart for flatness and weak characterization (which I would have to if I thought it were a novel), or to theorizing (the only other option) as to whether the novel is a portmanteau that will accommodate anything we should wish to pitch in.

Schneider's book has no dominant "plot," no key incident, and it does not yield to quick summary. Its axis is the constant presence—visually, politically, and psychically—of the Berlin Wall, and its progress is strung casually from incident to anecdote to meditation. The narrator, who does not name himself, is a writer living in West Berlin—I will be so presumptuous as to refer to him as "Schneider." We are given the basic lineaments of a life: he tells a few things about his past, describes his apartment building, introduces some of his friends, and indicates, most sketchily, what his love life is like. But there is no focus, no gathering surge. Incidents or personal notations are included only insofar as they afford some perspective on the "schizophrenia" of a culture. I use the term loosely—I don't think Schneider uses it at all. It is, however, the theme of the book (and, in a different way, the theme of his screenplay for Reinhard Hauff's *Knife in the Head*). As Schneider writes: "'I come from Germany.' Either it has no meaning, or I am speaking of a country that appears on no political map."

Why hasn't *The Wall Jumper* been written a hundred times before? Indeed, how could anyone living in Berlin, or even Germany, write about anything else? Those are the obvious—and most naïve—questions. The central, and unanswerable, question is: how did Schneider, a Berliner, manage to distance himself enough to see the Wall for what it is? For the schizophrenia he writes about is directly connected with one of the most primary human instincts—the impulse to internalize the features of our environment and adapt to them. To adapt is to lose the ability to see. That we have this kaleidoscopic meditation on the different styles of adaptation is in itself remarkable. And it's doubly so inasmuch as Schneider writes not like a detached alien but from the heart, like a native.

"The ring around West Berlin is 102.5 miles in length. Of this, 65.8 miles consist of concrete slabs topped with pipe. . . ." To call this the "real" Wall would be to diminish drastically the field of "the real." The concrete slabs are only the manifestation of a complex of political and ideological forces. Abstract and invisible though those forces are, the truth is that without their existence *in opposition* to another such complex, there would be no Wall.

That is one perspective. Another is the phenomenological: that the "real" Wall is the sum of its representations. That is, that every separate psyche sees its own picture and, on the basis of its experience, interprets it in its own way. Schneider is ever mindful of this, even in the face of his own strong feelings. In one episode, for instance, he is visiting friends in the East, listening as, one after the other, each tells stories of harassment by authorities, censorship, abuse. Schneider wants to cry out: "Why do you put up with this, even for a day? Get out; you can do it!" But he keeps quiet. He knows that his response does not take into account human complexity, that there are many kinds of reasoning. Blind adaptation cannot account for everything, and neither can fear. Everyone has something irreducibly irrational buried at the core.

Many of Schneider's anecdotes and speculations are fathom lines into this mystery zone; he relishes the irreducible. Consider the tale of Gerhard Schalter, the man for whom things are always "fantastic!" One day Schalter travels to East Berlin to meet his mistress, who is arriving by plane. She does not come. But this does not deter Schalter. He goes back to the airport every day to wait. In time, he forgets the real purpose to his going. He begins to make friends; he discovers that goods are cheaper. In the end the moving van comes to transport his goods to the East.

And then there's Schneider's friend Robert. Robert has come to the West because he could not publish his poems on the other side. He adapts to the new ways with astonishing ease, but he refuses to concede that they might represent any improvement. All is decadent and slack; people can't see that their lives are being manipulated from the top. In the East there are no illusions on that score. Still, he shops for a luxury car. His creed: "If you're going to live in the Western morass, then by all means do it as comfortably as possible." In arguments he gets worked up and screams about "Nazis" and "Western creeps." His accommodation is lacquer thin.

The issue of fascism versus communism is a live one for Berliners. Many Easterners righteously maintain that they were the ones who resisted the Nazi machine. For them the ghouls are very much alive—in capitalist disguise. Others, like Schneider's friend Pommerer, have stayed in the East because they truly believe that capitalism is dying and that communism, for all its "lapses" under Stalin, is just getting started. Pommerer regards himself as a dissident with respect to the current state—his writing is censored and restricted; but he prefers this to what he sees as the compromised freedom of the West. "If you could travel out, come back, and leave again," he says, "this would be the best place in the world . . . because of the people. They're more serious, more committed, hungrier." Most nights, though, he sits in a café and rails at the jukebox: "I'm sick of hearing that song. Here we sit in Berlin Center, the wall is only a few yards off, and beyond it are the all-night cafés of Kreuzberg."

These are just a few samples of the interpretive diversity among the citizens of the Berlins. Schneider's narrative, slight though it appears, manages, through juxtaposition and splicing, a thick weave of impressions. And though his prose moves from scene to scene and from one point of view to another, it never loses clarity or vigor. Descriptions of encounters are balanced by sharp vignettes about various intrepid adventurers: Mr. Kabe, for instance, the compulsive "wall jumper," who, for no ideological reason, and in spite of numerous arrests, must get himself over the Wall—because it's there; or else the three movie-starved kids who cross from the East to see the latest features and then dutifully make their way home again.

One tale tops the next in its improbability, but none quite satisfies Schneider. He wants the perfect emblem, the story that will in some way refract all the multiple meanings of the Wall in the lives of Berliners. "The only sure thing," he reports, "is that the man whose story I want is caught in a back-and-forth motion over the Wall, like a soccer goalie in an instant replay, always taking the same dive to miss the same ball." Schneider never does find the perfect story, but he captures its essence, perhaps inadvertently, in the image of "Frieda Loch."

Early in the book, Schneider mentions one of his neighbors, a smartly dressed elderly gentleman who always has an air of knowing something. "I thought I should follow him: behind his door there had to be some secret, a guide to serenity, to a carefree life." Late one night, in the courtyard of the building, he encounters a perfumed and blowsy-looking cabaret queen. "Don't you recognize me?" she asks. "Haven't you ever heard of Frieda Loch?" The transformation is perfect; only the "aquiline" nose tips Schneider off.

The incident is given in passing and is never elaborated upon, but it resonates no less for that. Frieda *is* the image of double identity, of the split in the soul. His/her unfixed, shifting sexuality is contradiction—the dress-up and the lascivious walk are the parody of contraction surmounted. That Schneider should have to search so resolutely for an image that would embody both dividedness *and* some possibility of triumph over dividedness—for this is what he ultimately wants—is distressing. It feeds our fear that the problem of the Wall, which is the problem of ideological opposition, is all but unsolvable. Schneider does speculate about this, and his assessment is anything but optimistic:

> What would happen if, say, both German governments took a year's vacation; if the journalists fell silent for a year; if the border police took a year to recuperate on the Adriatic and Black Sea, and

> the people started their own East-West negotiations? After a brief embrace, they would discover that they resemble their governments more closely than they care to admit. It would become evident that they have long since made their own crusade out of the biographical accident of growing up in different occupation zones—later, different social systems. As soon as someone asked which half offers a better life, the fight that both states carry on daily in the media would break out in the living room.

Throughout *The Wall Jumper,* Schneider upholds the truth of the particular, and resists the polemicist's kind of idea mongering. In his view, there are no freely floating ideas—there are only specific ideas in specific heads that are fastened to specific bodies that are in specific circumstances. He freely admits that if his own background had been different, that if he had grown up in Dresden, had watched Russian films instead of American Westerns, and had missed out on Bill Haley and Bob Dylan, his whole orientation—perhaps his very being—would be different. But that prospect troubles him. He does not want to agree to an out-and-out determinism. Instead, he wonders: "Would I have turned out so differently that no one would recognize me?" This is a key question. And how we answer it probably reveals whether we believe that the ideological impasse is permanent. Schneider hedges his bet and leaves the question hanging.

What are Schneider's politics? My guess is that he would set up camp with Max Frisch, who wrote: "I am not a political person, because I . . . take everything personally to heart." To take things "personally" in this way is to assert that truths are local, relative to a speaker, dictated by particulars. We can read this at face value, as an apolitical profession, or else we can put a higher and, I think, more accurate interpretation upon it. We can see it as a vision in which *everything* is political—in which politics is understood to be as intricate and relativistic as human social life. Living and working in his "Siamese" city, Schneider is such a politician of daily life. He avoids polemic, but at every moment he is aware of the webwork of political distinctions. He is not so much disengaged as multiply aware. This style has in no way undercut his humanity; it has not diminished his outrage at Western complacency or the repressiveness of the Soviet state. He has done with his prose what his instant-replay goalie could do only illusionistically—he has kept himself hovering in defiance of gravity.

Peter Schneider

Eva Demski

For I had to make him as you make a dead man, who has lost all the proofs and all the constituent parts of his existence, who has to be achieved entirely within you.

—RILKE, *The Notebooks of Malte Laurids Brigge*

Frankfurt, 1974. On the Saturday before Easter, an unnamed woman stands at the head of the stairs in a dark apartment building and watches two men trundling a zinc coffin down the narrow stairwell. Inside is the body of her estranged husband, aged thirty, dead of "natural causes."

The frame quickly expands. We find out that the apartment is swarming with police. The husband, it appears, was a radical lawyer who represented imprisoned members of the Baader-Meinhof gang (known henceforth as "the Group"). The police are looking for certain papers; an autopsy has already been ordered. As the woman stands in the corridor, in numb shock, she hears other officers interrogating a shabbily dressed young man—one of her husband's lovers. "They're enemies," she thinks, preparing to give her own deposition. "You have to fight them with cunning, dignified means."

Within a dozen pages, Eva Demski has put into motion all of the elements of a tough urban thriller: a dead man with terrorist connections, a host of prying cops, hints of night-side sexuality . . . but just as deftly she turns on her heel. The highly pressurized materials of *Dead Alive* (1986) do not explode into action. The woman attends to her business and then leaves, bearing the lurid images away into the stillness of her life.

Because of the Easter holiday and the required autopsy, twelve days must elapse before the body can be laid to rest. Demski has structured the novel accordingly, a chapter to every day. The strategy works to wonderful effect. We follow the woman through her days—she contacts friends and associates—through her stages of grief and realization; we heed the surges of memory. Ultimately the entire chaos of an epoch is forced through the aperture of those days of waiting. Sharp flashes disclose their history as a couple: the courtship, his early days as a flamboyant public defender, the travails of their shared activism, and the sexual conflicts that gradually destroyed their marriage. But, amazingly, Demski never detaches the private struggle from the larger context of the times. Every move is in some way bound up with the energies and pressures of the social sphere. Accounts from others sometimes vie with the woman's preferred version. By the time we finish the novel we feel as though we have participated in the life cycle of a whole generation.

Demski's woman protagonist is completely credible in her reactions and gestures:

> Fundamentally, she was one of those plump, vivacious women, a bit maternal without ever wishing to be a mother, good-natured and rather arrogant—one of those women who tend to cry easily when they go to the movies or listen to late-night radio talk shows. But on this first evening, and as the night wore on, her eyes were a desert. A couple of trial sobs, a feeling as if a rough brush

kept scraping back and forth inside her stomach; but not a single tear.

This is an inhabited character, not an invented one. Her emotional range is vast, and Demski makes no attempt to paint over her weaknesses. She becomes the perfect filter for the divergent voices that claim her attention.

Piece by piece, the woman begins to uncover the design of her husband's life. She talks with his parents and his former clients, colleagues and neighborhood cronies. The presentation is bare of easy sentiment. When the woman visits the hulking street-vendor Martina, for example, she hears: "You been off your feed for the last few days? You look better. Don't gobble it all back on. Have you had the funeral already?" The voices are worn, scarred, patched together—we trust them.

A lesser writer might have tried to force the plot to turn on the husband's hidden life. Demski is shrewder than that. These two people knew each other as well as any two complicated adults ever could—there are no sensational revelations. At the same time, though, the novel is faithful to the myriad ways in which other lives remain opaque. The woman is willing to face the truth about her husband's homosexuality, but try as she might she cannot understand what it meant to him. At one point she visits a leather bar that he used to frequent. Against the backdrop of a pornographic film, she sees an apparition. The subtle tics of its otherness are far more disconcerting to her than the images on the screen:

> Suddenly the wife saw her husband very clearly, standing in a rigid pose at the bar. His profile was half hidden and nothing was visible but his sharp nose and the shadows of his lashes on the curves of his cheeks. He was standing there as if he didn't see her, and observing the door with short, rapid movements of his eagle's head. She could see his white hands distinctly, lying side by side on the bar.

Soon after the news of the death has gone out, the woman is contacted by members of the Group. Terse voices instruct her over the phone. She arranges to meet a certain "Gloucester" in a café at the zoo. Posing as lovers, the two stage an embrace. She feels the young man tremble "like a taut wire from which a perching bird has just flown away: a movement not of fear but of alertness."

Their discussion concerns a valise that the lawyer had in his keeping: she must find it and deliver it to the Group. The woman is flattered, proud of having some importance for the revolution. But she is also confused and frightened. She cannot understand the impersonal intensity with which these people carry out their plans. Her husband's death, she sees, is nothing to them—it is a problem, an obstacle to surmount. Her emotions clash with her political sympathies. And when she finally does locate the valise, she realizes that there is no room for the striking of fashionable poses: she has to face for herself the real implications of her husband's commitment.

Again, Demski declines the more obvious narrative possibilities. Though the terrorist presence remains an important tensing spring, bringing into relief the moral and political interrogations, we end up seeing only a few surface traces of revolutionist activity. In the novel, as in German society, the Group stays underground.

Dead Alive delineates clearly how the euphoric solidarity of the sixties has given way to the most complicated polarizations. Former activists retreat into apathy, girding themselves with defensive righteousness. Small sects turn to violent praxis. And in the midst of everything else are the good liberal citizens who vote "law and order" but can scarcely conceal their glee at extremist actions. Demski's discursive plotting and her rendering of the woman's anguished indecision allow her an unforced examination of the differing stances and motivations. The woman listens carefully when her husband's associate proclaims: "At my age, one no longer cares about being something special, becoming famous. All I want is the revolution." But she is no less attentive when her old friend Paul, another lawyer, tells her: "I'm almost forty. When you reach my age, you have to watch out that you don't start to look comic as a revolutionary."

She realizes, finally, that she must choose for herself. She cannot be her husband, however much their ideals once converged. His anarchic temperament was able to accommodate, even foster, extremism—hers cannot. The woman surreptitiously destroys the materials in the case. Though her gesture is in one sense cowardly—she admits as much—it is also genuine, the result of profound self-examination.

A review cannot do justice to the woven quality of Demski's narrative. She shuttles with great ease between the crepuscular anxieties of the moment and the unexpected incursions of memory. At the same time, her wide range of concern and her nonjudgmental notation of character allow her to sustain a vivid sense of milieu. By the end of the tenth day, the reader has not only come to know the couple, but he has also penetrated the manifold layers of their social and political environment. What's more, he has watched, as if through a polished rearview mirror, the unceremonious end of an era:

> She still had one photo left from 1969. It showed the husband and wife looking earnest and excited, but also self-confident—he at twenty-six, she at twenty-five—both dressed in black, with the black silk flag draped over their shoulders.

On the day before the funeral, the woman suddenly throws herself into the project of making a collage scrapbook of faces from their shared past. Working with scissors and paste, she muses:

> How many different childhoods they had come out of; all of them approaching, like orbiting stars, a single point, where they then converged. Their childhoods hadn't been dream kingdoms. They had come from fine homes or from lower-middle-class obscurity; they had had anxious or megalomaniacal mothers; rich fathers or maybe no fathers at all—railroad conductors and generals, tradesmen and poets of the Thousand-Year Reich—and yet all of them, coming from far away, had met at this same point, a place of enchantment. There had been joy in the land for that brief spell in 1967, when all over the country they listened to the radio and heard how many they were and how, at least for that moment, the streets belonged to them.

When the book is finished, the woman takes it to the cemetery and places it in her husband's coffin. She has completed her mourning. At this moment, the tightened strands of the novel vibrate to make an eerie music: Demski is declaring both victory and defeat. Though the man is dead, something has been wrested from his life. The past, too, is gone, its promises spent—but we see that its outsized dreams can still flare up in individual lives.

At the funeral, the mourners group themselves in sharply defined factions: parents and family, the young lover and his friends, professional colleagues, a gang of black-jacketed cyclists . . . Plain-clothes police stand by, oblivious to the presence of a well-dressed woman from the Group. As the priest tries to speak, another young woman begins to shout obscenities. It seems that chaos will carry the day. But then, miraculously, silence supervenes—something more potent than divisive ideology moves through the room. For the space of a breath, the consecrating mysteries of love and death banish all distinction. Their presence cannot be sustained, of course. Animosity and strife return as soon as the procession gets under way. But now there is a hollowness, a boastful bravado, a quickening sense that the actors have had it with the play. With no sacrifice of austere realism, Demski has suggested that there may be other options.

PART II

Russian Writers

Osip Mandelstam
(1891–1938)
Joseph Brodsky
(1941—)

Literature under totalitarian regimes is a life and death business—that is the cliché and the truth. The perverse corollary is that these regimes confer upon the word a power unimaginable in the free West. Literature can bring imprisonment or death; its truths are the bread of life to victims of oppression. In our century, this has been most glaringly spelled out by the career of Osip Mandelstam. The supremely cultivated Mandelstam—one of the greatest poets and essayists in the history of the Russian language—was harassed for the duration of his writing life. He was finally arrested for reciting a poem against Stalin; he died in transit to a labor camp in 1938.

Thirty years later, Joseph Brodsky, a young poet from Leningrad, was put on trial for being a "parasite" and was sentenced to five years' internal exile. The sentence was commuted in 1972, and Brodsky was allowed to emigrate. He now makes his home in New York.

Brodsky is in many ways an heir to Mandelstam—in his outspoken manner, in his insistent moral seriousness. The poems and essays of both writers proclaim an absolute faith in language: the word alone guarantees the continuity of civilization. Mandelstam's essays look back to Villon, Goethe, and, above all, Dante. Brodsky, in turn, makes Mandelstam one of the objects of his homage. We can see how the links of the chain get joined.

Osip Mandelstam

Social differences and class antagonisms pale before the division of people into friends and enemies of the word: literally, sheep and goats. I sense an almost physically unclean goat breath emanating from the enemies of the word.

—MANDELSTAM

The poetry of Osip Mandelstam defies successful translation. This is because he worked with his superbly developed ear and his philologist's instincts from within the Russian language. What we get, in English, is at best a kind of camera obscura rendering of a phenomenon that is densely textured, quick with allusion, and that derives its internal propulsion from the intransmissible word itself. Anyone who doubts this need only refer to one or two of Clarence Brown's close readings in his book *Mandelstam* (1973). It would seem that any serious discussion of Mandelstam as a poet based upon translation is doomed. As for discussion about his world view—is it not part of the very nature of lyric poetry that its idea inheres in the prosody, that you cannot detach it and lift it out in the way you might lift out the backbone from a well-cooked fish? Mandelstam certainly believed this.

We are, therefore, quite fortunate that Mandelstam was a writer of prose as well, and that this prose was no mere footnote to the poetry, but its accompaniment. Here, particularly in the critical prose, we find the investigations, ideas, and arguments that in many ways form a counterpart to the poetry; here, too, we can speak of something that amounts to a world view. And, unlike the poetry, the prose does lend itself to a more or less sensible transposition into English. Mandelstam himself declares one of the distinctions between the two modes:

> The prose writer always addresses himself to a concrete audience, to the dynamic representatives of his age. Even when making prophecies, he bears his future contemporaries in mind. . . . Since instruction is the central nerve of prose, the prose writer requires a pedestal. Poetry is another matter. The poet is bound only to his providential addressee. He is not compelled to tower over his age, to appear superior to society.
>
> —"On the Addressee"

This impulse to instruction, which is not the same as didacticism, is present in Mandelstam's prose. It is what allows the close paraphrase of translation to succeed. The result is that we have access to a number of important statements from Mandelstam on the nature of language, poetry, and the position of the poet with respect to his culture and time. While this is not going to bring us any closer to the poetry—for that requires understanding of a different order—it will show us more about the thoughts and predilections of the man who wrote it.

There is enough prose so that it can be, and has been, divided into two groupings: *The Prose of Osip Mandelstam* (1965) and *Mandelstam: The Complete Critical Prose and Letters* (1979). There is no overlap in contents. In fact, the collections show decidedly different aspects of Mandelstam as a prose writer.

The *Prose* gives us the translated texts of "The Noise of Time" (written in 1925), "Theodosia" (1925), and "The Egyptian Stamp" (1928). "The Noise of Time" is the centerpiece of these three writings, all of which are philological in their method. The prose is poetic, deriving much of its rhythm and association from within the language. It is prose, however, and as such suffers less from translation.

Taken together, the three sections of the *Prose* provide a closely fashioned and intimately cluttered picture of time as it is transected by memory. There is not much of Mandelstam as persona in these pieces, for he has deliberately removed himself to the periphery, a tactic that is maddening until one grasps his purpose: that the time should enunciate itself as much as possible. Unlike most writers, he has no great interest in supplying a "portrait of the artist as a young man." His object is to re-create what he names in the one title: the noise of time. The technique is a careful amassing and rendering of detail. Here, for example, is a description of the premiere in St. Petersburg of Scriabin's *Prometheus:*

> In the dim light of the gaslamps the many entrances of the Nobility Hall were beset by a veritable siege. Gendarmes on prancing horses, lending to the atmosphere of the square the mood of a civil disturbance, made clicking noises with their tongues and shouted as they guarded the main entry with a chain. The sprung carriages with dim lanterns slipped into the glistening circle and arranged themselves in an impressive black gypsy camp. The cabbies dared not deliver their fare right to the door; one paid them while approaching, and then they made off rapidly to escape the wrath of the police. Through the triple chains the Petersburger made his way like a feverish little trout to the marble icehole of the vestibule, whence he disappeared into the luminous frosty building, bedraped with silk and velvet.

The prose reminds us in many places of the avid detailings of Proust, or Mandelstam's own countryman Nabokov. All three were equally consumed by the effort to graft memory to time. What emerges from these three pieces—and this is their success—is a picture so angled that the life of the artist does not emerge in relief. All is background, or, if you will, foreground.

The *Prose* repays careful reading. The contents will no doubt be sifted and resifted as Mandelstam's place in world literature continues to be reckoned. I would, however, like to focus on the critical prose, for it is in the essays that Mandelstam's sensibility steps forth most vigorously and contentiously.

The Complete Critical Prose and Letters is large enough to require both hands. Even if the letters, the more ephemeral reviews, and the scholarly apparatus were to be deleted, there would still be a good heft to the book. And this is as it should be. Mandelstam was a critic and essayist of major scope. There are, by my count, at least fifteen important essays, not to mention scores of intriguing passages and fragments. From "François Villon," written in 1910 when Mandelstam was nineteen, to "Goethe's Youth: Radiodrama," which came in 1935, when he was forty-four, the contents exhibit a remarkable internal unity. From first to last he is self-assured, consistent in his beliefs, and, above all, willing to risk. These risks were both literal—for he was writing what he believed right in the teeth of Stalin's storm—and figurative, the linguistic risks required to move away from the well-trodden paths.

It is one thing to discover internal unity in a scholar's quiet career, quite another to find it in the works of a man subjected to years of harassment, terrorization, exile, and proscription.* We must try to discover the secret of this unity. Where was it grounded, how was it achieved? In the case of Mandelstam it was, I believe, the result of an all-consuming will to organicism. His highest ideal, and this surfaces time and again in his work, was that of Hellenism: Man in natural concord with his world. It meant that he treasured above all else the free and organic development of his creative gift. In circumstances as hostile as those in the Soviet state, he was forced to sacrifice everything that belongs to an unimpeded life in order that this gift survive as it was meant to. He was at every moment paying heed to the destiny of his work, which he knew was more important than his destiny as a man. In the portrait we get from Nadezhda Mandelstam's

*I do not say much about Mandelstam's biography. It seems futile to do so when it is documented in such detail by his wife, Nadezhda Mandelstam. Still, the reader should keep a few important dates in mind. In 1933 Mandelstam writes a poem denouncing Stalin. Though the poem is not circulated except by recitation to friends, it finds its way to the secret police. He is arrested for the first time in 1934 and sent into a three-year term of exile. Upon his return to Moscow, he finds it impossible to find work or housing. He and his wife move from place to place until, in May of 1938, he is arrested once again. He reportedly dies in a transit camp in December of the same year.

memoirs, *Hope Against Hope* (1970) and *Hope Abandoned* (1974), he often appears curiously passive with respect to his fate. I think that the extraordinary energy he deployed inwardly just to secure the freedom he needed partially accounts for this passivity. It may likewise explain the organic integrity of his work, which, once it is grasped, works exponentially on every part until we confront a whole that has ramified internally to far surpass its assembled parts.

The beginnings of Mandelstam's career, as both a poet and a critic, are closely allied with the movement known as acmeism. Acmeism, briefly, was a reaction against symbolism, which was not only the dominant poetic mode at the turn of the century, but was to a large extent an expression of the prevalent world view of the so-called cultured elite. It was a cult of the beautiful and mysterious, a secular religiosity. There were similarities between symbolism in Russia and Pre-Raphaelitism in England. And the rise of acmeism, as Clarence Brown points out, strongly paralleled the emergence of imagism in England under Pound, Hulme, and Wyndham Lewis. Both movements stressed as guiding principles simplicity, clarity, and the elimination of the tone of otherworldliness. Both drew inspiration from what Henry Adams called the Dynamo—the beauty and functionalism of the new turbine-powered machines. But where futurism would emerge to celebrate the machine values to the exclusion of all else, acmeism referred with equal fervor to the past, specifically to the purity and economy of means of Hellenic classicism.

The presiding luminaries of acmeism included Nikolai Gumiliov, Anna Akhmatova, Michael Kuzmin, and, not long after its inception, a very young Mandelstam. He was only eighteen when his work began to appear in *Apollon,* the acmeist magazine, but from the very first it embodied the values and aspirations of the movement. "François Villon," Mandelstam's first published essay, is striking not only for its conviction and precocity, but also for an implicit identification with its subject. It is amazing to see, in retrospect, how the echoes multiply between the career of the great criminal poet of the fifteenth century and the great "criminal" poet of our own.

Mandelstam's development was, as I have stressed, organic; it was, even more particularly, concentric. He was at every point in his literary career a total sensibility. This is especially uncommon in a nineteen-year-old for it presupposes a deeply hermetic temperament. But clearly this is what Mandelstam had. Each consecutive work represents a further expression of the possibilities of the original fiber. The Villon essay predicates the grand exfoliation of the "Conversation About Dante" in 1933. Already compressed in its eight pages are a great many of Mandelstam's major concerns.

The piece opens with a clear sounding of the acmeist precepts. This is accomplished by a forthright act of historical identification. In choosing to speak about Villon, Mandelstam is already setting up the acmeist family tree. He begins: "Astronomers can predict the precise date of a comet's return over an extensive time interval. For those familiar with François Villon, the appearance of Verlaine represents the same kind of astronomical miracle." Among other things, the statement utilizes what is to be one of Mandelstam's favorite tactics, the application of the terminology of the exact sciences to the phenomenon of poetry and poetic creation. The statement is important, too, because it is a kind of self-prophecy—the next such "astronomical miracle" will be Mandelstam's own arrival. It is no use to object on scientific grounds of an insufficient time lapse between appearances, for Mandelstam was already incorporating relativity into his thought. He already recognized that historical time had become radically compressed.

Villon turned against the hothouse refinements of his time, as would Verlaine, as would Mandelstam and the other acmeists. He brought all the energies of his verse to bear on things, and he navigated among the here and now with the quickness and cunning that characterize the thief.

> Villon was exceptionally conscious of the abyss between subject and object, but he understood it as the impossibility of ownership. The moon and other such neutral "objects" were completely excluded from his poetic usage. On the other hand, he livened up immediately whenever the discussion centered on roast duck or on eternal bliss, objects which he never quite lost hope of acquiring.

Mandelstam already understood well, with his philological sense of the particular, how the life of great poetry depends upon time, and, vice versa, how time depends upon great poetry, and how it is linguistic precision that brings the two into their right relation. What he writes with regard to Villon's *Testaments* pertains closely to his own poetics.

> [The *Testaments*] captivate the reader simply by the mass of precise information they communicate. . . . The passing moment can thus endure the pressure of centuries and preserve itself intact, remaining the same "here and now." You need only to know how to extract that 'here and now' from the soil of time without harming its roots, or it will wither and die.

Thus, states Mandelstam, Villon has preserved forever the ringing Sorbonne bell that interrupted his work on the *Petit Testament* and that he promptly incorporated into a line. He touches here on what will later become a major statement: that it is only through language that one man's present can become another's, establishing thus a state of duration in which time is redeemed.

"François Villon" also introduces for the first time the architectural motif, one that Mandelstam will make much use of in his poetry and future prose. Here, deriving the character of a time from its use of certain building principles, he writes:

> He who first proclaimed in architecture the dynamic equilibrium of the masses or first constructed the groined arch brilliantly expressed the psychological essence of feudalism. In the Middle Ages a man considered himself just as indispensible and just as bound to the edifice of his world as a stone in a gothic structure, bearing with dignity the pressures of his neighbors and entering the common play of forces as an inevitable stake.

We find the same strategy, the derivation of an essence from a particular, that animates Spengler's attempt to write a "morphological history of the world." Spengler had not yet published, but we know from later citations by Mandelstam that he did eventually read *The*

Decline of the West. The similarities in method are worthy of remark.

Mandelstam's statement applies not only to acmeist poetics, the celebration of a structure for its "dynamic equilibrium of masses," but it also suggests something about the way in which he related himself to the social developments of his time. This was written, after all, only five years after 1905, and only eight years before 1918. Mandelstam identified closely with the original ideals of the revolution. Nadezhda Mandelstam emphasizes this point, that he believed that his "oath to the fourth estate obliged him to come to accept the Soviet regime." This belief he sustained so long as he could, well into the Stalin era. His ongoing attempts to work within the structure testify to this, as do his continuing appeals to his protector, Nikolai Bukharin. It was his retrospectively naïve faith that the aberrations he witnessed were temporary and would eventually come right. His trouble came, in part, from his desire to play a part in the life of his times. It was this that rendered conspicuous the divergence between his humanist values and the values of the emerging Soviet state.

The "Morning of Acmeism," written in 1912, but not published until 1919 (for reasons that are not clear), uses the imagery of architecture and building to clarify the acmeist credo. Mandelstam exhorts the poet to the same "piety before the three dimensions of space," with the implication that this must precede any successful projection into the fourth. This piety is what he finds in Hellenic culture, and in the builders of the "physiologically brilliant Middle Ages." It is the capacity for reverence for things as they really are that gives to a culture its sense of proportion and nobility. The materialism is not, however, as thoroughgoing as that espoused by Marx. Mandelstam's ideas about time and culture, as we will see, render the concept of progress in history specious.

The essay is noteworthy for two of its formulations. The first is of the poet as possessor of a special capability:

> The spectacle of a mathematician who, without seeming to think about it, produces the square of some ten-digit number, fills us with a certain astonishment. But too often we fail to see that the poet raises a phenomenon to its tenth power, and the modest

exterior often deceives us with regard to the monstrously condensed reality contained within.

Secondly, he iterates what will become an idea of great importance and one of the key articles of belief, namely, the power of the word. Here, as a preliminary, he declares that the word has a reality far deeper than its sign function.

> Deaf mutes can understand each other perfectly, and railroad signals perform a very complex function without recourse to the word. Thus, if one takes the sense as the content, everything else in the word must be regarded as simple mechanical appendage that merely impedes the swift transmission of the thought. "The word as such" was born very slowly. Gradually, one after another, all the elements of the word were drawn into the concept of form. To this day the conscious sense, the Logos, is still taken erroneously and arbitrarily for the content. The Logos gains nothing from such an unnecessary honor. The Logos demands nothing more than to be considered on an equal footing with the other elements of the word.

Form and content, then, are inseparable. This is the first movement toward the position that Mandelstam sets forth in the major essay "On the Nature of the Word" in 1922. It is here that he develops most explicitly his ideas about language, time, and culture.

Mandelstam begins the essay by posing a question: how can literature, specifically Russian literature, lay claim to unity? History—and he is obviously talking about the revolution—has accelerated with a geometrical ferocity. What will prevent the past from being severed entirely from the present?

Leaving the question for a moment, Mandelstam introduces the Bergsonian concept of duration. Duration can be thought of as the essence of time freed from the chain of linearly conceived units. It is what Proust, a follower of Bergson, sought along the paths of involuntary memory, and what Eliot, another adherent, meant when he wrote:

> Time present and time past
> Are both perhaps present in time future,

And time future contained in time past.
If all time is eternally present
All time is unredeemable.

The passage is Bergson in a highly distilled state. Mandelstam puts it thus:

> He [Bergson] is interested exclusively in the internal connection among phenomena. He liberates this connection from time and considers it independently. Phenomena thus connected to one another form, as it were, a kind of fan whose folds can be opened up in time; however, this fan may be closed up in a way intelligible to the human mind.

For Mandelstam, duration is manifest in language itself. This is a central point, and it becomes more clear as the argument develops. Mandelstam does not linger to explain anything—he moves immediately to answer the original question.

> Language alone can be acknowledged as the criterion of unity for the literature of a given people, its conditional unity, all other criteria being secondary, transitory, and arbitrary. Although a language constantly undergoing changes never freezes in a particular mold even for a moment, moving from one point to another, such points being dazzlingly clear to the mind of the philologist, still, within the confines of its own changes, any given language remains a fixed quantity, a "constant" which is internally unified.

What he is saying, in other words, is that literature and, by extension, the values of a culture exist in language, in a state of suspension that is not bound to linear time. The poet treasures language just as the archaeologist treasures the place where he is digging. Only by way of the past does he manage his thrust into futurity. Over and over Mandelstam dismisses the idea that there can be progress in literature. If language is duration, then all things in language are contemporaneous. He is entirely serious when he writes:

> One often hears: that is good but it belongs to yesterday. But I say: yesterday has not yet been born. It has not yet really existed. I

> want Ovid, Pushkin and Catullus to live once more, and I am not satisfied with the historical Ovid, Pushkin and Catullus.

Mandelstam continues the essay with an explication of what he sees as the Hellenistic nature of the Russian language. That nature, he says, "can be identified with its ontological function"—that is, the name of the thing is equivalent with its being. The idea behind this is that languages, at their origin, were originally entirely concordant with the world they named.

> Therefore, the Russian language is historical by its very nature, since in its totality it is a turbulent sea of events, a continuous incarnation and activation of rational and breathing flesh.

It could not really be less ambiguous: history is literally present in the totality of the language.

There is much in these pages that carries a religious tone, a constant use of words like "incarnation" and "sacred," but religion is not essential to the conception. It may or may not be adduced for the original creation of the world, but it is in no way implicit in the ontological connection between language and its objects. The Adamic overtones are inescapable (and acmeism had for a time the second name of Adamism), but in this case Adam is not naming things in God's created Eden, but on the soil of Hesiod, Homer, and Pindar.

Mandelstam characterizes this Hellenism beautifully:

> Hellenism is an earthenware pot, oven tongs, a milk jug, kitchen utensils, dishes; it is anything which surrounds the body. Hellenism is the warmth of the hearth experienced as something sacred; it is anything which imparts some of the external world to man. . . . Hellenism is the system, in the Bergsonian sense of the term, which man unfolds around himself, like a fan of phenomena freed of their temporal dependence, phenomena subjected through the human "I" to an inner connection.

And from this very naturally follows the idea that shows in clear relief how Mandelstam, holding to his convictions, could only become increasingly estranged from the world that Stalin was trying to force into being:

> Until now the social inspiration of Russian poetry has reached no further than the idea of "citizen," but there is a loftier principle than "citizen," there is the concept of "Man."

According to Nadezhda Mandelstam, the year 1928 was the high point of Mandelstam's public career as a writer. "The Egyptian Stamp" was published, along with *Poems,* the first collected edition of his verse. Mrs. Mandelstam suggests that a great deal was owing to the official presence of Bukharin, for he was still something of a man of culture. Still, to think of this year as being otherwise a high point is misleading. For one thing, Mandelstam had not written poetry since 1925 and would not resume until 1930. For another, Bukharin's opposition party was to be eradicated by Stalin that very year, and Mandelstam was to lose whatever official protection he had. The year, in fact, marked the beginning of the crackdown—witch-hunts began among ranks of party members and intelligentsia alike.

The first indication of trouble, for Mandelstam, came at the very end of the year. A journalist named David Zaslavsky led a virulent press campaign against him, accusing him of plagiarizing a translation of *Till Eulenspiegel.* The fault was the publisher's—he had omitted to list the credits of other translators—and the accusation was unfounded. The whole episode was blown out of proportion. Writers such as Pasternak and Zoshchenko came forth to defend Mandelstam. But nothing could prevent the change of official attitude that seemed to coincide with the incident. His public career was all but finished.

In the following year, 1929, Mandelstam wrote his famous "Fourth Prose." The significance of this work owes less perhaps to its contents than to its symbolic status as a turning point. His wife credits it as the explosion that freed him to write poetry again. He no longer had any doubts, she states, about where he stood. "Fourth Prose" represents his decision to speak his mind and accept the consequences, and as such it is as courageous and historically loaded a document as has ever been written. Any one of its sixteen sections would have sufficed for his arrest. It is Mandelstam's credo, his moral integrity affirmed at a time when no one dared affirm anything.

> I have no manuscripts, no notebooks, no archives. I have no handwriting, for I never write. I alone in Russia work with my voice, while all around me consummate swine are writing.

> Think how beautiful Mother Philology once was, and how she looks today. . . . How pure-blooded, how uncompromising she was then, but how mongrelized and tame she is today. . . .

> It was all as terrifying as a child's nightmare. *Nel mezzo del'cammin di nostra vita*—midway along life's path—I was stopped in the dense Soviet forest by bandits who called themselves my judges. . . . It was the first and only time in my life that Literature had need of me, and it crushed, pawed, and squeezed me, and it was all as terrifying as a child's nightmare.

> My work, regardless of the form, is considered mischief, lawlessness, mere accident. But I like it that way, and I agree to my calling. I'll even sign my name with both hands.

Apart from its beautiful fury and invective, "Fourth Prose" is remarkable for its stylistic acceleration. It signals the beginning of a change in his prose. What was formerly dense is now denser, and it is stenographically much quicker. More is assumed of the reader. Possibly this is because the reader had become an imaginary, future reader. The prose strides ahead in charged clusters. The remainder of Mandelstam's pieces are the closest thing we have to a truly poetic prose—not a prose that poetizes, but one that heaves great masses forward on the slightest of struts.

From now on everything he writes will be *sui generis.* To call his "Journey to Armenia" a travelogue, or his "Conversation About Dante" a piece of literary criticism, is to miss the point entirely. It is equally beside the point to say that Mandelstam changed his orientation in some fundamental way. What happened was far more interesting: a wholly organic phenomenon was subjected to an arbitrary and unnatural climate. But instead of atrophy there was hypertrophy. All growth was speeded up and intensified. By the early thirties he knew what his fate would be—he just did not know when it would come. He told Akhmatova that he was prepared to die. And so he wrote as one whose breath comes too quickly. Images were piled up, one hard upon the next. Progress on the page was analogous to the acrobat's progress from one flying ring to another.

This development reaches its *summa* in "Conversation About Dante." It is there that Mandelstam writes, with reference to poetry, a passage that characterizes itself and the essay perfectly:

> The quality of poetry is determined by the speed and decisiveness with which it embodies its schemes and commands in diction, the instrumentless, lexical, purely quantitative verbal matter. One must traverse the full width of a river crammed with Chinese junks moving simultaneously in various directions—this is how the meaning of poetic discourse is created. The meaning, its itinerary, cannot be reconstructed by interrogating the boatmen: they will not be able to tell how and why we were skipping from junk to junk.

I will pass over Mandelstam's other essays of the time, most notably the "Journey to Armenia," in order to spend more time on the "Conversation." Here the hypertrophic style is seen in its finest expression: not only is this one of the great documents on poetics and poetic gnosis, it is also one of the most unusual and penetrating valuations ever made about the phenomenon of Dante.

Dante was for Mandelstam the supreme poet and maker. He conferred upon him the title "internal *raznochinets,*" thereby cementing a bond of kinship and identification, for *raznochinets,* meaning "outside intellectual," was what he called himself. Nadezhda Mandelstam tells us that he had his Dante with him at all times from the early thirties on:

> Anticipating his arrest—as I have already said, everybody we knew did this as a matter of course—M. obtained an edition of

> the *Divine Comedy* in small format and always had it with him in his pocket just in case he was arrested not at home but in the street.
>
> —*Hope Against Hope*

The one exile carried the works of the other exile as if they composed a map—and the first of the three parts certainly did—of where he was going. Mrs. Mandelstam remarks later in her memoir that she does not believe that Mandelstam was allowed to carry his Dante with him into his final confinement.

The "Conversation About Dante" is Mandelstam's bid to free Dante from the clutches of scholars, and from his imprisonment in historical time as a classic—to release him into time itself, the realm of duration, where he belongs. Using the terminology of the modern sciences and music, contriving metaphor upon metaphor with the fervor of one who is repaying a great debt, he demonstrates that Dante's sensibility and poetic method were concerned, above all else, with process, impulse, and movement. The *Divine Comedy* is not some great static frieze, but a dazzling, kinetic thing:

> If the halls of the Hermitage were suddenly to go mad, if the paintings of all the schools and great masters were suddenly to break loose from their nails, and merge with one another, intermingle, and fill the air with a Futurist roar and an agitated frenzy of color, we would then have something resembling Dante's *Commedia*.

His purpose is to show just how the *Commedia* enacts itself at once in all three tenses: he has taken hold of the very root of his own poetic conviction.

He begins by establishing that poetry is transmutation and that Dante is a "strategist of transmutation and hybridization," that his purpose is not narration, as we have been taught to believe, but the "acting out in nature by means of [his] arsenal of devices."

> What is important in poetry is only the understanding which brings it about. . . . The signal waves of meaning vanish, having completed their work; the more potent they are, the more yielding, and the less inclined to linger.

Systematically he works to undermine the historical, static conception of Dante, and to replace it with the dynamic.

> Whoever says, "Dante is sculptural," is influenced by the impoverished definitions of that great European. Dante's poetry partakes of all the forms of energy known to modern science. Unity of light, sound and matter for its inner nature.

And then, pages later:

> A scientific description of Dante's *Commedia,* taken as a flow, as a current, would inevitably assume the look of a treatise on metamorphoses, and would aspire to penetrate the multitudinous states of poetic matter, just as the doctor in making his diagnosis listens to the multitudinous unity of the organism. Literary criticism would then approach the method of living medicine.

Once he has made his point about the absolutely dynamic character of the *Commedia,* Mandelstam begins to question the process of its composition. The magnitude of what he calls form creation astonishes him. To make sense of it he discovers a particularly rich metaphor:

> We must try to imagine, therefore, how bees might have worked at the creation of this thirteen-thousand-faceted form, bees endowed with the brilliant stereometric instinct, who attracted bees in greater and greater numbers as they were required. The work of these bees, constantly keeping their eye on the whole, is of varying difficulty at different stages of the process. Their cooperation expands and grows more complicated as they participate in the process of forming the combs, by means of which space virtually emerges out of itself.

It is impossible to disentangle from the "Conversation" anything like a single thread of argument. For one thing, Mandelstam is at every step referring his points to specific lines and sections and developing them as much as possible with reference to the Italian language. For another, he is working symphonically, or, recalling the last passage, stereometrically. Rather than attempt a paraphrase—as if a symphonic texture could *be* paraphrased—I would like to select a handful of passages, each of which compresses and suggests more than I possibly could.

Dante's thinking in images, as is the case in all genuine poetry, exists with the aid of a peculiarity of poetic material which I propose to call its convertibility or transmutability. Only in accord with convention is the development of an image called its development. And indeed, just imagine an airplane (ignoring the technical impossibility) which in full flight constructs and launches another machine. Furthermore, in the same way, this flying machine, while fully absorbed in its own flight, still manages to assemble and launch yet a third machine. To make my proposed comparison more precise and helpful, I will add that the production and launching of these technically unthinkable new machines which are tossed off in mid-flight are not secondary or extraneous functions of the plane which is in motion, but rather comprise a most essential attribute and part of the flight itself, while assuring its feasibility and safety to no less a degree than its properly operating rudder or the regular functioning of its engine.

Any given word is a bundle, and meaning sticks out of it in various directions, not aspiring toward any single official point. In pronouncing the word "sun" we are, as it were, undertaking an enormous journey to which we are so accustomed that we travel in our sleep. What distinguishes poetry from automatic speech is that it rouses and shakes us into wakefulness in the middle of a word. Then it turns out that the word is much longer than we thought, and we remember that to speak means to be forever on the road.

It is inconceivable to read Dante's cantos without directing them toward contemporaneity. They were created for that purpose. They are missiles for capturing the future. They demand commentary in the *futurum*.

For Dante time is the content of history understood as a simple synchronic act; and, vice versa, the contents of history are the joint containing of time by its associates, competitors, and co-discoverers.

Dante is an antimodernist. His contemporaneity is continuous, incalculable and inexhaustible.

That is why Odysseus's speech, as convex as the lens of a magnifying glass, may be turned toward the war of the Greeks and Persians as well as toward Columbus's discovery of America, the bold experiments of Paracelsus, and the world empire of Charles V.

When you read Dante with all your powers and with complete conviction, when you transplant yourself completely to the field of action of the poetic material, when you join in and coordinate your own intonations with the echoes of the orchestral and thematic groups continually arising on the pocked and undulating semantic surface, when you begin to catch through the smoky-crystalline rock the sound-forms of phenocryst inserted into it, that is, additional sounds conferred on it no longer by a poetic but by a geological intelligence, then the purely vocal, intonational and rhythmical work is replaced by a more powerful coordinating force—by the conductor's function—and the hegemony of the conductor's baton comes into its own, cutting across orchestrated space and projecting from the voice like some more complex mathematical measure out of a three-dimensional state.

Dante was chosen as the theme of this conversation not because I wanted to focus attention on him as a means to studying the classics and to seat him alongside of Shakespeare and Lev Tolstoi . . . but because he is the greatest, the unrivaled master of transmutable and convertible poetic material, the earliest and simultaneously the most powerful chemical conductor of the poetic composition existing only in the swells and waves of the ocean, only in the raising of the sails and in the tacking.

I do not exaggerate when I say that virtually every passage of this forty-five page piece is of comparable density and thrust. No one who works through it will ever be comfortable with a Dante who is not part dancer, part conductor, part quantum physicist.

It would be convenient to end on this high note, for the "Conversation" is above all a celebration of the word and the poetic process, but it is impossible to do so. The circumstances of Mandelstam, his tragic end, call us back into the historical element. We must somehow raise the question of how a sensibility of this order, believing what he did, could exist in the midst of a state that savaged every impulse to individuality and freedom.

The essay "The Word and Culture," written in 1921, shows us that Mandelstam was not blind to what was happening. Only four years after the revolution he could write:

> The separation of Culture and the State is the most significant event of our revolution. The process of secularization of the State did not stop with the separation of Church and State as the French Revolution understood it. Our social upheaval has brought about a more profound secularization. Today the State has a unique relationship to culture that is best expressed by the term tolerance. But at the same time a new type of organic inter-relationship is beginning to appear. . . . The isolation of the State insofar as cultural values are concerned makes it fully dependent on culture.

That relationship of "tolerance" was soon to take on the prefix "in"—but as far as Mandelstam was concerned, the dependence remained. The only problem was that the state did not realize the fact. Later in the same essay he proclaims:

> People are hungry. The State is even hungrier. But there is something still hungrier: Time. Time wants to devour the State. . . . To show compassion for the State which denies the word shall be the contemporary poet's social obligation and heroic feat.

Could Mandelstam have imagined when he wrote those words the extent to which their meaning was to be tested? Could he, at the very end, have still agreed—when it was not only the word that was denied but all human dignity? His faith in his poet's compact with time would have had to be absolute, present to him even when he wrote these words in his last letter:

> I got five years for counter-revolutionary activity by decree of the Special Tribunal. The transport left Butyrki Prison in Moscow on the 9th of September and we arrived on the 12th of October. I'm in very poor health, utterly exhausted, emaciated, and almost beyond recognition. I don't know if there's any sense in sending clothes, food, and money, but try just the same. I'm freezing without proper clothes.
>
> —letter to his brother Alexander Emilievich, October 1938

Osip Mandelstam's Armenian Journey

I had only one book with me, Goethe's Italienische Reise *in an expensive leather binding, as worn from use as a Baedeker.*

—addenda to "Journey to Armenia"

In the spring of 1930, Osip and Nadezhda Mandelstam set off for an eight-month trip to Armenia. So might run the deceptive syntax of the "shilling life." But as any reader of Nadezhda Mandelstam's *Hope Against Hope* or *Hope Abandoned* knows, there was no such propositional simplicity in their lives—ever. They did go to Armenia, yes. But it was a going attended by tremendous symbolic and circumstantial complexity. In retrospect, the journey would, like Goethe's abrupt flight from Weimar to Italy, stand for a great deal more than a set of remembered particulars. Armenia, with its sun and its ancient simplicity, was a gift bestowed upon one whose life was being clipped "like a coin." Before it could be viewed in retrospect, however, it had to hover before him as a prospect, a dream to hold against the anxious pressures of the present.

For the five-year period between 1925 and 1930, Mandelstam, without question one of the most gifted lyric poets of our—or any—age, wrote no poetry. As these were the ripest years of the poet's maturity—he was in his mid-thirties—this barrenness could only have had the most devastating inward effects. Of course, there is always a danger in trying to account for creativity, or its absence. But we have some warrant for considering the political and cultural situation of the day and Mandelstam's relation to it. Nadezhda Mandelstam reports, of the period in question, that her husband was trying, against his own instincts, to align himself with the attitudes and purposes of the emerging Soviet state. He believed, she writes, that his "oath to the fourth estate obliged him to come to accept the . . . regime." Whatever his outward demeanor at the time, it's not unlikely that the barometric pressure in his soul was dropping steadily.

In 1929, the storm broke. A journalist named David Zaslavsky accused Mandelstam publicly of having plagiarized a translation of *Till Eulenspiegel.* Mandelstam had, of course, done nothing of the kind. But the fury with which he was attacked, and the promptness with which official favor was withdrawn, showed him how things really stood; and, given the distribution of lines of force, how they were likely to continue to stand.

Mandelstam knew that his public career was scuttled. Privately, however, he appears to have experienced a tremendous liberation. Freed from a despised obeisance, sure now that his writing was for the drawer and not for the censor's eye, he felt a resurgence of creative energies. In December of 1929, he wrote his "Fourth Prose," a declaration of independence—and a pledge of self-allegiance—that still reads as if it had been seared onto the page with an acetylene torch:

> It was all as terrifying as a child's nightmare. *Nel mezzo del'cammin di nostra vita*—midway along life's path—I was stopped in the dense Soviet forest by bandits who called themselves my judges. . . . It was the first and only time in my life that Literature

had need of me, and it crushed, pawed, and squeezed me, and it was all as terrifying as a child's nightmare.

In the decade remaining to him, Mandelstam would write not only the "Journey to Armenia" and the "Conversation About Dante"—the most remarkable work of poetic interpretation ever written—but also some of his finest lyrics.

The Armenian journey came just a few months after the discharge of "Fourth Prose." (Arrangements and permissions came through the office of Nikolai Bukharin.) If Mandelstam had any specific premonition of his fate, he did not confide it to the page. The "Journey to Armenia," composed a year after his return, is almost pure celebration. The land, the people, his own rekindled senses—everything is heralded with energy and enthusiasm. Only in the very last passage does he remind us of the tyrant; only there does he reveal what he knows—that a happiness so pure will never come his way again.

If "Fourth Prose" represented Mandelstam's liberation, his acceptance of his poet's destiny, then "Journey to Armenia" is perhaps the first great bursting of the vocal pod. It is, like some of Mandelstam's other ventures into prose, utterly singular. Though we get all kinds of vivid glimpses—sensory and anecdotal—of Armenia, we could not really call the work a travelogue. It is as much about impressionist painting, naturalism, chess, and music as it is about places, customs, or people. In its midst we find oddly proportioned vignettes about the poet's Moscow neighbors. What's more, while some parts seem to be addressed to the general reader, other parts retain the intimate address of a personal letter; in fact, Mandelstam wrote sections of it for Boris Kuzin, a biologist he befriended in the course of his visit.

"Journey to Armenia" cannot be summarized or circumscribed in any fashion. The closest resemblance is to a writer's workbook. Reading through it for the first time, we suspect that the poet has culled through his insights and observations and has put them together pell-mell; that he is hoping to hold his reader through force of style alone. With a lesser writer we would absorb what pleasures the prose could offer and continue on our way.

But this is Mandelstam, who just a year later in his "Conversation About Dante" would write: ". . . where there is amenability to paraphrase, there the sheets have never been rumpled, there poetry . . . has never spent the night," and who would demonstrate in that work an unrivaled understanding of poetic structure. Anticipating wave-particle theory, Mandelstam grasped that the *Divine Comedy* was *simultaneously* a crystalloid construction of astonishing complexity and a sublimely energized system of flowing sound waves. Should we imagine, then, that he was capable of tossing off a loosely stitched quilt of notebook entries? More likely, we should give the "Journey" a second look.

If we read the work as we would a poem, attentively, not once or twice, but many times, and if we allow its casual-seeming elements to exert their magnetic waves, we begin to discern a most striking non-linear cohesiveness. Indeed, not only is the "Journey" not arbitrary in its construction, but it proposes an entirely new kind of prose—a poetic prose that is not merely the result of a poet applying himself to a new métier, but a prose that utilizes on a very refined level many of the associative dynamics of poetry.

Even the first-time reader of "Journey to Armenia" will be struck by Mandelstam's great interest in impressionist painting. We are only a few pages into the work before he introduces an enthralled—and seemingly irrelevant—passage on Signac (later there will be several pages devoted to his reactions to an impressionist exhibition). The whole section is, in fact, a flashback; Mandelstam is still in Moscow, anticipating his trip, when he finds a book that contains Signac's theory of optical blending. Mandelstam's was something more than a momentary enthusiasm. He writes: "I felt a shiver of novelty; it was as if someone had called me by name. . . . In all my long life I have seen no more than a silkworm."

There is no trace of silkworm blindness in the "Journey." On the contrary, it is as if Mandelstam is seeing, *really seeing,* for the first time in his life. His own elastic simile, which introduces the later encounter with the impressionist masters, conveys this excitement: "I stretched my vision like a kid glove, stretched it onto a shoe-tree, onto the blue neighborhood of the sea. . . ." The prose is studded throughout with the most exuberant sightings: "the light-blue policemanly phizzes of giant trout," poppies "bright to the point of surgical pain," "a lacquer painting the color of blood coagulated with gold," "a swampy parade ground the colour of billiard cloth," tea roses "like little scoops of yellow ice-cream" . . .

But there is something more involved here than just a celebration of the visual sense. Mandelstam did not insert the Signac passage casually. Rather, I believe that he discovered in Signac's book the clues, or justifications, for a new compositional method for prose, and that the disruptive placement of the anecdote is meant to alert the reader.

"The author," writes Mandelstam, "explained the 'law of optical blending,' glorified the method of working with little dabs of the brush, and impressed upon one the importance of using only the pure colours of the spectrum." What the impressionist attempts with color in three dimensions, Mandelstam will essay with units of prose—in four. The former destroys the tyranny of the subject in order to reveal the process of visual perception; Mandelstam explodes the linear and subject-centered progress of narrative so that he can expose the phenomenology of memory. His kind of impressionism has nothing of the slackness of arrangement that characterizes the efforts of second-rate talents. It is not a means of avoiding the structural imperative; rather, it implements a far more demanding—and poetic—organizational mode.

The key phrase in the above quotation is "the importance of using only the pure colours of the spectrum." As the writer cannot refer to an objectified spectrum, as his working materials are nowhere near as distinct as colors, the only criterion for "purity" is subjective. For Mandelstam, the pure was that which his poetic sensibility had naturally seized upon and preserved. However unprepossessing its outer contours—and many of Mandelstam's observations and anecdotes are strangely oblique—the event or observation had to have survived in memory with its aura intact. He was forcing himself to keep faith with the actual grain of his experience; heightening or artificial foregrounding was forbidden.

If we think of the "Journey" as a work of impressionism, then we have to think of each passage, each notation, as a pure color, as a patiently distilled dab applied to the narrative plane. And just as one does not *see* an impressionist canvas except by stepping backward in space, so one cannot gauge the effect of the "Journey" without allowing for an equivalent removal in time. Only as we recede from the actual reading can we see the work for what it is: a portrait, not of a place, but of an experience. Its larger life only begins in our afterimage, as it did for Mandelstam in memory.

In the addenda—material that was ultimately deleted from "Journey"—Mandelstam set down a particularly revealing observation about prose composition:

> Reality has the character of a continuum. Prose which corresponds to reality, no matter how expressly and minutely, no matter how efficiently and faithfully, is always a broken series. Only that prose is truly beautiful which is incorporated into the continuum as an entire system, although there is no power or method to prove it.

No finite prose, then, can match reality, just as no bounded canvas can faithfully represent a countryside. The creator (writer, painter) must not only select from among his perceptions, he must arrange them so that they form a self-contained system. For the impressionist painter, that system will be structured to the proportions and perspectives of the natural world. But for Mandelstam there is no discernible paradigm. His "system" need only correspond to the structure of the lived experience—rather, to the structure of the memory. Even though it is subjectively determined, however, it is not arbitrary. The distribution of elements—"although there is no power or method to prove it"—obeys the same psychic necessity that poetry does. And here we may add that poetic composition was, for Mandelstam, more a process of listening and discovering than of invention. "The poem," he wrote, "is alive through an inner image . . . which anticipates the written poem."

For all of this, we would nevertheless be wrong in trying to call "Journey" a poem in any sense. Though we find compression, metaphor, and a progress through association, the central propulsion does not come from the word unit. This, for Mandelstam, was the one essential attribute of poetry: its process was philological. Whatever power was released by a line came from collisions of strata in the individual words; semantic coherence was a by-product. Prose, however, was forced by its discursive nature to build itself up from semantic clusters—phrases and sentences. It is, therefore, axiomatic that prose will be more diffuse. Its echoes and cross-stitchings can only approximate those found in a poem. Still, working within these natural limits, Mandelstam created something not altogether unlike a poem.

In "Journey to Armenia," Mandelstam has given poetic-symphonic development to a specific array of elements. By this I mean something more than just an implementation of patterned recurrence. For Mandelstam was interested, above all, in transformation. His dynamic is Ovidian. The "pure colours" that he has gathered from his experience move in a force field animated by the currents of his obsession. He does not thereby distort his remembered account; if anything, he penetrates right to the springs of personal memory. In its overt particularity, "Journey" denies the very possibility of objective reportage.

At the beginning of his Dante essay, Mandelstam hails his subject as the "strategist of transmutation and hybridization," and as "the master of the instruments of poetry . . . not a manufacturer of tropes." And on the very next page, he describes poetic discourse as "a carpet fabric containing a plethora of textile warps differing from one another only in the process of coloration, only in the partitura of the perpetually changing commands of the instrumental signalling system." What Mandelstam has supplied, perhaps unwittingly, is a most astute characterization of his own prose in the "Journey to Armenia." It is, assuredly, a most intricately woven carpet, abounding in pattern and detail, and free of the autocracy of a governing figure.

The carpet analogy is quite useful, a means of access to a work almost entirely closed to analysis. With it we can make sense of the bewildering assortment of unconnected sections that comprise the opening pages. For if we keep in mind that any woven fabric, however complex, can be traced back at its borders to isolated threads—its constituent elements—then these disparate notations turn out to have a purpose. They present, often very subtly, the materials that will eventually undergo "transmutation and hybridization"; they are, to take an analogy now from twelve-tone music, the tones in the tone-row. Not until Mandelstam has laid out his separate notes is he free to begin working them together. But where music instigates its transmutations through the perpetual shifting of harmonic tension, Mandelstam's prose enacts its changing commands through the use of metaphor.

Metaphor was, for Mandelstam, less a device than an imperative; it was the mainspring, not the accompaniment, of his thought. This may derive from a clearly discernible polarization of sensibility. We find (and the following discussion will bear this out) competing drives—toward the structural and static, and toward the morphological and dynamic. We get simultaneously an absorption in the fixities of natural form *and* a fascination with the process of evolutionary change; archaeology and the live anarchy of the present; living speech and philology. In addition, we find recurrent reference to music and chess, both of which represent structure and change in their most intimate dialectical incarnation. As we shall see, Mandelstam's metaphoric transformations are the result of an incessant maneuvering between the poles of his own nature.

Mandelstam begins "Journey to Armenia" by locating himself, without any preliminary explanation, on the island of Sevan (in Lake Sevan, Armenia's largest), where he "spent a month enjoying the lake water standing at a height of four thousand feet above sea level. . . ." We expect, perhaps, a leisurely description in the best nineteenth-century manner. But we get nothing of the kind. Instead, the very next paragraph gives us a startling image of trout feeding at sunset, causing the water to roil up "as though a huge pinch of soda had been flung into it." And the following paragraphs rapidly catalogue wind conditions, the ubiquity of mischievous children, tall "juicy" grasses ("one felt like coiffing them with an iron comb"), and—everywhere—the "fiery red slabs of nameless graves."

We have scarcely begun to take in these descriptive cues when Mandelstam shunts us off onto another track. Quite abruptly, he begins an account of an expedition he took to a recently uncovered burial site. He introduces a certain Professor Khachaturian, "whose face was stretched over with eagle skin beneath which all the muscles and ligaments stood out, numbered and with their Latin names." But of the visit itself we learn little, except that Mandelstam carried away in his handkerchief "the porous calcified crust of someone's cranium."

The sections follow in quick succession. More uncentered anecdotes, more single-stroke characterizations. On another of his day trips, Mandelstam notices the completed frame of a barge and remarks upon its "fresh musical proportions." On yet another occasion, a visit to the Institute of Eastern Peoples, he reports, without much explanation: "Owing to my incorrect subjective orientation, I have fallen into the habit of regarding every Armenian as a philologist. Which is, however, partly right. These are people who jangle the keys of language even when they are not using them to unlock any treasures." And a few paragraphs later, we find him staring at the enormous head of one Conrad Ovanesian, musing all the while about the Armenian etymology of the word "head."

It is then, in the section entitled "Zamoskvorechie," that Mandelstam retails his discovery, while still in Moscow, of Signac's book on impressionism. Next, continuing the Moscow interlude, he devotes short passages to the toppling of an ancient linden tree, to his friend B.S.K. (Boris Kuzin), to a confused going-away celebration where the conversation is compared to "the knight's move, always swerving to one side. . . ." Narrative considerations, we now realize, will be irrelevant to the "Journey." What possible link could there be between the remembered farewell and this subsequent insert:

> When I was a child a stupid sort of touchiness, a false pride, kept me from ever going out to look for berries or stooping down over mushrooms. Gothic pinecones and hypocritical acorns in their monastic caps pleased me more than mushrooms. I would stroke the pinecones. They would bristle. . . . In their shelled tenderness, in their geometrical gaping I sensed the rudiments of architecture, the demon of which has accompanied me throughout my life.

However brilliant the prose—and already we have seen innumerable flashings from Mandelstam's quartz-light—we cannot quite shake the impression that these are inspired jottings. They simply do not add up to a narrative or a portrait, whatever their local merits. But now, one fourth of the way into the text, something begins to happen.

Mandelstam, it seems, has finished arranging his threads; he is ready to begin working them together.

"Only last year on the island of Sevan in Armenia, as I was strolling in the waist-high grass, I was captivated by the pagan burning of the poppies." The perplexing Moscow interlude is done with, and we are returned to our point of origin. The grass is again mentioned. And the poppies, as Mandelstam goes on to describe their astonishing color, recall for us the "pure colours" of Signac. Then, in the very next sentence, Mandelstam describes the flowers as "gawking butterflies" that grow on "disgusting hairy stalks." From now on, virtually every phrase will plait together with something else. The butterfly, for example, returns a few pages later. Observing a particular specimen, Mandelstam notes that its thorax "is strong, shaped like a little boat." We recall the skeletal barge with its "fresh musical proportions," not to mention a half-dozen other boats that have been mentioned in the narrative. As for the poppy's "hairy stalk," it reverberates perfectly with his later characterization of the Abkhazian language—with its "guttural compound sounds . . . one might say it was torn out of a larynx overgrown with hair." Mandelstam's repertory of sensory and imagistic crossings is inexhaustible. I have space to sample only a few.

"I gratefully recall one of my Erevan conversations . . ." writes Mandelstam. "The talk turned around the 'theory of the embryonic field,' proposed by Professor Gurvich." Then:

> The embryonic leaf of the nasturtium has the form of a halberd or of an elongated, bifoliate purse that begins to resemble a little tongue. It also looks like a flint arrowhead from the Paleolithic. But the tension in the field of force that rages around the leaf first transforms it into a five-segmented figure. The lines of the cave arrowhead get stretched into the shape of an arc.

Further along in the same passage, he asks: "What Bach, what Mozart does variations on the theme of the nasturtium leaf?"

The associative tensions move in every direction. A few pages earlier, for example, Mandelstam remarked of a fellow visitor: "The little children would show him their slender little tongues, sticking them out for an instant like slices of bear meat." We cannot read his description of the nasturtium leaf without a quiver of recollection. So, too, the flint arrowheads from the Paleolithic call up the visit to the burial site and the "crust" of cranium that Mandelstam wrapped in his handkerchief. The arrow itself materializes a few sentences down the page: "A plant in the world is an event, a happening, an arrow, and not a boring, bearded development." (It was for this innocuous-looking line, rumor goes, that the publisher of "Journey" lost his post; the offending words were "boring, bearded development," taken by authorities as a swipe at Karl Marx.)

The "force field" is taken up and reshaped in the very next section, where Mandelstam digresses on a chess game that he observed: "But these little Persian horses made of ivory are immersed in a solution of power. The same thing happens to them as happens to the nasturtium of E. S. Smirnov, the Moscow biologist, and the embryonic field of Professor Gurvich." Two subsequent observations then tighten the warp. "When the rays of a combination focus upon the chess figures," he writes, "they grow like mushrooms in Indian summer." This, of course, recalls the earlier passage where Mandelstam remarked on his reluctance to pick up mushrooms. It also exemplifies the poet's penchant for images that not only convert immobile artifacts into organic entities, but which impose dynamic potential upon the stationary. Fascinated as Mandelstam is by inorganic structure, he nearly always finds a way to blow a living breath upon them. Even the pinecones, architectural paradigms, were given a "shelled tenderness."

Still on the subject of chess, Mandelstam asserts boldly: "The [chess] problem is not solved on paper, and not in the camera obscura of causality, but in a live Impressionist milieu in Edouard Manet's and Claude Monet's temple of air, light and glory." This peculiar statement directly anticipates his visit to the impressionist exhibition, where, among other things, he will call Cezanne the "best acorn in the forests of France," and say of Matisse—in a beautiful phrase reminding us of his opening image of feeding trout—"The red pain of his canvas fizzes like soda." Again, the delight is in the unexpected synaesthesia, in the conferring of motion and tactile sensation upon an objectively stable color. In essence, it is the impressionist credo: paint not the thing, but the effect it produces.

As for "What Bach, what Mozart . . ." the musical motif comes to infiltrate nearly every section in the work. On the naturalist Pallas: "Whoever does not love Haydn, Gluck, and Mozart will never understand a word of Pallas." On Lamarck: "He hears the pauses and syncopes of the evolutionary line." And: ". . . I love it when Lamarck deigns to be angry and smashes to smithereens all that Swiss pedagogical boredom. Into the concept of 'nature' bursts the Marseillaise!" Still later, in the brashest of synthetic metaphors, he will describe the environs of Erevan thus: "Then suddenly a violin, sectioned into gardens and houses, divided up according to the system of the whatnot—with spreaders, interceptors, dowels and bridges." Even Tzara would have been tickled!

One could go on and on. The associative patterning is as subtle as that in the finest of Oriental carpets, yet it possesses the transformational fluidity that Mandelstam celebrated in Dante. We have to wonder whether the poet had it in mind to render Armenia in terms of a figured tapestry, or whether that impression is just a fortuitous by-product of his aesthetic. As I have said, I don't believe that Mandelstam set out to compose a portrait; he was just as much interested in getting into words the subjective sense of self-rejuvenation. The place and the event were most happily interfused.

"Journey to Armenia" begins with the laying out of fabric threads. It ends with a most affecting parable. On the last two pages—breaking with the prose pattern he has initiated—Mandelstam tells, in numbered sequences, the legend of Arshak and Shapukh. If we read past the accretions of legend, Arshak is clearly Mandelstam, Shapukh is Stalin, and Darmastat is, very possibly, Bukharin. I excerpt:

1. The body of Arshak is unwashed and his beard has run wild.
4. His tongue is mangy from jailer's food but there was a time when it pressed grapes against the roof of his mouth and was as agile as the tip of a flutist's tongue.
8. He [Shapukh] commands my hair and my fingernails. He grows me my beard and swallows me my spit so accustomed has he grown to the thought that I am here in the fortress of Aniush.
13. A certain Darmastat, the kindest and best educated of the

eunuchs, was in the center of Shapukh's army, encouraged the commander of the cavalry, wormed his way into his master's favor, snatched him, like a chessman, out of danger, and all the while remained in full view.

16. When the time came for his reward Darmastat inserted into the Assyrian's keen ears a request that tickled like a feather:
17. Give me a pass to the fortress of Aniush. I want Arshak to spend one additional day full of hearing, taste, and smell, as it was before, when he amused himself with hunting and saw to the planting of trees.

No problems with interpretation here, especially from our vantage in time. How closely that last section recalls Hölderlin's petition *To the Fates:* "Grant me just one summer, you mighty ones,/And one autumn to ripen my song,/So that my heart, sated with sweet playing,/May die more willingly." Mandelstam still had eight years to live, but he did not have to be a prophet to know that he would be harried to the limit of his endurance—and over it—by Shapukh. His well-known lyric, written just one month after his return from Armenia, marks the end of the idyll and the beginning of the odyssey:

Leningrad

I returned to my city, familiar as tears,
As veins, as mumps from childhood years.

You've returned here, so swallow as quick as you can
The cod-liver oil of Leningrad's riverside lamps.

Recognize when you can December's brief day:
Egg yolk folded into its ominous tar.

Petersburg, I don't yet want to die:
You have the numbers of my telephones.

Petersburg, I have addresses still
Where I can raise the voices of the dead.

I live on the backstairs and the doorbell buzz
Strikes me in the temple and tears at my flesh.

And all night long I await those dear guests of yours,
Rattling, like manacles, the chains on the doors.

—translated by Bernard Meares

Joseph Brodsky

In "Less than One," the autobiographical title essay of this 1986 collection, Joseph Brodsky writes:

As I remember my quitting school at the age of fifteen, it wasn't so much a conscious choice as a gut reaction. I simply couldn't stand certain faces in my class—of some of my classmates, but mostly of my teachers. And so one winter morning, for no apparent reason, I rose up in the middle of the session and made my melodramatic exit through the school gate, knowing clearly that I'd never be back. Of the emotions overpowering me at that moment, I remember only a general disgust with myself for being

Joseph Brodsky

too young and letting so many things boss me around. Also, there was that vague but happy sensation of escape, of a sunny street without end.

Though there is no way to isolate the germination of dissent in a man, this may have been its first consequential eruption—it was certainly not the last. From the confinement of those four walls, Brodsky went to work in the clamorous hive of a munitions factory, where his fellow proletarians drank "like sharks" and cursed their lot with such a steady ferocity that "a normal word, like 'airplane,' would strike the passer-by as something elaborately obscene. . . ." But the rebel managed to sustain his inner independence and to undertake his true education through books and the writing of poetry. In the closing essay, "In a Room and a Half," we are given a lengthy and loving depiction of the book- and armoire-armored cave that Brodsky contrived for himself in the tiny family apartment in St. Petersburg (attentive to the deeper implications of nomenclature, he never calls his native city Leningrad). From that lair he conducted his first literary campaigns.

That "sunny street without end" was not in the cards. As Brodsky's verse began to make its way among the Petersburg literati—earning the high praise of Akhmatova, among others—the authorities moved to muzzle him. After a trumped-up "trial" (the word should be construed in its nonjuridical sense), a transcript of which was smuggled out to the Western press, the "parasite" was sentenced to five years of hard labor in the swampy Arkhangelsk region. Protests by the international intelligentsia may have helped him to get an early release. In 1972, Brodsky was allowed to emigrate to Israel. His inner momentum, however, was westward; he changed his ticket in Vienna. Since landing on our shores nearly fifteen years ago, Brodsky has established himself as a poet, essayist, teacher, activist, and gadfly. *Less than One*—much of it, incidentally, written in English—shows us a good deal about the "heartwork" (Rilke's phrase) of exile.

We need these few biographical facts before we can assess the nature of Brodsky's contribution to prose. To call the essays "literary," for instance—what a sense of fussy irrelevance currently clings to that word!—would be misleading in emphasis. For what we feel as we read is that the words are coming out of life, not out of other books. If the subjects are often literary, this is because the works of certain writers came to matter very greatly to Brodsky. Not because he found them pleasing or interesting, but because they gave him the soul-saving bread of truth in a world that seemed to him bent upon the elimination of subjective inquiry. As Brodsky writes in that same title essay, remembering the early years of his schooling:

> It is a big room with three rows of desks, a portrait of the Leader on the wall behind the teacher's chair, a map with two hemispheres, of which only one is legal. The little boy takes his seat, opens his briefcase, puts his pen and notebook on the desk, lifts his face, and prepares himself to hear drivel.

Brodsky's self-education, then, was ultimately a war waged against drivel. Reading had to be simultaneously a passionate inner search and a desperate attempt to silence the canned monotone of the state. This may go some way toward explaining the depth of his immersion in the works of his chosen masters, that there is a will to get *to* something as well as *away* from something else.

At the core of Brodsky's canon are three of the four major Russian poets of our century: Anna Akhmatova, Osip Mandelstam, and Marina Tsvetaeva—Pasternak would be the missing fourth. All were magnificently gifted artists who witnessed and suffered the assaults of what Mandelstam called this "wolfhound" century. Only Akhmatova managed to survive the Stalin era; Mandelstam died in a transit camp and Tsvetaeva committed suicide. It's hard—and pointless—to say whom Brodsky admires the most. He seems to discover a different kind of spiritual power in each. Of Akhmatova's love lyrics, he remarks: "It is the finite's nostalgia for the infinite that accounts for the recurrence of the love theme in Akhmatova's verse, not the actual entanglements." While it is with a similar reverence, but a very different focus, that he tries to characterize Mandelstam's peculiar density:

> Using all the phonetic and allusory power of words themselves, Mandelstam's verse in that period expresses the slowing-down, viscous sensation of time's passage. Since he succeeds (as he

always does), the effect is that the reader realizes that the words, even their letters—vowels especially—are almost palpable vessels of time.

A similar metaphysical pressure is brought to bear upon the other objects of Brodsky's scrutiny, whether he is dealing with admired poets like C. P. Cavafy, Eugenio Montale, W. H. Auden, or Derek Walcott—or with larger topical obsessions, like tyranny, nonviolence, or Byzantium.

As I hope these citations suggest, Brodsky's is a sensibility bent upon thinking everything through from scratch. He is never, not even for the space of a sentence, derivative. Such an independent venture is, of course, bound to have its hazards. And, indeed, Brodsky can be didactic, biased (his "Flight from Byzantium" has drawn fire from certain quarters for its "Orientalism"), and dismissive (he gets rid of all of Tolstoy in a few paragraphs); at times, too, his thinking appears to be guided more by the quest for a startling apothegm than by a concern for scrupulous accuracy—this is one of the inevitable consequences of the aphoristic style. But his seriousness is such that even our disagreements force our thought into unexpected directions.

Brodsky's most effective tactic, which works in tandem with his uncanny image-making process, is to express the most sophisticated insights through the classroom tropes of plane geometry, simple physics, geography, biology, and so on; the abandoned textbooks seemingly left their mark. Thus: "The formula for prison is a lack of space counterbalanced by a surplus of time." And: "Memory, I think, is a substitute for the tail that we lost for good in the happy process of evolution." And, apropos Auden: "If time worships language, it means that language is greater, or older, than time, which is, in its turn, older and greater than space." I could find a hundred such assertions. Brodsky manages to keep the formulaic structure while changing the terms, the terms being, presumably, what his real education has taught him.

Brodsky's is a linguistic, not a rational, intelligence. We cannot call his forward motion on the page "thinking" unless we want to widen the boundaries of that word. For the progress from point to point is secured through analogy, metaphor, linguistic association, and a great deal else besides: the resources of poetry have been applied to prose. To follow, we must submit not just our minds, but our passional, intuitional, and spiritual selves. The participation is synthetic, not analytic. In these essays, whether Brodsky is discussing Cavafy's homosexuality or offering an *in memoriam* to his parents, he is not trying to *prove* anything. Even when he generates controversy—as he does when he insists upon the inferiority of Eastern creeds, finding in them the source of all despotism ("Flight from Byzantium")—it often seems to be more because argumentation and assertion activate the adrenaline flow of language and force the production of insight. And though insight is local and evanescent, lacking the stature of philosophical proof, it is, in the Brodskian universe, all we have.

Positioned at the center of the collection are two lengthy, and utterly singular, "readings." Brodsky works his way line-by-line through Auden's "September 1, 1939" and Tsvetaeva's "New Year's Greeting." Tedious though the explication can get at times—Brodsky is uncharacteristically methodical, and the reader cannot always see what he does in a rhyme or phrase—the pieces give us an astonishing glimpse of the tolerances of sound and rhythm that a poet works with. "On 'September 1, 1939' by W. H. Auden" especially will persuade anyone who needs persuading that the poet's braiding of elements is an activity as complex and calibrated as anything going on at Los Alamos.

Insofar as Brodsky has a deity, it's Language. If *Homo sapiens* is distinguished from his evolutionary brethren by his linguistic capacity, then the poet, Brodsky would say, operates at the summit of the anthropological pyramid; he is the supreme user. The essay "A Poet and Prose," which reflects upon the mechanics of acceleration in the prose writings of Tsvetaeva, is his most sustained exploration of this idea. Here is an exemplary passage—the reader may derive from it some sense of the pitch of the argument:

> Poetry is not 'the best words in the best order'; for language it is the highest form of existence. In purely technical terms, of course, poetry amounts to arranging words with the greatest specific gravity in the most effective and externally inevitable se-

> quence. Ideally, however, it is language negating its own mass and the laws of gravity; it is language's striving upward—or sideways—to that beginning where the Word was. In any case, it is movement of language into pre-(supra-)genre realms, that is, into the spheres from which it sprang. The seemingly most artificial forms for organizing poetic language—terza rima, sestinas, decimas, and so forth—are in fact nothing more than a natural, reiterative, fully detailed elaboration of the echo that followed the original Word. . . .

Brodsky, as I have said, is fundamentally an aphorist, stylistically speaking. His mind works with paradox, parallelism, reversal, and he strives to make every sentence the clincher. One can always look down the page and find a formulation that has built upon, and therefore tops, its predecessor. The writers that he dwells upon all reflect one or another of his obsessions, whether time/classical culture/language (Mandelstam, Montale, Cavafy), prophecy/totalitarianism/language (Dostoevsky), exile and language (Walcott), or ethics and language (Auden and, indeed, all of the others). The common denominator is, obviously, language, and as it fills the deity's spot in his cosmology, we should understand that it is in no way a neutral concept. Language, as his homage to Auden, "To Please a Shadow," repeatedly suggests, is at once the source and object of love. And the poet, though Brodsky never quite puts it in these terms, has the priest's role. All of this sounds strange in our secular and technocratic epoch. Not all readers will be able to share, or even feel comfortable with, this exile's passion, but few will come away unaffected by its force.

PART III

Twentieth-Century Constellations

Blaise Cendrars
(1887–1961)
Marguerite Yourcenar
(1905–1987)
Marguerite Duras
(1914–)
Michel Tournier
(1924–)
Primo Levi
(1919–1987)
Umberto Eco
(1932–)
Malcolm Lowry
(1909–1957)
Lars Gustafsson
(1936–)
V. S. Naipaul
(1932–)
Derek Walcott
(1930–)
Yaakov Shabtai
(1934–1981)
Salman Rushdie
(1947–)
Jorge Luis Borges
(1899–1986)
Julio Cortázar
(1914–1984)
The School of Gordon Lish
Docu-fiction

The pieces that follow are too various to be set under any one thematic grouping. Inevitably, however, common strands will be seen to pass from one to another.

I begin with an essay on Blaise Cendrars, the great French modernist-adventurer. His career encompassed wars and revolutions; he circled the globe like a satellite. He embraced wholly the modernist injunction: to make it new.

Among the other French and Italian writers, we find anguished responses to the tragedies of war. Marguerite Duras's The War *and Primo Levi's* Survival in Auschwitz *are both searing documents of witness. Michel Tournier, on the other hand, makes use of the symbolic possibilities of gnostic thought to pose the necessary questions about good and evil.*

This strain—gnostic, kabbalistic—turns up in several of the other writers under consideration. There is clearly a strong interest in doctrines that view creation as a contest between forces of light and darkness. Lowry, Borges, and Eco all find ways to implement central gnostic ideas about the postlapsarian inversion of values.

The work of non-European writers like V. S. Naipaul, Derek Walcott, Yaakov Shabtai, and Salman Rushdie is linked by a preoccupation with the tensions and conflicts faced by emerging societies. The pessimism of Naipaul, who finds that colonial incursion has condemned the third world to inferiority, is to some extent echoed in the novels of Shabtai and Rushdie. Walcott is the exception: his poetic task is to universalize and make central the experience of marginality.

Finally, I include two essays on recent trends in American fiction. "The School of Gordon Lish" takes a critical look at the present tendency toward fragmentation and minimalism. "Docu-fiction" argues that the fashionable blurring of the fact-fiction distinction ultimately weakens both terms.

Blaise Cendrars

. . . Alors, seven o'clock we take a taxi to the Chambre des Deputés . . . and then to Montmartre . . . Restaurant des Fleurs. What a place! The first time I have seen so many beautiful Frenchwomen. He [Cendrars] said we would eat cheaply and I thought we would go Dutch. Then he began ordering. Asked me did I like to eat. Why certainly! Alors, lobsters, oysters, pigeons, desserts I never saw in my life, wines extraordinary, fines, *chartreuse, coffee, etc. etc. I was embarrassed as hell. . . . Cendrars looks rough, like a sailor—he is one at bottom—and he speaks rather loudly, but very well. Has only one arm, the empty one, or half-arm, slung affectionately around my neck while he tells the whole restaurant what a great guy I am, what the book [*Tropic of Cancer*] *is about. . . . Perhaps the finest moment in my life, in one sense. But it went flat. I had nothing to say. I wondered how long it would continue. I was a perfect ass. And trying at intervals to break away. Finally we go out, four of us now, and we must have some more alcohol in the bars along the Boulevard in Montmartre. Whores hanging on to us, and Cendrars hugging them like a sailor, and urging me to take one, take two, take as many as you want. After two or three of these bars and more whores hanging on our necks I ducked—very unceremoniously too. An au revoir. I don't know what he must think of me. . . .*

—HENRY MILLER, *Letters to Anaïs Nin*

God, what on earth shall I look like when I emerge at last from my solitude in Aix-en-Provence . . . shall I look emaciated, as I did yesterday on board Papadakis's boat (after fleeing from Tehran, crossing Anatolia, embarking as a stowaway at Smyrna and landing at Naples, where Kim's cure failed completely), or shall I reveal my true face, no longer the face of a brawler and juggler, forever playing to the gallery, but that of the contemplative, which I have never ceased to be, even in the wildest moments of my eventful life? I know him so well, this inside-out brahmin, this boxer who trains by punching his shadow on the wall and studies himself in order to increase his speed, improve his technique, his reflexes, his counter attack, but who also knows how to take his punishment, for there are days when he faces a furious adversary, instead of his own shadow, in an adventure with a human being, outside the boxing ring and far from all spectators, and comes back thrashed and defeated. Count my scars! Not all of them are visible, and in any case they are nothing to be proud of. (If you play rough, you must expect to get hurt.)

I met Picasso one day, in front of his house in rue La Boetie. "Come up with me," said Picasso, "I'll paint your portrait. Nowadays I only work for posterity." "Then you can stick posterity up your arse," I replied, "I'm not coming."

—CENDRARS, *Planus*

In the last phase of his career, when he was already in his sixties, Blaise Cendrars wrote and published a series of autobiographical works that are as singular as anything in literature. Coming after a lifetime of publications, these books—available in England as *The Astonished Man* (1970), *Planus* (1972), and *Lice* (1973)—form a kind of entryway through which we pass to meet a rare, titan-scale individual. The life we encounter is as vast and variously textured as a composition by Stravinsky, and is as difficult to assimilate at first contact. Here is Cendrars in his full amplitude: wanderer, sailor, scholar, collector, entrepreneur, anarchist, soldier, pivotal figure in the Paris avant-garde, trickster, intimate of Picasso, Apollinaire, Stravinsky, Dos Passos (who translated him), Modigliani (who painted him), Duchamp (who probably played chess with him), Le Corbusier, Eisenstein, Satie, Chagall . . . The ellipses are rightfully suggestive. In these works we have him in many locales of his nomadic life: Africa, Russia, China, the Americas, the heartland of France, not to mention the great capital cities of the world. We have so much, and yet it feels like we are chasing quicksilver, or, better yet, like we are in the hands of a Scheherazade, a teller of tales with an ever-changing repertoire, a repertoire that will never be exhausted.

Cendrars is obscure. Few literate people will recognize the name. This is as unfortunate as it is comprehensible, for reputations flourish and wither in the hands of critics and litterateurs, and these types have always had a hard time with renegades. The situation is aggravated further by Cendrars's penchant for invention and exaggeration. Were it not that the life and writings are so intertwined—the two halves of a grand and mysterious destiny—this would not matter so much. But the fact is that Cendrars cannot be considered apart from his biography. To read anything that he wrote is to be implicated, present at the joining point of life and art. The two are intimately interfused. The writings have to be read as a footnote to the life, as an interlinear, if you will. It is as if to make this process even more forbidding and complex that Cendrars chose to write poetry, novels, reportage, criticism, autobiography, film scripts, radio plays—apart from which he also anthologized and translated. He could not have set his gift at the heart of a labyrinth any more artfully had he tried. And yet there will be those who will undertake to find their way in, for there is something in Cendrars that matters greatly and that is not to be found elsewhere. It is a vision fresh and authentic from a man who tunneled his way through considerable despair, who lived all aspects of life to the extreme, and who, for that reason alone, has more to tell us than the sort of academic epigone who seems to dominate the literature of our time.

> Cendrars: "No, no, no, no, not at all, you won't find me in it, I shall write a novel-novel, and I won't appear in it, because they don't see but one character in all my books: Cendrars: *L'Or* is Cendrars; *Moravagine* is Cendrars; *Dan Yack* is Cendrars—I'm annoyed with this Cendrars!"
>
> —*Paris Review* interview

In treating the life and writings of Cendrars, the main task is to establish the context of myth and self-creation. Some biography seems to flow more or less evenly from circumstance; in other cases, it is wrested forth with much turmoil, imagination, and daring, and this is the case with Cendrars.

"Blaise Cendrars" is a pseudonym for Frédéric Louis Sauser, who was born in 1883 in the Swiss canton of Neuchâtel. (Le Corbusier was born in the same little village just one month later.) The restlessness that would infect him lifelong was already present in the gene pool. His father, an inventor but also a man of many careers and aspirations, dragged the family from Switzerland to Egypt, then to Naples. It is no accident, especially in view of his late escapades, that Cendrars's poetic trademark became the listing of places—ports, cities, destinations.

Cendrars reports that his adolescence was wild, his character intractable. He was sent to one boarding school after another. In each he resisted, racked up absences. Then, when he was fifteen, he stole the family silver and made his escape out the window. For a time his career resembles that of Rimbaud. He wandered Europe, riding trains, hiking, finally ending up in St. Petersburg. There, the story goes, he met up with a jewel merchant named Rogovine, who took him into his employ. They rode the Trans-Siberian into Asia. In 1904—the testimony here, as everywhere, being as reliable as Cendrars—he worked stoking furnaces in Peking. Two years later, by whatever circuitous route, he was back in St. Petersburg.

It is hard to avoid making all this picturesque. The settings are right, the movement is swift and dramatic. But we must not forget that Cendrars/Sauser is only in his teens. Present, too, are his fear, his loneliness, his homesickness. These elements, compressed and matured, will show up later in his two long poems: *Prose of the Trans-Siberian* and *Panama, or, The Adventures of My Seven Uncles.* He will write:

And beyond, the Siberian plains the lowering sky
    and the tall shapes of the Silent Mountains that
    rise and fall
I am curled up in a plaid shawl
Motley
Like my life
And my life doesn't keep me any warmer than this Scotch
Shawl
And the whole of Europe seen through the windcutter of an
    Express racing ahead at full speed
Is no richer than my life
My poor life . . .

—*Prose of the Trans-Siberian*

There are more imponderable events. In St. Petersburg Cendrars falls in love with a young woman. She dies in a hotel fire. Nothing further is known of this. Cendrars, heartbroken, moves to Paris. The chronology is vague. Forty years later, writing in *Planus,* he states that his anguish and rage drove him to Finland, that he spent a summer manufacturing bombs for terrorists. A cryptic passage with much left unexplained, but the facts do correlate, at least imaginatively, with events in his doomsday novel *Moravagine.*

It is in Paris, in 1907, that Sauser rebaptizes himself Blaise Cendrars. He makes a compact with himself that he will henceforth be a writer, a poet. (He has produced a few fledgling pieces while in St. Petersburg.) But the wanderlust is undimmed. In the next four years he moves from Paris to Bern (where he takes up medicine for a year), then to St. Petersburg again. In 1911 he is in New York City, on the bum, starving. In one delirious night he writes *Les Pâques à New York* (*Easter in New York*), one of the first poems in the modernist canon, a work distinguished by its intensity and urban torsions. With this explosion his stay in New York ends. He returns to Paris via cattle boat and throws himself into the artistic life of the city.

Les Pâques foreshadows the *Trans-Siberian* and *Panama,* both of which were written in 1913. By that time Cendrars was already at the spearpoint of the avant-garde, consorting with Léger, Stravinsky, Apollinaire, Picasso, appearing in public attired in a demolished chair, or one of his painted suits. (Roger Shattuck gives a fascinating portrait of this era in *The Banquet Years.*) Cendrars was one of the first to embrace "the modern" in the full sense of the term. He saw clearly where the age was headed: toward speed, machinery, violence. The basis of human relationships was changing, and this change called for a new way of writing poetry. He responded. He wanted to do for poetry what the cubists were doing for painting. But where they worked spatially, looking for means by which to transmit all visual aspects of an object, Cendrars was concerned with time and events: he was after simultaneity, situations registered from all geographic and temporal perspectives.

Prose of the Trans-Siberian sent out shock waves when it first appeared. The poem made use of salad techniques: very long lines punctuated with lines of one or two words, abrupt transitions, shifting tenses, and imagery that anticipated the surrealists. By setting the narrative on a moving train, Cendrars was able to explore nuances of sound and tempo. This he did with the skilled ear of a jazz musician.

The poem was, in fact, dedicated to "the musicians." (Cendrars had studied music, and he claims somewhere in his writings that he very nearly became a composer instead of a poet.) The format of the poem was unprecedented: it was printed on a single sheet seven feet long, folded up like a railroad timetable. Sonia Delaunay painted an abstract accompaniment on the left-hand side of the sheet. Cendrars then announced that the full first edition of the poem, unfolded, laid end to end, would match exactly the height of the Eiffel Tower. If "the modern" was a religion in Paris, then the Eiffel Tower was its altar.

There was some controversy in academic circles as to whether Cendrars or Apollinaire was the first to write the modernist poem. No settlement was ever reached, though publication dates are in Cendrars's favor. There is no real point in arguing one way or the other. From a book like Shattuck's we get a clear picture of the cross-pollination that went on from one end of Paris to the other. Cendrars later professed indifference to the whole question of precedence. The war years were to bring decisive changes in his outlook.

> The war saved me by dragging me away and throwing me amongst the people in arms, one anonymous number amongst millions of others. No. 1529. What intoxication! . . . It takes a long experience of life, and many a tot of rotgut in the low dives Zola wrote about, amongst the common people, to relearn how to love your fellow man as a brother.

In 1914, calling upon his fellow poets to follow him, Cendrars rushed off to join the fighting. After many months in the trenches at the front lines, in September of 1915—a decisive date in his personal chronology—he was wounded by a mortar shell. His right arm had to be amputated. The injury threw him into despair. There are accounts of Cendrars refusing his prosthesis, pounding the walls of the hospital with his stump. It was not until he learned that his idol Rémy de Gourmont had died that same day that he was able to interpret his loss as a symbolic figure in his destiny. He will refer to this conjunction of events time and again.

The injury was to become a major turning point for Cendrars. Practically, it made it difficult for him to find work when he returned to Paris. For a period he begged alms in the streets, but that was not to be endured, and he fled the city. (Before the war, Cendrars had made a hasty marriage, a mistake. His wife, Fela, had borne him two sons, Rémy and Odilon. He left the family behind—an episode about which little is known.) In Cendrars's mythology this move was of great consequence. He was breaking with the past, leaving behind all literary and artistic circles, all family responsibilities. Henceforth he was to identify himself as a solitary, a member of no school, a man whose true home was among the poor and oppressed. He spent a part of the next year living and traveling with a band of gypsies, an experience that would later supply him with much of the narrative for *The Astonished Man*.

Cendrars was never one to occupy a place or a life-pattern for very long. In the epoch following the war he went through a number of careers. The personal changes, the motives, are only partially illuminated by his writings—once again the specific gravity of the man is hard to calculate. In 1917, for example, he announces that he is through with poetry. Two years later he reverses himself and issues the collection *Dix-neuf Poèmes Elastiques.* He has taken his techniques to new extremes—the lines are now short, the imagery sharp, concrete, the leaps rapid-fire and unpredictable. But Cendrars is right in one respect: poetry is no longer to be his major avocation. Five years later, with the appearance of *Kodak* and *Feuilles de Route,* his poetic vector reaches its terminus. *Kodak* is by far the more innovative. Cendrars pointed out, after publication, that every line in every poem had been lifted from a novel by Gustave Le Rouge.

During this period the poetic energies were deployed along other fronts. Cendrars was working as editor of Editions de la Sirène, publishing, among other things, a reissue of Lautréamont's *Les Chants de Maldoror,* a work that had been inaccessible for many years, and that was soon to generate a powerful influence on the surrealists. He also published his own *Anthologie Nègre,* a compilation and translation of African tales. But this was just one of his activities. In 1921 Cendrars was working with the film director Abel Gance on *The Wheel,* and was directly responsible for the montage sequences (which were said to influence Eisenstein). Afterward, continuing his involvement with film—which he celebrated as the modern art form *par excellence*—Cendrars went to Italy and formed his own film company, a venture that made him a fortune. The fortune disappeared shortly afterward in an international banking scandal. His last escapade in cinema was to be in 1924, the year that he went to Africa to film elephants. He would later spend time in Hollywood in a different capacity, supervising the work on the film version of his novel *Sutter's Gold.*

The next major epoch—if we can so divide a life (Cendrars himself spoke in terms of personal epochs)—came in 1924 with his first trip to Brazil. He discovered an immediate affinity with the South American geography, and for the next twenty years was to travel constantly between Europe and Brazil. During this long period Cendrars was conducting a number of highly mysterious business transactions, involving the import of motor fuel. He was also buying and operating a plantation in Brazil, and writing, but novels, not poetry. The publications continue: *L'Or* in 1925, *Moravagine* in 1926, *Le Plan de l'Aiguille* and *Les Confessions de Dan Yack* in 1929, as well as nearly a dozen volumes of reportage, translation, and anthology. Of the lot, *L'Or,* translated as *Sutter's Gold* (1926), scored the greatest popular success.

Sutter's Gold is the easiest of Cendrars's novels to assimilate. It deals in a compressed, minimalist prose with the epic downfall of his countryman August Sutter, the man who made the mistake of discovering gold on his property. The message of the book is as old as language itself: what shall it profit a man, if he gain the whole world . . . ? The tempo and simplicity of the work gained it a wide audience in many languages.

Moravagine, which did not appear in English until 1969, presents a wholly different side of Cendrars. Where *Sutter's Gold* is trim, concise, a parable, *Moravagine* represents inversion, excess—it is clearly the product of a tormented, even sadistic temperament.

Moravagine stakes out human extremity as its subject matter. The language is pained, exacerbated. Long, telescopic sentences carry us through revolution, terror, a zone of sexual and moral nihilism. To call the book depraved is to soft-pedal the issue. Nothing on that order, excepting Lautréamont, had appeared before. Moravagine seeks damnation and extinction with a glee unequaled in literature. The only parallels that come to mind are with Céline and Beckett. We can imagine an energized Molloy with limbs that function and a bomb in his pocket. Not a drop of sentimentality is to be found. Moravagine is projected as human nature stripped of culture and civilization—pessimistic, yes, but in view of the atrocities that Cendrars had witnessed (and of which he writes so well in *Lice*) not pure fabrication.

Le Plan de l'Aiguille and *Les Confessions de Dan Yack* both appeared in 1929. The former was published in English as *Antarctic Fugue* in 1948 and is unobtainable. The two were intended as consecutive novels, the latter meant to explain and fulfill the former—an effect never achieved in English since *Dan Yack* was never translated. Taken together, or separately, they are probably the least successful of Cendrars's writings. They represent an all too private working out of obsession. The settings and symbol constructions are fantastic—fascinating as well—but are not calculated to reach any but the most loyal partisans.

In the character of Dan Yack (the "hero" of both books), Cendrars gives us the polarities of his own nature: Yack is torn between his solitude and mysticism and his love of the world and activity among men, his self-sufficiency and his romantic will, his intellect and his senses. His realizations, accompanied by catastrophe and pain, come to him in the desolate silence of the Antarctic. In the course of the narrative he comes to terms with his past, his many selves, his loves, and, in an action of supreme self-transcendence, listens in to the way of the world. The message is not unlike Wittgenstein's "The world is everything that is the case." Yack has come to grips with renunciation and assent. The resolution, after so much of the fantastic, is his acceptance of the recognized proportions of things.

Cendrars did not find his ideal expression in the novel. The fact is that Cendrars was at his best when he worked either in loose associative verse forms, as in *Trans-Siberian* or *Panama,* both of which stand up as virtuoso performances; or when he worked in the autobiographical vein. The shorter poems, those of *Kodak* and *Dix-neuf Poèmes Elastiques,* strike us with their quickness and modernity, but hardly comprise a major testament.

In 1940, after a year or so as a war correspondent for the French press, disgusted by the reaction of his countrymen to the world situation, Cendrars withdraw to Aix-en-Provence and stopped writing. He once again drew the curtain on his literary career. What did he do, think? No one knows. Reports from friends and visitors had him meditating in an unheated kitchen. It was a period of sorrow for Cendrars. He was to learn from two separate telegrams that his sons, Rémy and Odilon, had been killed. Though his marriage had been brief and long since dissolved, Cendrars had felt close, at least spiritually, to the two boys.

The career does not end here, however. As before, Cendrars's pronouncements that he is "through" are reversed. After three years of silence his picks up his pen once again, this time to deliver a series of autobiographical chronicles. They are to be his major achievement. In a footnote to one of the volumes, *Bourlinguer,* translated as *Planus,* he writes: "The other day was my sixtieth birthday, and it is only today, as I draw towards the end of the present work, that I begin to believe in my vocation as a writer. . . ." Says Henry Miller, in his essay on Cendrars, "Put that in your pipe and smoke it, you lads of twenty-five, thirty and forty years of age. . . ."

What was it that detonated the man? Cendrars supplies one kind of answer in a dedication to his friend Edouard Peisson, who had come to visit him in his seclusion:

> If, in my desire to share that burden of responsibility, I ask myself how it is that your brief visit this morning triggered something in me so forcibly that I immediately started writing . . . I am not too sure how to answer. What you told me about your experience last night, the sky, the moon, the landscape and the silence must have rekindled similar reminiscences in me, stirred as I was by the reverberations of the war which seemed to echo through the bitter thoughts you had had. . . . Or do you not believe, quite simply, that sailors, like poets, are too sensitive to the magic of moonlight and to the destiny that seems to come down to us from the stars, on sea, on land, or between the pages of a book when at last we lower our eyes from the heavens, you the sailor and I the poet, and that when you and I write, we are prey to an obsession or victims of the distortions of our vocation?

* * *

> Today I am sixty years old, and the gymnastics and juggling I once indulged in to beguile the ship's boy, I now perform in front of a typewriter, to keep my body in training and my spirits lively, for it is years now since I went out; I no longer move, no longer travel, no longer see anyone, sliding my life under the roller of my typewriter, like a sheet of carbon between two sheets of white paper, and I type and type, recto and verso, and re-read like a somnambulist, intercalating the direct image with the reflection, which can only be deciphered in reverse, mirror-wise; I am master of my life, dominating time, for I have succeeded in dislocating and disarticulating it, sliding relativity into my sentences like a substratum, using it as the very mainspring of my writing. . . . It may be the literary novelty of the 20th century, the skill and art of applying the analytic procedures and mathematical deductions of an Einstein to the essence, the structure, the propagation of light in the technique of the novel!
>
> —*Planus*

Cendrars's return to literature at the age of sixty, his subsequent productivity, and the excellence and singularity of the works are matters for rejoicing. The three volumes, *The Astonished Man, Lice,* and *Planus,* originally *L'Homme Foudroyé* (published in French in 1945), *La Main Coupée* (1946), and *Bourlinguer* (1948), are not diminished by mention of Rousseau or Montaigne, though in their savor and energy they might more aptly be compared with Villon or Rabelais.

The content of these three works is at first glance diffuse. The diffusion is probably the major obstacle to Cendrars, but it is also a mark of his genius. The works *are* Cendrars, to the limit of the meaning of such a pronouncement. Adventure and reflection interpenetrate. Chapters, even paragraphs, even single sentences, zigzag back and forth through time. Nor are the sequences made any more accessible by Cendrars's penchant for rambling anecdotes, lengthy asides, footnotes, and the like. It is the content that excuses all the confusion. Familiarity with the voice and its owner provoke fascination. And as the reader submits to this fascination, the chronological jumble takes on a different aspect. He starts to experience the narrative with the acuity of one following a thread through a labyrinth. The time sense, the demand for sequence, are cast aside. The narrative, like the life, like *any* life, reveals that its true character is referential. A memory from childhood interlocks with an episode from later life—only a writer who has penetrated to the core of his being can offer us experience at this level.

Cendrars's life, I will not tire of repeating, was epic, the appetites gargantuan. *The Astonished Man* is a perfect title, for at the heart of this network is the figure of Cendrars—stripping himself of myth, layering himself with myth, we are never sure which—the astonishment of being alive always in his voice.

Miller again: "There were times when reading Cendrars—and this is something which happens to me rarely—that I put the book down to wring my hands with joy or despair. . . ."

The content? Cendrars's life. The volumes can be read in any order. They are simply tales, events, and encounters that Cendrars saw fit to put on paper. Reading them, picking up hints at every turn of stories and events not related, we wish there were more, but we find ourselves grateful, too, for what he has given.

There is no point in trying to invent a summary. What matters is not the content, but the man, our sense of his spirit and its amplitude. The spirit of the narrative voice is what alters a set of casually narrated tales into literature. Our sense of this spirit grows as we read and remains with us after we are finished. The reader who has persevered may find that Cendrars has become a taste, and, past that, an emblem for a whole way of looking at the world.

Cendrars was in his early sixties when the last of the chronicles was completed. In 1950 he returned to Paris from Aix. He was once again a married man; the rejuvenation he had experienced led him to cement a relationship that had been going on for some thirty years. This was with Raymone, the one true love to whom he alludes ever so discreetly in his works.

For the next ten years Cendrars was mainly active in radio work. His literary output diminished, consisting mainly of interviews and occasional pieces. One last novel, *Emmène-moi au Bout du Monde,* was published in 1956. It was translated into English as *To the End of the World* (1966). While it does not represent a major literary event, it was controversial upon publication—Cendrars took some well-aimed shots at Parisian society figures.

The last five years of his life were not happy. A deteriorative disease stopped his wanderings, confined him to a wheelchair. The writing stopped. In January 1961, three days after being awarded his only literary prize, Cendrars died. Had he been able to script it, he would probably have chosen a more dramatic exit. Perhaps something in the matter of Lord Mountbatten. Otherwise, though, he had less to regret than most. The life was rich. His testament is there for anyone who wants to find it.

Postscript: There is one major mystery yet to be solved. Cendrars stated many times that he had consigned a large number of manuscripts, unsigned, to various strongboxes in South American banks. He may have been exaggeration-prone, but he was not a liar. To date none of these manuscripts has been found.

Marguerite Yourcenar

In her "Reflections on the Composition of *Memoirs of Hadrian,*" Marguerite Yourcenar has described in some detail the halting yet seemingly fated progress of that book. Originally begun between 1924 and 1930, abandoned, resumed, it was abandoned again before the war, for the last time—or so the author thought then. In 1948, however, when Yourcenar was living in America, an old trunk full of papers and letters was returned to her. She tells how she seated herself in front of a fire and undertook the sad reconnaissance of her past. Letters were read and consigned to the flames, long-forgotten faces were recalled. Then: "I came upon four or five typewritten sheets, the paper of which had turned yellow. The salutation told me nothing. 'My dear Mark . . .' *Mark* . . . What friend or love, what distant relative was this? It was several minutes before I remembered that *Mark* stood here for *Marcus Aurelius,* and that I had in hand a fragment of the lost manuscript. From that moment there was no question but that this book must be taken up again, whatever the cost."

The long gestation bore magnificent results: the narrative, at once intimate and austere, reconstitutes with its burnished images the empire of second-century Rome. Largely on the strength of *Hadrian,* Yourcenar was elected to the Académie Française in 1981. She was the first woman ever thus honored.

During the period of the original drafting of Hadrian's letter to Marcus Aurelius, Yourcenar also completed the short novel *Alexis* (published in 1929), which appeared in English for the first time in 1984. *Alexis* is, like *Hadrian,* an epistolary self-accounting. But whereas *Hadrian* hoards the memories of a turbulent life against the onset of death, *Alexis* is little more than a congeries of hints and evasions. What Oscar Wilde called "the love that dare not speak its name" tries to come across in a low whisper.

Alexis, a successful young pianist, is writing to Monique, his aristocratic young wife, to explain his desertion. He has decided, after some agonizing (which is either genuine or pro forma—part of the trouble is that we're not sure), that he must be free to indulge his sexual preference. But this is Europe at the turn of the century, and with his refined sensibility, Alexis cannot come right out with the news. No, he constructs a lacework of hints and withholdings and coy reprimands to himself: nothing must injure the delicacy of feeling that is between them. It is of freedom that Alexis speaks, but his idiom is that of entrapment: "But, you see, I am hesitating; every word I write takes me a little further from what I wanted to express at the very outset. . . ." One thinks recurrently of Prufrock.

The apologia begins with some muted evocations of childhood. Alexis was a solitary dreamer; he grew up in a once-fine manor in Bohemia, surrounded by the ghosts of energetic ancestors and by the tranquil affections of his mother and sisters. We are to imagine the subtle ways in which a disposition is shaped, though from time to time Alexis supplies a speculative nudge. Recalling his sisters' girlhood friends, for example, he writes: "Nothing would appear to have prevented me from loving one of these girls, and perhaps you yourself find it strange that I did not. . . . One does not lose one's heart to what one respects, nor perhaps even to what one loves; above all, one does not lose one's heart to what resembles oneself—and it was not women I was most different from." To this he adds, bringing himself to the threshold of confession: "Monique, do you understand me?"

In time, of course, Alexis has to come to the point—a good letter, like any other prose, needs to develop in some direction. So, after endless tergiversation, he avers that there was an original incident, an initiation. Not that he is especially graphic: it happened somewhere along a road, by a hedge, with someone, somehow. He gives no name, face, or sensation. And yet we are to believe that this furtive, shameful event set him on his track. Not right away, naturally. Before he can accept himself, Alexis must suffer the lacerating cycle: penitence, denial, sudden abandoned indulgence, reaffirmed penitence. He comes to see that his marriage represents the supreme denial, and that the letter of confession is the record of his victory.

All of this could make for a fascinating narrative. The opposition of passion and the taboo has always been a source of the most irresistible tension in fiction. But this tension can neither gather nor release itself in the realm of abstraction. "I shall not describe the hallucinatory quest for pleasure," writes Alexis, "the potential mortifications, and the bitterness of a moral humiliation much worse than the sin itself. . . ." It's exactly what he *should* have done. Portrayed with such detachment Alexis's escapades do not have the force of passion that, from his perspective, is their principal justification.

Yourcenar wrote *Alexis* when she was twenty-four. She states in the recently written preface that she has resisted the temptation to revise or modernize the book; though she obviously recognizes the radically changed social perception of the homosexual, she contends that the difficulties facing the individual are much the same. Doubtless she is right, but my guess is that few homosexuals will find confirmation or self-recognition in the maunderings of this young man. Their value is mainly historical—they tell us something about the status of the unspoken, or unspeakable, in a certain milieu at a certain time.

How very different is the gravid fullness of *Hadrian* (1955) or the warts-and-all portraiture of *The Abyss* (1976). In those novels, too, Yourcenar represents love between men—Hadrian's devotion to the young Antinous is especially moving; but in both the rendering is so robust and unconstrained that it scarcely seems we are reading about a reality long proscribed. One could argue, obviously, that both novels are historical and treat of periods less distorted by sexual repression (Rome in the early empire, Flanders in the sixteenth century). At some point, however, the psychobiographer will get restive and demand his say.

Male love, not lesbianism, is a central subject in Yourcenar's novels. And yet Yourcenar has never made any secret of her own sexual preference. Clearly she has found in male homosexual love a useful figure, one that affords certain emblematic similarities and at the same time allows her to keep artistic distance. If this is so, then it is not unreasonable to speculate that the lapse of time between *Alexis* and *Hadrian*—more than two decades—coincided with a great personal liberation, that *Alexis* was the projection of a crisis that had been overcome by the time *Hadrian* was written. Or, to put it another way, that there was a tension about sexual identity that *had* to be overcome in order that *Hadrian* could take the form it does. Yourcenar's essay on that novel has a great deal to say about the difficulty of achieving historical empathy. Nothing is said about the matter of sexual empathy, which is hardly irrelevant.

Yourcenar's imaginative transformations raise some interesting, if unanswerable, questions. Why, for instance, does she not write about lesbian love? Or, if we accept that she has a need to distance and refigure the personal, then we have to ask whether there is, in fact, a ready interchangeability between lesbian and male homosexual love. Are the emotional and situational registers so parallel that one can stand in for the other, or is this possible only through some obscure private conversion?

Provocative though they may be, these are topics better left in the biographer's care. For us it is enough that Yourcenar in her best work is one of the great anatomists of the human psyche. The sexual disposition of Hadrian, or the philosopher Zeno in *The Abyss,* is less important, ultimately, than the highly kindled flux of inner life she depicts, that hovering between passion and detachment that, to a greater or lesser extent, characterizes us all.

Inseparable from this is her superb craftsmanship. Yourcenar is one of the last exponents of what used to be known, at least in France, as the "classical" prose style. Such a style aspires to lucidity and balance, a certain cool stateliness. In Yourcenar's hands it achieves a supple sensuousness as well, for she will freely modulate from the abstract to the concrete wherever appropriate. Here is Hadrian discoursing on love:

> That mysterious play which extends from love of a body to love of an entire person has seemed to me noble enough to consecrate to it one part of my life. Words for it are deceiving, since the word for pleasure covers contradictory realities comprising notions of warmth, sweetness, and intimacy of bodies, but also feelings of violence and agony, and the sound of a cry. The short and obscene sentence of Poseidonius about the rubbing together of two small pieces of flesh, which I have seen you copy in your exercise books with the application of a good schoolboy, does no more to define the phenomenon of love than the cord touched by a finger accounts for the infinite miracle of sounds. Such a dictum is less an insult to pleasure than to the flesh itself, that amazing instrument of muscles, blood and skin, that red-tinged cloud whose lightning is the soul.

With the passing of the classical style we have lost this kind of music. It may not be suited to the transmission of the modern sense of discord, but it embodies an element of human continuity that literature cannot easily do without.

Marguerite Duras

Minimalism is, for the practitioner, one of the more seductive literary modes. Like abstract painting, it looks easy, and as most of the action takes place in the realm of the unstated, the writer need not be bothered with the messy mechanics of plot or character development. Hemingway bewitched several generations of prose stylists with his primer-simple narratives and his aesthetic of exclusion: the unstated emotion, he maintained, can pack as much of a wallop as the stated one. In his hands the technique often worked—the early stories and novels, especially, quiver with repressed materials; but his legion of imitators the world over have given understatement a bad name. Few of them have bothered to learn the all-important corollary to that aesthetic—that the emotion, though not declared, must nevertheless exist. Most of us, I suspect, now balk when confronted with a page of fashionably lean prose. Dress it up how you will, I say it's spinach and I say to hell with it.

Rules make life ordinary, but exceptions make it bearable. A handful of unexpected masterpieces in the last few decades—Max Frisch's *Montauk,* James Salter's *A Sport and a Pastime,* and Lars Gustafsson's *The Death of a Beekeeper* come to mind—have shown that literary minimalism is still a viable enterprise. To this short list I would add Marguerite Duras's Goncourt Prize–winning novella, *The Lover.*

Duras's book presents, in flashback, the story of an adolescent French girl's coming of age—mostly in terms of her sexual involvement with an older Chinese man—in colonial Saigon in the 1930's. It is not, as some reviewers have suggested, a straight-faced remake of *Lolita.* The bond between these lovers is more existential than erotic. Indeed, the obsessive intensity of their coupling hints, according to minimalist precepts of exclusion, at the pervasiveness of the despair they hope to extinguish. Readers might find themselves blinking away images from Resnais's *Hiroshima Mon Amour,* for which Duras wrote the script.

The narrator—I will not make so bold as to call her Duras, though the biographical particulars seems to match up—begins her telling with an encounter from the present. An old acquaintance approaches her on the street and delivers the following compliment: "Everyone says you were beautiful when you were young, but I want to tell you I think you're more beautiful now than then. Rather than your face as a young woman, I prefer your face as it is now. Ravaged." The word echoes like a pistol shot in an empty street. We know we are in for anything but a lighthearted romp through the past.

The first third of the book hovers around a single image, a memory from the narrator's youth that is as composed and static as a photograph. "It might have existed," she writes, "a photograph might have been taken, just like any other, somewhere else, in other circumstances. But it wasn't. The subject was too slight." A girl, age fifteen and a half (the specificity tells us at once of the struggle between girlishness and precocity), stands by herself at the rail of a ferry crossing the Mekong River. She is on her way to her boarding school in Saigon; she's dressed in a hand-me-down silk dress, an exotic pair of gold lamé high heels, and a flat-brimmed pink hat with a broad black ribbon. Duras devotes several pages to her apparel, describing the acquisition of each item. But what we are really getting is a series of glimpses into a melancholy, fatherless childhood. An observation like the following tells us more about the family situation than pages of patient characterization:

> When my mother emerges, comes out of her despair, she sees the man's hat and the gold lamé shoes. She asks what it's all about. I say nothing. She looks at me, is pleased, smiles. Not bad, she says, they quite suit you, make a change. She doesn't ask if it's she who bought them, she knows she did.

There is, of course, another reason why the image is so painstakingly examined. The girl at the rail is just moments away from her fateful encounter. She has already taken note of the long black limousine and the gentleman watching her through the window; the promise of his otherness has already begun to penetrate her self-absorption.

A solitary, beguiling girl at a turning point in her life, inhaling the last air of innocence . . . The fantasy is an easy one to fall in with. But, as the puzzle books put it, something is wrong with this picture. And the more Duras keeps returning to it, the more we sense that. Carefully inserted vignettes and background details gradually force us to abandon the Pollyanna drift of our reverie. The girl on the barge is inwardly cauterized. Living in gloomy tropical houses with a half-mad mother and two tormented brothers has long since destroyed any joyous freshness in her. She is going through the paces of late adolescence with a cool detachment. Not lust, but a need even deeper—a need to be touched, to be certified as existing—makes her respond to the man's overtures.

Readers lured on by the promise of titillation will be disappointed. They will find no elaborate seduction scene, no fetishism (the gold lamé heels are a bit of naturalism, not a come-on), no variations on the themes of master/slave or colonialism-in-the-boudoir. These are just two strangers, adrift, frightened, and almost entirely opaque to themselves. He—no name is given—is a rich man's son, uncentered by wealth and idleness; he trembles when he offers her a cigarette and later can scarcely bring himself to touch her. She, in turn, tells him: "I'd rather you didn't love me. But if you do, I'd like you to do as you usually do with women." Their interchanges go largely unreported. But Duras does not need conversation to bring across the shuddering immediacy of the first bodily encounter or the emergent contours of their relationship:

> The skin is sumptuously soft. The body is thin, lacking in strength, in muscle, he may have been ill, may be convalescent, he's hairless, nothing masculine about him but his sex, he's weak, probably a prey to insult, vulnerable. She doesn't look him in the face. Doesn't look at him at all. She touches him. Touches the softness of his sex, his skin, caresses his goldness, the strange novelty. He moans, weeps. In dreadful love.

We wonder, momentarily, about that "dreadful love" but dismiss it as a young girl's ignorant perception. Neither do we find, as months pass, that anything resembling love develops between them. They have their ritual. He picks her up at school in his limousine, they go to his room in the city's Chinese quarter, he drives her back. We almost never hear them exchange words; their lovemaking is fierce, but in Duras's telling affectless: there is no apparent progress in their affections. When, from time to time, he takes the girl's mother and brothers out to dinner, no one talks. She explains to him that they are like that with everyone. The dominant impression is of claustrophobic unreality, as if this man and girl had been excerpted from the space-time continuum.

The affair continues for a year and a half. Then, one day, the girl is told that the family is returning to France, that passage has been booked. There is no shock or panic; any tremors they might feel travel inward. We get this flat report: "Once the date of my departure was fixed, distant though it still was, he could do nothing with my body any more."

The parting is simple, cinematic. The girl sees the black limousine on the pier as her boat pulls away. They will never see each other again. Years later she will learn that he has married a girl chosen for him by his parents. The unhappy business is consigned to memory, becomes a painful episode in what the French fondly call *l'éducation sentimentale.* Until, suddenly, in a time near the present ("years after the war, after marriage, children, divorces, books . . ."), he calls her. He is in Paris, traveling with his wife. He has followed her career, her literary successes. They converse nervously. "They didn't know what to say. And then he told her. Told her that it was as before, that he still loved her, he could never stop loving her, that he'd love her until death." With these words the book ends.

A sketchy chronicle like this cannot account for the power of *The Lover,* which derives as much from its silences as from its narrative. Duras's decision to present the story as a memory, to let a half century of vanished time function as a sounding chamber, is a brilliant one. Had the story been told in the present, the reticence, the terse notations, would have seemed mannered. This way, though, the spareness reveals as nothing else can the harsh abrasions of time. The woman with the ravaged face has given us a disturbing picture of the workings of destiny.

The Lover is saturated with a peculiarly Gallic ennui. As a result, the final lines break in on the gloom swiftly and unexpectedly. The telephone conversation transfigures everything. Both man and affair take on a retroactive profundity, invalidating our dismissal. This, in turn, makes the image of the limousine on the pier the very emblem of ill-starred love. The tale is rewritten in the space of a breath; its density, depth, and hopelessness become even more pervasive. Now, however, his love—its mysterious persistence—flings a beam of light into the darkness. And we can't help but steer our way toward it.

The Lover was published here in 1985 to considerable acclaim, garnering for Duras the wider recognition that had eluded her before through a long career as a novelist and script-writer. Readers were as much taken with the trembling staccato of her narrative style as they were with the narrative itself. That eerie and lacerating work will doubtless be invoked in most assessments of *The War: A Memoir* (1986). For this prose, too, is voiced through a numbed, life-scarred "I," and concerns itself, at least in part, with the ambiguities of love and the immense difficulty of bridging the space that exists between even the most kindred of souls.

Similarities do abound, but it is the primary difference that is most instructive. *The Lover* was written in the near present, after the passing of decades had stripped off emotional clutter and had left only the bleached residues of event. *The War,* on the other hand, comprises a diary and several memoirs and stories written by Duras in the 1940's; the main sections, she claims in a short preface, were put down in exercise books and forgotten. The first of these, "The War," is still mysterious to the author: "I recognize my handwriting and the details of the story. . . . But I can't see myself writing the diary. When would I have done so, in what year, at what times of day, in what house?" The congruity between works—the one remembered, the other forgotten—almost suggests that there is a deeper "writing self" that stands apart from the movements of time and circumstance.

The War has five sections. The longest of these, "The War" and "Monsieur X, Here Called Pierre Rabier," are directly autobiographical, and form, along with the thinly disguised (Duras admits it) story "Albert of the Capital/Ter of the Militia," the compelling core of the book. The two slight tales grafted to the end, "The Crushed Nettle" and "Aurelia Paris," lack the peculiar quiver that Duras's manipulation of her own persona invariably provides.

"The War" is, quite simply, a diary that was begun by the author when she heard that the German camps were being liberated. Her husband, identified only as Robert L., had been shipped to Belsen during the occupation for his resistance activities. Duras would not find out for a month if he was among the survivors or not. The entries—sometimes several for a single day—forge a nearly unendurable chronicle of fear and morbid fantasy. Time is registered not on the clock but in the nerve endings:

> You don't exist anymore in comparison with this waiting. More images pass through your head than there are on all the roads in Germany. Bursts of machine gun fire every minute inside

your head. And yet you're still there, the bullets aren't fatal. Shot in transit. Dead with an empty stomach. His hunger wheels around in your head like a vulture.

Duras tries to quell her agony by giving up hope. But, alas, one cannot control the mechanism with a resolve. She can only endure her dread. She works, spends long days in transit centers, helping others. Still, she cannot stop herself from prowling among the endless lines of returnees, scanning faces. The horror of it all nearly finishes her off. Then the call comes: Robert L. is alive.

Duras's pain does not end with Robert L.'s return—it just becomes more specific. For now the worst imaginings have been replaced by a reality that almost defies language. Every resource, we sense, is mustered to get the words to the page. No other choice is allowed. Only through the most precise accounting will history be served. Man must be able to look at what Man has done:

> The head was connected to the body by the neck, as heads usually are, but the neck was so withered and shrunken—you could circle it with one hand—that you wondered how life could pass through it; a spoonful of gruel almost blocked it. . . . You could see the vertebrae through it, the carotid arteries, the nerves, the pharynx, and the blood passing through: the skin had become like cigarette paper.

This, I may add, is the mildest of her reports.

The love we find here is not romantic, but biological. We feel Duras's struggle to reverse, through the most patient ministrations, the destruction wrought by an enemy that despised the human miracle. Astonishingly enough, the body is revealed to be the vessel for an entity more precious still: ". . . it was then, by his deathbed, that I knew him, Robert L., best, that I understood forever what made him himself, himself alone and nothing and no one else in the world. . . ." The diary breaks off with Robert L.'s recovery.

The other autobiographical sections are not nearly as harrowing. Both, however, give us sustained insight into the hectic and treacherous life in resistance cadres. In "Monsieur X," the more complex of the pieces, Duras depicts her desperate cat-and-mouse involvement with a young Gestapo officer (he claims to know the whereabouts of Robert L.). Fear, anxiety, and—yes—fascination are plaited with a slender filament of pity. Her devotion to justice—she finally denounces the man to her comrades—does not blind her to the uncertainty they share. Indeed, this is the quality that distinguishes Duras as a writer. On every page we hear a woman who is unable to hide from the truth, whose strength must take root in the hardest place—the far side of vulnerability.

Michel Tournier

The term inversions, *so oddly used by sexologists to designate heteromorphous erotic practices, would certainly have delighted the Gnostics: was it not their aim, in this domain as in all others, to bring about a total inversion of values between man, his fellow-creatures, and the world?*

—JACQUES LECARRIERE, *The Gnostics*

Roger Shattuck raised a few eyebrows not long ago when he announced that "the most exciting novelist now writing in French" was a man named Michel Tournier. It was a bold piece of advocacy for several reasons. On this side of the Atlantic, Tournier is virtually unknown. His novels have been published in small hardcover runs—mainly for the library market—and critical reception has been of the kind usually accorded to "interesting" but minor foreign imports. In France, however, where Tournier is known and read, the claim would probably have been construed by many as a calculated provocation. For in the eyes of the guardians of the French succession,

Tournier is perverse, crypto-mystical, reactionary, and morally subversive.

What, after Sade, Huysmans, Artaud, Céline, and Genet, could possibly ruffle the celebrated French sangfroid? The homoeroticism? The eager fetishism—for shoe leather, hair clippings, excreta? Or could it be the strange temperature pattern of his prose, the way the mercury climbs whenever details of a primary nature are touched upon; when, say, Abel Tiffauges slowly licks the "swollen pulp" of a schoolmate's wound in *The Ogre,* or when the exquisite Fabienne "plops" a tapeworm in the midst of an aristocratic soiree in *Gemini*? These things might have something to do with Tournier's contested status. But the controversy goes deeper than mere kinkiness. Shattuck's estimate was not capricious: Tournier is one of the few novelists alive who deserve to be called visionary. From one book to the next, he has been developing and extending a set of themes that are radically at odds with the common views of Western society. To the rationalist/Christian scheme he opposes a sensual Gnosticism; in the face of the "social contract" he flings an imperious, anarchic individualism. This is his real crime. In another age he would have been burned at the stake.

Friday, or, The Other Island (1967), Tournier's first novel, is relatively mild and playful in its heresies and is, for that reason, the most accessible of the four that have been translated. Already, though, the project of rereading the world has been undertaken and the key principles sketched: character as destiny, material reality as a Baudelairean "forest of symbols," the survival in the psyche of a lost wholeness, and the possibility given to the man of recovering this state through exceptional deeds of self-attainment. Mythic or textual reverberation is here, as in future novels, a crucial structural element.

Friday is Tournier's retelling of Defoe's *Robinson Crusoe.* Rather, it is a counterfugue to the original, a conversion of its solid substance into an airy parable of the spirit. The inversion is skillful. By turning the shipwreck into a stroke of destiny, Tournier turns the contingent life of Crusoe into the necessary life. From the moment of his awakening on the beach, his every step is toward the "real" Crusoe who has always been waiting inside.

Tournier's hero does things that Defoe's would never do. He suspends himself for days in warm mire; he conceives the fantastic notion that there is an animate and feminine "other island" beneath, or behind, the island he so doggedly cultivates; he lowers himself to the soil to make love to this entity and is only half-surprised when garish flowers grow up where he has left his seed. By the time Friday arrives, Crusoe is ready for complete transformation. And it is through his contact with the impulsive native, the tutelary spirit of the Other Island, that he reaches his apotheosis as the primal man, the sun-worshiping Adam who has learned to bear intact his original male-female "solar" sexuality.

In all of Tournier's novels, man is presented as a being reft from some original unity, condemned to wander in a world where the order of things has been scrambled and ciphered, as if by some calculating archfiend. But like the Gnostics, Tournier believes that a gleam of the pure light is still buried in our being. By this light one can make out the guiding signs, possibly even discover what pattern they make. There is no place for social order in this—social order is the very paradigm of the fallen condition. Only the private sense of destiny, the obscure proddings of self-intuition, can be relied upon.

> January 3, 1938. You are an ogre, Rachel used to say to me sometimes. An ogre? A fabulous monster emerging from the mists of time? Well, yes, I do think there's something magical about me, I do think there's a secret collusion, deep down, connecting what happens to me with what happens in general, and enabling my particular history to bend the course of things in its own direction.

This astonishing confession begins the tale of Abel Tiffauges, *The Ogre* (1972). From the first we are asked to accept the convergence of private self and outer world and to stand in the shower of portents and symbols that marks Tiffauges's "particular history." We are a long way from Crusoe's island: the track of Tiffauges's destiny will carry him down through the rings of a symbolist's inferno and into the sulfurous maw of Nazi Germany.

Tiffauges is the proprietor of an auto garage in Paris. When a shop accident one day incapacitates his right hand, he discovers that he can write a perfectly fluent but very different script with his left. What's more, the discovery prompts, *compels* him to set down his reflections and memories. The "accident," like Crusoe's shipwreck, signals the eruption of a hitherto buried identity.

It is impossible to record here the subtlety and intricacy with which outer and inner events are spun together, for it is Tiffauges's special bent to ponder every detail until its larger significance declares itself. With the liberation of his left, "sinister," side, his past has come to life. He remembers everything: his miserable childhood at St. Christopher's School, the punishments and bullyings he suffered; the unexpected intercession of Nestor, the janitor's son; the boiler room explosion in which Nestor died . . . Tiffauges suddenly recalls how Nestor used to insist upon holding his left hand while they sat together at the back of the class. Could it be that his guardian has come back to direct his life? Pondering that enigma, Tiffauges gets the first inklings of his "phoric" (from the Greek *pherein:* "to carry") vocation.

Already this sounds like enough to perplex all but the hardiest of kabbalists—it is just the beginning. With the "phoric" thread in hand, Tiffauges goes fishing. He recounts to himself the legend of the school's patron saint, Christopher (Christo-phoros: Christ-bearer), how the river rose around the giant Canaanite while the child on his back "weighed as heavy as lead." The tale merges with his memories of Nestor to become a vivid self-premonition: "carrying" will in some way figure in his yet unknown mission.

The fascination of Tiffauges's ruminations derives from his absolute conviction that life is an arcane puzzle and that these most unlikely insights and connections are essential to the solution. Sure enough, the day comes when his speculations are galvanized by the real. When one of his mechanics is wounded by a flying blade, Tiffauges hurries over; as he lifts up the young man's body he is transfixed by a "phoric ecstasy." At a stroke his course is revealed to him: he must tear down his illusory existence and replace it with another. He must, henceforth, follow the tumult of his strange inclinations.

The Ogre is in many ways a shapeless book. Its narrative hews to the logic of obsession, private and, later, collective. We follow along as Tiffauges abandons, stage by stage, all belief in volition, until he finally obeys only the configuration of events and his reading of signs. When he discovers, for instance, that he is stirred by the innocence of children, he spends whole days lurking in schoolyards, with a camera. At night, alone in his apartment, he searches among the snaps of faces for a hint about the reality he seeks. Staring at the negatives in their bath, Tiffauges starts to contemplate the principle of inversion, how "in a naked body . . . the parts which are softest and pearliest in reality . . . appear darkest and murkiest." The idea of reversed values provokes him—he cannot say why exactly—and he adds it to his interpretive kit bag.

Tiffauges's peregrinations have their consequences. A young girl that he has befriended is raped, and through a "malign inversion" (he has discovered that there are different kinds of reversals), Tiffauges, connoisseur of the innocence and joy of children, is charged with the ultimate desecration. He is strangely calm. According to his reading of things, some frightful retribution must fall upon his accusers.

The retribution is the war. Tiffauges is released without trial and sent to the front—"to get a bayonet stuck through [the] . . . gizzard." From this point on the strands of private and collective obsession will be tightly plaited. As Stendhal registered the uncontrollable surges of war through the eyes of his Fabrizio in *The Charterhouse of Parma,* so Tournier refracts everything through the symbol-hunting passion of his "ogre." Tiffauges is captured by the Germans, and after all kinds of uncanny experiences he ends up working in Kaltenborn, a training center for Nazi youth. Volunteering as a recruiter, he prowls the countryside on his black steed, searching out the finest blond specimens. Each "find" grants a new ecstasy. The youths are going to certain death, Tiffauges knows that, but his "eu-phoria" will not be suppressed. He is living out the dark lines of Goethe's "Erlking": "Who rides so late through the night and the wind?/It is the father with his child. . . ."

Just days before Kaltenborn is overrun by the advancing Russian army, Tiffauges finds a starving child in the woods: Ephraim, a refugee from Auschwitz. He is the sliver of light that has passed through darkness, the being that has proved miraculously impervious to evil. Ephraim mutters gnomic biblical pronouncements while Tiffauges carries him around on his back. And when the Russians break through, the two escape into the night. However, it is not until they are crossing a vast swamp that Tiffauges realizes that his mission is finished. He feels the elfin rider get heavier and heavier as legends and signs converge in his being. He pushes on—for "all was as it should be." When he looks up for the last time, he sees only "a six-pointed star turning slowly against the black sky."

The Ogre has been reviled both for its attentiveness to the unseemly—the book is full of anatomical fetishism, prolonged caresses, coprological excitements—and its cool, unflinching depiction of Tiffauges as a Nazi yes-man. Tournier plunges his ogre into a hell, but the fellow flourishes, witnessing and enacting horrors with little trace of remorse. But to interpret this as authorial sanction is foolish. *The Ogre* is a gnostic fable. It may be peculiar, but is redemptive as well. For the whole to succeed, Tiffauges must be fully immersed in the corrupted element—only then can he achieve his apotheosis. As Dante had to penetrate to the deepest cavity of hell before he could pass through Lucifer's thighs and see the stars again, so Tiffauges must bear the growing weight of Ephraim right into death before he can see the symbolic triumph of spirit.

With *Gemini* (1981), Tournier took his obsessions in new directions. Destinies and mysteries of inversion were still dominant, but the field of research was now that of human identity. The tale of the perfect geminate pair, Jean and Paul, is played off against the bizarre homosexual adventures of their uncle, Alexandre. The plot instigates and survives every kind of improbability: Alexandre, president of TURDCO, an enormous refuse-collection empire, investigates the deep symbolic secrets of garbage; Paul circles the world in quest of his lost twin, self-consciously replicating the travels of Verne's Phileas Fogg. Pattern folds into pattern until the most provocative ideas come to life. The divided twins become the drifting halves of Diotima's sacred whole described in *The Symposium*. Alexandre's priapic search becomes the reverse of Jean's, its profanation. And so on. On the surface we see the deft play of mirrors; at the root we are caught up in an interrogation of the foundations of the psyche. Tournier is interested above all in locating the source of the primal imbalance that sponsors our relentless bonding and mating. Like Crusoe's "solar sexuality," the idea of the lost twin becomes a mythic strand in Tournier's separatist cosmology.

What *does* the author finally believe? What is the basis of his vision of destinies? The spiritual need is certainly at the core of each of the novels: we are always hovering on the brink of hidden orders, superior realities, transcendent states. But for all that, there is little that refers to any orthodoxy, even such as the Gnostics—in spite of their hatred of orthodoxy—might have unwittingly held. Christian allusions abound, but invariably they seem to be more a part of a mythic substratum than hints of a proferred solution. *The Four Wise Men,* the fourth of Tournier's novels, hardly dissolves this impression of heterogeneous spiritual drives.

In *The Four Wise Men* (1982), Tournier presents us with yet another retelling. This time he has adapted the Bible story of the journey of the Magi, refurbishing it completely with the addition of an apocryphal fourth traveler. With his singular narrative gifts, he animates a time and place and brings to life four very different—and very troubled—men. Three of them are driven by uncanny twists to follow "the comet with the golden tail," and they converge upon the manger in Bethlehem. The fourth, Prince Taor, is a spoiled innocent who has set off with a fleet of ships to find the recipe for *rahat loukoum*—"Turkish delight"—to appease his mania for sweets. But as the Bible teaches: the last shall be first. It is Taor the purehearted who, after the most awful calamities, after thirty years of servitude in the salt mines at Sodom, finds his way to the site of the Last Supper. Crazed with hunger and thirst, almost dead from his ordeals, Taor stands over the table. He has come too late. Christ and the disciples have left. In despair, he takes a crust of bread and drinks from a goblet:

> Then he toppled forward, but he did not fall. The two angels who had been watching over him since he left the salt mines, gathered him into their great wings. The night sky opened, revealing a sea of light, and into it they bore the man who, having been last, the eternal latecomer, had just been the first to receive the Eucharist.

This is as subversive as it is spiritual. Is Tournier making sport, playing versions on a sacred text, or is he trying to shake the scales from our eyes, to make us see the grace embedded in the rough matter of creation? Is he mocking or pointing? How we answer will depend largely upon how skewed or straight we believe the order of things to be.

There is much to question in Tournier's enterprise, and many, out of refinement or faith, will not approve it. But I can think of nothing that matches the verve and daring of these imaginings. They open the sluices wide to the unconscious materials that are the very stuff of art's pity and terror. His way of transforming these into the legends of spirit restores to the novel a sense of "high stakes" that has long been missing.

There are signs that Tournier may yet find an American readership. Several of the novels have recently been reissued, and with the publication of *The Fetishist* (1984), a collection of Tournier's stories, the statistical odds have further improved. Indeed, here is the perfect back-door entry for latecomers. As oddly angled as anything by Tournier, these stories progress in vivid flashes and have little of the recondite speculation that makes the novels at times forbidding.

Tournier has a way of tricking us into the realm of the perverse. We accept and absorb some deviant tic, our curiosity is piqued—and then, all at once, we are caught up in the strange logic of compulsion. In "Veronica's Shrouds," for instance, a photographer with a professional interest in a young man's torso is gradually revealed to have a vampire instinct—image by image she is robbing her subject of identity. When the possibilities of the lens have been exhausted, she turns to other expedients. Too bizarre even to summarize, every one of these fourteen stories in some way extends Tournier's gnostic attack on order. He manipulates relentlessly the anxieties with which we surround the taboo. Where we repress, he exalts. Where we discern only darkness, he finds illumination. By flipping the underside of the psyche up into the light, he achieves the desired inversion—we stare at the world as if it were a negative that has yet to be printed.

Primo Levi

Like any other Holocaust document, Primo Levi's *Survival in Auschwitz/The Reawakening* (1986) raises certain questions before you even start reading. Is it possible to narrate the personal and collective experience of suffering once it exceeds a certain magnitude? What *is* that magnitude? At what point do words betray the contours of event? And is there a way in which language, however honest its intent, distorts more than it clarifies? To tell of a horror using the ordering patterns of syntax, working up paragraphs and chapters—doesn't this already imply that it *makes sense,* that memory has drawn its taming comb through? "No poetry after Auschwitz," wrote the philosopher T. W. Adorno. Levi's books are not, of course, poetry—they are memoirs, acts of witness. Should we consider applying Adorno's injunction, or even Wittgenstein's: "Whereof one cannot speak, thereon one must remain silent"? For to break silence is to insist that one *can* speak, that a subject is speakable. But is this subject—Auschwitz—not *unspeakable*? Do we say that testimony, however distorted, is better than silence? Or is the lateral movement of the reader's eye a kind of acceptance of the passage of horror into language? Can language take in this experience without a shiver? Levi's balanced prose suggests that it can.

Levi, an Italian Jew, was arrested by the fascists in 1943 and deported from Turin to Auschwitz. *Survival in Auschwitz* is the narrative of his twelve months of imprisonment. You must understand, however, that the duration of his sufferings bears no relation to time as we conceive it: Levi and his fellow prisoners—starved, brutalized, humiliated at every turn—lived in hell, and time is the first thing that stops in hell. The memoir was written soon after his repatriation to Italy. But as he states in his afterword, he did not have an easy time finding a publisher: "The public did not want to return in memory to the painful years of the war that had just ended." The small publisher who undertook the first edition folded shortly after. The book's eventual success (it was reissued by Einaudi, one of Italy's major publishing houses, in 1958) encouraged Levi to write a sequel volume recounting his difficult path from Auschwitz back to Turin: *The Reawakening* appeared in Italy in 1963. Trained as a chemist, Levi resumed his career upon repatriation; it is only in recent years that he has devoted himself more fully to writing. (He is perhaps best known for *The Periodic Table* [1984], which amalgamates chemical metaphor with personal reminiscence and historical documentation.)

Levi's two memoirs are now available between one set of covers, and they represent a kind of *Iliad* and *Odyssey* of the soul. What is curious is that though nearly twenty years elapsed between the writing of the two, the tonal continuity is seamless. You could argue that the detachment of *Survival in Auschwitz* was a product of numbness and spiritual shock, and that a similar distancing was gained for *The Reawakening* by the passage of years. More plausible, I think, is the idea that the whole experience seared itself into his being so completely that the time differential became irrelevant. Levi himself seems to hold with the latter explanation. In his preface to *Moments of Reprieve* (another, much slighter account of Auschwitz published here in 1986), he writes: "Without any deliberate effort, memory continues to restore to me events, faces, words, sensations, as if at that time I had gone through a period of exalted receptivity, during which not a detail was lost."

Levi tells, without faltering (indeed, often with the stolid imperturbability of Defoe's Robinson Crusoe), the full sequential tale of his ordeal. Although he speaks for the most part in the first person singular, he slips quite readily at times into the plural. But this makes perfect sense: the sinister Auschwitz machine was perfectly contrived to turn an "I" into a "we," and, almost inevitably, a "we" into an "it." (Of the 650 Italian prisoners in Levi's railroad convoy, only 20 survived.) The paradox of a historical narrative like this is that the single voice can speak with authority for the speechless millions who died.

Looking at them from a strictly literary point of view—which is, without question, a sacrilege—you're apt to find that the plots of accounts by Holocaust survivors are invariably the same. Sudden arrest, the terrors of transit in a suffocating cattle car, the ritual humiliations inflicted upon arrival at the camp. Loved ones were separated, possessions were confiscated; every prisoner was stripped, disinfected, shorn, tattooed with a number, and then thrust into a barracks. Survivors quickly separated themselves from the *Muselmänner* (literally, "Muslims"), what Levi calls the drowned, those who could not adapt themselves to the primal struggle for space and food that ensued. These *Muselmänner* were quickly taken by disease, malnourishment, or the regular "selections" (the motto over the camp gate was ARBEIT MACHT FREI—work will make you free—and those who could not work were promptly exterminated).

Given the uniformity of camp procedures and the limited range of possible human response to them, one Holocaust memoir ought to be enough. Reading the descriptions, however, in Levi's book—or those of Bruno Bettelheim, Viktor Frankl, Elie Wiesel, or any one of a hundred others—you realize that the word "enough" is not only irrelevant, it's outrageous. You might better ask how anything *else* can be written. It is with this realization that we abandon the category of literature and turn toward the category of the sacred.

For just as sacred books are not read for plot, information, or entertainment, but are a way of pointing the self, again and again, toward a spiritual destination, so these memoirs impose their own liturgical obligation. Only with this difference: whereas the holy books present the legend of the good, telling of purpose and salvation, these texts mark out the empery of evil. Their deeper dimension, and their importance, are not to be comprehended through a strict adherence to historical surfaces. Levi himself suggests this. Referring to the fervent exchange of stories by camp inmates, he writes: "We tell them to each other in the evening, and they take place in Norway, Italy, Algeria, the Ukraine, and are simple and incomprehensible like the stories in the Bible. But are they not themselves stories of a new Bible?"

This is as reflective as Levi gets in his writing. He is almost entirely concerned with bearing witness, with detailing the endless privations that the Germans inflicted and the resourceful strategies that the would-be survivors adopted. This avid, relentless documentation, and the necessary avoidance of speculation, give Levi's document its compelling texture of veracity. For existence inside the electric wires of the camp bore no relation to anything outside. An inquisitive or reflective intellect was a distinct liability; to think was to squander valuable protein and to risk the paralysis of despair. It was far more important to be vigilant, to snatch an extra mouthful of soup, to listen in the dark in order to gauge the level of the night bucket (whoever found it full had to carry it out into the snow to dump it). Levi insists that such a focus was to be preferred; survival was not otherwise possible. The rare days of respite from brute toil were in many ways the worst. One began to think of home and family. . . .

The bulk of *Survival in Auschwitz,* then, takes us through the round of days and seasons. We feel the punishing cold as the inmates gather for reveille and work assignments. They shiver in muddy pits and dream of nothing more sublime than an extra ration of gruel. The most cunning and venturesome conduct intricate campaigns to get their hands around a husk of hardened bread. Indeed, only bread can still quicken these men into theoretical debate:

> None of us old ones are able to preserve our bread for an hour. Various theories circulate to justify this incapacity of ours: bread eaten a little at a time is not wholly assimilated; the nervous tension needed to preserve the bread without touching it when one is hungry is in the highest degree harmful and debilitating; bread which is turning stale soon loses its alimentary value, so that the sooner it is eaten, the more nutritious it is; Alberto says that hunger and bread in one's pocket are terms of opposite sign which immediately cancel each other out and cannot exist in the same individual; and the majority affirm justly that, in the end, one's stomach is the securest safe against thefts and extortions.

Auschwitz was, finally, an antiworld. And in the strange economy of such a place—where death was more common than food—perverse market laws prevailed. We hear far more about crusts of bread and spoonfuls of soup than we do about the deaths of individuals. ("How many absent? Three absent. Homolka gone into Ka-Be this morning, the ironsmith dead yesterday, François transferred who knows where or why.") This skewing of emphasis seems horrifying, but perhaps it's Levi's way of conveying his most damning indictment of the Nazi inferno. By remaining true to his perceptions, by deliberately *not* tilting the scale to the side of the human, he reveals more clearly than anything could the disfiguring force of evil.

The last section of *Survival in Auschwitz* is as harrowing as anything in Holocaust literature. As the Reich collapses and the Red Army advances, Auschwitz is suddenly evacuated. Twenty thousand prisoners (none of whom will survive) are sent on forced march. Levi, who is in the Ka-Be infirmary with scarlet fever, is left behind. "The Story of Ten Days" describes this final nightmare. Faint from hunger and fever, surrounded by the dead and dying, Levi must forage for necessities. Here is part of the entry marked "25 January":

> It was Sómogyi's turn. He was a Hungarian chemist, about fifty years old, thin, tall, and taciturn. Like the Dutchman he suffered from typhus and scarlet fever. He had not spoken for perhaps five days; that day he opened his mouth and said in a firm voice:
>
> "I have a ration of bread under the sack. Divide it among you three. I shall not be eating anymore."
>
> We could not find anything to say, but for the time being we did not touch the bread. Half his face had swollen. As long as he retained consciousness he remained closed in a harsh silence.
>
> But in the evening and for the whole of the night and for two days without interruption the silence was broken by his delirium. Following a last interminable dream of acceptance and slavery he began to murmur *"Jawohl"* with every breath, regularly and continuously like a machine. *"Jawohl,"* at every collapsing of his wretched frame, thousands of times, enough to make one want to shake him, to suffocate him, at least to make him change the word.

The Russians—exhausted, unenthusiastic liberators—finally arrive, and Levi's maddeningly circuitous homeward journey begins. *The Reawakening* chronicles all of the delays and frustrations that he endures. He is shunted from transit center to transit center; each move carries him deeper into Russia and farther from Turin. But no obstacle can quench the joy he feels: freedom is freedom no matter where one stands. After the darkness of the first volume, the sequel is like a gift of light—you cannot fail to share some of Levi's giddy disbelief: that anyone could have survived Auschwitz, that *he* survived it.

And yet the questions raised by Levi's account remain—raised not by his telling of it, but by its very existence. What are problematic are the seductions of narrative. Time and again I found myself reading *Survival in Auschwitz* with interest—horrified interest, it's true, but interest nonetheless. I had to pinch myself to remember that I was not moving within the closed order of literature, that these descriptions matched up with things that had happened *in the world.* Putting words to certain kinds of experience does falsify, if only because the act implies the adequacy of language. Auschwitz cannot be translated, though there are good reasons for trying to do so: amnesia is more to be feared than are the illusions of chaos mastered. Still, the reader must exert every effort to remain critical of both self and text. He mustn't forget for a moment the gulf that exists between the sign and its referrent. How vast is that gulf? Think of it this way: we have the option of closing the book and turning out the light; Primo Levi didn't.

Umberto Eco

There are two mysteries connected with Umberto Eco's *The Name of the Rose* (1983). One comprises the bulk of the plot and involves a trail of murdered monks in a fourteenth-century Italian monastery; the other has to do with the book's sudden explosive celebrity. Are there really that many intrepid readers out there? It's an exalting thought. To be sure, the demand for good whodunits never slackens, and this one reads—in its whodunit parts—like vintage Doyle, with esoteric clues, strange reversals, and an engagingly empirical sleuth, Brother William of Baskerville(!). But this rose is a many-petaled contraption, as much history as mystery. And the history portion, studded with ecclesiastical lore, Latin tags, learned discussions on heresy and the interpretation of writ, is demanding. What's more, the whole has an ulterior life as a meditation on the meaning and nature of signs. Chic it may be, easy beach-blanket reading it is not. Nevertheless, the prospect of an intricate solution can exert a powerful magnetic effect on readers' minds, and Eco's solution is as intricate as an Egyptian stamp. The more minds he can inveigle into his subtle net, the better. For there are other mysteries well worth pondering in these pages.

Eco is professor of semiotics at the University of Bologna. Before the publication of *The Name of the Rose,* he was known mainly in scholarly circles as the author of *A Theory of Semiotics* (1976) and *The Role of the Reader: Explorations in the Semiotics of Texts* (1979), forbidding tracts that are not about to be elucidated here. Semiotics, in its most general sense, is the science of signs, and, as clues are nothing more or less than signs, there is a natural affinity between the discipline and the mystery genre—which Eco, naturally, exploits to the full. But the matter is quite complex. As Baskerville at one point explains to Adso, his assistant (the name cleverly echoes "Watson") and eventual recording angel (for these are Adso's memoirs, set down half a century after the events): "The print does not always have the same shape as the body that impressed it, and it doesn't always derive from the pressure of a body. At times it reproduces the impression a body has left in our mind: it is the print of an idea."

This is essential. Through signs the world of ideas is established as continuous with the material world, and word and deed are seen as equally consequential. A copy of the second book of Aristotle's *Poetics,* presumed lost, becomes an object worth killing for—not for its scarcity, but because its contents may be interpreted in a most inappropriate way. Bibliomania figures here in all of its permutations. Indeed, even Adso's memoir is presented as a "found" text of dubious provenance. Eco, in a straight-faced preface, details his own unsuccessful attempts to trace the history of the document. He suggests that there has been an ongoing conspiracy to suppress Adso of Melk. How else to explain a trail that opens onto a void at every turn? Before Adso ever begins his narrative the potency of words has been underscored. And when he does begin, we read: "In the beginning was the Word . . . ," the ultimate sense of which locates all material origin in the sign.

The year is 1327. The monks of the not-to-be-named monastery are in furor. The Antichrist is come! One monk's body has been found at the foot of a cliff, another's has been stuck head down in a vat of pigs' blood. Baskerville, on hand to mediate a parley between envoys of Pope John XII (who is in Avignon) and an entourage of dissenting Franciscan Minorites, is asked to press his deductive abilities into service. Baskerville can no more refuse a mental challenge than Holmes could. He sets to work instantly to disentangle the widely flung net of possible causes and effects. And, as the monastery is one of the foremost centers of learning of the time, the clues soon direct him to the library and the texts housed in its labyrinthine arrangement of rooms—their plan adapted from Borges's descriptions of the library at Babel.

Baskerville is a monk of the new dispensation. He worships reason and believes in God because God planted reason in man. He is, like his mentor Roger Bacon and his friend William of Occam, a herald of Renaissance energies and ideas: he speaks of the possibility of flying machines, and he astounds the other monks when he clips two oblongs of glass over the bridge of his nose in order to read. As detective, he follows a principle that Vico will proclaim three centuries later—that man can understand what man himself has wrought. Naturally, he is an anomaly. The monastery and the world at large are still steeped in the sense of *mysterium tremens.* As Adso declares at the beginning of his narrative: "But we see now through a glass darkly, and the truth, before it is revealed to *all,* face to face, we see in fragments (alas, how illegible) in the error of the world, so we must spell out its faithful signals even when they seem obscure to us and as if amalgamated with a will bent wholly on evil." Obviously, Baskerville will have two kinds of signs to consider, those bound by cause and legible to reason, and those created into the fabric of the world (or imprinted in zealous minds) by God, the interpretation of which is tricky even for the semioticians of the church. Eco has great sport mixing the two, and the pattern that Baskerville finally uncovers is most unempirical: the murders appear to be symbolically linked to the opening of the seals in the Apocalypse of John.

Umberto Eco

Eco's learning is prodigious. Fortunately, it does not interfere with his keen satiric sense; if anything, it supplies him with targets. The parley between the Pope's charges and the Minorites is, for instance, a comic *tour de force.* We might call it a clash between styles of interpretation. At issue is the poverty of Christ, whether or not He and His disciples owned their goods or had them *usus facti,* in use alone. A small point on the face of it, but one that might determine which way heresy lies, and thus might have larger application to the fate of the Church. Each faction puts its keenest men on the rostrum and a hermeneutic fireworks ensues. There is wit enough on either side to reverse any proposition, and then reverse the reverse, until it is obvious to all that black is white and up is down. At which point the solemn friars resort to the ultimate logic—they charge at each other with fists flailing. So much for the semioticians of the Church.

But Eco is not entirely lenient with brilliant Baskerville either. Though he finally does solve the murders, his success is made to depend as much upon serendipity as cerebration. As often as not it is some fumble by Adso that gets him over a hurdle that reason alone cannot clear. Holmes demystifies the world entirely; Baskerville runs reason to the end of its tether and then has a pratfall. Near the end of the book we find him complaining to Adso: "I have never doubted the truth of signs . . . they are the only things man has with which to orient himself in the world. What I did not understand was the relation among signs." I leave it to the reader to discover what these signs are and what bizarre pattern they finally sketch.

The Name of the Rose is a first-class mystery, but it does have higher claims as well. Eco asserts these by using the genre itself as a trope: the mystery is a figure for all epistemological questioning—how do we know things, what can we know? Tale and higher concern have been stitched together so artfully that we are hard put to spot a seam. But here we come to an unfortunate paradox, for in the process of stitching these "higher concerns" together with the exigencies of a whodunit, Eco has also undermined himself. For the tension of gradual disclosure, which is the mainspring of mystery narrative, exhausts itself once and for all (barring the reader's memory lapse) in the first reading. Though intricate and challenging on many levels, *The Name of the Rose* is a hard book to return to. Certainly it cannot be read in the same way a second time. The plot machinery prohibits it: once the casual chain is known, the links stand out in greater relief. Nor are the characterizations strong enough to take up the slack. With the exception of Adso, who is a wonderfully fresh and ingenuous narrator, the figures are cleverly done cutouts. Even Baskerville is not, in the last analysis, Holmes redivivus. analysis, Holmes redivivus.

Still, something of importance does survive after the mainspring is spent. Eco has set into motion—fantastical though that motion may be—a piece of old tapestry. And this in itself may draw us back for a second look. Besides learning something about the intellectual and spiritual passions of fourteenth-century Europe, we glean all manner of details about the workings of scriptoria, the symbolism of gems, herb cultivation, and truffle hunting. And Eco has registered with great art the fevers and anxieties of a world on the very edge of transformation. Monastic life has had its hour on the stage; the first prototype flying machines are little more than a century away. The powerful determining forces of history have been drawn down into the close circuitry of the abbey on the mountaintop.

Eco seems to have anticipated the problematic second-life status of his book. As Adso and Baskerville are about to leave the monastery, the latter announces: "The order that the mind imagines is like a net, or like a ladder, built to attain something. But afterward you must throw the ladder away, because you discover that, even if it was useful, it was meaningless. *Er muoz gelîchesame die leiter abewerfer, sô er an ir ufgestigen . . .*"

"Who told you that?" Adso inquires.

To which Baskerville replies: "A mystic from your land." The mystic was, or is, or will be, Ludwig Wittgenstein. The German is a close paraphrase of Proposition 6.54 of the *Tractatus,* published almost six hundred years later. If Eco's constructed ladder is not as useful as Wittgenstein's, it nevertheless should not be thrown away. Even renegotiating it, the mind is moved from word to world and back, covering in the process more than a few ells.

Malcolm Lowry

*"Oh, I know, but we got so horrible drunkness that night before, so perfecta*mente *borracho, that it seems to me, the Consul is as sick as I am." Dr. Vigil shook his head. "Sickness is not only in body, but in that part used to be called: soul. Poor your friend, he spend his money on earth in such continuous tragedies."*

—*Under the Volcano*

On November 2, 1936 (el Día de los Difuntos, or "Day of the Dead"), Malcolm Lowry first set foot on Mexican soil. Though he was only twenty-seven years old at the time, Lowry already had a published book, *Ultramarine,* to his credit, a drinking problem that verged on the epic—and that would, in time, destroy his life and his talent—and a marriage that had faltered many times before and would soon collapse altogether. Lowry and his wife, Jan, had come to Mexico to give their marriage one more chance. There, they reasoned, the allowance that Lowry got from his father (and that was his sole means of support) would enable them to live without financial strain. By the beginning of 1937, they had established themselves in a small house in Cuernavaca. Within weeks Lowry was working on a story that he entitled "Under the Volcano."

Whatever idyll there may have been at first, it was only a short while before the old pattern reestablished itself: Lowry pitching from cantina to cantina, disappearing for days at a time, and Jan making feeble, hopeless attempts at rescue. It was not long before Lowry was to hear the clicking of her "faithless heels" as she turned elsewhere for solace. In January 1938, Jan left him for the last time. Lowry's Mexican nightmare began in earnest.

To read the letters from this period—at least one of which he actually phrased as an SOS—is to glimpse the real-life source of the visionary hell that Lowry created in *Under the Volcano.* The five months that he stayed in Mexico after Jan's departure were an unrelieved torment. Lowry drank constantly, was arrested several times by the police—and was, he averred, terrorized and spied upon constantly. He was also destitute. What is miraculous is that the story "Under the Volcano" grew during this time into novelistic proportions, and that by the time he returned to the United States—in July of 1938—it stood as a completed first draft.

This contradiction, creation versus self-destruction, is the very core of Malcolm Lowry. The biographical details, most of them heartrending, can be found in Douglas Day's *Malcolm Lowry* (1973), a monument of humane and penetrating disclosure. What emerges, not only from the Mexican account, but from the account of the next eight years, is a picture of exceptional doggedness, strength, and faith.

These years were to be the best of Lowry's life. Upon his return from Mexico he met Margerie Bonner, whom he was to marry in 1940, and who was to be at his side until his death in 1957. After a long series of Lowryesque (which is to say, improbable) circumstances, he and Margerie came to live in a squatter's shack in Dollarton, Canada. There, in the wilderness, Lowry spent years rewriting—laminating, layer by layer—the manuscript of *Under the Volcano.* It was completed on Christmas Eve 1944. Then, for the next two years, it was to travel from publisher to publisher, rejected at every turn for having no plot, for being too much obsessed with alcohol, for being too obscure.

The Lowrys were traveling in Mexico when word of *Volcano*'s acceptance reached them. Two telegrams arrived on the same day, one from Jonathan Cape in England, the other from Reynal and Hitchcock. Lowry gleefully reported to his friends that they were handed to him by the same postman who handed Yvonne's postcard to the consul in the novel. But if this seems like an interesting coincidence, one should read Day's biography carefully: Lowry's life never left the rails of portentousness. He fully believed in Baudelaire's pronouncement that "life is a forest of symbols." This is clear to anyone who has read *Under the Volcano*.

From the acceptance of *Under the Volcano* in 1946 until his "death by misadventure" in 1957, Lowry wrote nothing that even approached the brilliance and intensity of that book. His life ran amok. No effort or discipline was able to prevent him from sinking more and more deeply into alcoholism. His output, in terms of drafts and stories, was impressive, a mark of his effort to hold off doom, but all the writings suffer from the same faults: solipsism, an inability to create drama or tragedy, and an obsession with private "signs" that fails to sustain any action or emotional interest. Lowry had mined his tragic heart once, thoroughly. He was unable to repeat that performance.

What we have in *Under the Volcano* is a nearly perfect coincidence of subject, style, and author. It is perhaps the most single-mindedly intense novel ever written. The prose is resonant, crafted, and from time to time even outdoes Proust in excess and sinuosity. The themes—if we imagine writing a book report—are themes of doom (private and collective), death, salvation versus damnation, Sin (capitalized), expulsion from Eden, and, in the last analysis, the wonder and mystery of all the above. The narrative, which Lowry has described as a kind of "infernal machine," takes only twelve hours to unwind. It unwinds to perfection.

The day is November 2, 1938, the Day of the Dead—the one time of the year when the spirits of the living and dead are said to mingle. The place is Quauhnahuac (the Nahuatl name for Cuernavaca). It is to be the last day in the life of Geoffrey Firmin, ex–British consul to the district. On this day the consul's ex-wife, Yvonne, returns to him—she is hoping to salvage the marriage and to save the consul from his drinking. It is the very thing that he has been praying for during his months of isolation and despair, and now that his prayer has been granted, he finds that he cannot take the step to save himself. There are forces active in the consul (in the world) that are stronger than the simple desire to reform. These forces and their devastating effects are the true protagonists of *Under the Volcano.* Apart from the obligatory movement from place to place, and the few spots of recognizable human activity, almost all the action is internal, in the hell of the consul's soul. This word—"soul"—as will be seen, is used literally, and not as a figure of speech.

The structure that Lowry has chosen, as well as the hellish, beautiful, overripe setting, allows him to create a work of seemingly infinite resonance. The surface meaning, as Lowry insisted, is perfectly wrought, and the book can actually be read without any reference to Dante, Christ, Faust, or the Kabbalah. But it is just beyond the surface texture that the eerie vibrations begin. *Under the Volcano* starts echoes and then multiplies those echoes until it is impossible for anyone to say, "This is what he means," or "Here is what the symbols point to." We are fortunate nevertheless, in having David Markson's *Malcolm Lowry's Volcano* (1978)—though not nearly so fortunate as Dante was in having Virgil.

Markson intends, quite literally, to supply the reader with a guidebook to the intricacies of symbol and allusion in Lowry's book. In his afterword he tells on what basis this is justified:

> But is any *single* fictional achievement—and I include *Ulysses* in the question—quite so fecund in evocation, so *diverse* in amplification? Indeed, my ultimate suspicion is that *Under the Volcano* should not be read as we read other fictions at all. It is a poem, and a poem in kind with several of its grandest models. I mean with the *Aeneid,* the *Divine Comedy,* with Goethe's *Faust*—each of which, for the *apparatus criticus* of centuries, remains ever open to this same sort of enriching interpretation and delight.

A strong statement, but there are many, present reviewer included, who would not say *too* strong. It is interesting to compare, at this point, Markson's declaration with a remark of Lowry's:

> Nor was the book consciously intended to operate on quite so many levels. One serious intention was to create a work of art—after a while it began to make a noise like music; when it made the wrong noise I altered it—when it seemed to make the right one finally, I kept it
>
> —*Selected Letters*

The key word here, undoubtedly, is "consciously." Lowry's words should be inscribed on the flyleaf of Markson's book to serve as a counterweight whenever we feel that Markson is getting too assiduous in his quest for connecting threads and symbols.

Markson follows the text carefully and consecutively, modeling his approach to some extent on that used by Stuart Gilbert in his guide to *Ulysses.* In the opening chapters he frequently apologizes to the reader for appearing to make more of an allusion or reference than may seem justified; but each apology carries the assurance that as meanings and textures proliferate the method will bear fruit. And so it does—maybe too much fruit. By the end of the book Markson has nearly convinced us that Lowry out-Joyced Joyce. The reverberations have become overwhelming. We don't believe that Lowry intended everything that Markson has discovered. He probably did not. Nevertheless, to the extent that Markson can make them work, the correspondences and patterns exist.

Comparing Lowry's densities with Joyce's, we can see that they result from different methodologies. Joyce's method was the more conscious. His symbols and correspondences were meticulously implanted in his work. He was also, as Lowry was not, a man of prodigious learning. Lowry's craft depended far more upon the activities of the unconscious. In that sense it was more "artistic."

Lowry lived in a world of signs and believed in those signs. He was incapable of supplying the consul with any kind of psyche other than his own. Therefore, what in Joyce is created is, in Lowry, and in the consul, discovered. This proliferation of correspondences results in a kind of madness. There seems to be no way of stemming the movement, except by dulling the mind—a purpose to which drink is wonderfully suited. After a time, though, it appears that even alcohol cannot arrest the sense of doom and persecution. Lowry was to say often that he felt that he had actually implicated his life in his writings, that his narratives became prophecies. Even more frightening was the sense that his own life was being authored. He did not say "by God" either. He suspected, rather, that there were unidentified malevolent forces, forces that had turned on him, as they had turned on the consul, because he had misused his powers. Lowry's conviction of being implicated in his own fiction became, in its turn, the subject matter of a never-completed novel, *Dark as the Grave Wherein My Friend Is Laid* (1968).

In a writer so obsessed with hidden and semidisclosed meanings, it is inevitable that this kind of patterning will dominate the narratives. Markson conveys much information about the extent to which these patterns operate. His one mistake, I believe, is that he fails to discern in every case where they are consciously used and where they appear fortuitously. For is it not inevitable that in working out certain thematic concerns there will appear innumerable unintended links or "sympathies" with epics or mythologies that use a similar tonal range? Surely Lowry intended this as a part of his method, just as he intended specific symbols and references.

To give some idea of the level upon which we are working, let me cite one example, to my mind a successful piece of literary detection. In the first chapter of *Under the Volcano,* Jacques Laruelle, a boyhood friend of the consul's (who has, coincidentally, met up with him again, in Mexico), recollects an incident from the far past. He and Geoffrey, vacationing at the seaside, met two girls and took them walking on a golf course in the dark. There they parted ways, each to attend to his own amour.

> Laruelle didn't know to this day why there was no understanding about the Hell Bunker. He had certainly no intention of playing Peeping Tom on Geoffrey. He had happened with his girl, who bored him, to be crossing the eighth fairway toward Leasowe Drive when both were startled by voices coming from the bunker. Then the moonlight disclosed the bizarre scene from which neither he nor the girl could turn their eyes. Laruelle would have hurried away but neither of them—neither quite aware of the sensible

> impact of what was occurring in the Hell Bunker—could control their laughter. Curiously, M. Laruelle had never remembered what anyone said, only the expression on Geoffrey's face in the moonlight and the awkward grotesque way the girl had scrambled to her feet.

Lowry never informs us as to the real nature of what Laruelle witnessed. Markson writes:

> Describing the "Hell Bunker" Lowry writes that it "lay in the middle of the long sloping eighth fairway"; he also refers to it as an "abyss," and remarks further that it "yawned." Hell in quotation marks, an abyss that yawns in the middle of a field, the field numbered as the eighth of a sequence. Whereas in Dante's description of the eighth circle of his own hell: "Right in the middle of the malignant field yawns a well." Some few lines later, as Dante peers into that other "bunker," we discover what Laruelle saw: "In the bottom," Dante writes, "the sinners were naked."

So much for obviousness. This example should illustrate how, on the one hand, Lowry was capable of refined, if obscure, allusiveness, and, on the other, to what extent Markson is willing to track him down.

It would be a mistake to suppose that the whole of *Under the Volcano* is constructed on as rarefied and subtle a level. This is not to say that Lowry's gifts or persistence were insufficient; certainly they were not. It is, rather, that he wanted most of his signs to work as portents, not explicit symbols or correlatives. And this choice is what makes *Under the Volcano* what it is, something more on the order of a symphony or tonal composition. Working with repetition, leitmotiv, cinematic recurrence of names, places, objects, and numbers, Lowry creates a rich, shifting narrative that enables him to portray mood and movement in the psyche as few writers have ever managed. The elements, though they can and do refer outward—to other texts, mythologies, events—also function for themselves: it is possible to say that they have no more "meaning" than musical sounds. It is because of this tonal depth and integrity that *Under the Volcano* endures. The multiplicity of meanings is, as it were, a function of the superstructure.

> The Consul dropped his eyes at last. How many bottles since then? In how many glasses, how many bottles had he hidden himself, since then alone? Suddenly he saw them, the bottles of aguardiente, of anis, of jerez, of Highland Queen, the glasses, a babel of glasses . . . built to the sky, falling, the glasses toppling and crashing, falling downhill from the Generalife Gardens, the bottles breaking, bottles of Oporto, tinto, blanco, bottles of Pernod, Oxygenee, absinthe . . . How indeed could he hope to find himself, to begin again when, somewhere, perhaps, in one of those lost or broken bottles, in one of those glasses, lay, forever, the solitary clue to his identity? How could he go back and look now, scrabble among the broken glass, under the eternal bars, under the oceans?

In his essay "Tradition and Individual Talent," T. S. Eliot asserts: "The more perfect the artist, the more completely separate in him will be the man who suffers and the mind which creates; the more perfectly will the mind digest and translate the passions which are its material." It seems that there is no way to tailor this so that it will fit Lowry. Alas, we say, for the inability to stand apart from his sufferings and the subtle workings of his own psyche was largely responsible for his failure—post-*Volcano*—to write anything of enduring value. It is, on the other hand, this very creation via immersion that makes that one book so powerful and unique. The consul's suffering is Lowry's; it is less transformed than transposed. How, then, are we to account for the fact that it *works,* that it succeeds on the level of high art? An important question. Answering it, one exposes the central tension of the book.

First the heretical statement: for all its genius, *Under the Volcano* just barely succeeds on the level of high art. Its passion and suffering threaten time and again to become confession and self-flagellation. It is only Lowry's prodigious discipline and the grandeur and control of his prose that performs the saving action. That he can succeed in the face of such likely failure cancels that "just barely" and makes the performance all the greater. The best analogy might be that of the bullfighter: the more grace and control he can demonstrate in moments of extreme danger, the more of a master he proves himself to be.

Many of the early criticisms of *Under the Volcano,* especially those from publishers' readers, contended that there was too much alcohol in the book. Indeed, there is hardly a page where the consul is not either taking a drink or preparing to take one. (Some industrious scholar will soon, no doubt, make a list of everything that this poor man consumes—enough, I suspect, to fill a child's swimming pool.) In spite of this, it is not a book about alcohol. It is about the sickness of the soul. Alcohol is the only thing that can hold that soul in equilibrium from moment to moment, and the gargantuan consumption only demonstrates what terrible straits that soul is in.

This insistent use of the word "soul" marks a departure, I realize, from any of the assumptions of modern criticism. We are to believe that, since Freud, such a thing as the soul cannot exist. But Lowry, writing after everyone else learned the news, seems not to have been listening. *Under the Volcano* is directly concerned with salvation and damnation—for which a concept of soul is required—and he is *not* using these terms as conceits.

On a more immediate level the book is about love—sacred and profane. It insists that love is the only possible salvation, the only way to break the demonic circle of the self. NO SE PUEDE VIVIR SIN AMAR—"One cannot live without love"—is the motto that the consul has at one time scrawled on the wall of Laruelle's house. The motto, through repetition, becomes a major indictment of all concerned, to the point where neither the consul nor Yvonne can bear to look at it, much less confront its truth in their own lives. The consul, we realize, understands the meaning more profoundly than the others. At the same time, he has the greatest difficulty in taking the step. It is the step that would save him, would revolutionize his life. There are times when he appears to be very near taking it. He wants to tell Yvonne, means to. And does not. The reader cannot understand. Why will he not accept what Yvonne has come to give? This question, slightly altered, is the very core of the book: Why does the consul refuse to save his soul? The answer is to be found in the second of the book's three epigraphs, a quotation from John Bunyan:

> Now I blessed the condition of the dog and toad, yea, gladly would I have been in the condition of the dog or horse, for I knew they had no soul to perish under the everlasting weight of Hell or Sin, as mine was like to do. Nay, and though I saw this, felt this, and was broken to pieces with it, yet that which added to my sorrow was, that I could not find with all my soul that I did desire deliverance.

The most wrenching, pathetic, and, in the psychology of belief, actual of situations.

The question of why the consul will not save himself actually belongs in the past tense. This is not immediately clear. Reading *Under the Volcano,* we at first view it as a kind of contest, what used to be described in terms of God and the Devil wrestling for the soul of a man. It seems possible that the consul may yet save himself, or be saved. Later we realize that this is not the situation. The consul's soul is already in the Devil's clutches. What we see are but the final devastating images of that lost battle. That we can continue to believe in the consul's salvation even when we know his doom to be sealed is one of the astonishing features of the book.

In the consul are the ruins of a soul. We apprize its former health and wholeness much as we might imagine a temple from the positioning of a few broken columns. This, paradoxically, is where the book strikes its most positive meaning. Having given us the reality of the soul, Lowry has also established the *possibility* of its rescue. And the consul, of course, becomes Everyman—with a twist, and a few bitters. What is unclear—and, judging from the biography and letters, as well as Markson's book, seems to have been unresolved in Lowry's life—is where this redeeming force resides, through what agency it works. Lowry was not more Christian than he was occultist or kabbalist. References and correspondences are invoked from all areas, without apparent preference. What are we to make of this?

In *Under the Volcano* the reality of the soul is connected with a nameless but all-pervasive order, an order that accommodates all mythologies and forms of belief. These forms appear as aspects or illustrations of the workings of this order. In this sense, then, the consul's damnation is read not only as Christian, but is at the same time equated with serious, fatal violation of kabbalistic tenets. It is this positing of a greater, nonspecific order that allows Lowry to allude freely to all the religious texts, as well as the great visionary literatures (Blake, Rimbaud, Baudelaire, et al.). The implication seems to be that Lowry saw the potential for meaning and wholeness *in man himself,* that this potential has been created into his very being. This does not clear up the final ontological questions—created how? whence?—but it renews that questioning from yet another point of view.

The consul's actual death, the novel's culmination, does not supply any final answers. The movement of the narrative has led the consul inexorably to the darkest, most doom-ridden place of all, a cantina called the Farolito. There, alone, he moves from room to room, each place darker, more hopeless, each a deeper circle of hell. When he has penetrated to the deepest place—there taking a whore in a loveless embrace—his death is inevitable. He can go no further in the denial of love. It is at this point, having prepared the ground carefully, that Lowry plays an unexpected hand: he makes the actual circumstances of the consul's murder a fiasco, nothing more than a case of mistaken identities. A local fascist leader, believing the consul to be a Communist agitator, pushes him outdoors and, a moment later, shoots him. The consul is left to die in the grass, a supreme anticlimax after so much psychic tension.

Dying, the consul experiences visions that are confused and inconclusive. There is a suggestion that he has attained to something, reached a peak, but then that vision is undercut, disqualified. Unidentified arms lift him and fling him into the *barranca.* The last flaring of vision has the consul falling into the very heart of the volcano. He is Marlowe's Faust going "headlong into the earth." He has taken on hell for all of us (would that it were true)—his fall is meant to illuminate again the straight way that has been lost.

The last word belongs to Lowry:

The book should be seen as essentially *trochal,* I repeat, the form of it as a wheel so that, when you get to the end, if you have read carefully, you should want to turn back to the beginning again, where it is not impossible, too, that your eyes might alight once more upon Sophocles' *Wonders are many, and none is more wonderful than man*—just to cheer you up.

—letter to Jonathan Cape, *Selected Letters*

Lars Gustafsson

I took one personality, mainly my own childhood, my own youth up to the age of eighteen, and then varied it into five different lives, strengthening one property of my personality here, weakening it in another by giving myself a little more of a certain talent, subtracting a talent there. That resulted in alternative lives, what I call cracks in the wall. These five novels are an experiment with the possible lives of a certain organism. They are a set of premises.

—GUSTAFSSON

The *Death of a Beekeeper* (1981) is the fifth in a series of five novels, the only one available to date in English. It is, with Max Frisch's *Montauk* or Beckett's *Company,* one of those pared-down, compressed pieces beside which other novels look like Biedermeier furniture. I hope that the rest of the series—*Mr. Gustafsson Himself, Woe, The Family Reunion,* and *Sigismund**—follows soon. If the quality of the other novels proves at all comparable to that of *Beekeeper,* we would have to say that a major literary event has been taking place in the last decade.

**Sigismund* was published in translation in 1985.

Beekeeper, like Tolstoy's *Death of Ivan Ilyich,* is a novel about a man who is dying. It is, therefore, by virtue of that time-honored interdependence, about living. The comparison of Tolstoy's treatment and Gustafsson's is a kind of object lesson about the differences of temperament and sensibility. Where Tolstoy works the pedals of his organ furiously to drive home the message that death is the big event, the grand horror, the reckoning, Gustafsson turns his attention to the psyche, its strategies of refusal, the stages through which it moves to assimilate the unknowable. His depiction, because it is oblique, is finally more moving. He has not set out, as Tolstoy did, to make our hair stand on end.

Beekeeper consists of a compilation of "found" notebooks. They belong to Lars Lennart Westin, who, we learn from the prelude, is thirty-nine, divorced, prematurely retired from teaching. He lives in a hut on a rural peninsula and makes what little money he requires by selling the honey his bees produce. The description we get from the author/editor is the kind we might expect from an uninquisitive neighbor: "He has a telephone, a television set, and a subscription to the *Vestmanlands Lans Tidning.* Since obtaining his divorce he has had no notable relationships with women." Then we learn, with an abrupt switch of tense: "What follows now are the notes he left behind. Left behind: for in this spring of 1975 in the middle of the thaw he finds out that he will not live to see the fall. He has terminal cancer. . . ." There is a deception here, to me inexplicable. The fact is that Westin *does not* find out anything of the kind. He has undergone tests because of pains that he has been experiencing, but when the results are mailed to him he refuses to open the letter. The whole book revolves around his attempt to cope with an unidentified process in his own private fashion, without medical intervention. The re-formation of his psyche in response to pain and doubt is the substance of the book.

The journals introduce disease in the most indirect yet telling manner. Westin's dog has run away, and when he finds the animal he cannot understand why it behaves as though it cannot recognize him. He considers all manner of possibilities, adding, almost as an afterthought:

There is another explanation, of course, but it is so crazy that I can't believe it.

That all of a sudden I have taken on a different smell in some damnably subtle fashion which only the dog can perceive.

When the hospital report finally arrives, Westin leaves it unopened and goes for a long walk. While walking he comes to a decision: he will ignore the letter, he will treat the situation as a kind of Pascalian wager: "Either this letter says that it's nothing bad. Or it says that I have cancer and am going to die. . . . The smartest thing for me would be not to open it, because if I don't open it, there is still going to be some kind of hope." With this calculated aversion Westin signals his determination to die his own death. He also gives us a perfect glimpse of the contradictions of his character, his speculative turn face to face with his refusal to confront facts squarely. Westin does not really believe that he's *not* going to die—the tone of his journal tells us that—but he knows that the margin of doubt is precisely the freedom his mind requires: it will hover and explore; otherwise it would be transfixed by certainty.

No reversal could be more complete than the one we go through as we exchange our first "outside" impression of the lone beekeeper for the almost instantaneous absorption into his skin. The journals are so forthright, so actual, that we take on the lineaments of Westin's personality from the first. What is so masterful about Gustafsson's writing is that he can accomplish this with such an economy of means. He has the minimalist's gift, the ability to make the unstated present as a force. Combined with this is the composer's instinct—he knows when to amplify, when to fade, when to modulate. He achieves the credible texture of consciousness without ever straining for it.

Westin, monitoring his pain, denying it, courting it, pretending to accept it, sets down a series of reflections. These take the form of reminiscence, abstract speculation, fantasy, and constitute, in their sum, a drawing up of accounts. His has not been a very eventful or exciting life; he admits as much. There were idle, dissipated student days, a sober courtship, a distant marriage, one love affair, a divorce. But it is all in the telling. Gustafsson knows well that there are layers and layers in the psyche, layers of varying density and substance that are governed by ineluctable laws of relativity. The shifts and transformations, the precedence of one detail over another, the elisions of memory, are what is fascinating. It is the process, not its objects, that concerns us. Thus, Westin can report one day that his whole career and wedded life mean less to him than the recovery of certain images from his childhood.

Midway through the book there is an interlude during which the pain subsides. Westin begins teasing himself with the thought that the worst may be over, that he might be getting well. His hesitation, his constant self-admonishment that he must not let himself begin to hope, are unbearably poignant. He has, simply, come to understand what it means to have the gift of life, that it *is* a gift. In the end, when the pain starts up again, he writes: "I knew that I had only been granted a pause. . . . Strangely I have the feeling that I have used it well."

Susan Sontag, in *Illness as Metaphor* (1978), has argued vigorously against the mystification and mythification of disease, cancer in particular, against the notion that the disease can be said to derive from the character of the individual. *The Death of a Beekeeper* does, in a sense, promote the latter idea. The equivalence between the repressed life, unfulfilled relationships, and inability to face oneself directly, and cancer is suggested. Consider the following passage. Westin has brought Ann, the woman he has fallen in love with, to meet his wife. The unexpected happens: the two women take to one another and develop a relation that finally excludes him. He writes, parenthetically:

> (And I think that in doing so they took from me my last chance for achieving independence, for achieving a clarity about myself and my own dimensions, for which I had been destined all my life, toward which everything had pointed.
>
> (What the two women succeeded in blocking was an eruption of reality, of personality.)

That the cancer would be, eventually, the consequence of such failures is an idea that Sontag would not assent to. On the other hand, it conforms exactly to the theories that Reich had about the etiology of the disease. The dispute is not one that can be engaged in a trivial manner. I can only affirm that in Gustafsson's book the connection is well imagined and convincing.

The profound and subtle texture of Westin's dying is not to be captured in paraphrase. It has a tonal integrity, a skillful manipulation of tenses, and it depicts very truthfully the complex emerging awareness of one human being. The reader's final impression is that between the first journal entry and the last (in which he learns that an ambulance has been summoned) a great psychic transformation has been effected. The tools of language are not very useful with respect to these processes in the psyche and the precise character of the change is not to be specified. We can say that the arrow has moved from lesser to greater, outside to inside, surface to depth, denial to acceptance. We cannot say, however, that Westin has grasped the full meaning of his experience. That would be too facile. It would be more accurate to say that he has begun to see. The pathos is that he did not begin to see earlier, but the triumph is that he did begin.

In one of the later journal passages Westin writes:

> I am of the opinion that the soul is spherical (if indeed it has any form at all), a sphere, in which a faint light penetrates just a little ways below the rainbowlike shimmer of the surface, where sensations and reactions of consciousness whirl about like soap bubbles, constantly changing their color, but it's only a very little ways.
>
> Deeper inside there are only feeble traces of light, approximately like those in very great ocean depths, and then darkness. Darkness, darkness.
>
> But not a threatening dark. A motherly darkness.

It is Gustafsson's intent to show how slight the "I" really is, but to show, at the same time, what miraculous pirouettes it can perform. This is not a contradiction but a tension of opposites, a tension that keeps us vibrating within our constructed selves while everything that is Other is perilously near.

Lars Gustafsson

V. S. Naipaul and Derek Walcott

On Isabella when I was a child it was a disgrace to be poor. It is, alas, no longer so. And it astonished me when I first came to England to find that it wasn't so here either. . . . Politicians proclaimed the meanness of their birth and the poverty of their upbringing and described themselves with virtuous rage as barefoot boys. On Isabella where we had the genuine article in abundance, this was a common term of schoolboy abuse, and I was embarrassed on behalf of these great men. To be descended from generations of idlers and failures, an unbroken line of the unimaginative, unenterprising and oppressed, had always seemed to me to be a cause for deep, silent shame.

—V. S. NAIPAUL, *The Mimic Men*

A writer dies inside when he betrays, like a paid spy, the rhythm of his race.

—DEREK WALCOTT

There is no simple answer to the question of why languages and cultures gain and lose vigor and expressiveness, and why at certain times one portion of a language culture can be in ascendancy while another suffers decline. Consider, in this regard, writing in English at present. It is of more than passing interest, I think, that two of the most accomplished, energetic (and by this I mean linguistically *and* in terms of output), and serious writers in our language were born only two years apart in the same little-regarded pocket of the world, the West Indies. Derek Walcott and V. S. Naipaul, the former a black poet and playwright, the latter, of Indian extraction, a novelist and essayist—both are writing as if to compensate for centuries of cultural waywardness, both are striving to speak in the way that the great writers have always spoken, prophetically, to grand concerns, past regionalism. But what is surprising, finally, in view of the superficial similarities, is that they should occupy such divergent positions with regard to the Caribbean, issues confronting third-world peoples, and, on a grander scale, the fate of the human enterprise. The first indication of what these stances might be is in the fact that Naipaul lives in exile in London while Walcott spends most of the year in Port of Spain, Trinidad. What in some circumstances would be insignificant here is not.

Of the two writers, V. S. Naipaul is certainly the more conspicuous. In fact, one of the most interesting developments in literature in the last decade or so has been the rapidity with which Naipaul has advanced from the status of respected and "interesting" third-world writer to, most recently, in the words of several estimable reviewers "one of the world's foremost living novelists." This advance coincides closely with the publication of Naipaul's last four works, the novels *Guerrillas* (1975) and *A Bend in the River* (1979), and the documentaries *India: A Wounded Civilization* (1977) and *The Return of Eva Perón* (1980). The quality of these writings is high, very high, and *A Bend in the River* is already being cited as a masterpiece, which in many ways it is—but the fact is that there are many other things to study, too, if we are to understand the arrival of Mr. Naipaul.

V. S. Naipaul has been writing steadily, with no apparent letup, since 1954, publishing since that time, all told, sixteen books. Many of these have been awarded prizes in England and elsewhere. He is not a newcomer. What is interesting is that what we now refer to as the Naipaul vision—a vision that is unique, pitiless, and that indicts man in no uncertain terms—has really come to the fore only in these most recent works. It is with this new, famous Naipaul that we are here concerned, the Naipaul that gives us, often at the expense of balance and compassion, those supposedly central attributes of great writing, his remorseless view of collapse, futility, the betrayal of the human by the human.

"The world is what it is; men who are nothing, who allow themselves to become nothing, have no place in it." With these words Naipaul begins *A Bend in the River.* The stern, biblical cadence has already become a sort of emblem for the world view of the coming decades. Like his other novel, *Guerrillas, A Bend in the River* presents us with an uprooted, disenchanted protagonist, a man who comes to understand that the violent thrusts of history—which in large measure determine his life—are beyond his, or anyone's control, and that their underlying determinants are the rapacity of some and the fear and inertia of others. Communication is doomed to fail because no one is sufficiently in command of the truth. The supremacy belongs to those who can act, however mindlessly. In short, Naipaul is giving us his analysis of the situation in the countries of the third world, countries he sees as doomed to reenact the same dreary scenario until some global catastrophe finally delivers everyone from everything. The reason for this perpetual frustration is, according to Naipaul, clear: these countries have never had a viable culture or base of their own, they have always parroted the culture of the oppressor; things are now, alas, too far advanced, the corruption too deeply implanted, and there is no more Eden to return to.

The final passage of *A Bend in the River,* which is set in a country much like Zaire, has the narrator, Selim, fleeing from yet another eruption of senseless violence. The passage depicts, in the best Naipaul style, the human limit and the extent to which nature and the force of inchoate events overpower the individual.

> It was in this darkness that abruptly, with many loud noises, we stopped. There were shouts from the barge, the dugouts with us, and from many parts of the steamer. Young men with guns had boarded the steamer and had tried to take her over. But they had failed; one young man was bleeding on the bridge above us. The fat man, the captain, remained in charge of his vessel. We learned that later.
>
> At that time what we saw was the steamer searchlight, playing on the riverbank, playing on the passenger barge, which had snapped loose and was drifting at an angle through the water hyacinths at the edge of the river. The searchlight lit up the barge

> passengers, who, behind bars and wire guards, as yet scarcely seemed to understand that they were adrift. Then there were gunshots. The searchlight was turned off, the barge was no longer to be seen. The steamer started up again and moved without lights down the river, away from the area of battle. The air would have been full of moths and flying insects. The searchlight, while it was on, had shown thousands, white in the white lights.

It is, I think, this vision in all its intensity, excellence, and pessimism that is being touted. Why is this? It is not as if no one has ever ventured to be pessimistic about man's nature or his prospects, nor as if corruption and decline were being discovered for the first time. What is most important, apart from literary strength, is the fact that this is being written by someone *from* the third world, someone we must trust. As critic Jane Kramer shrewdly noted in a recent review in *The New York Times Book Review:*

> We turn appreciating Naipaul, even reading Naipaul into a kind of exemption from his fury. No wonder he forgives no one—not when he is being praised so often as that Indian writer who, being "one of them," can expose the depravities of "his" world in ways that we Westerners, with our colonial past and our complacent present, could presumably never get away with.

Kramer has here identified the guilt that is real enough to demand a scourge, but that, in the eyes of the educated Westerner, can by and large be projected onto the neighbor, the person in power, the bureaucrat, anyone who is implicated but less self-reflectively aware of what Naipaul is saying.

Disorder is the terrain he claims, and he has the arrogance and talent to defend his vision against all comers. He is not, as so many of his contemporaries are, content to serve us the hairline crack on the living-room wall. No, Naipaul's scenarios are replete with gunfire, senseless violence, senseless death, forces spilling from their customary sluices. The events of our day, and the absurdity and failure that seem to attach to them, vindicate this sort of vision, even lend it an aura of prophecy.

It seems that this new Naipaul has come at just the right time. There has been a substantial gap in the truth spectrum, so substantial, in fact, that many in their excitement confuse this utterance with the whole truth. The avidity with which so many rally behind his flag indicates that some kind of dialectical correction is in process, a movement from complacency to too great a willingness to find everything on the verge of collapse. Why is this? Perhaps it is because after so many years of misplaced confidence—in the rightness and decency of those who wield power—eruptions everywhere are showing that these qualities have nothing to do with what is really dominance and expropriation. The reaction to the news is fear, paralysis in the face of an uncertain future, a feeling of helplessness before a corruption that has eaten too deeply into the governing structure. Further, anger, a sense of having been betrayed, and a crude satisfaction at the thought that those who have nothing further to lose are picking up their guns. The fallacy, which is planted in the psyche, is the fallacy of exemption: that it will happen everywhere but here, and if it happened here it would be the man next door who would catch the bullet. These are some of the emotions and this is the fallacy—they attend our attraction to Naipaul.

The more attention that is accorded to Naipaul, the greater the demand placed upon the critic. The kinds of claims that are advanced tell us a great deal about the contours of educated sentiment here and elsewhere, and educated sentiment has as much to do with the state of civilization as anything else. It is vital that guilt reactions and the sort of blood-lust/last-days sentiment that emerges from ennui and helplessness do not become our criteria for the truth value of a writer. And Naipaul is just the sort of writer who can polarize segments of society, whose prized precision and truth-telling are calculated to be provocative. Trying to account for Naipaul's popularity with liberal Westerners, Edward Said has written in *The Nation:* "Why? Because he exorcises all the 1960's devils, national liberation movements, revolutionary goals, Third Worldism—and shows them to be fraudulent public relations gimmicks, half native impotence, half badly learned 'Western' ideas." What has happened, and this is as much a result of cultural shifts as it is of Naipaul's own intentions, is that this kind of vision has moved from the periphery of our concern right into the center, and that with this movement many of our ideas about the "state of the art" have been altered. The applicability of the vision must be examined carefully.

The one thing that we are always taught about masterpieces is that they reflect life in its full amplitude, and that their underlying stance is compassion for humanity. Compassion is supposedly the fruit of deep meditation and deep insight into the plight of mortal, self-reflecting creatures. What troubles us as we read Naipaul is that he fulfills so many of the other prerequisites for greatness—he creates character, milieu, situation, and tension brilliantly—and yet, at least in the most recent works, reveals a thoroughgoing lack of compassion. It is almost as if he thinks that to indicate compassion is to violate some high criterion for objectivity. Naipaul presents himself as a detached, exact, unaffected, even ironic observer, a man holding his hand to a flame and recording the various sensations in an uninflected voice. Which is the paradox: one cannot hold flesh to flame and speak calmly.

We are inclined, then, to suspect the opposite, that beneath the precision and calm are frustration, rage—indeed, were it not for the works that issue at a rate of one per year, impotence. The rage would clearly be at the backwardness of these countries, at the very movements of history that "conspired" to keep these places out of the mainstream of culture and enterprise and condemned them to the status of second-rate. One wonders, too, the extent to which there might be private rage, at a destiny that had him born in the West Indies rather than elsewhere, that ensured that his career, no matter how successful, would always be regarded as an exception or freak. We know how anger, when successfully sublimated, can become exactitude, an inflated vigilance with regard to details, facts. Naipaul has tailored the language of the educated Englishman into a style of scalpel precision. But one cannot shake the sensation, reading the prose, that the lash, sparkle, and edge have been bought at a high price.

One of the main features of the Naipaul style is its obsession with evidence, the care taken in marshaling the facts that will support a negative contention. Naipaul demonstrates an extraordinary ability for coming up with certain kinds of information, for fusing facts together, for making it appear that there is no other kind of information. This is not a writer's trick so much as a feature of his personality. At the core he is bitter, convinced that the world is a place of exploitation, and convinced that what has made things this way, colonial greed and the ignorance and acquiescence of the colonized, will engender violence and collapse. He is also deeply ashamed of the backwardness and speciousness of third-world cultures. Whether he is, further, ashamed of being ashamed is less clear. Looking for culprits he finds, in combination, vanity, moral laxity, covetousness—character attributes that show up, for example, in *Guerrillas* in the persona of Jimmy Ahmed, bogus black-power spokesman, and, even more glaringly, in the Englishwoman Jane, who courts Ahmed's chic, who imagines that she can board a plane and leave the islands when things get "hot," and who is finally hacked to death by Ahmed's henchmen in a scene of supreme viciousness. It is at points like this that we sense Naipaul taking pleasure in his linguistic detachment, his ability to narrate a piece of savagery without a syntactical flinch. The pleasure is, perhaps, the pleasure of avenging himself on the kind of presumption and laxity he has embodied in the character of Jane.

Naipaul is so skillful a writer that his pictures are at first entirely persuasive. Evidence is presented in such a way that we omit to think that life is ever any different, though of course it is. But after the spell wears off one starts to wonder—could it be that life in these places, these worst of places, is such an unrelieved round of cruelty, betrayal, and decline? The headlines are always there to indicate that it is indeed—but we must not forget, either, that the newspaper is not a digest of things as they are. Nowhere is there life that is totally without pleasant or neutral mediation, the things that partly compose *any* mosaic of the truth, and that are the very scrim we position between ourselves and the world in order that we may live. People have their illusions, fall in love, and that love is composed of tenderness and sacrifice and is something more than plunder. Naipaul is entitled to deploy sexuality metaphorically, but if he is concerned with a context of truth then he must find a place for the rest of the emotional spectrum. In these later works love is scarcely permitted. When there is sex it is generally presented as buggery, or else in its moments of *tristitia*. He seems to forget the extent to which the human being secretes affection and order.

What we have, finally, is a crafted picture of our worst imaginings: rats in the garbage, termites in the beams, guerrillas in the brush. Things are presented without center. There is no God and the flex of power is random, or else determined by laws that we cannot find or measure. Naipaul appeals to chaos. And this, I think, is the central fallacy. For this chaos, which rings so true in our private paranoia, is simply insufficient vision. What appear as the random workings of power are but the insufficiently understood workings. All events take their shape in a social fabric and can be viewed as a sum total of stresses: push, pull; cause, effect. There is no meaning until the subjective, psychic factors are interpolated. Naipaul, presenting events, carefully bones them of their subjective layer. We are given sequences, chronologies, highly accurate renderings of surfaces—but there are no connections of meaning. As events proceed toward their violent terminus, as in his celebrated essay "Michael X and the Black Power Killings in Trinidad" (which supplied much of the underpinning for *Guerrillas*), the reader is forced to supply the psychic counterpoint. The narration of senseless events builds until there is only one conclusion possible: that a portion of the race is living in a state of savagery. Still. Or once again.

If I strike a note of reservation it is in spite of my admiration for Naipaul. My effort is to pin down where and why he might be wrong about "things as they are." The problem is not, I think, in his perception of events—it is, rather, that he seems to infer what human nature is like from the violence happening in the "hot spots" of the world. We need this vision, of course, as purgative, as preparation for various disenchantments, but the fact that we need it is not to say that it is the most reflective of the human condition at present. It deals with phenomena that have been neglected, neglected mainly because so few of those who have the language and ability to relate them convincingly also have the firsthand experience. We must bear in mind, even against the current of Naipaul's excellence, the subtle but important ways in which his art is a compensation for an insufficiency of this brand of truth.

Naipaul, in his self-imposed exile, in his eminence, is, perforce, an object of interest to any third-world writer. Derek Walcott is no exception. I would hazard, even, that Walcott is obsessed by this figure. References, some blatant and some quite subtle, appear throughout the collections. In one of the earliest, *The Castaway* (1965), he dedicates a poem, "Laventille," to Naipaul. There, throughout, Walcott says "we," views himself and Naipaul as united in a condition of uprootedness. This would have been written, most likely, in the early sixties. In 1977, however, in an interview with Sharon Ciccarelli in *Chant of Saints* (1979), Walcott said:

> A man, for instance, might say: "All this fuss the niggers are making (to make the statement crude and succinct) is a pain and I'm withdrawing from it, and that's my attitude, and I'm going to live in my black ivory tower and not involve myself in any revolution. . . . As a matter of fact there is a terrific West Indian writer, V. S. Naipaul, who is very cynical of Caribbean political and racial endeavors. That has been his consistent position, and yet one is able to admire him as a writer, and respect his stance because he writes out of it, and even to admit that he is a very good writer.

Walcott is clearly soft-pedaling the issue here, for the poems of this period are full of bitter allusions to a personage that can only be Naipaul. In his collection *Sea Grapes* (1976), for instance, in a poem entitled "At Last" and dedicated "to the exiled novelists," he writes:

You spit on your people
your people applaud,
your former oppressors
laurel you.
The thorns biting your forehead
are contempt
disguised as concern,
still, you can come home, now.
Before, in your finical gut,
the bowels of compassion
petrify to a gallstone

and your ink deliquesces
into bile. In your eye
every child is born crippled,
every endeavor
is that of the baboon;
can you hear the achievement
of this chimpanzee typing?

And this past winter, in his Chapin Memorial Lecture in New York—the subject: West Indian writing—Walcott pronounced *A Bend in the River* "a racist joke." By this he means that Naipaul's attitude toward and depiction of the black supports the colonial bias of racial inferiority.

The sources of their divergence are not hard to guess at. In Walcott's eyes Naipaul has honed his considerable talent at the expense of his people, and he has put his irony and detachment in the service of exposure, derision, and humiliation. That he has placed himself in exile in order to do this only makes matters worse.

It would be simple if we could now say that Walcott represents the opposite of Naipaul, that he is a man of his people, engaged. To some extent he is, it is true. He lives in the Caribbean and expends great energy in writing and producing plays and directing the Trinidad Theatre Workshop. His personal and political involvement in the Caribbean is evident, and his plays, which seem to be a vehicle for one part of his concern, bear this out. Their intent is to find in situation and idiom the mythic and racial taproots of the Carib peoples. But any serious study of his output, which to date includes six collections of poetry, one verse epic, and three collections of plays, reveals that he is a man of profound conflicts and some degree of ambivalence with respect to these very issues. Much of that ambivalence has been overcome, and his pronouncements now reflect great conviction, but one needs only to survey the early work to see that it is a conviction born of struggle. Walcott too has spent time in exile, has agonized over his attraction for a language that is, in one sense—always in one sense—the glory and instrument of the enemy. In an early poem he writes:

Where shall I turn, divided to the vein?
I who have cursed
The drunken officer of British rule, how choose
Between this Africa and the English tongue I love?
Betray them both, or give back what they give?

Every career has its own complexities, baffles, barriers. In Walcott's case they are not open to public inspection. There is no major turnaround as in the case of Naipaul, no dramatic change. Rather, there is a steady growth and deepening. The epic *Another Life* (1973) marks his maturation and is the first expression of his powers working in unison. From that point on, right up to the most recent magazine publications, what we witness is an authority and power that seems to grow with each performance.

In the earlier collections the Walcott voice is still diffuse. He shows himself capable of vigor and freshness, but his love of writers like Traherne and Thomas Browne has not yet been taken into the marrow. Still, as early as 1963 Robert Graves could pronounce: "Derek Walcott handles English with a closer understanding of its inner magic than most (if not any) of his English-born contemporaries." Many of the poems in these collections—up to and including *The Gulf* (1970)—invoke the Caribbean. We see Walcott trying to mediate his sense of the islands with his sense of the world beyond. Description is powerful, and anger and tenderness are handled well, as are themes of exile, solitude, and conflict, but the effect is still that of a composition that verges on resolving into a major key.

To read *Another Life* with some experience of Walcott's earlier work is exciting. We hear a voice detach itself from other voices and acquire a resonance peculiar to itself. Here is Walcott's turning point. He discovers how to make the personal the universal. He gives us the myth, and all the pain, of a young man growing up in the West Indies. The aspirations are there, the will to express, to be great. The work is associative, layered, and suggests by its movement the unfolding consciousness of the narrator. His struggles, whether by intention or inadvertently, fuse in our mind with the political and cultural identity struggles of that portion of the world. The tension that is struck between the personal and the racial is powerful and helps carry the narrative.

Prominent in *Another Life* is language, rich, at times simple, full of chop, at other times baroque, sinuous. The tonal and textural reach is full and yet the voice hovers out of reach of any sort of pathos or confession. Here, for example, is a passage in which the speaker addresses his mother:

Mama,
your son's ghost circles your lost house, looking in
incomprehensibly at its dumb tenants
like fishes busily inaudible behind glass,
while the carpenter's Gothic joke, A,W,A,W,
Warwick and Alix involved in its eaves
breaks with betrayal.
You stitched us clothes from the nearest elements,
made shirts of rain and freshly ironed clouds,
then, singing your iron hymn, you riveted
your feet on Monday to the old machine.

Then Monday plunged her arms up to the elbows
in a foam tub, under a blue-soap sky,
the wet fleets sailed the yard, and every bubble
with its bent, mullioned window, opened
its mote of envy in the child's green eye
of that sovereign-headed, pink-cheeked bastard Bubbles
in the frontispiece of Pears Encyclopedia.
Rising in crystal spheres, world after world.

They melt from you, your sons.
Your arms grow full of rain.

An indication, I think, of Walcott's graciousness and inventiveness.

The matter of language is, of course, central for any writer, but for the third-world writer the importance is underscored. Language is not something simply acquired and used unreflectingly; its meaning is also political. The specter of servitude is there, for one thing. The writers and artists of the third world are obsessed with the notion of mimicry, either in their desire to re-create admired forms, or in their determination to avoid this. As Walcott said in his Chapin Lecture: "Is this language I use my own? If it is mastered am I a servant of the power where it originated? . . . Am I creator or conspirator?" Questions like this reveal the extent to which Walcott and others in his position regard language as an emblem of the innermost soul.

The choices available to the third-world writer are several, each with its implications. For as a writer chooses his expression, he likewise chooses his audience. Sharon Ciccarelli asked Walcott about this in her interview.

> C: Do you think black writers should write in the language of their ex-colonizers; for instance, Cesaire writing in French, or Soyinka writing in English? Should they attempt to master a traditional language—Swahili, Yoruba? Or should they work towards a fusion, say the way McKay used the Jamaican *patois* . . . ?

> W: I think the writer writing in English or Spanish is lucky in the sense that he can master the original language, or the language of the master himself, and yet have it fertilized by the language of dialect. Someone who knows what he is doing, a good poet, recognizes the language's essential duality. The excitement is in joining the two parts.

Walcott's English carries just this sense; syntactically and in terms of word usage it is open to all the resources of the language. The result is that he is writing the richest and freshest lines anywhere.

Despite Walcott's pronouncement, one can imagine that writers in his position might feel ambivalent toward a Naipaul. The ease with which the latter adopted the English of the educated classes, his supremacy in its use—which is the supremacy of the outsider outdoing the insider—could easily give rise to a blend of envy and contempt, the portions determined by the extent to which that path represented a temptation. Walcott was certainly not immune to temptation.

It is *Another Life* that seems to mark the crisis, the choice of one path over another, the acceptance of destiny, place, and time. Walcott invokes and accepts his past without a trace of cynicism or patronage. The process is largely the laying to rest of ghosts, a confrontation with the situations that shaped his identity as a man. The narrator confronts much pain, the suicide of his mentor, the failure of a great, deep love, the need to cut the root of place and leave, and finally, the need to return and face the works of time. All of these events are presented at their full pitch of pain, bodied forth and, in other places, counterpointed by imagery of the island and the sea. We are, at times, in a place of great openness and natural beauty, at other times in a dank, confined locus. Likewise the sea—wild, sluggish, Penelope's shuttle making and unmaking a garment, waves that are like turning leaves in a book "left open by an absent master/in the middle of another life . . ." The steady pressure behind the language, the love, and the skill with which inner and outer worlds are imagistically twined make this a mighty work.

From that book on Walcott's voice has not faltered. Two published collections, *Sea Grapes* and *The Star-Apple Kingdom* (1979), plus a dozen or so subsequent major magazine publications show him moving in the direction of the bard. By this I mean that the sureness now is very nearly the prophetic one that we associate with our image of bard. And, too, the grandness of his themes: questions of history and empire, the destiny of Man conceived *sub specie aeternitatis.* Implicit is his solidarity with the great Roman poets. But there is another allegiance as well, this with the Russian poetry of this century, Akhmatova, Mandelstam, and more recently Joseph Brodsky. Walcott shares with the latter a vision of empire in decline, a vision that underlies his most recent work and lifts it apart from the closed-circuit lyric that dominates the scene.

Walcott's strengths in this regard are those of a poet. We don't expect analysis, but we do expect articulate moral response—it is there in abundance. Also, we get the deep, purgative experience of powerful emotion powerfully enunciated. His conception of history is a poet's; it is cyclic, metaphoric, and, as a result, dimensional in a subjective manner. How different this is from Naipaul's conception, which is linear, event determined, and accurate in its specifics. There is a place, of course, for many versions, those rendered in the tones of a journalist as well as those that seethe, praising, condemning, pronouncing upon man as great poets always have.

Here, as illustration, is a portion from an uncollected poem entitled "North and South":

Now, at the rising of Venus—the steady star
that survives translation, if one can call this lamp
the planet that pierces us over indigo islands—
despite the critical sand flies, I accept my function
as a colonial upstart at the end of an empire,
a single, circling, homeless satellite.
I can listen to its guttural death rattle in the shoal
of the legions' withdrawing roar, from the raj,
from the Reich, and see the full moon again
like a white flag rising over Fort Charlotte,
and sunset slowly collapsing like the flag.

It's good that everything's gone, except their language,
which is everything. And it may be a childish revenge
at the presumption of empires to hear the worm
gnawing their solemn columns into coral,
to snorkel over Atlantis, to see, through a mask,
Sidon up to its windows in sand, Tyre, Alexandria,
with their wavering seaweed spires through a glass-bottom boat,
and to buy porous fragments of the Parthenon
from a fisherman in Tobago, but the fear exists,
Delenda est Carthago on the rose horizon,
and the side streets of Manhattan are sown with salt,
as those in the North all wait for that white glare
of the white rose of inferno, all the world's capitals.

The Star-Apple Kingdom embodies these latest trends in Walcott's writing. We see him working his voice with confident ease, using long lines that carry tension, much texture, and a rough elegance. The long opening poem, "The Schooner *Flight*," is probably the most powerful piece in the book. Walcott evokes in the person of Shabine a kind of latter-day Odysseus, a sailor among modern islands, a truth-seeker, a misfit, a man in need of great doses of sky and sea. Shabine has the gift of language and he uses this gift to excoriate his demons. The world is corrupt, in decline, getting worse all the time, and yet, if a man can feel the call to courage and beauty, all is not lost. The poem finally celebrates what is to be celebrated more than it denounces. And there is a margin left for meaning. The poem ends:

> Sometimes it is just me, and the soft-scissored foam
> as the deck turn white and the moon open
> a cloud like a door, and the light over me
> is a door in white moonlight taking me home.
> Shabine sang to you from the depths of the sea.

Viewing Naipaul and Walcott, their separate natures and modes of response, we get a sense of the complexities—emotional, political, linguistic—facing the writer and, by obvious extension, the citizen of the third world. There is no profit, at this level of attainment, in extolling the one writer at the expense of the other, for what we confront, finally, is the multiplicity of truths. Their opposition, on a moral level, may be expressed as follows: whether one thinks that the process of value corruption is too vast and its evils too deeply rooted for there to be any use in trying, or whether one thinks that some effort can avail. Both writers, I think, acknowledge futility, but Walcott cannot find it in himself *not* to try, whereas Naipaul can, and does, insisting by his effort, his exile, that his truth is unvarnished and constitutes his contribution. As Pascal knew well, there are reasons and there are reasons.

Yaakov Shabtai

Yaakov Shabtai's urgent and innovative novel *Past Continuous* was first published in Hebrew in 1977. That we got it in English only in 1985 reminds us yet again of the difficulties we've had since the scattering of tongues at Babel. In this case, the lapse is frustrating because Shabtai had such a keen diagnostic sense about the crisis of meaning and values that we are currently living through; as with any crisis, no insight can come too soon. I use the past tense here because the author died suddenly of a heart attack in 1981; he was forty-seven.

The narrative performance in *Past Continuous* is extraordinary. Shabtai found a new use for the stream-of-consciousness mode, adapting what is almost by definition a subjectively centered idiom into a means for expressing the collective life of an extended human network. Shifting adeptly between daily life in modern Tel Aviv and the nerve-pattern intricacies of the remembered past, the novel renounces customary kinds of structure. No character or incident is given special status. We feel, as a result, that we have walked in upon an epic family gathering. And as we move through the crowd, we are not only introduced to every person, but are given sharply registered personal histories as well. It is seldom clear whether we are in the author's mind or that of the character whose past we are tracing. As the same figures keep reappearing—differently angled, of course—we are almost overpowered, both by a sense of flux and by a recognition of the extent of human interconnectedness.

Where ties are so interwoven, and where the precipitate of affections and enmities is so dense, there is no perception of time possible except that named in the title. In Shabtai's world, what we are accustomed to call the present is really only the outermost projection of an ongoing past. And indeed, Israel, Caesar, and Goldman—the three friends whose doings during a nine-month span compose the book's surface integument—move like wraiths before the accumulation of generational history that surrounds them.

The nine-month span, which generally recalls gestation, is here possessed of a grimmer significance. *Past Continuous* begins with this charged declaration: "Goldman's father died on the first of April, whereas Goldman himself committed suicide on the first of January. . . ." All subsequent narrative is tinged for us by this knowledge; we look at everything through the lens of Goldman's concealed despair. Goldman will be, in the terminology of family therapeutics, the member who "expresses" what the others cannot. Moritz Heimann's aphorism, cited by Walter Benjamin, sheds light on this opening stratagem: "A man who dies at thirty-five is at every point of his life a man who dies at the age of thirty-five." Through the novelist's art the reader shares the perspective of the fateless gods.

The opening, however, is somewhat misleading. For we would naturally expect that Goldman will be at the novel's center. But he is not—at least no more than is his father, or his mother, Regina, or his uncle Lazar, or his friend Caesar, or Caesar's wife, or any one of a dozen others. Shabtai uses the period between the two deaths as a frame, and allows the tension of expectation to exert binding force on what might otherwise be a shapeless mass of anecdote and recollection.

To the reader who is unwilling to proceed with care, who refuses to pencil out a genealogy as he reads, *Past Continuous* may appear to be just that—shapeless. For no sooner do we join Israel and Caesar at the wake for Goldman's father than the floating digressions begin. Each glance or handshake initiates a new account. The plumb line pauses in the immensity of the past, the story is told, and then the next level is sounded. The immersion can become almost unbearable at times. But we never get the sense—and this is the secret of Shabtai's power—that these are privately hoarded details. No, each time the room comes back into focus, we realize that the narrative is part of the collective memory of all present. And with this realization comes a great feeling of inner expansion. Identities, and the problematic particulars of time and place, are diffused within the larger life of the clan.

> Shoshana had lived in the little room. Naomi's room, where she slept and sewed and also cooked meals for herself and her son on a little kerosene stove, partly because the kitchen was unbearably crowded, but mainly because Grandfather Moshe David, Regina's father, who had lingered on for a few years after his wife died, terrorizing the household with his religious fanaticism and his gloomy, irascible temper, which would flare up from time to time and erupt into passionate and vociferous scandals, was afraid that she would defile the food and dishes by bringing nonkosher things into the kitchen and mixing up the milk and meat dishes and the separate soaps and towels.

Seldom in literature do we penetrate so far into the mysteries of family life, or comprehend so intimately the changes that work their way through generations. Shabtai's novel shows us how the sterner, cruder life of earlier times has given way to the anxious anomie of the present. Where Goldman's father once bludgeoned a neighbor's dog—because he could not bear the woman's capricious manner, and because the dog was eating better than most people in wartime Israel—Caesar, fickle-hearted man of the present, can think of nothing more pressing than his next assignation or his growing bald spot. On his way to the funeral for Goldman's father, he hums "Ob-La-Di, Ob-La-Da" to himself. The very grain of things has altered.

The events of the past, so weighted with suffering, repressed passion, and the will to endure, increasingly take on the bold lines of legend. Goldman's Aunt Zipporah toils without rest from earliest childhood to make sure that her family survives. Uncle Lazar, who had been captured in the war, makes his way home after years of imprisonment in a Siberian labor camp, only to have his wife refuse to shake his hand when he walks into the house. In the face of such stark histories of pride and pain, the aimlessness of Goldman and his friends is almost an affront.

Lazar underscores this in his conversations with Goldman. At one point Goldman discourses on suicide, claiming that it is the one true freedom, the only way to cheat death of its dominion. Lazar has a hard time meeting his gaze; it is as though he is ashamed. Finally, though, the memory of his own suffering gives him voice. "I don't know," says Lazar with the most rending understatement, "but it seems to me that a person has to endure a great deal before he can say the kind of things you've been saying."

Shabtai has arranged his time dissolves in such a way that we experience by increments the profound changes that have engulfed this world. They are not so much addressed as glimpsed from the corner of the eye. We note that the makeshift dwellings chronicled by the elders have been torn down to accommodate modern high rises; that apartments and houses now have the latest appliances. A son or a cousin is drafted into the army and never returns. Characters remark, in passing, that Tel Aviv is overrun with strange faces. Perhaps the older generation is not constitutionally different from its heirs. Perhaps it is the impersonal force of circumstance—social, economic—that is responsible for the erosions of character. The transformations that other nations have undergone over centuries have in Israel been compressed into decades. The elders were faced with clear obstacles and did what had to be done. Goldman and Israel and Caesar have had no such luck.

To them has fallen the task of defining the values of the culture, and they do not know where to begin.

The implication of *Past Continuous* is that the faith—in God or country—that makes life endurable is all but impossible to sustain where there is no hardship. This becomes more obvious as the novel draws to a close. Goldman, who has hitherto been peripheral, is brought forward. A creature without faith, without deeper goals or connections, he inches toward his awful self-recognition. First, though, he will try the various panaceas of the age. He exercises on a contraption called the Bull-worker to build up the outer man; he undertakes a dilettantish study of astronomy and begins translating the *Somnium,* an ancient cosmological treatise. The study eventually becomes oppressive, "filling him with a feeling of the nothingness and meaninglessness of the universe in the light of the infinite finiteness and the complete neutrality of time and of space. . . ." Life without higher sanction is unendurable. He sees, after Lazar dies, that there is no longer sustenance in his relationships; he has no reason to go on.

If this were all, if Shabtai had served up a vision of generational decline and nothing else, *Past Continuous* would stand as one of the bleakest contributions to modern literature. What mitigates the horror, paradoxically, is Shabtai's vision of time. For the past that presses forward at every instant is also the repository of legends and their lessons. It is the *living* repository—for frail though these elders may be, many of them are yet among us. Long after Caesar's empty buffoonery and Goldman's suicide have dimmed in the memory, the image of Zipporah endures. Here she is arriving at a wedding in the final pages of the book:

> . . . at that moment there was a stir and Zipporah appeared in the doorway to the hall. She was sitting in a wheelchair and Esther pushed her slowly among the guests, who came up to her one after the other and respectfully, admiringly, and also affectionately shook her hand and kissed her cheek and exchanged a few words with her, and Goldman remained standing where he was and he looked at her and saw her approaching him in her wheelchair—a

small, erect woman in a dark woolen dress, with one foot shod in a white canvas shoe peeping out from under it, her short, curly gray hair tied in a black ribbon and her little face, as rosy and wrinkled as an old apple, shining with an intelligence and authority which were nothing but the expression of her own integrity and her confident and tireless affirmation of life with all its difficulties and suffering.

Salman Rushdie

"I tell myself this will be a novel of leavetaking, my last words on the East from which, many years ago, I began to come loose." So writes Salman Rushdie in an aside in his novel *Shame* (1983). Readers familiar with his Booker Prize–winning *Midnight's Children* (1981) are sure to arch a skeptical brow, for Rushdie is a writer demonized by place. His every phrase seems to blossom from the soil of Eastern myth and legend. What kind of leave-taking does he have in mind? Can a writer decide this kind of thing? Or is this a feint, an announcement made to short-circuit his canonization as our Writer of the East?

Bombay born, Rugby and Cambridge educated, Rushdie now lives in London. Although he is only in his mid-thirties, he has already established himself as one of the preeminent tale-tellers of his generation. *Midnight's Children,* his second novel (the first was *Grimus,* published here in 1979), attempted nothing less than a myth of modern India. With its sprouting, bougainvillea prose, its daring manipulation of time, its insistence on the fantastical character of the real, its outsized personalities and grotesque humor, it resembles García Márquez's *One Hundred Years of Solitude* and stands up well to the comparison. *Shame,* piping a similar cobra music, promulgating its own impossibilities, is like a partitioned-off piece of *Midnight's Children.* And "partitioned" is the right word here—for *Shame* is Rushdie's myth of Pakistan, or someplace very much like Pakistan. He cautions us not to limit the sphere of reference. "My view," he states, "is that I am not writing only about Pakistan." That "only" is the freighted word.

Shame begins with the death of the patriarch Old Mr. Shakil, and ends many years later with the violent murder of his grandson, Omar Khayyam Shakil, in the same decrepit mansion in the town of Q. Omar is conceived by one of Shakil's three daughters during the festivities arranged to honor the old man's death. We never learn who his father is, or, for that matter, his mother—as soon as they detect pregnancy, the three haughty sisters sequester themselves and divide their shame: "Identically, their wombs ballooned towards the pregnancy's full term. It is naturally possible that all this was achieved with the help of physical contrivances, cushions and padding and even faint-inducing vapors; but it is my unshakable opinion that such an analysis grossly demeans the love that existed between the sisters."

Omar has a predictably odd and precocious childhood. Locked away from the world, he passes his days in the dark corridors of that "improbable mansion." He stares at the distant mountains through his telescope, masters innumerable languages; finally, with the aid of his grandfather's books, he teaches himself the art of hypnosis. We prepare ourselves for marvelous exploits. He is certain to be, like Saleem Sinai in *Midnight's Children,* the carrier of a grand destiny. But suddenly, with a snap of the narrator's wrist, the figured carpet is plucked from under us. Some fifty pages into the book Rushdie sets Omar aside and begins to spin the tale of Bilquis, the mother-to-be of Omar's bride, Sufiya Zinobia.

With this shift, the strong linear flow is broken. The plot will now be parceled out among Bilquis; her husband, Raza Hyder; Hyder's cousin Rani Humayun; and Rani's husband, Iskander Harappa (whose drinking and debauching partner, we hear, is a young Dr. Omar Shakil); later we pick up Sufiya and Naveed (the two Hyder daughters) and Arjumand, daughter of Rani and Iskander. Omar never earns our full attention again. We are caught up, instead, in an elaborate snake dance involving the Hyders and Harappas, two of the families of power in Rushdie's not-quite-named emerging nation.

It sounds confusing, and it is. Not only does the focus shift from character to character but Rushdie juggles verb tenses as if they were so many colored balls. He has discovered the inexhaustible fourth dimension: any event both *has* consequences and *is* a consequence. The past-future axis can be speared through the story line at any point. Time and again Rushdie will halt action for a peep into the future ("Many years later, when Iskander Harappa stood in the dock of the courtroom . . ."—the García Márquez echo is surely deliberate) or leapfrog backward with a "many years ago" construction. The splices are well done and the time swings can be exhilarating. Only the reviewer suffers, for an elegant précis is impossible.

Raza Hyder and Iskander Harappa are fatally entwined as accomplices/rivals in the struggle for political power. Echoes of Zulfikar Ali Bhutto and Zia ul-Haq abound—Harappa, like Bhutto, awaits trail in a Lahore jail; he is finally executed, as Bhutto was, after the trial results in a hung jury. But again, Rushdie warns us not to read *Shame* as a *roman à clef:* "There are two countries, real and fictional, occupying the same space, or almost the same space."

The political vicissitudes of the two power brokers propel the plot, but the domestic consequences of their mania supply its substance. And here Rushdie indulges his appetite for the fantastic. If the political realm is depicted with little exaggeration (after all, who needs to heighten anything in the daily news?), the private is set out with different truths in mind. Thus Sufiya, the first Hyder daughter, is "gifted" with an uncanny sensitivity to shame—her own and others'. As Raza Hyder climbs to power, Sufiya is transformed into a murderous demon. For in Rushdie's scheme, shamelessness and shame are dialectically hitched, each engendering the other, until they produce violence.

Tracing his obsession, Rushdie tells the story of a Pakistani in East London who murders his daughter because she made love to a white boy. "My Sufiya Zinobia," he writes, "grew out of the corpse of that murdered girl." In that incident Rushdie saw the elements of the culture in relief: pride, rage, furious righteousness. And shame? He admits that the *sharam* of the Moslem world does not translate directly into the "shame" of ours. Rooted in the religion, *sharam* is as difficult to take hold of as it is pervasive. But one thing is clear: the women are the martyrs. Sexually oppressed, hidden behind the shielding and enticing veil, they have had to express the contradiction between law and human instinct in blushes.

A similar division of labor exists in the social and political realm. There the men wield the power and the women take on the emotional consequences of the men's actions. Shame, for men, is injured pride; for women, it is more like an expiation of sins. The father who killed his daughter reveals one aspect of *sharam;* Sufiya Zinobia reveals another. In a culture where the men repress and the women express, the compensatory dynamic makes the bestialization of Sufiya possible.

Shameless power—in one way or another it perverts the natural lives of the characters. Each becomes a grotesque of a different stamp. The once-beautiful Rani Harappa ends her days embroidering hellish visions onto shrouds; the daughter, Arjumand, differently attuned, worships her father and makes herself into the icy "virgin Ironpants" to please him; Iskander Harappa, as we already know, is executed by his old colleague. *Shame* is, in one sense, a vivid dramatization of Lord Acton's too often cited, never sufficiently heeded maxim, "Power tends to corrupt. . . ." But for Rushdie the corruption seeps through the social world and into the most private reaches of the individual psyche.

Rushdie has put together an intricate tale and his sustained sinuosities are a delight. Problems arise, though, when he tries to bring everything together into a properly Sophoclean ending. He is forced to do some heavy-handed maneuvering. First, the neglected Omar—now obese and aged—is brought back. He marries Sufiya, hoping to cure her through hypnosis. But shame has scoured away her last human resources. She escapes into the countryside and begins her orgy: to quote Ted Hughes, her "manners are tearing off heads." Meanwhile, Raza Hyder, who has executed Harappa and assumed the presidency, is toppled by a coup. Bilquis, Raza, and their son-in-law, Omar, don disguises and flee, naturally, to the old mansion in Q., where, after all these years, the trio of weird sisters is still clucking. Horror, violence, death. We have been brought full circle to be cleansed at the grand union of effects with their causes.

But we are not cleansed. At least, not fully. For Rushdie's tale-telling impulses have overwhelmed his moral purpose. He has spun his threads with considerable art, but he doesn't allow every fate to ripen separately. There is a sense of forced, hothouse development; the finale lacks tragic resonance.

In a similar way, Rushdie's complex inventiveness undermines his treatment of the grand theme: shame. He is, abstractly speaking, on to something. The violent imposition of political nationhood on a traditional and religious culture cannot but have powerful consequences. When people act in new ways, against themselves, against the past, monsters are created. Raza Hyder and Harappa are inhuman in their will to power. Sufiya's shame and rage are, in effect, the reaction of the human in the face of the inhuman. The cause-and-effect dynamic, as Rushdie knows well, operates on both the physical and psychic planes. But all too often we are simply told that there is shame—we are seldom permitted to feel its burn. When shame finally does avenge itself on shamelessness, we cannot feel the full *frisson,* and *that* is a shame.

There are, however, compensations for these failings. The writing is supple, descriptions are charged (Raza Hyder has "enough energy to light up a street," a young movie magnate is a "kiss-lipped boy") and for all its fragmentation, the story surges forward with no wasted motion. We come away shaken, though more by the implications of the tale than by the tale itself. If what Rushdie says about shame is true, if it does well up wherever power turns against the commonweal, and if it does, in fact, turn into violence, then there is more darkness in store—and not "only" for Pakistan.

Salman Rushdie

Jorge Luis Borges

Geneva. June 14, 1986. The newspapers of the world report that he's gone, that ludic, lucid man, the Euclid of the secret orders of time, the confectioner of paradox, the artificer. With the exhalation of the last breath, he surrendered destiny—the moment-by-moment choosing of a life—to fate, the sum of a life finally chosen. Only then was it revealed: that every step and turn and tap of the wooden cane had been moving him toward that room in Geneva.

There are things that we will never know, and they are the most important of all. Jorge Luis Borges had been in Geneva before; he attended the *lycée* there from 1914 to 1918. The young man was already inclined to arcane meditation. Did he at any point feel the brushing wing of futurity? Did his gaze—he would not begin to lose his sight until 1927—ever pan the facade of that final place? If so, was there a catch of the breath, a shiver? It's not impossible. Destinations were always charged in his imaginings. Think of his detective Lönnrot ("Death and the Compass") arriving at the dark villa of Triste-le-Roy, exploring its eerie symmetries, finally reaching the oriel room where he will die. "An astonishing recollection struck him," writes Borges. *Recollection,* that's the key. Borges, like Plato, believed that all knowing already exists, inscribed in the cells, that we come to truth through anamnesis, a remembering. Did it all come back to him, too, there in that last room?

Borges's genius was to elaborate and insist upon an order of reality hidden from the five senses but accessible to the speculative intelligence. Like the kabbalists and Gnostics, he spoke in terms of a once-known universal meaning that had somehow gotten scrambled and was now beyond human recognition. The paradigm for this is, of course, the legend of the hubris at Babel and the subsequent dispersal of the one speech into myriad warring tongues. The mystic would insist that the original speech can be reconstituted, that bits of it inhere in the scattered vocables. Borges (who was for years the director of Argentina's national library) has great sport with this possibility in "The Library of Babel," where he posits a near infinity of volumes to represent every conceivable combination of letters of the alphabet. Among the billions of pages of nonsensical chaos, he reasons, there must also be the book of books:

> At that time it was also hoped that a clarification of humanity's basic mysteries—the origin of the Library and of time—might be found. It is versimilar that these grave mysteries could be explained in words: if the language of philosophers is not sufficient, the multiform Library will have produced the unprecedented language required, with its vocabularies and grammars.

But the cleverness of Borges's inventions and paradoxes is not enough to explain their enormous appeal. In their idiosyncratic exactitude, with their cunning appurtenances of footnotes and bibliographic references (many of these invented), they are telling us fables we want to believe in: that time and consciousness are mysteries our vaunted sciences have not explained, that our lives are, at a deeper level, journeys marked with signs and portents, and that each of us may have an ordained destination where, at an appointed time, the reason for our pilgrimage, will be given to us.

To read Borges, especially the collections of his middle period—*Ficciones* (1962), *Labyrinths* (1964), and *The Aleph and Other Stories, 1933–1969* (1970)—is to feel the self gradually divested of its conceptual armor. Underneath the crust of the glib and reasonable, the reader encounters a reality of haunting coherence and connectedness. This reality, Borges hints, has always been there, the pleasure ground of a spiritual elect. We may be tempted to call it the world of the imagination and leave it at that. But Borges himself is so possessed by it, he guides us toward it with such persistence, that we relinquish our doubts. And then it strikes us: these are not stories at all. These fanciful narratives are the author's way of telling us his truth; they are whimsical-looking ciphers in a most serious code. If you stop the reader on the street and ask him, he will say that it's all nonsense. But catch him with the book in his hand and it's a different story. Borges knew that we cannot read and disbelieve, that to the extent that we disbelieve, we are not reading.

My own favorite tale is "The Garden of the Forking Paths," in which the narrator solves the enigma of a seemingly indecipherable text when he understands how it enfolds all events and all possible outcomes. He explains it thus:

> In all fictional works, each time a man is confronted with several alternatives, he chooses one and eliminates the others; in the fiction of Ts'ui Pên, he chooses—simultaneously—all of them. He creates, in this way, diverse futures, diverse times which themselves also proliferate and fork. Fang, let us say, has a secret; a stranger calls at his door; Fang resolves to kill him. Naturally, there are several possible outcomes: Fang can kill the intruder, the in-

> truder can kill Fang, they can both escape, they both can die, and so forth. In the work of Ts'ui Pên, all possible outcomes occur; each one is the point of departure for other forkings.

With this, Borges founds a more encompassing form of time, one in which everything is always happening and everything has already happened. Though we have never encountered such a form ourselves, we recollect the feeling of it from certain of our dreams. Borges—who has been alive forever, who has been breathing his last breath in a room in Geneva through eternity, who has never existed and therefore can never die—may be at home in it now.

Julio Cortázar

"After the age of fifty," wrote Julio Cortázar in his last book, "we begin to die little by little in the deaths of others. The great magi, the shamans of our youth, successively go off." I don't know that we have to be fifty, or forty, or any great age at all to experience this dying by proxy. When I heard in February 1984 that Cortázar had died in a Paris hospital, some little part of me turned to ash. He had been one of the shamans of my youth, yes, but there was something more: I had come to believe in the legend of his permanent youthfulness. The photographs were part of it: even in his late sixties, Cortázar had the face and look of a man in his thirties. I was convinced he had a secret. He knew something about mirrors and reversible stairs and the abracadabra that can make time flow backward. Somewhere inside the alphabet he had come upon the spring of youth. Then I opened the paper. I saw that the man in the picture was wearing a gray vest of column inches.

Born in Brussels, in 1914, Cortázar was taken to Buenos Aires by his Argentine parents when he was four. The numerology of his life—and Cortázar was a writer very much interested in numbers and coincidences—works out perfectly: he lived for thirty-three years in Argentina and thirty-three in Paris. The symmetry would have pleased him, as would the march of threes. Perhaps these thoughts ran through his mind when he knew that the end was near.

The Argentina period represents Cortázar's long apprenticeship; by his own account, he spent years and years just reading and honing his craft. In the forties he published only a small volume of sonnets and a highly polished and abstract series of dialogues on the Cretan Minotaur (neither has been translated). Then, in 1951, the year of his self-exile to Paris, he released *Bestiario,* the first of his many luminous story collections. The fruit of his patience is a maturity and consistency—a number of the *Bestiario* tales are collected in *The End of the Game and Other Stories* (1967)—almost never witnessed in a debut collection. Even Borges claimed to be enchanted, though this was perhaps less an honor than one might suppose: the stories were very much influenced by the old master's conceptions.

Cortázar was, from the first, determined to subvert our customary expectations of reality. These stories were the guise of fantasy—the narrator of "Axolotl" stares at an amphibian in an aquarium with such intensity that their identities are finally reversed; the photographer in "Blow-up" finds that the shapes and figures in a particular enlargement are anything but frozen—but behind the mask is a serious questioning of our ideas of order. Like Borges, or Poe, Cortázar was fascinated by the liminal—by strange convergences of events, by the permeable boundaries between psyches. He devoted himself to unstitching the seam between anarchic reality and the fabric of reasonable explanation that we so carefully stretch over it.

Entering Cortázar's world, we leave behind our ordinary time perceptions. Sequence and succession, the lockstep of ticking seconds—

these have almost no place in the fiction. The time of a glance or a caress is elastic: the psyche dilates and opens onto expanses of experience. And in the face of the experience, the sweep of the clock hands is irrelevant, if not absurd.

> Think of this: When they present you with a watch they are gifting you with a tiny flowering hell, a wreath of roses, a dungeon of air. . . . They gift you with the job of having to wind it every day, an obligation to wind it, so that it goes on being a watch; they gift you with the obsession of looking into jewelry-shop windows to check the exact time, check the radio announcer, check the telephone service. They give you the gift of fear. . . .
>
> Death stands there in the background, but don't be afraid. Hold the watch down with one hand, take the stem in two fingers and rotate it smoothly. Now another installment of time opens, trees spread their leaves, boats run races, like a fan time continues filling with itself, and from that burgeon the air, the breezes of earth, the shadow of a woman, the sweet smell of bread.
>
> —*Cronopios and Famas*

Assumptions about identity are likewise undermined. The link between self and world is never fixed; it can be shifted or erased as the situation requires. A man reading a novel loses himself in the identity of a killer who is stalking through a house to kill a man who is reading a novel about a killer. . . . A woman crossing a bridge in a mist encounters a *Doppelgänger* coming from the other direction. And so on. Summarized like this, the stories may sound merely clever. But Cortázar is the most artful of storytellers. He knows how to set up improbabilities and how to pace them so that the reader is always at the edge of the possible.

In 1963, Cortázar published his landmark antinovel, *Hopscotch* (it appeared here in 1966). *The Winners,* his first novel, had come out three years before and been published in this country in 1965, but its impact had been minimal—and these days it reads like a dry run for *Hopscotch*. Success for the latter was instantaneous. Here was a book to demolish the myth of Latin American provinciality: Cortázar was outdoing the modernists at every turn. Indeed, the much-talked-up "boom" of the South American novel began with these pages; *One Hundred Years of Solitude* was still gestating.

Cosmopolitan and daring, *Hopscotch* defies categorization. Chapters and time sequences are broken up; we are invited to read in whatever order we please (a chart is provided for the less adventurous). The result is a remarkable essay in the provisionality of narrative and the inexhaustibility of telling. *Hopscotch* could be said to represent the application of the principles of cubism to the novel. Just as we know that in a cubist painting we are looking at a guitar, a bottle, and a tabletop, so we know that we are reading about Horacio Olveira's memory search for La Maga, the woman whose love he had betrayed and lost. But as we assemble and reassemble the planes of narrative—scenes from Paris and Buenos Aires, quotations and jottings, Olveira's complex writerly ruminations—we realize that we are also reading a tract on the hazards of intellectual hypertrophy, a parable about the relativity of madness and sanity, a treatise on the limits of language, and, not least, a slow blues for the mind on the theme of exile.

Fragmentation continued to fascinate Cortázar. After *Hopscotch* he published a maddening hall-of-mirrors text/novel entitled *62: A Model Kit* (1972). He was attempting a new reading of identity, an exploration of the possibility that we may, without being aware of it, form part of a constellation of other individuals—a constellation that, from a certain detached point of observation, has a life of its own. In *62: A Model Kit,* the life of a network of friends and acquaintances is presented without sequence, without plot, and without the tensions of narrative expectancy. It remains Cortázar's least accessible work.

In his last decade, Cortázar completed the whimsical, sporty prose of *A Certain Lucas* (1984), as well as two story collections. *A Change of Light* and *We Love Glenda So Much* have now been combined as a compendious paperback (1984); the two fit together perfectly. On the strength of this volume alone, Cortázar's place as a master of the genre is secure. The vision is intense, pure, and utterly singular; the Borges influence, still conspicuous in the early collections, has been absorbed and transformed.

The earlier stories were just a little too neat. The reversals were smooth, the surfaces refined, and when they ended it was with a click. But the open-form experiments of *Hopscotch* and *62: A Model Kit* obviously influenced Cortázar's conception of the short story as well. Here are fictions that dare to sustain ambiguity, plots that move—in the manner of late-period Henry James—among innuendos, that leave in their wake the most tantalizing ellipses and question marks.

In "Footsteps in the Footprints," Jorge Fraga sets out to write the biography of the elusive poet Claudio Romero. He tracks down every scrap of information, interviews a legion of relatives and associates—he even locates a few revealing letters that Romero wrote to his mistress. The biography is a coup, and Fraga is notified that he has been awarded the prestigious National Prize. But something starts to nag at him. He has an intuition that his telling is wrong, that there is more to the story. He returns to interview the daughter of the mistress a second time. And it turns out that, yes, there is another letter, a most compromising document. Fraga demands to see it. "While he watched her bending over the music case, going through papers, he thought that what he knew now he'd already known (in a different way, perhaps, but he'd known it) the day of his first visit. . . ." With this, the plot modulates to a new key, becomes a penetrating inquiry into conscious and unconscious motivation. What did Fraga *want* to know? Why? What has changed?

Fraga is finally compelled to torpedo his own career. At the awards ceremony, he delivers an "absolutely wild" version of the life. He is, of course, disgraced. And as the story ends, we find him lying awake in bed, debating his alternatives. He thinks about the pistol in his desk drawer; he thinks about retiring quietly to the country until the scandal blows over:

> It was all a matter of choosing. And even though he'd already decided, he still thought, just for something to think about, choosing and giving reasons for his choice until dawn began to brush against the window, against the hair of Ofelia asleep and the silk-cotton tree in the garden, imprecisely outlined like a future that

takes shape as present, hardens little by little, enters into its everyday form, accepts it and defends it and condemns it in the morning light.

Cortázar gradually developed a prose style that could move with confidence and discrimination among the murk of the interior life. The plots in these stories are saved from out-and-out improbability—and thereby rendered all the more unsettling—by the deftness with which event and perception of event are merged. "In the Name of Bobby," for instance, presents an aunt interrogating her young nephew about his terrifying dreams—dreams in which the mother keeps perpetrating unspecified cruelties. The boy is evasive. But then the aunt begins to notice his strange fixation: whenever he is in the kitchen he seems to be sneaking looks at a certain "long" cutting knife. She says nothing, and the story shifts among silences and unspoken surmises. The hot afternoons grow increasingly tense. And then—well, nothing dramatic happens; the knife is never "used." As we finish, however, we feel we've slipped in through the mesh of surfaces, into a dense precipitate of Oedipal confusions. The blade is more real and more menacing in the sharp focus of fantasy than in the hand.

The range of the twenty-eight stories in *A Change of Light* and *We Love Glenda So Much* is vast. Attenuated intimations are balanced by concretely plotted episodes; though Cortázar could not resist the lure of border zones, he was nonetheless acutely aware of the contours of our shared reality. Indeed, several of the more disturbing stories deal face-on with torture and political repression. Throughout his life, Cortázar distinguished himself as a tireless publicist for human rights and an outraged opponent of right-wing dictatorships in his hemisphere. Like so many writers of our time, he understood that exile is not an escape; it is, if anything, a condition of heightened responsibility.

An author's final book is invariably received by his readers as a kind of testament. How pleased we should be that Cortázar left us as charming and personal a work as *A Certain Lucas.* The book is brimming over with absurdist humor and razor-tipped *aperçus.* It's like a magician's hat packed between hard covers: every short chapter conjures another unexpected pink-eared rabbit. The unifying principle is simple—most of the sections relate in some oblique way to the life and thoughts of a certain Lucas (or a certain Julio). But unity hardly matters here. What does matter is the joy, the airy, associative romping of the sentences, the delightful holiday feeling we get as soon as we realize that syntax and logic are off playing hooky:

> In the center of the image are probably the geraniums, but there are also wisteria, summer, mate at five thirty, the sewing machine, slippers, and slow conversations about illnesses and family annoyances, a chicken suddenly leaving its calling card between two chairs or the cat after a dove that's way ahead of him.

Surrealism always appealed to Cortázar as did the droll "pataphysics" of Alfred Jarry and the escalating mayhem of the brothers Marx. Antic as the canvas may be, though, we cannot but notice two real eyes peering out from slits in the painted face. In a passage that has already become, through citation, a kind of unofficial epitaph, Cortázar—lifelong lover and player of jazz—wrote:

> At the hour of his death, if there is time and lucidity, Lucas will ask to hear two things: Mozart's last quintet and a certain piano solo on the theme of "I Ain't Got Nobody." If he feels that there won't be enough time, he'll only ask for the piano record. Long is the list, but he's already chosen. Out of the depths of time, Earl Hines will accompany him.

The rest, really, is a matter of black keys and white, and of black letters cakewalking down galleries of white paper.

The School of Gordon Lish

When I had my interview with Arnold Gingrich at Esquire *and he asked me what kind of fiction I was going to be publishing, I said, "The new fiction." He said, "What's that?" I said, "I'll get out there and find it, Mr. Gingrich."*

—Lish

Longtime readers of American fiction will probably have noticed certain changes in the product during the last few decades. A good deal of the gravity, scope, and narrative energy seems to have gone out of our prose. Formerly there were lives, fates. Now, increasingly, we greet disembodied characters who move about in a generic sort of present. Events on the page are dictated less by complex causes than by authorial fiat. While adherents of the poststructuralist disciplines may find this exalting and confirming, the "dear Reader" tacitly addressed by a more traditional ficton registers a growing despair.

The first signs of disturbance came during the late sixties, when writers like Donald Barthelme, Kurt Vonnegut, Robert Coover, John Barth, and E. L. Doctorow began to assault the narrative norms. Different as their subversions were—they included surreal disjunctions, the mixing of high and low genres, and the use of self-reflexive "metafictional" techniques—the end was the same: the sustaining pretenses of fiction were powerfully undermined. The influence of this attack was felt in every quarter; even professedly rearguard stylists found it ever more difficult to generate the necessary authority.

The spirit of playful subterfuge and interrogation vanished, however, along with the counterculture. In its place there appeared a deep unease. Fiction writers neither resumed the old ways nor went on with the dare of the new. In a climate of social instability, both the novel and the story drew in their wings. Raymond Carver, Ann Beattie, Frederick Barthelme, and others tried to forge a prose out of whatever had not been decimated by their predecessors. Rooting their work in an indefinite present, they refused to essay the creation of coherent fictional worlds. Their example caught on. Styles everywhere became numbly diaristic. Structures were collage derived. The episode, the paragraph, the sentence, the phrase were the new units of composition. The literary glamour of the seventies attached to the fragmented writings of Renata Adler and Joan Didion, and an army of epigones rose up to follow.

If fiction was once an empire on which the sun never set, it is no longer. Nowadays we rarely meet with a work that tries to bring a larger social context to life, or that explores with any conviction what it means to live in an era of broken connections. In this media culture, fiction seems no longer charged with the mirroring of reality. And yet words keep coming. A whole new generation of prose stylists advances behind the Barthelmes, Carvers, Adlers, and Beatties, a generation that studies the moves and devices of these "masters" as avidly as mid-century writers studied Hemingway, Faulkner, and Joyce.

In casting about for some way to give the new tendencies a habitation and a name, we might do worse than fix upon a particular office at the firm of Alfred A. Knopf, in which sits an energetic and outspoken editor named Gordon Lish. Lish is right now very much at the epicenter of American literary publishing. For one thing, he edits a fair number of "hot" young novelists and story writers. But there are his other activities as well. Lish has for years conducted highly selective fiction workshops in New York and elsewhere—not infrequently assisting his stars into print and into publishing careers. He has also launched a magazine, *The Quarterly,* which is subsidized and distributed through the Random House network. (The first issue appeared in the spring of 1987.) On top of all this, Lish is himself a determined practitioner of post-Carver fiction, with a story collection and two novels to his credit.

Lish's diversified enterprise, and his literary and practical influence, have drawn extremes of response. Nothing could have been more worshipful, for instance, than Amy Hempel's 1985 article in *Vanity Fair* ("Captain Fiction," it was called), which opened with this bold-faced blurb: "Gordon Lish is the Lee Strasberg of American fiction." Writing as a student and a published discovery of Lish's, Hempel fizzed exuberantly about his qualities as a teacher, dwelling upon his idiosyncrasy, his assertive candor, his engagement ("For thirteen weeks it is a class in which first Lish and then his students get the spirit and testify"), and not least, his willingness to perform extramural services for the deserving.

A more astringent view of this activity of discovery and promotion is to be found in Joe David Bellamy's essay "A Downpour of Literary Republicanism" in a recent issue of the *Mississippi Review* (1986). Bellamy suggests that Lish is in some ways as important as *The New Yorker.* Calling him a "cultural commissar" and identifying his aesthetic with Republican conservatism (for its interest in outer, documentary narrative, as opposed to inner, subjective experimentation), Bellamy concludes by goggling at the power that Lish commands: "possibly enough to make it rain if he wants it to rain."

Hempel has evidently passed too many mesmerized hours staring at her book contract, Bellamy too many brooding over his Saul Steinberg poster of New York; but surely some truth can be shaken out of both. Lish does command power. He has gone on from his early days of publishing and proselytizing for writers like Carver in *Esquire,* where he was fiction editor for eight years, to put together a distinctive, if not universally appealing, roster of talents for Knopf. His list includes

Anderson Ferrell, Barry Hannah, Hempel, Bette Howland, Janet Kauffman, Raymond Kennedy, Nancy Lemann, Michael Martone, Bette Pesetsky, Mary Robison, Leon Rooke. And he has abetted a career or two; a few years back, for instance, Lish secured a contract for his student Anderson Ferrell on the strength of a few paragraphs of prose.

Still, it's obviously foolish to think of the man as omnipotent. While he will extol the trust placed in him by Knopf's president, Robert Gottlieb—"No question," says Lish, "I am able to indulge my fantasies at the expense of a powerful organization"—he does have a tether. He has tried for years to put across one of his favorite stylists, Stanley G. Crawford, author of the novella *Log of the S.S. The Mrs. Unguentine,* without success. Nor could Lish be called capricious. Ferrell's short novel *Where She Was* (1985) is a sharply realized work of prose; it amply deserves to have been published. The issue, perhaps, is not so much that Lish can indulge his fantasies, but that so few other editors manage to do the same.

What finally makes Lish exceptional among editors is his devotion to the young. A photocopied announcement for *The Quarterly* advised that the magazine "is open to all comers, but will doubtless prove to be particularly hospitable to the work of the young and unsung." Lish is frank about his predilections and his agenda. "If I were given the option of publishing the fourth great work by author A," he states, "and the OK first book by author B, I would be inclined to go with the OK first book."

But he also admits to an ambition greater than just discovering the publishable young. Lish wants to find and train the next titleholder, the future Great American Novelist. He uses the analogy of a boxing coach: "I can tell you how to take the guy, though I can't do it myself." And the guy, the writer that Lish admires above all others and hence is determined to unseat, is . . . Harold Brodkey.

Harold Brodkey? Yes, emphatically. Lish admits no reservations to his adoration. Brodkey-love swamps every other subject of conversation, though Lish will, to be fair, also sing arias of praise for Cynthia Ozick and Don DeLillo. He is convinced, in part on the strength of published work, but especially by what he has read of the legendary (some would say too legendary) work in progress *A Party of Animals,* that Brodkey is the prose master of our century. He acknowledges, of course, the credibility problem that comes with declaring the preeminence of a novelist whose major work is still under wraps, but as he puts it, "The evidence is before me . . . and there it is."

Lish cites as the cardinal virtues of Brodkey's prose its intelligence, its moral seriousness, its relentlessness. He particularly admires what he sees as the author's willingness always to remake himself. "I don't think there's anyone who is coming onto the page so ferociously," he says. "I read Brodkey and I can't catch my breath." Brodkey presents, for Lish, in every way the opposite of the writing represented by Saul Bellow, whose fiction he derides as pretentious and predictable. Asked if anyone can challenge this Goliath, he smiles. "Somewhere out there is a young writer who has what it takes."

It's hard to get things square. Here we have Lish's testimony on behalf of Brodkey, a writer well along in his career, who is working with a perfectionist's resolve on a grand novel, refusing to publish before he's ready. There we have the example of Lish himself, editor and evangelist of the unsung, doing everything he can to get their young work in front of an audience, hoping that one of them will be the next Brodkey. But there is still a greater contradiction. Where Brodkey's prose aims at grandeur, at a dynamic totality that can embrace ideas, psychological motivations, moral and spiritual questioning, Lish's progeny come across almost without exception as purveyors of the slight and the fragmented. They are sculptors of sentences rather than worlds. Their hunt for essences bypasses existence. Ferocity is nowhere in evidence.

Of course Lish's authors are not all of a single stripe. Though they tend to youthfulness, and their productions to slimness—each one can be read in an evening—there seems to be little similarity between a book like Leon Rooke's *Shakespeare's Dog* (1983), which looks at the bard through the eyes of his randy and highly verbal dog, Mr. Hooker, and the pruned contemporaneity of a story collection by Mary Robison or Amy Hempel. And between these two poles we get the denser domestic portraits of Janet Kauffman and the airy biographical fantasies of Michael Martone. But underneath the variegated surface, behind the sentence-by-sentence expertise, are indications of what is either a new aesthetic or else a crisis in the art. Whichever it is, it has very little to do with Brodkey, Ozick, or DeLillo.

Joe David Bellamy's charge of "literary Republicanism" is misleading when applied to this group of writers. Doubtless Bellamy had Carver's fiction in mind when he coined the epithet. And while Carver's fidelity to grim middle- and lower-class exteriors, and to a tactic of unstated motivation, has been influential, things have changed since his heyday in the early seventies. Lish's writers take a much freer hand with subject matter, voice, and narrative exposition. And what has passed into their fiction, whether from Carver, Beattie, or the spirit of the time, is a total refusal of larger social connection. Indeed, in this respect, Lish's authors are only a case in point. Most of contemporary fiction is similarly skewed. Characters are shown as moving in contained worlds, alone, or with family, friends, and lovers. Everything beyond the local is alien chaos. The social fabric, once the complex and comprehensive subject of fiction, can no longer be found. Nor is there any attempt, as in the novels of Don DeLillo, to make a subject out of this very absence of social bonds. Among these writers a centripetal isolation prevails; the world never extends illusionistically beyond the cast assembled on the stage. This might explain why so many of these books are slight. The writers have shorn themselves, or they have been shorn of, a central resource.

Lish's own work is relevant here, for he preaches what he practices. The stories in his 1977 collection, *What I Know So Far,* progress by way of an anxious staccato, building their episodic structures along the fault lines of discontinuous speech patterns. The sentences capture the reader with their erratic and colloquial beat: "Alan Silver moved in. He moved in when there were seven houses and four still going up. He was twelve. Maybe I was nine by then. So that's the boys from two houses. The other five had boys in them too." They deny him, however, any kind of stable fictional order. Lish's novel *Dear Mr. Capote* (1983) worked similarly, though the subject matter was horrific: the colloquial jumps came out of the mouth of a demented serial killer. But *Peru* (1986), his most recent novel, achieves an eerie profundity absent from the other work. For Lish has finally matched his talky, nipped-off style to its ideal subject—the gradual recovery of a repressed childhood memory. The flat word-sounds and incessant repetitions eventually reveal the violent psyche of a lonely child. Needless to say, nothing exists beyond the recursive monody of the narrator's voice and the handful of images that it summons up. Lish, then, is the paradigmatic Lish author.

The others can be parceled into several roughly bounded camps. Mary Robison, Bette Pesetsky, and Amy Hempel would definitely fit together into one of these. They might be described as the main legatees of the Carver influence. Their collective muse owes a great deal to his opaque technique and his close-focus scene building. In their stories (though Robison and Pesetsky have written novels, their talents favor brevity) we encounter sudden, brightly lit tableaux animated by characters that have either been damaged into eccentricity or else scorched to blankness by the inchoate forces of modernity. Strange behavior and terrifying revelations are set before us in neutral, nonjudgmental tones. Scenes are generally given in the present tense, and all background has been carefully cut away. The reader's job, it appears, is to supply the excised humanity, to be shocked and stricken on behalf of the affectless.

In Mary Robison's "Weekday," from *Days* (1979), a divorced couple have a short reunion that is at once intimate and edged with hostility. As Christine, the ex-wife, cuts Guidry's hair—both have been swilling vodka all morning—we hear the following exchange:

> "I think you hang around with faggots," Guidry said.
>
> "Don't forget I'm cutting your hair. You could come out of this looking pretty funny."
>
> Guidry said, "I don't think you're taking your life seriously."
>
> "Probably not."
>
> "Not," Guidry said. "Just not. Your father died last year. Your daughter had her first period, which you don't even know about."
>
> "Michelle?" Christine said.
>
> "That's the one," Guidry said. "I had to send her up to Mom's. I know a little about it, but."
>
> "When?" Christine said.
>
> "A month ago."

"She's only ten."
"She's eleven."

The title piece of Bette Pesetsky's *Stories up to a Point* (1981), meanwhile, presents this give-and-take between husband and wife on the subject of their estranged daughter:

> My husband sits down at the breakfast table and slams the *Times* across the toaster. "If she ever calls," he declares, "if she ever calls, you are to hang up at once, do you hear?" "I will," I reply. "No, wait," he says. "Don't do that. Talk to her first. But coldly. Let her ask to come home or for money. Then tell her about her room. Tell her how I sold everything—her furniture, her pictures. Be sure and tell her how I burned her papers, her books, her clothes, and her record collection. Tell her that her room is now an upstairs den. Mention the console television in the corner. "She'll hate that." "I'll do just that," I say. "Swear it to me." "I swear," I say. "How do you want your toast?"

Finally, Amy Hempel's story "In the Cemetery Where Al Jolson Is Buried" moves from scene to scene by tracking the tough wisecracking between two friends, one of whom is dying in the hospital:

> She is flirting with the Good Doctor, who has just appeared. Unlike the Bad Doctor, who checks the IV drips before saying good morning, the Good Doctor says things like "God didn't give epileptics a fair shake." The Good Doctor awards himself points for the cripples he could have hit in the parking lot. Because the Good Doctor is a little in love with her, he says maybe a year. He pulls a chair up to her bed and suggests I might like to spend an hour on the beach.
>
> "Bring me something back," she says. "Anything from the beach. Or the gift shop. Taste is no object."
>
> He draws the curtains around her bed.
>
> "Wait!" she cries.
>
> I look in at her.
>
> "Anything," she says, "except a magazine subscription."

The doctor turns away.
I watch her mouth laugh.

Here we have a finger on one of the central pulses of contemporary fiction. This stuff is state of the art. The same tonality can be heard in thousands of stories coming out of workshops and writing programs. It is choking the pages of literary magazines as well as glossies. This manner is what results when talent and inexperience go out looking for subject matter. The cuttings above show three orders of tragedy—a lost marriage, a lost daughter, the imminent loss of life—and a single mode of response. In each case there is a displacement of crisis by repartee, an avoidance of human depths that a different sort of author would choose to plumb and to illuminate.

In the understated scenarios of Carver, who learned much from Hemingway, the unspoken or avoided material has a chance of reaching the reader. The opaque surfaces are designed to transmit suffering. Carver's characters do not reveal emotion, either because it overwhelms them or because muteness is seen as a talisman of resistance; but the reader does believe that somewhere, perhaps only in the author's heart, the real emotion existed, was felt. No chance of that here. The diction of Robison, Pesetsky, and Hempel ensures that we will remain unaffected. Everything genuine has been transposed into the key of the one-liner. We are to remark, rather, the disjunction between the presentation and what it buries, and so we do. But we can do nothing about it. We know that there is no payoff.

This prose has been styled to look "real." It vigorously mimes the banalities and discontinuities of ordinary speech. And yet, reading these stories, I am struck by nothing so much as their falsification of the grain of experience. These writers may owe some of their tricks to Carver, but their real antecedents are not literary at all. They're televised. The pace and pitch, the timing—everything has been deftly lifted from the screen, even from the prime-time sitcom. Not intentionally, I imagine. Still, listen in as you read. Do you hear human voices, or something closer to TV gabble? In certain passages I almost expect to hear the laugh track start up.

Fortunately, not all of the fiction, not even by younger writers, has been bent by these pressures. Within this same Knopf corral, a very different, and in some ways more salutary, approach has been taken by linguistically attuned stylists such as Barry Hannah and Leon Rooke. In their work we at least get the freshening pleasures of language and a feeling of anarchic sport. Their fiction does not derive from the imperatives of plot or character; it has its source in the rhythms and soundplay options of the sentence. Hannah, whom Lish credits with "more of an impact on how sentences get written all round than Raymond Carver," takes obvious delight in his ability to jump through hoops with a flourish. Opening his novel *Ray* (1980) quite at random, I find his amoral but tenderhearted doctor reminiscing as follows:

> One night, when I was in Saigon, a chicken colonel's wife walked past my Yamaha motorbike on the street. My eyes got wide and my heart was molasses. She walked by me, clicking her heels, tanned legs so lean, a fine joyful sense of her sex uplifted at the juncture of her thighs.

We see the craft and care of making, but only later, after we have siphoned up the pleasure.

And here is Rooke's Mr. Hooker, dilating on the charms of his beloved bitch, Marr:

> I have always liked her feet: the hobgoblin tufts of brightness growing up between the black pads like weeds through stone; the smooth nails that curve as little moons to reach points sharper than my own. Her deft ankles, too. The beauteous knees. She shook herself, then licked her upper thigh.

Hannah and Rooke are word men. Sprinters. Sentence acrobats. They can peg to a millimeter a physical sensation. They can start a rumble between clauses, if they've a mind to. This is what we turn to them for. And this is their limit. No use looking for excavated depths of character or immersions in plot. As in the stories of Robison and company, lives are caught midflight. The past is alluded to randomly, in fragments, if at all. What keeps us going in Robison's work are the promises of incongruous surprise and the blandishments of paradox. (Meager fare, I'd say.) With Hannah and Rooke, it's the velocity of the prose, and the flash that comes when word sounds touch and ignite in the ear.

Two novellas of the Lish school, Ferrell's *Where She Was* and Kauffman's *Collaborators* (1986), come slightly closer to rewarding conventional expectations. Each undertakes, in its way, to develop a character portrait through a succession of carefully placed vignettes. Again, there is nothing so overt as plot. *Collaborators,* the more successful of the two, reveals to us the complex, yet distinct, stages of a mother-daughter relationship. A tragic event is at the root—the mother has a disabling stroke midway through the book—and Kauffman meets the emotional demands squarely. The mother's efforts to recover speech and motor skills press sharply on the daughter's maturing sensibility:

> She pointed at the ground, saying, Dare, dare, or There, there.
>
> What is it?
>
> There! she said.
>
> In the ditch at the edge of the field was a groundhog hole. That's all I could see.
>
> That? You mean that groundhog hole?
>
> Yes! Her face was red with the explosive sounds of the word.

Kauffman's novel is set, for the most part, on a tobacco farm in Pennsylvania. Ferrell's *Where She Was* is also located, interestingly enough, in tobacco country. The focus, however, is much less on relationships. Ferrell is after a more solemnly mythic, a more truly existential, portrayal. His Cleo Lewis, a hardworking mother and wife, is full of inarticulate longings. In the face of these, the husband and children appear peripheral. But she does not know what she longs for. When local churches and preachers fail her, she succumbs to the call of a mysterious drifter.

Though Ferrell tends to overwrite in places, to layer atmospheric effects with a loaded brush, he does at times achieve a genuine force. Building periodic rhythms account for much of the effect:

> They walked through the forest. The trees began to be farther apart and taller. Cleo smelled creek water. It was as if the smell came from his hair and blew around her, a cool smell, a smell so strong Cleo could feel it against the back of her throat, a damp, rich smell as rank as the dirt—a smell that would grow things.

How different from this is Nancy Lemann's light-handed conjuring of New Orleans in *Lives of the Saints* (1985). Where Ferrell is dense and portentous, Lemann is nimble and casual seeming. The ghost of a story—no more—emerges from the vignettes she convokes. A young woman, Louise, is in love with a gallant and eccentric ne'er-do-well named Claude. He moves in and out of her sights, mostly against an impressionistically dabbed backdrop of New Orleans. Louise's voice trips erratically through the vast registers of love, coaxing, denying, breaking down in admission:

> Yankee girls probably sat around having philosophically inquiring conversations about the meaning of art. But Claude would never talk about serious things. He was always too busy making lamebrained jokes or talking about the small things. He would probably tell them that the dress they were wearing reminded him of some huge thing—all he wanted to do was plummet to the depths of factuality about what you were doing at that exact moment, and what you were really like. He was just a simple, dark-haired Tareyton smoker, completely wry.
>
> My heart was not trained to love anyone but him.

This, then, is Lish's squadron, most of it. The writers are, as I say, outwardly various enough. But from a certain angle, taking a tight noon-hour squint, one can discern a common style. It is all very modern, or postmodern. The byte-sized perceptions, set in an eternal present, are the natural effluence of an electronically connected, stimulus-saturated culture. In a sense, they are what we have earned for ourselves: these writers may satisfy themselves that they have, intentionally or not, mirrored our world to us, mimicked the sensations of contemporary experience. Still, in another sense, their work represents an abrogation of literary responsibility. If fiction is to survive as something more than a coterie sport, it must venture something greater than a passive reflection of fragmentation and unease. Indeed, it must manifest some of the very qualities that Lish has attributed to the work of Harold Brodkey: intelligence, moral seriousness, and relentlessness. And, I would add, comprehensiveness and scope.

I am not calling for a curmudgeonly return to the tradition of the nineteenth-century narrative. Far from it. The modernist revolution in the early part of the century left the writer with an arsenal of new devices and modes—interior monologue, shifting narrators, collage, and temporal modulation, to name but a few—as well as a high injunction: to dare a prose that can face chaos and master it with vision. Woolf, Joyce, Lawrence, Faulkner, Musil, Broch, Kafka—these artists did not finish off fiction; they opened new sluices for it. And in our own time American novelists like Pynchon, Bellow, and Percy have carried on the hard task of probing our place in the turbulent cultural present. All three have managed to keep their focus wide and their grasp on the particular steady. Not one of them has fallen back upon convention for its own sake.

Of course these are all masters in late career. Theirs will not be the shaping voices of the coming decades. It will fall to the younger authors, Lish's among them, to bring the world over into words. But this will not be possible without more exertion and more willingness to risk than many young writers have shown. The careful construction of sentences and paragraphs is a first step, not a final goal. The world of the future is bound to be more dispersed and more synthetic than it is now. There is a real danger, then, that reality will outstrip the writer's ability—if expression fails, understanding fails too. It is necessary to believe, with Gordon Lish, that there is undiscovered greatness in the young. But it is hard to rest easy with the growing cult of small-stage pyrotechnics. The impending challenges are of a different magnitude.

Docu-fiction

In 1917, Marcel Duchamp submitted to the world his *Readymade Fountain,* which, as any student of art history can tell you, was a porcelain urinal mounted on a pedestal. He took an object that was fairly dripping with prosaic—no, low—associations and subjected it to the cleansing context of the aesthetic. His act of framing made the point that the art was not in the thing, but in the *perception* of the thing. Mostly, though, he was tweaking the nose of the bourgeois museum-goer. So coolly skeptical a man would not have believed, surely, that he would revolutionize our way of looking at the world. The tyranny of daily life and daily perception are all but absolute. Everyone knows that. Art remains, at best, a sequestered order we escape to when we can.

Still, Duchamp's gesture has become a point of reference for all serious visual artists who have come along since. And insofar as their work manifests something of his conception, it continues to move through the bloodstream of the culture. Progress in the arts (if indeed it *is* progress and not just change) has always come about as the result of pressures and protests against the constraints of genre.

The novel, too, has been subjected in our age to one attempted renovation after another. Shaping subversions have ranged from stream-of-consciousness narration, which came to stay, to the collage cutup experiments carried out by William Burroughs, which may never be assimilated. Whatever their thrust, though, most of the moves were made with open reference to the reigning norm—they went against it.

Conceptually speaking, it may have been middlebrow novelist Truman Capote who carried out the most threatening assault—a coup d'état from within. In 1965, Capote began to publish installments of his eventual bestseller *In Cold Blood* in the pages of *The New Yorker*. The material itself was straight tabloid stuff—an account of the savage slaughter of a Kansas farm family by two ex-convicts. What was different was that Capote set out his documentary sequences much as a novelist would have, staging scenes for dramatic tension, even going so far as to work up a structure of parallel narratives. But the real shocker came when the book was published: Capote had the temerity to bill *In Cold Blood* as a "nonfiction novel."

This may not seem very significant. Who cares, finally, what an infamous party-boy writer decides to call his book? Apparently, though, it was just the signal that a whole army of journalists had been awaiting. Overnight—almost literally, to hear Tom Wolfe tell it—the New Journalism was born. Wolfe, Jimmy Breslin, Gay Talese, Hunter Thompson, George Plimpton, Terry Southern, Joan Didion, and countless others began churning out a prose that felt entirely fresh. Nonfiction writers had fallen in love with the devices of fiction.

Magazine journalism has not been the same since. You cannot find a feature article in the popular press that does not make use of some, if not all, of the techniques that Wolfe enumerated in his canon-making anthology, *The New Journalism* (1973): scene-by-scene construction, realistic dialogue, third-person point of view ("presenting every scene to the reader through the eyes of a particular character"), and the precise recording of "significant" details. A formerly cut-and-dried mode has become a vital, exciting genre.

I am less sanguine, however, about the impact of Capote's framing maneuver on the so-called serious novel. What he instigated, Norman Mailer quickly turned to his own ends. *The Armies of the Night* (1968), Mailer's account of the 1967 march on the Pentagon (and his own prominent participation in it), was subtitled *History as a Novel, the Novel as History*. Then, a decade later, after a number of similar exercises in cross-dressing—*Of a Fire on the Moon* (1970) and *Marilyn* (1973) among them—he brought out his enormous "true-life novel," *The Executioner's Song* (1979), which detailed the criminal career of convicted murderer Gary Gilmore. More than simple nomenclature is at issue—the conflation of genres ultimately threatens the status of both fact and fiction.

Wolfe writes as follows of the docu-fiction procedure:

> It consumes devices that happen to have originated with the novel and mixes them with every other device known to prose. All the while, quite beyond matters of technique, it enjoys an advantage so obvious, so built-in, one almost forgets what a power it has: the simple fact that the reader knows *all this actually happened.* The disclaimers have been erased. The screen is gone. The writer is one step closer to the absolute involvement of the reader that Henry James and James Joyce dreamed of and never achieved.

Wolfe has always enjoyed floating helium-filled assertions toward his readers, but his optimistic burbling here has an almost born-again vapidness about it. Facts are stranger and more involving than invented things, he says, so let's just report the facts and make great literature. Wolfe is essentially ignoring the whole history of Western art. Was it out of sheer blindness—an inability to see the forest for the trees—that man set out to render the world as *other* than what he saw? Hardly. Art (fiction included) came into being precisely because no accounting of the real facts, no matter how expertly done, could ever be enough. Long before Socrates, the perceptive understood that facts were facts, and that truth was what they *meant*. Meaning only begins when the contingent circumstances have been stripped away. And fiction moves in the realm of meaning—it is the afterlife of facts.

The "nonfiction novel" is an oxymoronic phrase and a moronic idea. The etymologist would ban language altogether before allowing it. "Fiction" comes to us from the Latin: *fingere*, "to feign." A novel, meanwhile, is defined in the Oxford dictionary as "a fictitious prose narrative of considerable length." Neither Capote nor Mailer had any trouble with that last stricture—*The Executioner's Song* breaks the thousand-page barrier—but if we trust that words still mean things, then what these authors claim to be offering are nonfictional fictions, or unfeigned feignings.

Just where does the fiction come in? If the events really took place, then the feigning must consist in giving them narrative form, in the excerpting and arranging. But then virtually all written works, histories and biographies in particular, would have to be classed as so many different kinds of novel. What are histories or biographies but judicious orderings of selected bits of information? The logical extension of this would be to say that *all* human information exchange is selective, and therefore fictional. Doubtless there is a grain of truth here, but it is not enough. Indeed, the moment at which everything becomes provisionally fictive is also the moment when we have to let go of the idea of fact. And without that idea, fiction itself becomes a meaningless concept. When you start thinking like this, you are in grave danger of becoming a deconstructionist. Deconstructionists deem all meaning indeterminate, all discourses suspect, and would like nothing better than to boil all separate disciplines and genres down into one primal soup.

My point is this: that real life has always outdone fiction in inventiveness, in twists of irony and sensationalistic flourishes. And the novelist has always known it. His ancient motto—*primum vivere, deinde scribere*—attests to his willingness to study and learn. In his terrible pride, however, he has invested his art with the prestige of higher truth. Something that *may* have happened but didn't is seen as having superior value, for by not being tethered to factual surface, the writer can attribute consciousness and volition to his creations. He is thereby free to explore the ways in which real-life circumstances might come to have human meaning.

The docu-novelist's claim that "all this actually happened" effectively replaces the imaginative creation of character and situation. Remove the claim and the reader has nothing to feed on. If *In Cold Blood* or *The Executioner's Song* had been *made up,* their artistic impact would have been negligible. By recording sequences of real events and saying "Look, they make a story," Capote and Mailer were not making art so much as they were celebrating an artistic perception. This, I think, is what their use of the word "novel" really signaled. We come back to Duchamp. If he had actually *created* a urinal, he would have been reviled for debasing the artistic function. By calling it readymade—which caused furor enough—he could be received as a conceptual revolutionary.

The showcasing of real-life events in a fictional frame does not, finally, enlarge the genre. Rather, it weakens both the event and the art. For art and life, fiction and fact, stand in an eternal face-off. "We have art," said Nietzsche, "that we may not perish of the truth." The truth he referred to was that of an unanchored, godless existence. But if we think of it differently—truth as deeper meaning—then we can twist his formulation to read: we have truth that we may not perish of the facts. To bring the raw materials of life directly into the sphere of art leaches off something of their obdurate otherness. Bring enough real life into art and you will have real life everywhere you look. Is this what we want? Oscar Wilde, that old artificer, knew what the game was about as early as 1891. He wrote the following in his dialogue *The Decay of Lying:*

> Art begins with abstract decoration with purely imaginative and pleasurable work dealing with what is unreal and non-existent. . . . Then life becomes fascinated with this new wonder and asks to be admitted into the charmed circle. Art takes life as part of her rough material, recreates it, and refashions it in fresh forms, is absolutely indifferent to fact, invents, imagines, dreams, and

keeps between herself and reality the impenetrable barrier of beautiful style, of decorative or ideal treatment. The third stage is when Life gets the upper hand, and drives Art out into the wilderness. This is the true decadence, and it is from this that we are now suffering.

PART IV

Critics and Thinkers

Erich Heller
(1911—)
Walter Benjamin
(1892–1940)
Cyril Connolly
(1903–1974)
George Steiner
(1929—)
Eugenio Montale
(1896–1981)
Roger Shattuck
(1923—)

Critics and thinkers. They are at once a part of the labyrinth and spinners of the thread that would guide us through it. They are all, without exception, preoccupied with the collapse in our age of the certainties of civilization. Though they write out of, and about, different language-cultures, their bearing is universal.

These writers share a determination to uncover the sources of our crisis and to point a way forward. To some degree, that way must connect us with the past. This recognition makes them conservators, humanists. Their effort has been, and continues to be, heroic. These essays assemble the perspectives that have most stimulated and influenced my thinking.

The roots of the collapse extend far into the past. Nietzsche's announcement of the death of God at the end of the nineteenth century was a culmination of distress, not a beginning. Erich Heller looks to the preceding century, to Goethe—poet and scientist—and finds the fissure that will become the deadly rift between the organic and analytic approaches to experience. He traces the progressive stages of our disinheritance through the works of key nineteenth- and twentieth-century German writers.

Roger Shattuck obeys a similar impulse in making his assessment of twentieth-century French culture, but he goes back to the distinction drawn by Pascal between l'esprit de finesse *and* l'esprit de géométrie. *His search for a possible ground of synthesis leads him to figures as diverse as Valéry, Monet, and Apollinaire.*

The responses of the other essayists testify not only to their temperamental differences, but also to the complex realities of the condition. In critics like Walter Benjamin and Eugenio Montale, despair and faith are almost inextricably intertwined. Their interpretations of decline are alloyed by a profound belief in the cultural inheritance.

The contrast between Cyril Connolly and George Steiner raises a central question. Where Connolly, in many ways the ultimate aesthete, sought the salvation of culture in works of artistic purity, Steiner questions if the refinements of Western civilization might not have been bought at a price—the atrophy of our human instincts. The men who stoked the crematoria, he reminds us, came home at night to their Beethoven and Goethe. But even in his anguished interrogations, Steiner does not turn his back on humanism. Like the other critics, he would find out where it failed, and why.

Erich Heller

The background to my writing is the political and cultural catastrophes of this century, and my attachment to things overtaken by them. My aims: to preserve the memory of the things I love, to be truthful to them and therefore to write as well about them as I can.

—HELLER

By general consensus we live in something called the Age of Criticism. Yet put to the test, whom would we tick off as our outstanding critics—whom could we find to set beside, say, Edmund Wilson, Randall Jarrell, or T. S. Eliot? The question is, of course, deceptively posed. For when we say "Age of Criticism" we mean one thing—by "critic" we mean quite another. The former is a catchall epithet for a pervasive cultural bias toward reductionist thinking and academic specialization; it implies a truth criterion bounded by the empirical ideal of the sciences. When we speak of a critic, however, we still hearken to a more general, and genial, image. A critic is expected to be a broker between realms of the imagination and the culture at large; he is to proctor values. If we have so few outstanding critics nowadays, it's because the job has become almost impossible to perform. The culture is too diffuse, and drastic changes and accelerations in the social sphere have made value determination hopelessly relativistic. For a critic to *presume*—and what good is a critic who does not?—he must have, besides erudition and intuition, a confidence that verges on hubris. It is far more difficult to be a generalist than a specialist.

I don't intend here to puzzle over names and reputations or to make lists—except to say that any list, long or short, would be incomplete if it did not include Erich Heller. *Erich Heller?* I anticipate a certain surprise on the reader's part. Heller does not have a wide popular renown, nor would it seem, on the surface of it, that he has any truck with the general. His are the appurtenances of the specialist: he is a professor, a scholar; his writings, almost without exception, treat of thorny topics in German letters. I admit, Heller makes it onto my list through the back door.

Born in Bohemia in 1911, educated in Prague and Cambridge, England, Heller is, like Auerbach and Curtius, one of those rare broadly civilized scholars—he opens wide the scope of whatever subject he fastens upon. Not that he has restricted himself unduly. The whole of German literature and thought is within his empery; he writes with equal clarity and penetration about Goethe, Nietzsche, Kafka, Mann, Spengler, and Wittgenstein, to name a few. But even this substantial territory is expanded by his approach. For if there is a single premise behind his work, it is that an understanding of German culture is essential to an understanding of *all* modern culture, that otherwise we cannot hope to grasp the nature of the crisis of values that increasingly afflicts us. Why German culture? Apart from its astonishing contribution to literature, science, philosophy, and psychology in our time, it may be, for mysterious linguistic reasons, a barometer of our spiritual climate. As Heller (who writes in English) puts it:

> A sober view of the matter may well be that modern German, having become a literary idiom later than French or English, is an adolescent language, malleable and ready to manifest the inarticu-

> late, which lies buried beneath all languages, within its articulations. It is easily seduced by genius, idiot or villain. Of course no language is immune from the mendacity of rhetoric and pretentiousness, but German has the lowest resistance. No translations of Hitler's oratory, alas, could convey the resonance of hell in it (had it been otherwise, perhaps the resistance of the world might have come earlier and at less cost). And if, to pass from the base to the sublime, all great lyric poetry can only be approximated in translation, Hölderlin's is nearly unapproachable; and this is so largely because he is a German poet.

The passage comes from Heller's most recent collection of essays, *In the Age of Prose* (1984), but it could as well have been taken from any of his other books. Indeed, the organic consistency of his work is such that an isolated review of a single book would be unenlightening: it would be like trying to study a tree by taking hold of its outermost branches. No, Heller's has been, from the first, a sustained enterprise, and one ought to treat him as he unfailingly treats his subjects—with a view to the whole development.

"Ah, the old questions," exclaims Hamm in *Endgame,* "there's nothing like them!" This might serve, as well, as a motto for Heller. If he comes across in all the grand diversity of his work as a hedgehog (and he does call himself that, citing Archilochus' maxim "The fox knows many things, but the hedgehog knows one big thing"), it is because he is singlemindedly concerned with the meaning of the intransitive verb "to be." He is a man on an ontological mission. This, more than anything, sets him apart from most other critics of our day. He wants to understand. And though he hardly ever declares himself on the page—he prefers a stance that might be characterized as passionate self-effacement—we feel his compulsion clearly. Here, in a paragraph about Goethe and Darwin, Heller gives us a glimpse of his own critical program:

> Willingly or unwillingly, Darwin had to give still greater force to that system of unsystematized, inarticulate metaphysical fallacies which one might term the Creed of the Ontological Invalidity;

> both in the sense that it dismisses *a priori* as invalid all . . . assertions about the nature and meaning of Being . . . as well as in the sense that it has made an incurable invalid of that faculty of the human intelligence which . . . is capable of responding positively to questions asked about *what* the world is. To such questions the modern intelligence is prone to respond with a mixture of shame, embarrassment, revulsion and arrogance which is the characteristic reaction of impotence to unfortunately unmanageable demands.

Needless to say, Heller repudiates that creed.

Were this not enough to separate him from the academic herd—as naturally it is—his unapologetically biographical approach would clinch the matter. Heller insists upon the flesh-and-blood reality of the writer, as well as the particulars of time, place, and circumstance. The text is, of course, sovereign, but it is so by virtue of the artist's transformation of his material, not because of some preconceived critical dogma. That material is nevertheless of compelling interest—for it is only by studying *how* it has been transformed that the critic can make his full assessment. A complete separation between writer and text (I shall touch on this later) would make Heidegger's complicity with the Nazis irrelevant to the philosophy; Heller declares, in no uncertain terms, that this is a most appalling evasion of truth. The lives behind the letters matter supremely. And from the fullness of his presentations, we know that Heller has taken in everything by and about his subjects. Rilke, Nietzsche, Hegel, Kafka, Mann (Heller has written separate books on these last two), among others, come across with a rare dimensionality. They are perceived simultaneously as unique individuals *and* as agents in the larger life of their culture. With no one is this more evident than with Goethe. He is the keystone, the origin and moral terminus, of Heller's *oeuvre*.

The Sage of Weimar has not traveled well into English, either in terms of translated texts—which read more like paraphrase, especially the poetry—or of general image. The popular conception of Goethe is of a pompous, self-regarding bore, and little has been done to reverse it. T. S. Eliot's essay demoting Goethe to the lower slopes of Parnassus is much better known than his later retraction. What portraits we have—most notably Tischbein's—show a proud, forbidding countenance. We see Literature with a capital *L* and we shy. Heller's essays on Goethe, while they do not campaign actively for a revisionist picture, do set up fresh perspective and give us a better idea about why the Germans revere him above all other mortals. The essay "Goethe and the Idea of Scientific Truth" (in *The Disinherited Mind,* 1952), in particular, ruffles our image of the serene Olympian. We see, perhaps for the first time, the enormous range of his interests and abilities, and get a sense of the powerful inner contradictions that underlay that range.

Heller begins with a carefully culled bit of biography: Goethe, forty-five years old, out of sorts with himself—torn by the conflicting claims of poetry and scientific interest—bitter about the literary tendencies of the times, attends a meeting of naturalists in Jena. (The year is 1794.) Also present is Schiller, whose celebrated play *The Robbers* has disgusted Goethe: "because it poured out over the country, in a gushing, irresistible torrent, precisely those moral and theatrical paradoxes which I had striven to eradicate from my own work." As chance would have it, the two meet at the exit and begin conversing.

"In no time at all," writes Heller, "their conversation had reached the crucial point." Working from Goethe's accounts, he reconstructs the scene, and locates the crux of their disagreement, the roots of which go back into Kantian philosophy. The issue is not just literary. Goethe, explaining to Schiller his ideas on plant metamorphosis, persists in equating experiences and ideas. Schiller maintains that the two are very different: the symbolic plant that Goethe has been describing cannot possibly exist in nature. Goethe restrains his anger, the dispute remains civil. But later he notes: "If he takes for an idea what to me is experience, then there must, after all, prevail some mediation, some relationship between the two."

Heller does not go on to complete the story of what soon will become one of the most celebrated friendships in the annals of literature. Instead, he breaks off, taking up the history of Goethe's scientific researches. "Palermo, April 17th, 1787"—Goethe is traveling in Italy, observing nature; he suddenly experiences an overwhelming desire to verify his intuition: that a prototype plant—an *Urpflanze*—

actually exists. If he could find it he would be able to demonstrate to one and all that there is a principle of transformation whereby every plant attains its unique shape. He could then prove that the diversity of the plant world is a result of the varied responses of this *Urpflanze* to restrictions or advantages conferred by climate, soil, etc. Goethe writes to Herder that same year that he is "very close to discovering the secret of the creation and organization of plants." His optimism, scientifically speaking, is a bit premature.

Goethe's idea, is, in some respects, an anticipation of Darwin's principle of natural selection. But there are differences. As Heller remarks: "This responsiveness . . . is not a mere giving in to external influences, it is rather like a creative conversation between within and without, a kind of dialectical education through which the individual form becomes in actuality what from the very beginning it had been potentially."

With this idea of a "creative conversation" we are very near to the central problem—if it is a problem—of Goethe's science. For in this research, as elsewhere—his *Theory of Colors,* for example—Goethe insisted, against all of the precepts of materialist science, that nature was animate and purposeful. His theories, by our criteria, are all fanciful, "poetic," and wrong. And Heller could easily have left matters at that. His chapter would stand as a fascinating excursus along one of the byways of the scientific imagination. Typically, though, he chooses to raise the discussion to a higher level. Might not Goethe's convictions, he asks, have some relevance to our time? Soon the most vexing "larger" questions are brought into the light.

Heller is not cowed by the sanctities of the empirical world view. There are perspectives, he claims, from which our sciences appear to be just another mode of imaginative organization:

> But it is not only this exuberant dance of scientific hypotheses which is revealed by Goethe's history of science. What, above all, emerges most clearly is the fact that every scientific theory is but the surface rationalization of a metaphysical substratum of beliefs, conscious or unconscious, about the nature of the world. . . . The totems and taboos of the savages, the pyramids of Egypt, the

> Acropolis of Athens, the cathedral of Chartres *pragmatically* prove as much, or as little, of the ultimate nature of reality as any scientific experiment. It is indeed amazing how malleable the world is and how easily it models and remodels itself according to the inner vision of man, how readily it responds to his "theorizing"!

It is possible, then, to see the Goethean endeavor in another light. If we grant the relativity of truths, then we must shift our interrogation to a moral plane: what is the *best* truth for man? And this, Heller believes, was the underlying impulse of Goethe's thought, the key to his greatness. He had no use for a knowledge that would only cause man "to fret away his days in the narrowest and most joyless limitation."

Goethe's concern about the human impulse for knowledge and truth (two very different things) found its ultimate expression in *Faust*. It is, for Heller, the central myth for our times. Faust, in love with knowledge, lacking any sense of limit, bartering his soul away to the Devil in spite of the certainty of damnation, is the very image of modern man. His hubris is ours. But Goethe's version, in Heller's view, is not the cautionary tale, the *tragedy,* that it ought to be. His Faust is redeemed, as other Fausts (the original, Marlowe's, Mann's) are not, in order to teach "the insatiable Speculators his morality of knowledge." In "Faust's Damnation" (*The Artist's Journey into the Interior,* 1965) and "Goethe and Tragedy" (*The Disinherited Mind,* 1952), Heller searches for the sources of this redeeming urge.

Faust ends as it does, he believes, with its hero saved from the Devil's clutches, because Goethe was constitutionally incapable of writing tragedy. He worked on the play throughout his life without finding a satisfactory, unambiguous resolution: he could not bring his subject in line with the needs of his own character. "Nature is fundamentally innocent," writes Heller, "and Goethe's genius was in communion with Nature." Tragedy requires a vision of evil that Goethe simply did not have. He saved Faust because it was Nature itself that was in the soul:

> What is Faust's sin? Restlessness of spirit. What is Faust's salvation? Restlessness of spirit. . . . What the heavenly powers mean

> by that striving which carries its own salvation must surely be different from the striving the goal of which Faust hopes to achieve with the help of black magic and the Devil.

Heller's great admiration for Goethe in no way blinds him to the inconsistencies at the heart of his masterwork. And his skillful disentangling of distinctions bears importantly on the question of whether modern Faust, with all his striving after mastery of the cosmos, will or will not be rescued.

Goethe, in his inconsistency and dividedness, as well as in his will to wholeness, is crucial to Heller's project. He is the harbinger of crisis, the representative man who carries within the tensions and contradictions of his time; he is also, by virtue of his balance, sanity, and faith, the last German writer to live in essential concord with his world. The larger part of Heller's work deals with the progressive dissolution of Goethean harmony and examines how this dissolution afflicted the writers and thinkers who followed. There is urgency in these investigations—Heller's own soul, we sense, is very much implicated.

The Disinherited Mind takes its title from Rilke: "Each torpid turn of the world has such disinherited children . . ." What is it in time, or history, or the destiny of the race that creates in us a growing sense of displacement, or, to use Heidegger's word, "unhousedness" (*Heimatlosigheit*)? Heller finds one kind of explanation in the philosophy of Hegel: that Spirit, or *Geist,* that grand and all-but-indefinable entity that moves over and through human history, is proceeding, through its own obscure necessity, toward fulfillment in itself. That is, this Spirit is steadily withdrawing from its commerce with the material realm, into self-contained inwardness. Heller is well aware of the Germanic abstruseness of the concept (at one point he quotes Nietzsche's *mot,* that Hegel had "the art of speaking about the soberest things in the manner of a drunk"), but he nonetheless exerts himself to render it as intelligible as possible. Abstract and elusive though it may be, it pertains figuratively, if not otherwise, to this ontological crisis.

Heller's long essay "The Artist's Journey into the Interior" is a *tour de force* of explication. Economical, focused, it puts Hegel's idea to work in a broad context. Beginning with the philosopher's own ideas about Greek sculpture, Heller moves on to survey changing styles in painting, the linguistic self-consciousness of *Hamlet,* and finally, the *Duino Elegies* of Rilke; at every point he maps the widening rift between spirit and matter.

For Hegel, Greek sculpture of the classical period was the first and only instance of spirit and matter in a state of perfect accord. The Greek sculptors created the human figure not out of any cunning of mind, but thoughtlessly, out of the fullness of their being. "Here," writes Heller, "what is ugly, repugnant and oppressive about the body—the body that was soon to become the deplorable prison cell of the soul—is not prudishly glossed over or sentimentally denied; it is truly extinguished." The marriage of elements was destined to be short-lived. Spirit would soon give up its free mingling with the sensuous and take the first steps toward its appointed destination. Heller remarks the palpable traces of its movement:

> He who happens to travel from the temples of Greece to the churches of France can almost follow the course of this retreat with his own eyes. To strain one's sight . . . in the holy dusk of the Lord's residences across the Auvergne . . . then to recall the sanctuary of Aegina, visited only a few days past, is like tracking the Hegelian spirit from its marble pasture under the open skies to its secret lair enclosed by stone—the very stone which, in its turn, falls victim to the most astonishing campaign ever conducted by the Spirit against the native heaviness of matter. These ribbed vaults and pointed arches, these clustered columns, ogives, spurs, and buttresses, these pinnacles and traceries, these vast roses and panels of glass—they all conspire, in Vezelay, Bourges, Chartres, or Saint-Chapelle of Paris, to break and transform the massive masonry into the inner soul's essays at casting off the rocky weight. . . .

And as we read it seems that we have, for a moment, caught hold—if not logically then with our inward sight—of this improbable processional.

Heller is keen and discriminating in his discussions of painting and sculpture—his pages on the *Arnolfini* portrait by van Eyck should be required reading for art historians—but the play of ideas reaches its finest pitch when he discusses Rilke. For the *Duino Elegies* fulfill and express the Hegelian prophecy to the letter. There Rilke works out his grand idea of the redemption of the world through inwardness: "Nowhere, my love, will be world but within"; "Earth, isn't this what you want: an invisible/re-arising in us?" It is as if Hegel himself had come back to recast his thought in lyric form.

Heller tracks the complex, slow maturation of Rilke's poetry in four different essays—it is obviously a matter of some compulsion for him. And time and again he returns to examine the dramatic reversal in midcareer: just a few years before the sudden inspiration of the *Elegies,* Rilke was immersed in the writing of his so-called "thing poems"; poems like the celebrated "Panther," in which he tried to extinguish all inwardness in a pure identification with creatures and objects outside himself. As late as 1908, four years before the first of the *Elegies,* Rilke wrote a "Requiem" for a young friend who had committed suicide. Its import was that a greater attention to the material order could perhaps have saved him. Heller writes:

> In the *Duino Elegies* saviour and saved have, in a most drastic maneuver of reversal, changed parts: no longer is it the visible things that save the unquiet inner spirit by granting it a refuge in their unshakable "objectivity"; on the contrary, it is the invisible spirit that redeems the visible world threatened with destruction.

By "destruction" Rilke does not mean actual annihilation; he means the surrender of that world through the loss of meaning. One of his main themes is the gradual alienation of man from his surroundings and its reflection in linguistic insubstantiality—almost as if Hegel's withdrawal of Spirit meant, for him, the attenuation of the language bond. Words like "House, Bridge, Fountain, Gate, Jug, Olive Tree, Window" no longer carry their designated meaning. They still *refer,* but that Adamic spirit—which has always been their real content—has been worn away. The only possible reclamation (and here we find resemblances to Nietzsche's program of self-transcendence) is though the performance of "heart-work." Man must strive to somehow take into himself the things of the world, to imbue them with meaning. Henceforth it will be in the soul—invisibly—and not in the open air, that the world will have its real being. What prompted such an about-face in Rilke's attitude remains largely obscure.

What Hegel saw as the progressive march of Spirit, Nietzsche perceived in very different terms. It was his burden and, perhaps, mission to suffer through his being the implications of "the death of God." Where Hegel's Spirit was an autonomous entity, Nietzsche's God was not; man had killed Him. And on the heels of this murder came the crisis of values. Nietzsche's thought, for Heller, straddles a century and a half of cultural life. The crisis was there before he named it and it continues today, eighty-some years after his death. A look at the titles of the Nietzsche essays is instructive: "Nietzsche and Goethe," "Burckhardt and Nietzsche," "Rilke and Nietzsche," and "Wittgenstein and Nietzsche." In every case, Heller finds, there are important affinities. How is man to live without faith in a transcendent God; how is he to face the terrible emptiness? For Goethe there was still the nature bond, a pantheism that did at least guarantee connection to an unspecified immanent force. Rilke, before the declarations of the last *Elegies,* was more modest: "There remains, perhaps,/some tree on a slope to be looked at day after day. . . ." Nietzsche's need, however, was all-consuming. Man had to perform the impossible: he had to surpass himself and become godlike.

Nietzsche's dramatic assessments have by now become the catchphrases of college philosophy surveys. Heller realizes this, and it is the aim of his essays to muscle past rhetorical surface and received opinion in order to recover the terrifying truth underneath. He forces us, by dint of repetition and widening inference, to recognize that Nietzsche is not yet—and will probably never be—safely behind bars.

Possibly the most fascinating of these essays is the one entitled "Rilke and Nietzsche" (*The Disinherited Mind*). By setting these two very different personalities side by side, and comparing carefully their separate developments—Rilke's into prophetic poet, Nietzsche's into prophetic thinker—Heller discloses some startling similarities. At times, indeed, we get the uncanny feeling that the two men are just different refractions of a single impulse, that it is—to fall back on a cliché—the age that is speaking through them. As Rilke moves toward his celebrations of inwardness, Nietzsche formulates, with ever greater daring, his Superman. (The parallelism is, of course, thematic, not chronological.) The Rilkean Angel—"the being in whom the transformation of the visible world into the Invisible . . . is already accomplished"—bears more than a family resemblance to Zarathustra, who, on his mountain, draws from his soul the courage and will to become a god among men. "Rilke," concludes Heller, "is the poet of a world of which the philosopher is Nietzsche."

In the Age of Prose, Heller's most recent offering, does not diverge thematically or tonally from the earlier books—at least not dramatically. We find essays on Rilke and Hegel, Thomas Mann (three incisive readings), Kafka, Fontane, Kleist, Nietzsche, Hamsun (one of Heller's rare departures from German letters), and the illustrator Wilhelm Busch. Where we sense a change, a more impassioned and frontal stance, is in the chapters devoted to Karl Kraus, Heidegger, and Hölderlin, and what Heller calls "The Broken Tradition." Central to each is a preoccupation with language.

Heller has written about Karl Kraus before. In *The Disinherited Mind* he gave us one of the first presentations in English of the great Viennese satirist. But that treatment was an overview and an introduction; this exposition focuses on Kraus as a guardian of the German language. "Karl Kraus" is lit up by Heller's own sympathy and conviction. He is in complete agreement with the Kraus position: that the abuse of language correlates directly with social, cultural, and political decline; that the rectification of abuses and deflation of rhetoric have to be the preliminaries to any larger improvement. Kraus's journal, *Die Fackel* (*The Torch*), which he wrote entirely by himself, mocked and mimicked the bombast and cant of politicians, celebrities, journalists, and writers. No one was immune and everyone was suspect. A badly written sentence was like a slap in the face: for Kraus, as for Wittgenstein, ethics and aesthetics were synonymous.

> "What an order of life were to evolve if the Germans obeyed no other decrees but those of language," he [Kraus] wrote; and also said that nothing could be more foolish than to assume that it

> was merely an aesthetic need which is awakened or satisfied by the need for linguistic perfection. No, for Karl Kraus, this was an ethical demand, although at the same time he knew that the deep love for language was like the passionate love for Pandora or Helen: a sublime folly, even a chimera, within the instability of world and history; and yet to him, the enslaved lover of language, it was the binding, unchanging image of eternity.

If Heller does not openly identify his values with those of Kraus, it may be because of modesty. But modesty in no way prevents him from speaking out against Martin Heidegger. His invective is suffused with the spirit of Kraus:

> One who is unable to forget the Heidegger of 1932 and 1933 and 1934, a picture above all that shows him mustachioed like Hitler, sitting at a platform table in the company of other committed academic personalities and surrounded by an ecstasy of swastikas and S.A. men—one who is plagued by such memories is tempted to ask whether it was not the ambiguities resulting from such twin-nature and such a strained relationship to his time that made this interpreter of Hölderlin for quite an extended moment deaf to the resonance of hell conveyed by the voice and the language—yes, the *language*—of the *Führer* and his companions, creatures in whom abysmal inferiority uniquely mingled with the demonic. Be this as it may, it should not be forgotten because it was not the private person Martin Heidegger but unmistakably the author of *Being and Time,* for again and again, in speeches, pronouncements, and official letters he verbally behaved as if, with the arrival of Hitler, Being had unexpectedly and triumphantly returned to Time, choosing as its vessel the German vessel in the manner of Jehovah's once electing the Jews.

Language, for Heller, represents the last line of defense against the disappearance of meaning and value from the world. It may ultimately betray us—for it *is* us: we have made it—and it may, by the same token, yet save us, because we have invested it with our traditions, our knowledge, and our aspirations. In "The Broken Tradition," an address commemorating the two thousandth anniversary of Virgil's death, Heller maintains that it is still an open game. Against the Hitlers and Heideggers we can, so long as we retain our bond to the word, oppose our Goethes and Virgils. He notes, concluding the piece, that the heirs of Virgil and Kafka did not burn their unpublished manuscripts as requested: "Perhaps it is not always ashes that the mythic bird needs for new flights."

I read that as a tempered sort of optimism, or faith. Heller has spent a lifetime assaying our spiritual condition. He has worked without blinders, and without the usual humanist pieties. I would pay him the highest compliment that I can think of for a critic—to say that I trust him.

Walter Benjamin

To the memory of Norman Dukes

The collector destroys the context in which his object was only part of a greater, living entity, and since only the uniquely genuine will do for him he must cleanse the object of everything that is typical about it. The figure of the collector, as old fashioned as that of the flâneur, could assume such eminently modern features in Benjamin because history itself—that is, the break in tradition which took place at the beginning of this century—had almost relieved him of this task of destruction and he only needed to bend down, as it were, to select his precious fragments from the pile of debris.

—HANNAH ARENDT, *Walter Benjamin, 1892–1940*

The writer mysteriously exceeds his reader—any attempt at true reading confirms this. I say "mysteriously" because the language, the face that we inspect, and that inspects us, originates in the unconscious and is out of reach. It is at once the living source and the core of privacy. Thus, the more complex and profound the writer, the deeper his linguistic roots, the less we are able to throw out nets around the phenomenon—his work—and bind it to us. We respond by looking for ideograms that can encompass it symbolically; we draw out threads where we can and follow them. In the case of a writer whose work is as evolved and compacted as Walter Benjamin's (to call him a "critic" is to misplace him), the ideogram must be of Byzantine complexity, as subtle and singular as a fingerprint. But he supplies it for us himself: in his essay "A Berlin Chronicle" (*Reflections,* 1978) he refers to his life, and his work, as a labyrinth. And, truly, a labyrinth is very much like a large fingerprint, its runnels deepened into passageways, its fleshy parts raised to wall height. But a labyrinth is not a labyrinth if there is not the possibility of negotiating it successfully, and for this we need a thread. Possibly the most serviceable guide through the passages of Benjamin's thought is the figure of the *flâneur,* the wandering observer who confronts the chaos of the modern world as if it were a labyrinth that only he can penetrate.

The style maps the man: Benjamin's prose style represents as nothing else can the stresses and conflicts in his character and the drive that seeks to surmount all contrariety. Each sentence is a reconciliation effected between concept and living detail, the difficulty of true speech and the necessity of it, between rigorous logic and the belief that the real contents of life will always flee logic. Reading Benjamin, we feel that here is a man climbing a Matterhorn by incising each step. With each attainment he stops, takes his chisel to the next piece of rock, begins again. Another metaphor comes to mind: Benjamin as both Theseus and Daedalus, the hero over obstacles and the creator of obstacles. The sentences themselves are labyrinths; the meaning that coils through them is a slight but durable filament.

To talk about the flâneur in Benjamin's sense—and Benjamin's flâneur is a motif, a concept in many ways different from the historical flesh-and-blood stroller who wandered the boulevards and passages of nineteenth-century Paris—we must first remark Benjamin's vision of complexity. For he was a man acutely aware of the world as layered sense. Like the kabbalists, he spoke in terms of forty-nine levels of meaning; if something was not difficult it could not be true. Indeed, perception itself was a hermeneutics. Looking at the external world he saw the ramified density of history. The present was at every moment the net result of all that had ever happened. Looking inward he saw the complex ramifications of personal history, the self as net result of every decision and event ever experienced. Small wonder that the simplest act of perception was, for Benjamin, the confrontation of vast networks of complexity. The discovery of meaning through analytic operations was defeated by the sheer multifariousness of relevant detail.

Benjamin's flâneur is a response to a world in which sense is disjected, scattered, crystallized in detail. The flâneur is the collector and connoisseur of detail. He is a sensibility as opposed to an intelligence. His highest aspiration is to become a medium, a precipitate in which the scattered particles of sense can reconstitute themselves. The original whole (and Benjamin's conceptions are never without their biblical sense) has been shattered, by time, by history, by the hubris of progress; but the flâneur, by drawing together bits and pieces from the rubble, can discover its echo. The flâneur is, thus, dedicated to the surveying of space, for it is only in space, in the network of layered particulars, that the successive images of time are concretized. Space exists to take the print of time.

> The flâneur, Benjamin once wrote, is the priest of the *genius loci* when that genius has lost its sacred and unique place, when it has become a wandering spirit or homeless voice. It is in the air as a startling image; the poem, then, or Baudelaire's quasi-priestly activity is to recover and inscribe these exilic images, to restore spirit to place, if only in poems.
>
> —G. HARTMANN, *Criticism in the Wilderness*

> . . . all these things think through me or I through them (for in the grandeur of reverie the ego is quickly lost!); I say *think,* but musically and picturesquely, without quibblings, without syllogisms, without deductions.
>
> —BAUDELAIRE, *Paris Spleen*

Stroller, dandy, saunterer, idler, man of the crowd—there is no exact English or, presumably, German equivalent for the word *flâneur,* no single word that can carry the overtones that Benjamin intended. The flâneur is a phenomenon specific to Paris—Paris of the nineteenth century—which, not coincidentally, was the locus of Benjamin's most sustained literary, sociological, and historical investigations. Benjamin discovered that in tracking the gradual extinction of the historical flâneur he was able to diagram the progress of the "modern": mechanization, urbanization, the incorporation of "shock" into daily life, and the erosion and withdrawal of spirit ("aura") from the interaction of man and his environment. The processes were correlate. Benjamin's studies (especially his unfinished work on Paris in the nineteenth century) are, in a sense, projections of the principle of natural selection upon the human sphere. The flâneur, as the delicate vessel of sensibility, was not constituted for survival.

For Benjamin, the flâneur is at once a genuine historical manifestation and a personal emblem, the representation of a sympathetic sensibility. The two are not to be confused. The historical flâneur was already an extinct species in Benjamin's day. But this did not prevent him from appropriating the term for his own uses, or from viewing his own peregrinations as *flâneries*. But what we must keep in mind is that Benjamin's flâneur *emblem* is to a large extent a construct, a collection of attributes—real and imagined—around a vanished historical entity. By excerpting the flâneur from the past, by projecting his image upon modern urban life, Benjamin conferred a shock upon the word. He turned a phenomenon into a type, a mask.

To the historical flâneur belonged certain traits, a specific self-conscious style: he was idle, whimsical (Nerval was seen walking a lobster on a leash on the streets of Paris), casual. He celebrated the gratuitous, the serendipitous. His leisure, particularly in nineteenth-century France, presupposed a sound economic base. But the flâneur was not a dandy. In spite of certain shared attributes, flâneur and dandy were quite different. The dandy represented the elevation of class distinction into style; his detachment was a deliberate underscoring of the prerogatives accorded to lineage and wealth. The flâneur, on the other hand, represented an elevation of values into style. He was the protest of spirit in the face of encroaching materialism, of human time in the face of artificial acceleration. Thus, he made a cult of the materially useless. His prized possession was the observation, the insight.

Baudelaire's descriptions of the painter Constantin Guys are the finest characterization of the type:

I would willingly call him a dandy and for that I would have a sheaf of good reasons; for the word "dandy" implies a quintessence of character and a subtle understanding of all the moral mechanisms of this world; but, from another aspect, the dandy aspires to cold detachment, and it is in this way that M. G., who is dominated, if ever anyone was, by an insatiable passion, that of seeing and feeling, parts company trenchantly with dandyism.

To be away from home and yet to feel at home anywhere; to see the world, to be at the very center of the world, and yet to be unseen of the world, such are some of the minor pleasures of those independent, intense and impartial spirits, who do not lend themselves easily to linguistic definitions. . . . Thus the lover of universal life moves into the crowd as though into an enormous reservoir of electricity. He, the lover of life, may also be compared to a mirror as vast as this crowd; to a kaleidoscope endowed with consciousness, which with every one of his movements presents a pattern of life. . . . It is an ego athirst for non-ego. . . .

If in a shift of fashion, the cut of a dress has been slightly modified, if clusters of ribbons and curls have been dethroned by rosettes, if bonnets have widened and chignons have come down a little on the nape of the neck, if waistlines have been raised and skirts become fuller, you may be sure that from a long way off his eagle's eyes will have detected it.

We may rest assured that this man . . . has a nobler aim than that of the pure idler, a more general aim, other than the fleeting pleasure of circumstance. He is looking for that indefinable something we may be allowed to call "modernity." . . . The aim for him is to extract from fashion the poetry that resides in its historical envelope, to distill the eternal from the transitory.

—*The Painter of Modern Life*

If we simply change "fashion" to "phenomena" we will have secured the primary function of Benjamin's flâneur.

Walter Benjamin

It is not always easy to disentangle the image of the original crowd-walker from the overlay of attributes and values that Benjamin conferred upon it. Benjamin's rendering of the flâneur, for instance, emphasized the cognitive possibilities of his "style." But Benjamin was fully aware of this distortion. When he spoke of the flâneur he was speaking not so much of the flâneur's historical manifestation as of his latent possibilities. These are equally vital to the concept, and equally real. And it was by developing and extending these latent possibilities that Benjamin was able to identify himself with the flâneur. It was, for him, a necessary identification—it clarified his psyche to himself. Benjamin's interest in the flâneur, and his conception of himself as flâneur, was part of a process of self-reconciliation. His sense of failure, peripherality, his inability to do the right academic thing, these were gathered into an intellectually acceptable image, attached to a type with some historical precedent. The image of the flâneur gave a certain fashionable legitimacy to Benjamin's socially marginal predilections: wandering, collecting, observing. Likewise, it made his self-exemption from marital and familial responsibilities appear less an indication of failure than of resolve: the flâneur *wants* to preserve his peripherality; it is the basis of his existence. By highlighting the unique virtues of the flâneur—virtues established as such by Benjamin himself—he was, in effect, making a case for his own persistent nonconformity.

Still, it would be a mistake to identify Benjamin completely with the flâneur. There is a sense in which the flâneur represented everything that Benjamin was not, as if the image were a carefully elaborated alter ego. The flâneur, for example, was at home on the street, at ease in the deeps of the metropolis. Benjamin was not. He was a timid, civilized, fastidious man. He yearned for ease but could not have it. The flâneur moved freely in all directions on the societal grid. Benjamin's ventures always represented approaches to the threshold, the Other, the forbidden. To gauge the kind of tension he experienced—tension between his nature and his desire—we have only to consider this passage from his essay "Hashish in Marseilles" (*Reflections*): "The music that meanwhile kept rushing and falling, I called the rush switches of jazz. I have forgotten on what grounds I permitted myself to mark the beat with my foot. This is against my education, and it did not happen without inner disputation." There were boundaries and borders everywhere for Benjamin. In some cases they were class lines. But these he set out topographically. Certain streets or districts represented the forbidden. The precincts of the poor he always associated with vice and prostitution. For Benjamin, crossing class lines was a spatial exercise, a way of exacerbating the tension between the self and the Other. He writes: ". . . the places are countless in the great cities where one stands on the edge of the void." The void is, of course, internal. And crossing these boundaries—in one case he speaks of a sensation of "trembling and sweet fear."

The idleness of the flâneur represented a calculated affront to the time-money equation that was institutionalized with the advance of technology and the organization of the labor process. His gait was a sign of his mockery. Benjamin (whose own gait writer Max Rychner described as "at once advancing and tarrying, a strange mixture of both") typically raises this to the status of an epistemological problem. In "Theses on the Philosophy of History" (*Illuminations,* 1968) he writes: "The true picture of the past flits by. The past can be seized only as an image which flashes up at the instant when it can be recognized and is never seen again." The flâneur, whose idleness is the result of his peculiar reorganization of sensibility, is the only one who, as Hannah Arendt observes, "receives the message." The implications are profound, two-sided: it is not just the aptitude of the flâneur, it is the character of reality itself. Idleness becomes a prerequisite for cognition. Or, more accurately, idleness sponsors indirection, and indirection proves to be the only access to certain aspects of the truth. Not only is the flâneur's casual progress a form of protest, it is an evolved adaptation to the complexity of transformed urban life.

Given Benjamin's assumption—that "the true picture of the past flits by" and that data vital to understanding are concretized in scattered details and inaccessible to immediate inspection—what then is the flâneur's tactic of cognition? To say that he is a reader of signs and a correlator of particulars presupposes that there is something to be read, a hidden picture. And, indeed, this is the very conviction (or longing) that underlies and animates Benjamin's thinking. He believes, like Kafka, that an order once whole has been broken up and scrambled; a metaphysical reality once present to man is now concealed in fragments. The prototype is, of course, the hubris at Babel and the ensuing disaster: the one true language was deformed into countless different tongues. What prevents Benjamin's vision of the situation from being entirely hopeless (as it is in Kafka) is the belief that the scattered pieces still possess some residual attraction for one another, that the original reality can theoretically be rediscovered. The flâneur, because he has abandoned the hierarchy of accepted values and modes of perception, is the medium through which the original connections and relations have a chance to disclose themselves. His task is threefold: to gather detail, to remain sensitive to all possible correlations, and to refrain from judgment or the imposition of theoretical constructs.

> . . . the failure of the systematic thinker constitutes the true triumph of the master of hermeneutics who, in "reading" the things of the world as if they were sacred texts, suddenly decodes the overwhelming forces of human history.
>
> —PETER DEMETZ, introduction to *Reflections: Essays, Aphorisms, Autobiographical Writings* by Walter Benjamin

"Decoding" is one way to think of it. If we take up the original analogue of the labyrinth, then we can think of "reading" as the process of tracing a thread. This is more appropriate, I think, for decoding suggests understanding in the form of sudden revelation, a form Benjamin would probably have rejected. Hannah Arendt characterizes the process less dramatically:

> What fascinated him [Benjamin] about the matter was that the spirit and its material manifestations were so intimately connected that it seemed permissible to discover everywhere Baudelaire's correspondences, which clarified and illuminated one another if they were properly correlated, so that they finally would no longer require any interpretive or explanatory commentary. He was concerned with the correlation between a street scene, a speculation on the stock exchange, a poem, a thought, with the hidden line

that holds them together and enables the historian or philologist to recognize that they must all be placed in the same period.

—*Walter Benjamin, 1892–1940*

This obsession with proper correlation found expression as well in Benjamin's lifelong fantasy: to assemble a book consisting entirely of quotations from his readings, the pieces selected and arranged in such a way that they would make a seamless whole. The fantasy is nothing less than the flâneur's original desire—to assemble the true picture of history (and, thereby, the present)—projected onto the image of a book. It incorporates neatly the whole secondary realm of Benjamin's *flâneries,* those that took as their field the vast territories of the printed word.

Ideally speaking, then, the flâneur sets himself up as a kind of neutral medium through which the hidden connections among phenomena reveal themselves. Practically speaking, however, the various relations are seldom self-announcing; the flâneur must exercise his highly intuitive discrimination. He must know which detail "speaks" and he must have some sense about how it may relate to another. This already suggests some prior intuition of form or pattern on his part. And where might this originate? Second-guessing Benjamin, I would say that the flâneur—indeed, every person—possesses some prelapsarian residue, and that the discovery of external pattern is connected to the uncovering of the concealed essence within. This should not sound too foreign—it is precisely Plato's theory of knowledge as *anamnesis.*

Finding and relating, this is the sum and substance of the flâneur's obscure art. The process is, of course, complex. On one level there are relations across the surface; that is, the relation of detail to detail, like to like, the forging of connections among disparate entities. On another level there is the relation of detail to cause, manifestation to underlying phenomenon, or, in Marx's terms, superstructure to infrastructure. Benjamin's unfinished "Arcades" project, provisionally entitled *Paris, Capital of the Nineteenth Century,* was to be the apotheosis of his method, a study of the origins of "the modern" that would combine the flâneur's ambient perspective with the more rigorous methodology of Marxist "science."

> Haussmann's urban ideal was of long perspectives of streets and thoroughfares. This corresponds to the inclination, noticeable again and again in the nineteenth century, to ennoble technical necessities by artistic aims. The institutions of the secular and clerical dominance of the bourgeoisie were to find their apotheosis in a framework of streets. Streets, before their completion, were draped in canvas and unveiled like monuments. Haussmann's efficiency is integrated with Napoleonic idealism. The latter favors finance capital. Paris experiences a flowering of speculation. Playing the stock exchange displaces the game of chance in forms that had come down from feudal society. To the phantasmagorias of space to which the *flâneur* abandons himself, correspond the phantasmagorias of time indulged in by the gambler. . . .
>
> —*Paris, Capital of the Nineteenth Century*

Benjamin submitted portions of the "Arcades" project to his friend Theodor Adorno at the Institute for Social Research. Adorno's carefully worded reply indicates that Benjamin's Marxist formulations were anything but orthodox:

> This, I think brings me to the centre of my criticism. The impression which your entire study conveys—and not only on me and my arcades orthodoxy—is that you have done violence to yourself. Your solidarity with the Institute, which pleases no one more than myself, has induced you to pay tributes to Marxism which are not really suited to Marxism or to yourself. They are not suited to Marxism because the mediation through the total social process is missing, and you superstitiously attribute to material enumeration a power of illumination which is never kept for a pragmatic reference but only for theoretical construction.
>
> —letter, November 10, 1938

Adorno's statement underscores the fact that Benjamin's mode of relating detail to structure could not be assimilated entirely to Marxist methodology. It is too impressionistic and favors the suggestiveness of details over the rigors of causal explanation. But we must keep in mind that Benjamin's purpose is not to explain history—he wants to arrange its concrete details in such a way that it will enunciate itself and disclose its true patterns. Benjamin is not committed to a Hegelian march of reason or the eventual emancipation of mankind. His vision of futurity—and therefore his whole vision of history—is deeply penetrated by the teleology of Judaic messianism. In his "Theses on the Philosophy of History," written one year before his death, he presents this image of the angel of history (based upon Klee's drawing *Angelus Novus*):

> His face is turned toward the past. Where we perceive a chain of events, he sees one single catastrophe which keeps piling wreckage upon wreckage and hurls it in front of his feet. The angel would like to stay, awaken the dead, and make whole what has been smashed. But a storm is blowing from Paradise; it has got caught in his wings with such violence that the angel can no longer close them. This storm irresistibly propels him into the future to which his back is turned, while the pile of debris before him grows skyward. This storm is what we call progress.

To relate Benjamin's vision of history to his practice of prospecting for the telling detail would require a major excursus. Suffice it to say, for the present, that while his method of correlation resembled that of Marxist practice in some ways, Benjamin was in no sense attempting a thoroughgoing material analysis of history. He was, as the following passages show, too much alert to the singular, tactile actuality of his surroundings; he could not refrain from the "enumeration" that Adorno chides him for.

Benjamin's *flâneries* (from *Reflections*):

> Travel by streetcar in Moscow is above all a tactical experience. Here the newcomer learns perhaps most quickly of all to adapt himself to the curious tempo of this city and to the rhythm of its peasant population. And the complete interpenetration of

technological and primitive modes of life, this world-historical experiment in the new Russia, is illustrated in miniature by a streetcar ride. The conductresses stand fur-wrapped in their places like Samoyed women on a sleigh. A tenacious shoving and barging during the boarding of a vehicle usually overloaded to the point of bursting takes place without a sound and with great cordiality. (I have never heard an angry word on these occasions.) Once everyone is inside, the migration begins in earnest. Through the ice-covered windows you can never make out where the vehicle has just stopped. If you do find out, it is of little avail. The way to the exit is blocked by a human wedge. Since you must board at the rear but alight at the front, you have to thread your way through this mass. However, conveyance usually occurs in batches; at important stops the vehicle is almost completely emptied. Thus even traffic in Moscow is to a large extent a mass phenomenon.

—"Moscow"

In their materials, too, the street decorations are closely related to those of the theater. Paper plays the main part. Red, blue, and yellow fly-catchers, altars of colored glossy paper on the walls, paper rosettes on the raw chunks of meat. Then the virtuosity of the variety show. Someone kneels on the asphalt, a little box beside him, and it is one of the busiest streets. With colored chalk he draws the figure of Christ on the stone, below it perhaps the head of the Madonna. Meanwhile a circle has formed around him, the artist gets up, and while he waits beside his work for fifteen minutes or half an hour, sparse, counted-out coins fall from the onlookers onto the limbs, head, and trunk of his portrait. Until he gathers them up, everyone disperses, and in a few moments the picture is erased by feet.

—"Naples"

Suburbs. The farther we emerge from the inner city, the more political the atmosphere becomes. We reach the docks, the inland harbors, the warehouses, the quarters of poverty, the scattered refuges of wretchedness: the outskirts. Outskirts are the state of

> emergency of a city, the terrain on which incessantly rages the great decisive battle between town and country. It is nowhere more bitter than between Marseilles and the Provençal landscape. It is the hand-to-hand fight of telegraph poles against Agaves, barbed wire against thorny palms, the miasmas of stinking corridors against the damp gloom under the plane trees in brooding squares, short-winded outside staircases against the mighty hills.
>
> —"Marseilles"

For Benjamin the historical appearance of the flâneur coincided meaningfully with the transformation of social life in nineteenth-century France. Indeed, the latter determined the former. The bases for this transformation were to a large extent economic and political, but Benjamin directed his attention less to their underlying structure, more to their conspicuous manifestation in public life. Changing architecture, the appearance of the first arcades, the widening of the streets, the dramatic increase in traffic, new forms of public entertainment—these developments were all linked. And in this public arena the flâneur appeared as a kind of warning light: what was in danger was the life of the spirit. The flâneur was a moral protest, a figure of witness. He was made necessary by the dramatic extrusions in the material realm. But these same extrusions finally brought about his eclipse. As the material forces increased, his social position changed from the marginal to the absurd. The disproportion between values had stripped the relationship of its tension. Paris outgrew the flâneur; the man of the crowd was overwhelmed by the crowd.

> The greater the share of the shock factor in particular impressions, the more constantly consciousness has to be alert as a screen against stimuli; the more efficiently it does so, the less do these impressions enter experience, tending to remain in the sphere of a certain hour of one's life.
>
> —"On Some Motifs in Baudelaire," *Illuminations*

Benjamin sees the adaptation to modern life as a schooling in shocks. He places the concept of shock at the very center of his analysis. And here, for him, is the importance of Baudelaire. Baudelaire was the last fighter, the last flâneur—he sacrificed himself in the effort to parry the shocks of modern life. "He indicated the price for which the sensation of the modern world may be had: the disintegration of aura in the experience of shock." "Shock" we may define as the collision of the adaptive faculties and the stimuli of a rapidly changing environment. "Aura," an essential Benjamin term, designates authenticity, an original or primary relation of man to his world, or, more precisely, the product of a relation in which the perceived object "has the ability to look at us in return." The presence of aura is the guarantor of the sacredness of experience. As shocks increase and intensify, the possibilities for genuine perception and a genuine relation of the self to the world diminish. The flâneur was only meaningful so long as he could sustain or represent the genuine perception or response. Baudelaire's was the last stand; the *Fleurs du Mal* is to be read as an elegy.

Benjamin's appropriation of the image of the flâneur for himself was to some extent an ironic gesture. He knew that the harmony between man and his world had been all but irreparably violated. But it was precisely this knowledge—this hopelessness—that forced him to effect a major transformation. Moving from the objective to the subjective, he brought the flâneur sensibility to bear upon the inside life. And thus, the flâneur becomes a bridge connecting Baudelaire to Proust; and Benjamin's autobiographical "A Berlin Chronicle" can be read as his complex mediation of these two figures.

The key insight and connection point is to be found in Benjamin's discussion of aura in the Baudelaire essay. He writes: "To perceive the aura of an object we look at means to invest it with the ability to look at us in return. This experience corresponds to the data of the *mémoire involontaire*." It was Proust who, drawing upon the philosophy of Henri Bergson, articulated the distinction between voluntary and involuntary memory. Voluntary memory, habit-conditioned, depending upon the projection of a chain and cause and effect upon one's own past, has no bearing upon the real "lived" contents. It represents the destruction of the aura of the past; its premise is explanation. Involuntary memory, on the other hand, obeying laws of its own, ignoring every command of the will, is our sole means of contact with the real experience of the past. As Samuel Beckett wrote in his study *Proust:*

> Involuntary memory is explosive, "an immediate, total and delicious deflagration." It restores, not merely the past object, but the Lazarus that it charmed and tortured, not merely Lazarus and the object, but more because less, more because it abstracts the useful, the opportune, the accidental, because in its flame it has consumed Habit and all its works, and in its brightness revealed what the mock reality of experience never can and never will reveal—the real.

Thus, just as the flâneur, by virtue of his lingering walk and his radically dissociated sensibility, is able to garner in its particularity the "true picture of the past," so only a susceptibility to the gracelike workings of the involuntary memory could return to the individual the genuine experience, or aura, of his personal past. What Benjamin writes about the historical past ("Theses on the Philosophy of History") is virtually identical to the Proustian formula: "The past can be seized only as an image which flashes up at the instant when it can be recognized and is never seen again." Underlying both is the presupposition that the life of the past concentrates its essences into detail. Only thus can the taste of the madeleine cake unfold a forgotten world around the narrator Marcel. And just as there is no telling *when* the involuntary memory will yield its hoard, so there is no knowing which stray detail will bear the impress of a world.

The only record we have (at least in English) of Benjamin's *flânerie intérieure* is his piece "A Berlin Chronicle," which was written in the late 1930's. It is a remarkable document, not only because of its dense, compacted style and its temporal montage effects, but also because of what it reveals to us of Benjamin. The sixty pages of text are all but unpopulated: what memory has restored to him are the images and sensations of space. The paradox is significant. Benjamin's flâneur, perambulating space, discovers time; Benjamin, casting his net back into time, discovers space. As space bears crystals of time, so time itself proves to have crystallized into space. Nothing could be further from Proust's experience. In *Remembrance of Things Past* the restored world is rich with emotion and the delicate shadings of personality. "A Berlin Chronicle" is as barren as a moonscape. In this respect, curiously, it recalls Osip Mandelstam's autobiographical memoir "The Noise of Time"—also a sequence of precisely rendered interiors that are all but unpopulated. Psychologists might find something to ponder in the convergence: both memoirs were left by intellectually and linguistically precocious sons of well-to-do Jewish families. Mandelstam: 1891–1938; Benjamin: 1892–1940.

One of the curious features of "A Berlin Chronicle" is that, despite the static character of each section, the progression and organization of the specific memories suggest that the material was not consciously called to mind, but that it was, in fact, given by the *mémoire involontaire*. If this was the case, we are left with pressing psychological questions. Is this depopulated image of the past a result of repressive energies? How else could active emotion crystallize so completely into the static pictures of places and things? Whence the need for repression? The questions can be fairly raised, but given the paucity of evidence about Benjamin's early life, I do not think that they can be satisfactorily answered.

> I have long, indeed for years, played with the idea of setting out the sphere of life—bios—graphically on a map. First I envisaged an ordinary map, but now I would incline to a general staff's map of a city center, if such a thing existed. . . . I have evolved a system of signs, and on the grey background of such maps they would make a colorful show if I clearly marked in the houses of my friends and girlfriends, the assembly halls of various collectives, from the "debating chambers" of the Youth Movement to the gathering places of the Communist Youth, the hotel and brothel rooms that I knew for one night, the decisive benches in the Tiergarten, the ways to different schools and the graves I saw filled, the sites of prestigious cafes whose long-forgotten names daily crossed our lips, the tennis courts where empty apartment blocks stand today, and the halls emblazoned with gold and stucco that the terrors of dancing classes made almost the equals of gymnasiums.
>
> —"A Berlin Chronicle"

The passage speaks for itself, as does the following, where Benjamin is referring to the suicide of his close friend, the poet Fritz Heinle:

> No matter how much memory has subsequently paled, or how indistinctly I can now give an account of the rooms in the Meeting House, it nevertheless seems to me today more legitimate to attempt to delineate the outward space the dead man inhabited, indeed, the room where he was "announced," than the inner space in which he created.

A pronouncement of this kind only makes sense if we keep in mind the aesthetics of indirection practiced by the flâneur. But even so the contradiction is not resolved. It is, finally, the contradiction that stands at the heart of Benjamin's work, at the Minotaur's place in the labyrinth: that a man so vulnerable to the real should spend his life so doggedly—and by way of such intricate mental maneuvering—in pursuit of it. His whole intellectual effort was aimed at devising a position that would enable him to dispense with intellectuality. He wanted desperately to get his hands on the real. The flâneur was his chosen emblem because the flâneur moved about in the world unencumbered by concepts. But in adapting the emblem to his needs Benjamin could not but turn it into a concept as well. And so, Benjamin's flâneur is in many ways the opposite of the original man of the crowd: he is the subtlest of mental constructs, the divinatory creature who wants the redemption of pure meaning, meaning anterior to all mental constructs.

Cyril Connolly

Habent sua fata libelli. So runs the old tag: books have their fates. Years ago, working in the antiquarian book trade, functioning as turnstile between past and present, the popular and the obscure, the market economy and the secret economy of passions and obsessions, I learned the truth of it. There are certain books that do not die when they go out of print, that take on, instead, a shadow life more mysterious and interesting than their shelf life ever was. By word of mouth, by way of catalogues, by serendipity, they find the readers they were meant to have.

"Do you have anything by Cyril Connolly?" That was one of the more common requests, and one that puzzled me. I had pegged the man as yet another feather in the British peacock's fan that was Bloomsbury. (Bloomsbury, I later found out, loathed Connolly.) His essays—I had only looked at them—seemed flouncy and slight. I wondered what the fuss was all about.

One day I came across a slim, unusual-looking volume called *The Unquiet Grave* by an author who identified himself only as "Palinurus." It was a case of the right book finding the right reader at the right time: I was completely taken. Meditation, private journal ("word cycle," it called itself), there was no tidy slot for it. The author discoursed freely on writers and writing, the austere sadness of the ancient world, the waning of culture and value in an age of global insanity (the book was published in 1944); and interspersed with the broodings were sudden bouts of self-flagellation: he was lazy, debauched, faithless, a failure. The mix was irresistible. He exhumed both his own heart and that of a dispirited era:

> On the American desert are horses which eat the locoweed and some are driven mad by it; their vision is affected, they take enormous leaps to cross a tuft of grass or tumble blindly into rivers. The horses which have become thus addicted are shunned by the others and will never rejoin the herd. So it is with human beings: those who are conscious of another world, the world of the spirit, acquire an outlook which distorts the values of ordinary life; they are consumed by the weed of non-attachment.
>
> There is sanctuary in reading, sanctuary in formal society, in office routine, in the company of old friends and in the giving of officious help to strangers, but there is no sanctuary in one bed from the memory of another. The past with its anguish and injuries breaks down all the defenses of custom and habit; we must sleep and therefore we must dream.

I forget how I learned that Palinurus was Cyril Connolly, but when I did, I too began to hunt for the books of his essays. When I found one, I would savor it slowly—dipping, lingering over turns of phrase, siphoning its contents much as Connolly reported doing with his Petronius,

Leopardi, Flaubert . . . That ellipsis represents a set of footprints left by a man who wandered slowly and purposefully through the vast territory of the written word. For Connolly brought erudition, discrimination, and passion to bear upon everyone from the Roman elegists to Sade to Robert Lowell. He loved literature, and his whole life was given over to expressing that love.

Connolly's extraliterary peregrinations took in the sunsets of Greece, the Botticellis in the Uffizi, the burial tombs at Luxor, and the rich, deep image-world of his boyhood in Georgian England and his schooldays at Eton and Oxford. The fuss, I saw, had to do with something more than just literary excellence; it was a question of personal style. Connolly's was the sensibility of an epicurean, devoted to pleasure and beauty and obstinately secure about its likes and dislikes. But at the same time he was obsessed with ranking and enumerating, always measuring his own stride against that of the greats. His character abounded in contradictions. He could sound like an elitist prig, or suddenly discharge a venomous spray of self-loathing. "Approaching forty," he wrote, "I am about to heave my carcass of vanity, boredom, guilt and remorse into another decade." How could any charge of high-handedness stick? His adoration of genius could not but lead him into the most bitter self-reproach: "Why not me?"

The vigor and precision of the prose, however, were a rebuttal, for they partook, often, of something like genius. It was as if he had to contradict himself into brilliance. Whatever the obstacles, whatever the gravity of his temperament, the prose could rise like a helium balloon:

> The hexameter may well be the "stateliest measure ever molded by the lips of man"; the couplet has proved the more enduring. Often have I fancied, though this kind of statement can never possibly be proved, that the rise and fall of the elegiac couplet bears some relation to the waves breaking on the Greek islands with the retreating backwash that follows. "The surge and thunder of the Odyssey" has been celebrated—what of the less positive assertion and milder withdrawal of the Mediterranean sea? It is not impossible that listening to this eternal susurrus awoke in

> these island peoples an instinctive poetry of flux and re-flux expressed in the alternation of the long and sonorous with the short and melodious line.
>
> —"The Elegiac Temperament,"
> *Selected Essays*

> My thrill of the week was to visit a little shop on Landsdowne Hill in the early dusk of winter afternoon and receive a rolled-up bundle of "Comic papers," Chips and Comic Cuts, the Rainbow, the Gem and the Magnet—I hold them, as I did everything, to my nose, the smell is excruciating—damp paper, newsprint; I feel I shall burst. Ahead of me stretches the evening with my grandmother; the gas lit, the fire burning, the papers unrolled and untied, the peace and security of the literary life, though even then I am depressed by the knowledge that nothing I find inside will come up to the sensation of opening them.
>
> —"A Georgian Boyhood,"
> *Enemies of Promise*

Connolly was born in Coventry in 1903, the same year as George Orwell. In fact, the two were classmates at Eton. "I was a stage rebel," writes Connolly in *Enemies of Promise* (1939), "Orwell a true one. Tall, pale, with his flaccid cheeks, and a matter-of-fact, supercilious voice, he was one of those boys who seem born old." Their early differences became only more pronounced as time went on. Orwell threw himself into the social and political agitations of the day; he went to Spain to fight fascism, espoused causes, aimed his prose against class privilege and the mentality of empire. Connolly followed the call of belles-lettres: he did Latin and ancient Greek, studied the modern Romance languages, and was quite proud about matriculating with a "classical education." Although he did not exactly turn his back upon politics (he traveled to Spain several times in 1936–37 as a reporter for *New Statesman*), issues of politics and culture were, for him, weighted in terms of the latter. A glance at his recently published journal, in *Journal and a Memoir* (1984), reveals the extent to which his own emotional turmoils shouldered everything, social concerns included, to one side.

He was emotionally and sexually (Connolly was homosexual in early manhood, heterosexual later) bound to his class milieu in a way that Orwell was not—he never broke with aesthetic ideals that he had absorbed at Eton and Oxford.

Connolly succeeded his formal education with a lifetime of reading and connoisseurship. In his earliest pieces he's erudite and sure; he never seems to lack for a reference. By the time he reached his stride as a critic in the late 1930's (he founded the influential journal *Horizon* in 1939), he had brought to maturity the cunning, quicksilver style that would remain his trademark. His prose was the very antithesis of the straightforward, elbows-on-the-table prose of Orwell. Drawing upon the elegance of Horace, Pope, and the earl of Rochester and at the same time tapping his own deep spring of melancholy, Connolly made his writing a link to what he saw as the verities of higher civilization. He did not, however, become a thorough mandarin: dense and repressive rhythmic clusters are broken up by energetic, even romantic surges. Syntax can reveal character as well as anything else.

Connolly toiled on behalf of the higher continuities for nearly half a century. By the time he died, in 1974, he was England's, and maybe the world's, leading critic. But he was a critic in the journalistic, workday sense—a watchdog and pen for all occasions. He did not venture off, as Edmund Wilson did, into the more demanding and enduring forms of cultural criticism and serious "literary" essay—not often, at any rate. Apart from *The Unquiet Grave, Enemies of Promise* (which is part literary chronicle, part memoir), and a light, glittery novella, *The Rock Pool,* which he wrote in the thirties, his *oeuvre* consists entirely of book reviews. But what a panorama! The entire development of literature in our age is there refracted through his prism. And right alongside, similarly refracted, are the greater and lesser figures of every era. Although Connolly knew he was working in a compromised genre, he did everything he could to infuse it with "civilized" values. Such a vast perspective had never been squeezed into column inches before. Propertius breathes as freely in that space as Auden or Huxley:

> The reading of this first book of Propertius is an outstanding literary experience. One is altogether enraptured by this strange

> gusty music, by the glimpses of Greek mythology, of drunken quarrels and heavenly reconciliations, of the moon gliding across the window over Cynthia's bed, of her basking among the sun bathers on the beach at Baiae, of a group of weekend guests, wine glasses in hand watching the fast skiffs and slow barges drift under the woods along the Tiber, of Propertius battering in vain at the locked door of her whom he called his mother and sister . . . while the little breeze of early dawn blows across him. . . .
>
> —"The Elegiac Temperament"

I am not surprised that Connolly's work was out of print in this country for so long. The world that he represented, with its ideals of discrimination and its assumption of cultural continuity still rooted in the fantasy of empire, is itself out of print, blasted by two world wars and the collapse of political hegemony. Although Connolly knew this, he continued to project in his criticism the values of Eton and Oxford as he had known them in the twenties. His style was, to some extent, a calculated act of defiance: by committing himself to artistic nobility, he pointed himself deliberately at obsolescence. He did nothing to placate the philistines. If civilized culture was going down, he would damn well go down with it.

What does it mean, then, that Connolly is now being "rediscovered"? *The Unquiet Grave, The Rock Pool,* and *Enemies of Promise* are all sporting the ephemeral gleam of the new paperback. Peter Quennell, one of Connolly's old friends, has put together a *Selected Essays* (a hit-and-miss mélange of travel writings, reviews, and satires, published in 1983), and a combination package of early journals and a memoir by David Pryce-Jones has been issued. Connolly's sad, impertinent, toad-featured face has been turning up in magazines everywhere, accompanied by fond, celebratory, or patronizing assessments by the likes of V. S. Pritchett and Hilton Kramer. Does this mean that he's back, garnering deserved recognition, or is it all just a queer flare-up from a media machine that must have something to gnaw on day in and day out? How has he worn—the man who in *Enemies of Promise* adjured himself to write something that would last for at least a decade? How do his words resonate in a world that has been so thoroughly changed in so short a time?

Few will deny that the decades since the war have brought a sense of culture in decline. In the arts, this has manifested itself as a loss of direction. Styles come and go, surfaces change, but with little suggestion of progress or goal. The pessimists argue that we have come to a cul-de-sac, that with no basis of authority chaos must follow; the optimists maintain that the new pluralism—or postmodernism—is a salutary condition. That the pronouncements of the latter are coming from within the walls of the universities is not just happenstance. If the arts have declined, the theories of art are prospering as never before. Indeed, there appears to be an ominous parallel between diffusion in the cultural arena and the consolidation of power and influence in the hands of theoreticians. It is hard not to establish a causal connection, or to deny that the long-prophesied Age of Criticism has arrived at the expense of spirit.

Critic Frederic Jameson, by no means an advocate of postmodernism in the arts, posits in his essay "Postmodernism and Consumer Society" (in *The Anti-aesthetic: Essays on Postmodern Culture,* edited by Hal Foster, 1983) that there is a connection between the development of artistic (in the most general sense) styles and the process through which a culture defines itself. He suggests that there has appeared in all the arts a reaction against the "established forms of high modernism": the architecture of Robert Venturi, the musical compositions of Philip Glass and Terry Riley, the poetry of John Ashbery, the fiction of Thomas Pynchon. Of course, waves of reaction are nothing new; our culture is used to absorbing subversive developments—Joyce, Stravinsky, Mies van der Rohe—and domesticating their influence. But the great modernists were omnivorous, simultaneously summing up and exhausting tradition. Joyce recapitulated the history of literature; Stravinsky did the same for music, Picasso for painting. The newcomers are, therefore, forced to assail the idea of tradition itself. And this assault takes two forms: first, the elimination of the old boundaries between serious and popular culture; second, a systematic breakdown of the distinctions between "kinds" of disciplines:

> A generation ago there was still a technical discourse of professional philosophy—the great systems of Sartre or the phenomenologists, the work of Wittgenstein or analytic or common language philosophy—alongside which one could still distinguish that quite different discourse of other academic disciplines—of political science, for example, or sociology or literary criticism. Today, increasingly, we have a kind of writing simply called "theory" which is all or none of those things at once.

We can see this declassification in artistic disciplines as well. There is an eclectic insouciance, a refusal of the grand or "serious" gesture of historical identification. History is present only as ironic quotation. Ashbery, Glass, Venturi, and Pynchon can be taken as exemplars: each makes it his program to rummage among forms and, through combinations of high and low effects, deny the idea of continuity.

Jameson's argument soon takes a frightening turn; at the far end of its arc we will once again encounter Connolly:

> We need to introduce a new piece into this puzzle, which may help to explain why classical modernism is a thing of the past and why postmodernism should have taken its place. This new component is what is generally called "the death of the subject" or . . . the end of individualism as such. The greater modernists were . . . predicated on the invention of a personal style, as unmistakable as your fingerprint, as incomparable as your own body. But this means that the modernist aesthetic is in some way linked to a conception of a unique self and private identity . . . which can be expected to generate its own unique vision of the world and to forge its own . . . unmistakable style.

He goes on to announce that "the older bourgeois individual subject no longer exists." Postmodernism, in his eyes, is just the harbinger of this momentous cultural change; it is an effect, not a cause. The causes are social and economic. We are by now familiar with the litany: bureaucratic standardization, the concentration of capital, the erosion of local power bases, technological advancements. These and a host of other postwar developments have stripped the individual of his sense of selfhood. The rate of social change has engendered paralysis, destroying the bedrock stability without which there can be no private worlds or private styles. We no longer have the individual substance necessary for the production of "great" art in the classical or modernist sense. Instead of major works we have theory. The indeterminacy of culture has created an insatiable appetite for interpretation.

Connolly begins *The Unquiet Grave* with the following: "The more books we read, the sooner we perceive that the true function of a writer is to produce a masterpiece and that no other task is of any consequence." From the forties to the eighties—on the time line of Western culture a few decades are as nothing. But what a difference! Has that much really changed? Should we regard Jameson's analysis as a paranoid fantasy, or should we suppose that Connolly was hurling his challenge in the face of an already discernible dissolution? In either case, it's clear that Connolly's aesthetic, which is succinctly summarized in that one sentence, is radically at odds with contemporary suppositions—even if Jameson has exaggerated their impact somewhat.

And this brings us to the "Connolly question": does the classical-humanist-modernist tradition (as celebrated by Connolly or anyone else) have any place in our postindustrial consumer culture? Do works of sensibility and spirit from Greece, or Rome, or Renaissance Europe—the Arnoldian "touchstones" of Western imagination—matter in themselves, or are they just fodder for academics and "names" for cognoscenti? Has theory usurped their place? Do we share Jameson's belief that the individual is being supplanted and that the new arbitration of meaning will exist in different form—collective?—if it exists at all?

What our culture is presently witnessing is, on the one hand, the demotion and demystification of the work of art and, on the other, an elevation of the concept. Indeed, the theoretical seems to be investing itself with the very sanctity that it has banished from the arts. And this trend is linked to the expansion of technology and the empirical sciences and the revolution in information processing. Roland Barthes breaks a Balzac story into small units, or "lexies," so that five different "codes" can be applied; what Terry Eagleton writes, in *Literary Theory,* with reference to Barthes can stand in for the whole program of literary theory:

> The most intriguing texts for criticism are not those which can be read, but those which are "writable" (scriptible)—texts which encourage the critic to carve them up, transpose them into different discourses, produce his or her semi-arbitrary play of meaning athwart the work itself. The reader or critic shifts from the role of consumer to that of producer . . . literature is now less an object to which criticism must conform than a free space in which it can sport.

Mallarmé once said that "everything exists to end up in a book." We can now carry that thought one step further: every book exists to end up in a theory. The world of spirit is to be converted into mind, and art is to be negated. What other consequence could there be? Not only are art and theory mutually exclusive, but the latter cannibalizes the former; it makes use of it while at the same time denying its original intent, its human circumstance. The concrete particularity of the past—both personal and cultural—that inhabits and determines the work is processed into neutral, ahistorical mental contents. "Structuralism," reports Eagleton, "flees from history to language."

Connolly's enterprise, needless to say, went in the other direction. Implicit in his valuations, supporting and authorizing them, was an active recognition of historical process. This awareness was at once particular—he grasped the dynamic interactions of person, place, and milieu—and relativistic. Connolly believed that history behaves organically, that cultures grow and diminish, and that it's foolish to suppose that what's most recent is naturally superior. England in 1944 represented, in his eyes, no advance over sixteenth-century Florence or seventeenth-century Holland. Material progress was one thing, quality of life was quite another. As he put it in an essay on Lord Chesterfield:

> All of us who allow the sense of a past a certain play in our lives come sooner or later to adopt a special period, to fall in love with a few decades of history which we cannot read about without

a certain quickening, an interior voice affirming "This was the time."

—*The Condemned Playground*

For Connolly, every realized work had an equal claim to our attention, not in spite of its pastness, but because of it. "Culture" and "history" were words referring to a single ever-changing entity—human life—in which we are all implicated. And of which every part mattered. The critic's job, along with greeting and assessing the new, was to keep alive in the present an image of the whole. In this capacity, Connolly patrolled the past incessantly—as a seeker, not an archivist. He tested the works and reputations of other periods for their value to our ongoing endeavor. And when he brought a neglected treasure into the light, he celebrated not only its beauty, but its capacity to recall to us the mysterious larger life of culture.

The reappearance of Connolly's books may be a sign of reaction against the prevailing thrust of critical theory. If so, it will generate the slightest of ripples, nothing more. The various doctrinaire isms have taken their place at the table and are happily masticating the legacy of centuries. They will not disappear. New styles of "reading" will succeed one another, but the underlying tendency—toward reduction and abstraction—is no more likely to die out than is the collateral trend toward the technological transformation of the social and natural order. Where will Connolly fit in? Nowhere near the center, that much is certain. His books—those wonderful auscultations of the tradition—are fated to return to the underground. There they will command interest among a small public of unregenerate back-pedalers. How could it be otherwise? The arrow of modern life and the arrow of private sensibility have passed going in opposite directions.

George Steiner

A few years ago I went to hear George Steiner lecture at Boston University. Afterward, we happened to be standing on the same crowded curb, and he gallantly invited me to share a cab to Harvard Square. I was thrilled. I would like to say that we talked animatedly for the duration of the ride, but we didn't—he did. I was the sole auditor of a twenty-minute lecture on Walter Benjamin's untranslated opus about nineteenth-century Paris. I remember concealing my astonishment—not so much at what Steiner was saying as at how perfectly he was managing to say it. Ornate, precisely balanced sentences assembled in the air, paragraphs shaped themselves in sequence. And there was no sign of effort on his features. By the time we pulled up in front of the Wursthaus, he had extemporized a perfect little essay. I'm sure it could have gone verbatim into *The Times Literary Supplement.* Maybe it did.

I was enthralled and demoralized. My own tongue felt as unwieldy as a rubber doormat. I could barely say goodbye to the man. But he wasn't waiting for any eloquence from me; he gave a cheerful nod, paid the fare, and was off.

That ride did clear up one mystery for me. For I had always wondered how Steiner was able to be at once so well read and so prolific. Apart from his larger thematic studies—on chess, translation, tragedy, Tolstoy and Dostoevsky, Heidegger—he has published bushels of essays on the most recondite topics. I understood then that he was a man gifted with a rare degree of mental clarity and great organizational abilities; he could absorb and distill large quantities of heterogenous material quickly. It was obvious, too, that he made the most of his time: twenty minutes in a taxi were twenty minutes to be used. Perhaps I'm being catty. The gift may come with its own curse—the inability to stop.

When I heard that Oxford University Press was issuing *George Steiner: A Reader* (1984), I was distressed to see that venerable old house giving in to the bonbon sampler trend—and shocked to find Steiner a party to the deed. Ordinarily he would be the first to deplore such a venture. Indeed, if there's one thing he stands for—consistently, militantly, even shrilly—it's our obligation to hold the line against any further diluting or trivializing of serious culture. As he says elsewhere, in an essay entitled "After the Book?": "Among the very many students I have met and taught in several countries over the past few decades . . . fewer and fewer reject the prepackaged selectivity of the paperback in order to own *complete* works of an author." He goes on to lament this as a symptom of eroding literacy. But if this compendium isn't "prepackaged selectivity" I don't know what is. I, for one, will keep my various Steiner volumes—each has something interesting that is not in the *Reader.* But I did, I admit, stop to think through the question: how essential is the essential Steiner?

Steiner's is a most vexing case. His books and essays are almost iridescent with intelligence and brio. He is bold, polemical, and alive to the fingertips with moral concern. He has a nose for the hot topic and a knack for posing the controversial question. What's more, his area of competence dwarfs most contemporary fiefdoms: he is schooled in languages, classics, philosophy, linguistics, music, painting—and who knows what else. World literature is his central field of expertise. To read him, or to share his cab, is to be dazzled.

And yet ultimately the very quality that makes Steiner so special—his breadth—works against him. So zealous is he about knowing everything, and about convincing the reader of this (with a glancing reference, a beautifully obscure citation), that he never gets his spade in past the topsoil. He formulates problems brilliantly, he churns out the most effervescent prose, but he does not think—that is, his ideas are nowhere near as deep as his subjects. Steiner can go as far as the best thinker in many a field, but only after that thinker has left tracks. He does not have in him the force needed to bend, or extend, or destroy an idea. He can only remark it in another.

Even Steiner's magnum opus, *After Babel: Aspects of Language and Translation* (1975), with its formidable command of the relevant history and its sure description of problem areas, does not advance to anything. It asks questions, sketches hypothetical directions of inquiry; the questions, alas, remain largely unanswered, and the hypotheses, beguiling though they are, go unexplored.

The most conspicuous and representative example of this ledge standing is Steiner's impassioned interrogation of the Holocaust. He has nailed down a central paradox, one that if unraveled would explain a great deal about the deeper tensions of twentieth-century culture. In essay after essay he thrusts it in our faces:

> The barbarism of our time did not spring out of the steppe or the jungle. It arose in the very heartland of high civilization. Men tortured and gassed in the very neighborhood of the museums, schools, concert-halls, libraries which constitute the anatomy of humanism. Neither Bach nor Goethe, neither Pushkin nor Cervantes, proved any barrier to the actual inhuman. . . . Were there powerful elements inside humanism, within civilization, that not only failed to oppose barbarism but helped produce it? Is the no-

> tion of "civilization" itself flawed or tragically implicated in the coming of bestiality? Do the habits of mental abstraction, of fictional conceptualization which liberal humanism placed at the center of its educational process, in some way incapacitate man's more immediate political reflexes?

Steiner's obsessive interest in these questions is a noble testament to his own anguished humanity. By asking and asking throughout his work, he keeps the moral paradox alive in our minds, and this is salutary. But for all his relentlessness, he does not get very much farther. I have not found in any of Steiner's writings any deeper kind of psychological, philosophical, or political investigation.

He has, it is true, written at length about the art historian Anthony Blunt, whose erudition and scholarly integrity coexisted with his treasonous devotion to Soviet spies, and about Martin Heidegger, who could address with full philosophical force the problem of Being while maintaining a complicit silence on the Führer's atrocities. The terminologies of connoisseurship and attribution are knowingly deployed, as are the ontological distinctions of Heideggerian philosophy. But the brief against Blunt (which is a *tour de force* of controlled invective) does not leave us with more than a recognition of a profound split between "intense emotional power" and "rational detachment" in his character. The Heidegger study, meanwhile, puts the pressing question: "Is there, then, anything one can argue to account for or to justify the total silence of one whose later works, according to Martin Buber, 'must belong to the ages'?" And then answers: "Only conjecture is possible."

Steiner follows up this disclaimer with a few speculative motions. Either "the enormity of the disaster . . . may have seemed to Heidegger . . . absolutely beyond rational comment," he writes, or else the philosopher was left speechless by his recognition that "Germany's pre-eminence in just those activities which may be the highest in reach of man, namely philosophy and music," was somehow inseparable from its potential for plumbing "the last depths." What these suggestions establish most clearly is that the passion of the questioning is not matched by an equally powerful determination to give answer. It is *the* problem at the core of Steiner's enterprise.

Still, we must admit that he is both engaged and engaging. There is, for one thing, the pure pleasure of reading his prose. He can write about literature with an élan that sends the reader hurrying to the book in question. Here, for example, he remarks upon the scene from *War and Peace* in which Pierre lies gazing at the sky:

> All the implicit contrasts, between celestial motion and earthbound growth, between the uncontrollable play of natural phenomena and the ordered, humanized cycles of agriculture, are relevant. In the macrocosm, the tail of the comet is uplifted; in the microcosm, the soul is uplifted. And then, through a crucial transformation of values, we are given to realize that that universe of the soul is larger.

Discrimination and love are seldom so effortlessly fused.

I think of Steiner as pursuing a kind of shuttle diplomacy among the ever more insular areas of specialization, bringing an insight from linguistics to bear upon a passage of eighteenth-century prose, or applying a precept of anthropology to a problem in the theory of translation. It is for this that we ought to cherish him. If he does not break new ground in any discipline, he does nevertheless impart to everything he touches the sense of its deeper interconnectedness. Only a sensibility of vast cultivation could do this kind of brokering. To say that Steiner has erected bridges between specialized areas would be going too far. But his example shows that diverse and meaningful signals can still be exchanged between fortifications.

I would not like to leave the impression that Steiner is nothing more than a popularizer. His critics have been unfair in this respect—he is a peregrine, not a parrot. Indeed, following him in his peregrinations, we find all kinds of intriguing suggestions. Any one of them, followed up in depth, could become a thesis of compelling power. Opening to the *Reader*'s introduction, I find Steiner musing *en passant:* "We ask ourselves whether there is in the genesis of great art and its effects upon us some analogy to the coming into being of life itself."

Or else, in the selection entitled "Future Literacies," in the midst of a long paragraph on the time orientations of the sciences and humanities, this: "Because it carries the past within it, language, unlike mathematics, draws backward." My delight in nuggets like these will keep me reading whatever Steiner writes. His refusal to follow up his own glimpses of true discovery may keep him from attaining the higher reaches of Parnassus. But to those of us grazing in the flatlands below he will always be superior company.

Eugenio Montale

Literary traffic between Italy and America has always been fitful. The greatness and complexity of Dante have proven, in a sense, a liability. After all, who can undertake to read Italian literature without first knowing Dante? It is partly because of Dante that Petrarch and Leopardi are so little known, and that the Italian masters of our century—Montale, Ungaretti, Saba, and Quasímodo in poetry, Pavese, Gadda, and Svevo in fiction—have been more heard of than read. Translators have worked hard, but in spite of their efforts the graft has not taken well.

But we have more to blame than just the stature of Dante. There is also the arrogant view of Italy as the small country where ruins are eternal and the president's name changes every few months. The accumulations of the past once represented wisdom, and wisdom, in turn, was power; but now it is the opposite: traditions and ancient patterns are seen as dead weight. The brutal eruptions of history have shouldered them to the side.

The reader of Eugenio Montale's essays in *The Second Life of Art* (1982) will have to rid himself of this preconception, for they are the speech of a supremely civilized man, a cosmopolitan in the old sense, a poet and thinker for whom writing was for more than fifty years an intense vocation. What might once have been just an important collection of literary essays has taken on the symbolic aspect of a last stand. Montale carried on the European cultural tradition until he died in September 1981, while that culture eroded around him.

Montale was born in 1896 in Genoa. He died at eighty-four in Milan, roughly a hundred miles away. Though he traveled widely in his time, he remained wholly Italian, bound to his region, his time, and, most of all, his craft. Montale was one of the fortunate artists who discover their gift early and never relinquish it. After 1925, when he published *Ossi di Seppia,* the work that changed modern Italian poetry, his stubborn presence exerted its influence on Italian letters. He weathered two world wars and the fascist interregnum without ever compromising his liberal humanism. The slow, patient work continued. He published few volumes of poetry, but each was a major event; he wrote hundreds of essays and *feuilletons.* During his years as literary critic for Milan's *Corriere della Sera,* 1946 to 1973, he published several pieces a week. But in spite of this large *oeuvre,* he remains an incalculable figure, hard to place. His private life, his emotional sources, were kept hidden. In his poetry he practiced an aesthetic of reserve that kept his most intimate thoughts away from gossip; antecedents and connecting threads were sketched, suggested, but never explained. His prose, on the other hand, is civilized, ironic, in certain places warm or humorous, but nearly always public. We see both the emotional and the intellectual sides of his sensibility in his work, but the private man remains remote.

Still, Montale was not playing a sly game. From time to time, when he deemed it appropriate or necessary, he would use a personal or confessional anecdote. In *The Second Life of Art,* for instance, we find this:

> For many years I carried with me a rusty metal shoehorn I was so ashamed of that when I stayed in a hotel I'd hide it so the maid wouldn't see it. It was the only thing that had been with me since childhood. One day in Venice I forgot where I had hidden it, or rather forgot the shoehorn itself, and I never had the courage to inquire about it. In all probability it is sleeping today at the bottom of the lagoon. Still, I feel remorse, and when they tell me that a cosmonaut has circled the globe six, ten, or sixty times, I think the greatest discovery would be the one that would bring me back my old rusty shoehorn. I know perfectly well that if the shoehorn were to reappear on my table I would feel more terror than joy. Consciously or not, I rid myself of it. I must therefore accept the assistance of chance and continue to live without that magic, silent, rusty Oliphant, as I must confess that I have dared to replace it with a red plastic model which I now set out in plain view and could lose without regret.

I cite this passage because it expresses concisely Montale's temperament, and gives a glimpse of the associative intelligence that informs his essays: the ability to leap—from shoehorn to cosmonaut—, the contrast between the values of public and private life, the use of telling detail. If Montale had a method for writing essays, it was the subtle method of the flâneur, the method of no method. Somewhere in his writings he speaks of this, comparing his approach to that ancient practice of searching for water with a hazel rod, the water in this case being those crystallizations of insight not available to the reasoning faculty, and the rod being the receptive sensibility.

One finds in this passage, obliquely stated but unmistakable, Montale's uneasiness. This is what makes him an exemplary modernist: the perpetual strain in his work between the vanishing certainties of the past and the onslaught of a most frightening future, a future in which all received values would most likely be compromised, if not negated altogether. Expressed emotionally in his poetry and somewhat more intellectually in his prose is Montale's vision of the present as a perilous strait between two very different kinds of time, the vision of a man acutely sensitive to the velocity of historical change.

The essays in *The Second Life of Art,* a small selection from Montale's prose, span a full fifty years of activity. The book begins with ten general meditations, the first, "Style and Tradition," published in 1925, and the last, "Is Poetry Still Possible?," the poet's acceptance speech for the 1975 Nobel Prize. The titles show Montale's central preoccupation and his growing pessimism over its future. The perspectives of these opening essays help to define the concerns of the shorter pieces that follow, which are largely appreciations of writers and artists. For everything connects, implicitly, with one question: how will the culture of the past survive into the future? How will human values, as they are exemplified in great works of art, weather political barbarousness and the vacuity of mass society?

Montale is not much interested in stating those values or investigating the great artists of the past. The values are understood. As for past artists, with the exception of his essay on Dante—in which he asks, "What does the work of Dante mean for a poet today?"—they are treated as a patrimony; they are not discussed. Montale is interested in the present and the struggle of the artist in the twentieth century. These are mainly sympathetic essays, sensitive to the particular problems in each writer's career. Montale is rarely judging: he cannot seem to sustain the attitude of superiority that is required. And he hardly ever condemns.

The first section of literary pieces is called "On Italian Writers." At least three of those writers—Dino Campana, Giovanni Pascoli, and Gabriele D'Annunzio—may be unfamiliar to American readers; their works are either not yet translated, or, in the case of D'Annunzio, little read and out of print. Of the others, two, Italo Svevo and Benedetto Croce, are better known, but probably only Dante is truly familiar. Even without knowing these writers, however, the attentive reader will be repaid by his experience of the relaxed flow of Montale's prose style, the rhythm of his sentences, and by seeing what impressions and ideas influenced the poems in *Ossi de Seppia* and the later work.

Montale's poetry, like his prose, followed no program, but hewed closely to the shifts of his inner life. Nevertheless, at various points in his career the critics were eager to link his work with this or that school, most often with "hermeticism"—the movement that espoused the aesthetic of difficulty and veiled reference. Montale would have none of it. In one of the self-interviews reprinted in *The Second Life of Art,* he asserts:

> The intentions I'm outlining today are all *a posteriori.* I obeyed a need for musical expression. I wanted my words to come closer than those of the other poets I'd read. Closer to what? I seemed to be living under a bell jar, and yet I felt I was close to something essential. A subtle veil, a thread, barely separated me from the definitive *quid.* Absolute expression would have meant breaking that veil . . . an unreachable goal.

Montale's profession of no profession gives him a remarkable critical openness. He never has to defend one school against another, or attack in the name of a poetic ideology, in a country that has been in this century a vat of isms. It is instructive to read his essays on Campana, Pascoli, and D'Annunzio, to see how carefully he read his predecessors and contemporaries. Although he could not make use of the style or approach of these poets, he could still judge them on their own ground. Of Campana, for example, whose excessive Rimbaudian style was far from Montale's own idea of compression and clarity, he wrote:

> Dino Campana, who, as Cecchi has said, "passed like a comet," may not have exercised "an incalculable influence," but the traces of his passing are anything but buried in the sand. There was nothing mediocre in him; even his errors we should not call errors but inevitable collisions with the sharp corners that awaited him at every step. The collisions of a blind man, if you will. Visionaries, even if they happen to be "visual" like our Campana, are inevitably the most artless, the blindest of creatures on this earth.

Many critics writing today could learn something from the combination of sympathy and discrimination Montale displays here.

In a charming sketch Montale describes his friendship with Italo Svevo, his friendship as an eager young poet with an aging *grand seigneur* of letters. As he carefully assesses Svevo's career, Montale gives us a clear interpretation of the successive self-portraits identifiable in Svevo's characters, a sequence that culminated in the unforgettable Zeno Cosini: in Zeno, Montale suggests, the artist created his *Doppelgänger.* But in doing so, by showing the interplay of character and locale, he achieved something even more remarkable. He brought a whole city to life.

> We have said that Trieste lives at the edges of [Svevo's] *Una vita* and absolutely invades *Senilita;* but at this point Trieste is the very weft of *La Coscienza di Zeno,* the first warp, so strong that it could be called the producer of its characters themselves, as if the fundamental tone (the tone and rhythm of a city with a double aspect, intensely European and yet unmistakably linked to a very different stock by language, blood, and traditions)—as if the fundamental tone had created figures, characters, situations, by parthenogenesis.

Three sections of the book are made up of some twenty short, idiosyncratic pieces, each having at its center some odd, revelatory incident or some striking observation. Most of them were written as *feuilletons* for the *Corriere della Sera.* The *feuilleton* is not the precise equivalent of our "column." Though it is as brief, its conceits are generally more literary and less self-consciously ephemeral. Montale's seem to me masterpieces of the genre. Casual, impressionistic, they are like the ink and wash sketches of a sixteenth-century master—one or two lines, a touch here and there of the perfect shading.

The lightness of touch can be deceptive at times, allowing us to forget that Montale was among the most erudite and cosmopolitan of writers. When he was young he translated Fitzgerald, Steinbeck, Hemingway, Faulkner, and Melville into Italian. He was a passionate lover of opera, and in his youth had trained with the baritone Ernesto Sivori. When he grew older he took up painting. The passion for culture in all its forms animates—however subtly—these pieces. Montale perceived the life of his time in the music of Stravinsky, the painting and sculpture of Braque and Brancusi, the vastly different poems of Pound, Eliot, Auden, Char, and Cavafy.

Of a reception given for T. S. Eliot, Montale wrote:

> Eliot had not yet won the Nobel Prize, but he was considered the most likely of the *papabili* and his fame among the young of two worlds was undisputed. Which did not preclude a feeling of embarrassment among those present who, as they entered, were unable to make out the poet on first sight. Naturally, those who had seen his photograph did not hesitate; but the rest—attracted by a name that remained simply a name, unrelated to some physical image—were unable to choose among so many heads of hair, so many pairs of glasses, so many authoritative faces. Then a murmur rose among the uncertain, a direction was pointed out, an indicating arrow shot in the air toward a distinguished gentleman, thin and unbearded, somewhere between fifty and sixty, more "clergyman" than professor but for his limpid and penetrating gaze, which was protected by a pair of tortoiseshell glasses.

The effect is that of a camera rolling through a crowded room. The confusion of "so many heads of hair, so many pairs of glasses" is at once cleared away. Before we have caught our breath we are face to face with the famous tortoiseshell glasses.

In the piece "On the Trail of Stravinsky," Montale is a cultural reporter, in Venice to cover the world premiere of the Auden-Kallman-Stravinsky opera, *The Rake's Progress.* Though he claims to be on the trail of the composer, he never gets to meet him. There is always some obstacle or failed connection. But chance brings him to the restaurant where Auden, Spender, and MacNeice happen to be eating a mussel stew.

> Wystan Hugh Auden, the librettist of the *Rake* in collaboration with Chester Kallman, is forty-four years old and five feet seven inches tall, and lacks, or has lost, the youthful expression and the flowing hair that certain photographs lent him. He is a strong, cordial, human man whom one seems to have known forever. He divides his time between Ischia and New York; now an American citizen, he has taken the opposite route from Eliot, who was American and became English. According to Stravinsky, who chose him on the advice of Huxley, Auden is the Bach of modern poetry. He does what he likes and knows every secret of technique. And in

> fact his poetry is sweet like Spenser's, ironic and witty like Pope's, dry and discursive like Eliot's. He jumps from the old to the new with perfect nonchalance, enjambs his stanzas like the best of Byron's *Don Juan,* juggles modern thought with acrobatic agility; moving through time and space among the ghosts of Kierkegaard and the invective of Karl Barth, he has abandoned the religion of Marxism for the Anglo-Catholicism into which he was born; and finally (and for me, today, this is his greatest attraction) he loves opera and in the libretto of the *Rake* has succeeded in writing a masterwork of the genre.

Two pages later, the premiere over, when Montale runs into Auden at the airport, he cannot resist adding a final stroke. Auden "jumps aboard the plane like a roebuck. His carrot-colored head enters the cabin, disappears."

Montale was much interested in English and American poetry and he has a great deal to say, both directly and by inference, about Eliot, Pound, and Auden. Of the three, he was temperamentally closest to Eliot, in whom he found a poetics not unlike his own. Montale had worked out on his own notions similar to Eliot's "objective correlative." But even more than Eliot the poet, I think, Montale admired Eliot the critic-essayist. He valued Eliot's search for a usable past, for ways to enrich modern art and thought with the best of the European tradition. That he did so in a lucid, classical manner was for Montale a great achievement.

Montale was somewhat harder on Pound. He was irritated by the "abridged, night-school, accelerated-course" approach that Pound took to that same cultural past. He thought Pound's energies were deployed superficially and lacked a center. Nevertheless, he had respect for some of Pound's work, particularly the early collection *Personae.* As to the question of Pound's fascism, Montale, who had distinguished himself by his uncompromising opposition to Mussolini, gave him the benefit of the doubt. He was convinced that Pound could not have known about the crematory ovens. "Pound," he writes—and he knew the poet for many years—"was a profoundly good man, of this I am sure."

Montale went several times to see Malraux, Brancusi, and Braque.

Three less kindred personalities cannot be imagined—the diplomat *engagé,* the misanthrope-perfectionist, and the sage of cubism. What is so fascinating about these accounts is Montale's ability to absorb the imprint of a personality from the briefest and most formal of circumstances. Braque is detached, monumental. Brancusi is rude, and this meeting is our one chance to see Montale's equanimity shaken. As for Malraux, Montale spends several hours letting the man reveal himself. Montale is awed. Soldier, diplomat, art historian, novelist, Malraux has managed to do everything with Gallic flair. What's more: "He has spoken for an hour and a half, giving the illusion of talking to a friend and of having opened himself up for the first time." But finally the visit is over, and Montale is on the street searching for a taxi.

> I go out under the first raindrops and skirt the deserted pool. I don't know whether to envy the regal destiny (or anti-destiny) of André Malraux, but this evening I am less unhappy with my own. And for this too I can thank the regal author of *The Voices of Silence.*

Tact, at times, can be the deadliest weapon of all.

In a beautiful untitled poem in *Ossi di Seppia,* Montale, not yet thirty, wrote his credo. It is an apostrophe to the sea, and at one point he proclaims:

> It was you who first taught me
> my heart's puny tumult
> was only a moment of yours—
> that at bottom I kept your
> hazardous
> law: to be vast and various
> yet steady
>
> —translated by Sonia Raiziss
> and Alfredo de Palchi

Vast, various, steady—Montale's work was all these. And if the sketches seem diffuse, the meditations that open the collection have a steadiness, as well as vastness and variety. Here, where Montale deals with the issues that usually are printed in capital letters—Man, Time, Culture, History—we find his curious blend of humaneness and pessimism at its strongest. The same sensibility persisted for fifty years. Montale himself tried to account for this persistence. In one of his self-interviews, he describes his temperament as something autonomous, an entity with its own laws and almost immune to history. "From birth I have felt a total disharmony with the reality that surrounded me," he writes. And then, taking into account fascism and two world wars, he adds: "I had reasons for unhappiness that went far above and beyond these phenomena." The reader should not suppose that Montale was unmoved by the larger tragedies; he is merely saying that he felt his own more deeply, that they had been present from the start. Ultimately, though, the public and private forms of despair are fused in a quietly charged tone present in everything Montale wrote.

Fascism, collectivism, the erosion of a great tradition—all are, for Montale, manifestations of the same tendency. There is no name for it. To call it historical decline or entropy is not to define it. But recognizing this tendency can result only in a tragic view. Montale also recognized that one is still forced to act and decide, and every act and decision has bearing upon the surrounding world. Thus, despair notwithstanding, there is the choice to be made: to submit to history, or to live "in spite of it." Montale's career exemplified the latter choice. His vision of decline did not prevent him from putting his life into the service of ideals of beauty, goodness, truthfulness. Perhaps deep down he did not exclude all hope. As late as 1944, in an essay entitled, fittingly, "A Wish," he wrote:

> It is simply the old battle of good and evil, the struggle of divine forces fighting in us against the unchained forces of bestial man, the dark forces of Ahriman. Thus in us and through us a divinity is brought into being, earthly at first, and perhaps celestial and incomprehensible to our senses, which without us could not develop or become cognizant of itself. And because of this we must simply say no to every exploitation of man by man. . . .

This seems uncharacteristically Manichaean, out of keeping with Montale's secular nature. Yet the vision here of man creating the divine for himself is not that of a practicing Christian.

A later essay, "Man in the Microgroove," published in 1962, presents a view that seems more characteristic. The conceit in this piece is that history can be likened to a phonograph record, in whose grooves the future is already pressed. The terror is, of course, that nothing can be altered, that history is not a struggle of opposing forces but a *fait accompli.* Worse still is the possibility—or probability—that the future is one in which the contours of humanistic culture and its traditions have been completely eradicated. Montale closes this speculation with a double negative that is anything but reassuring:

> And yet the real history, the one that counts and is not to be found in books, is precisely this one, the one made by simple men; and it is the only one that still rules the world. Tomorrow perhaps it too will disappear and then science will be able to record a truly unheard of man, a new zoological specimen whose distinguishing features I fortunately don't know. I am not entirely sure that this portentous individual is not already hidden within the microgrooves of the record.

If anything will save culture, it will be the work of a few artists. So Montale believed. This is less, I think, a profession of elitism than the considered view of a man who saw a whole generation swept by fascism. How were the values and lessons of the past to be carried into the future if not in the hearts of a few special people? The public at large would not undertake such a salvage operation. And how were civilized values to be kept alive and disseminated if not through art? In the light of these questions, the thesis of the title essay is of central importance. In "The Second Life of Art," Montale argues that art does not attain its full meaning until it is seen apart from the setting in which it was created. That is, the melody does not really live until it is recalled outside the concert hall; the line of poetry only matters when it has come to the reader in a situation detached from the actual reading of the poem. This is a controversial idea, for it postulates "memorability"—whether conscious or unconscious—as a requisite attribute of art. For Montale such experiments as Dada, aleatory music, or Duchamp's "found objects" preclude the possibility of a second life in the experience of the viewer. Montale's position is conservative, to say the least. But then, conservation was his mission. He simply feared that the past would not reach the future on such rickety bridges.

Montale's tendency in his poetry, his prose, and, I suspect, his life was to avoid final pronouncements. He needed to be in a state of uncertainty; for him it was tonic. He saw himself as living in the breach between the diminishing past and the fearsome future. There are more comfortable places to station oneself, but I don't think it ever occurred to him to move. Montale's path required that, having lost his rusty shoehorn, he make do with his "red plastic model." He would carry on, but he was not going to pretend that the replacement was just as good. He could lose it, he says, "without regret."

Roger Shattuck

I've been having a curious experience with Roger Shattuck's *The Innocent Eye* (1984). Even though I've read—and, in most cases, reread—all of the essays, I cannot pick up the book without the certainty that there is one very important piece that I've somehow overlooked. It's like a scene that I remember, or have invented, from an old movie: the detective paces back and forth through the rooms of the house, tapping the walls, muttering calculations, finally announcing to all assembled, "There has to be another room here." The stroke of the pickax proves him right. Of course, the dimensions I'm figuring are nonspatial, the walls invisible. But my findings are similar. There is a very specific, albeit unwritten, essay between these covers. Its absence exerts a considerable distorting force on the whole book.

This whimsical conceit (which I will return to) is not inappropriate to a review of Shattuck. He is a longtime celebrant of the odd, the fanciful, the perdurable strangeness that haunts the margins of culture. Indeed, his own key opus, *The Banquet Years: The Origins of the Avant-garde in France, 1885 to World War I* (1968), set out to capture the spirit of an era not through the exploration of leading figures and key works, but precisely the reverse. Shattuck took as his coordinates four of the most idiosyncratic creators of the age and fashioned not only a thoroughly charming narrative, but a portrait that was all the more incisive for its obliquity. A brilliant move, really—to look at French culture in terms of its most unlikely extrusions: Alfred Jarry's "pataphysics," Henri Rousseau's tropical dream-scapes, the puckish compositions of Erik Satie, and the frenetic innovations of Guillaume Apollinaire.

In *The Innocent Eye,* Shattuck once again walks with his dowsing rod through the literary and artistic culture of twentieth-century France. Though the book lacks the thematic organization of *The Banquet Years*—it is, after all, a compilation of twenty-some years' worth of essays—the intellectual underpinnings are coherent and consistent, and the fascination it exerts is irresistible. There are several reasons for this. First, nothing is prepackaged; every essay embodies a conviction and a singularity that persuade us that Shattuck is following the track of his own obsessions. These are not academic exercises, but private researches. They are marked by unexpected departures, unique juxtapositions, and all manner of divagations. We become enthralled with the subjects because he is.

The other reason is so obvious that it may get overlooked. Simply, Shattuck is the best of possible guides; his energetic and synoptic temperament is perfectly suited to the *Zeitgeist* he pursues. For if anything characterized French modernism, it was the synthetic impulse. Diaghilev's collaborative productions were only the most striking example; artists, writers, and composers everywhere were looking to break through the confines of their genres. Shattuck does not lose sight of this for an instant. What's more, he is versed in the principles and terminologies of all the arts. In *The Innocent Eye,* we find him discoursing lucidly on the interplay of visual and sonic elements in Apollinaire's calligrams, on the corporal and choreographic qualities of Stravinsky's music, on Magritte's manipulation of figural and linguistic puns, and so on. His conceptual range is not only impressive, it's essential.

The hybridization of the arts is one central theme in the book. Another—as pervasive, but even more important in its implications—is the affirmation of a deep-seated continuity between the scientific and artistic (or humanist) world views. Shattuck's argument, taken up in a number of the pieces, centrally or *en passant,* warrants some comment.

In "The Tortoise and the Hare: Valéry, Freud, and Leonardo da Vinci," one of the cornerstone essays of the book, Shattuck recalls to us Pascal's well-known distinction between *l'esprit de géométrie* and *l'esprit de finesse.* He writes:

> After the seventeenth century it is possible to trace a deepening split in the higher levels of culture. A scientific cast of thought bent on reducing all phenomena including men to material causes, mathematical principles, and (after Darwin) chance operating within a vast expanse of geologic time, stood opposite a widespread faith in feeling, instinct, the spirit, and the irreducibility of life and humanity to material causes.

A familiar litany. But Shattuck quickly departs from predictable paths. First, he pounces upon a luminous bit of information: in the fifty-year period between 1869 and 1919, more books were written about Leonardo da Vinci than about any other human being, apart from "the institutionalized figure of Jesus." Of these, two were written by thinkers of genuine power and are of great interest to Shattuck—Paul Valéry's *Introduction to the Method of Leonardo da Vinci* and Sigmund Freud's *Leonardo da Vinci and a Memory of His Childhood.*

I will not try to account for the sinuosities of Shattuck's exposition, except to say that he discovers a most suggestive link between the two men: both at one time proclaimed their interest in the work of the mathematician Poincaré, especially his articles on the psychology of the scientific imagination. Shattuck makes the most of his lead:

> Valéry's attack on Pascal's irresponsible dividing of the mind into two parts, Freud's reluctance to see Leonardo as a man at odds with his own most precious talents, and their common interest in Poincaré's psychology of scientific and creative thinking—these circumstances reinforce what should already be clear about the coincidence that Valéry and Freud both wrote about an Italian painter and thinker who lived four hundred years before their time. They did not see in him a universal genius who represents a variety of human faculties vying with each other in a great divergence of roles and activities. His versatility led them in another direction. Their two highly contrasting books restlessly trace the multiplicity and contradiction of Leonardo's activities back to a mind. And above all, that mind is one, an integrity of scientist and artist, of sensibility and intelligence.

Shattuck follows this up with a fascinating hypothesis of his own. Connecting this idea of "one mind" to the Einsteinian conception of a space-time continuum, he advances the idea that thought may be a single entity capable of various "speeds," and, therefore, may partake of various states; that, in short, analytic and intuitive thought—*l'esprit de géométrie* and *l'esprit de finesse*—might just be two modalities of a single process. I do not have the competence to determine how original, or fanciful, Shattuck's notion is, but the presentation is most stimulating.

"Claude Monet: Approaching the Abyss" is another attempt on Shattuck's part to push the arts and sciences into an alliance. In his carefully documented account of Monet's years at Giverny, he leads us through the developments that culminated in the gigantic canvases and the artist's painstaking explorations of strategically cultivated landscapes:

> . . . Monet did not anticipate the full effect on himself of his own last water-lily and wisteria compositions; they swept him away by their scale and by the importunacy with which they substituted their colored surface for every other aspect of painting, including vibrating field and retinal impression.

Shattuck's thesis, much abridged, is that Monet's astonishing sensory endowment brought him into creative contact with the flux behind appearances—the very electromagnetic field that James Clerk Maxwell was working to establish theoretically; that he registered and expressed what science could only touch with formulae.

These are not the only examples of artistic-scientific complementarity. In "Vibratory Organism: Baudelaire's First Prose Poem," Shattuck discerns in a passage from *Salon de 1846* a phonic and semantic oscillation that prefigures eventual discoveries about the "energy and periodicity of the very stuff of the universe." And in a far-ranging essay entitled "The Demon of Originality," he makes some provocative statements about the contradictory uses of the concept of experimentation in the arts and sciences. Opposed though they clearly are—the one seeking to open new possibility, the other to reduce it through testing—both spheres may be facing an undreamed-of cul-de-sac. In Shattuck's view, the limits of the discoverable are not eternally extendible; the future may very well see a "flattening" of the curve of invention and force a radical reassessment of the idea of progress.

I don't want to create the impression that Shattuck writes about nothing else but the rift between the two kinds of *esprit. The Innocent Eye* also includes absorbing discussions of Artaud, Valéry, Malraux, Magritte, Jarry, Apollinaire, Duchamp, and Meyer Schapiro, as well as lesser pieces on Michel Tournier and Balzac (this last appeared as an afterword to an edition of *Eugénie Grandet* and sits awkwardly among the other essays). In terms of both focus and command of perspective, these studies are far more satisfying than the more generalized polemics included at the back of the book—"How to Rescue Literature" and "The Poverty of Modernism." The latter, couched in the form of a conversation between a professor of literature and his ex-pupil, drifts unconvincingly among abstractions, only to end with the pupil trumpeting his admonition: "All that modernism framework carries you further and further from individual writers."

"How to Rescue Literature," on the other hand, contrasts the pedagogic styles and implicit value-systems of textualist theorists and old-line humanists, and concludes by advocating that works of literature be read aloud in the classroom. Sympathetic as I am with Shattuck's desire to free works of spirit from the clutches of theoreticians, and persuasive as some of his comments on *viva voce* performance are, I am disappointed by the sleight of hand. Instead of drawing upon his great learning and argumentative intelligence to demonstrate just how analytic schemata bleed the life from their host, he turns his back on the whole issue. Every such abdication can serve only to buttress the case made by the theoreticians: that humanism is an old bitch gone in the teeth.

Shattuck probably has a deeper grasp of French culture than any American critic. He is aware of the historical and political heritage (read his opening essay on a gathering of world intellectuals in Paris for the International Congress of 1935), as well as the complex influences that pass among the different arts. He is also attuned to the larger—and more diffuse—osmotic exchange among all areas of intellectual and spiritual endeavor. Moreover, his writings give every indication that he has thought a great deal about the problems raised, not just by the various expressions of modernism, but also by their passage from the center of the stage to the wings. His concluding statements, simplistic though I made them sound, make their assertions out of hard-won wisdom, not naïveté. If Shattuck decries the contaminations of theory, it's because he has wrestled with its claims and knows whereof he speaks.

This wrestling, implied but nowhere evident, is what composes the unwritten chapter; it is the missing link. For apart from a brief digression in the essay on Tournier, and a few remarks in the final "polemics," there is no mention of the theoretical inferno that France has become in the last thirty years. The subject may not fall strictly within the compass of the book—its subtitle is *On Modern Literature and the Arts*—but it cannot be avoided. The modernist impulse did not simply fade away. In one way or another it prepared the soil for *Tel Quel*, poststructuralism, and deconstruction. What are the links between the synthetic intellectualism of a Valéry and the ingenious dismantlings of a Roland Barthes? Is there a relation between Duchamp's ironic subterfuges and the work of Derrida? Without some understanding of the complete trajectory of modernism, we cannot fully appreciate its efflorescence. Shattuck's stance at the end of *The Innocent Eye* leaves no doubt about his profound antipathy for the so-called postmodern developments. I would like to see him roll up his sleeves and engage in some real polemics—we may not be able to change history, but we can certainly argue with it.

PART V
General Essays

Notes from a Confession

Rereading

The Leaning Umbrella:
A Reflection on Flaubert

Television:
The Medium in the Mass Age

An Open
Invitation to
Extraterrestrials

Some Notes Concerning
the Impossibility of
Literary Biography

These last essays reflect some of my general interests and concerns. As all of the preceding pieces have been "readings" of a sort, I include a trio of reflections on the process of reading itself. "Notes from a Confession" and "Rereading" question the ways in which texts involve the sentient creature behind the eyes; "A Reflection on Flaubert" describes my successive interactions with a single novel.

"Television: The Medium in the Mass Age" and "An Open Invitation to Extraterrestrials" try to pin down some of the more elusive implications of living in a media culture. "Some Notes Concerning the Impossibility of Literary Biography" emphasizes the need to respect the line between the life and the work. Miraculously engaging as it sometimes is, literature is not life—it is life transformed.

Notes from a Confession

The primal scene. It is a Saturday afternoon, summer, weather temperate. I am lying on the bed in my room reading a novel. I am ten, or twelve, or fifteen—it doesn't matter. Once again, in my absorption, I have not heard my father come home from the office. Now he stands in the doorway. Not a word has been exchanged, but already I've put the book out of sight and donned a false nonchalance. "Come help me in the yard," says my father. Shorthand. For we're both loath to go through the argument again. Not even an argument. Because I'm not vertical, not engaged conspicuously with the so-called real world, I'm in the wrong. I know that. No use in my arguing the value of reading. "There's enough to think about with real problems," he would say, "why add on the problems of make-believe people?" I have not yet, at that age, formulated a rejoinder. My rejoinder is my persistence. As soon as he is out of the house again, I am back on the bed.

Mea culpa. Confession. One generally confesses to make a clean breast of things, to bring some misdeed or inadequacy into the light. Reading? Well, yes—behind everything, in spite of any high-flown pronouncements I might make, there is still the residual sense of something not altogether praiseworthy about my habit. Is it the activity, or is it more a question of *my* involvement, my reasons? How to explain?

Quite recently, I watched *Days of Wine and Roses* on the late show. Jack Lemmon and Lee Remick as an alcoholic couple. Lemmon finally takes the cure, Remick cannot be convinced to stop. In the final scene, Lemmon is pleading with her: why won't you save yourself? Remick looks around the room in anguish; it is as if she's looking through the walls at the world itself. "When I'm not drinking," she says finally, "everything looks so *dirty.*" I come to attention—I'm not even sure why. I don't think that I feel disgusted in that way. But why did I sit up? And why did I think of that episode just now?

There is reading, and there is reading. Reading as a means to an end, for information, to cultivate oneself; reading as an end in itself, a process, a compulsion.

I think of the following scenario: I am imprisoned in a room for a week. There is a bed, a chair, and one book—the most trivial of romances. How many hours must pass before I devour it? How many times will I reread the thing before my jailers release me? Should I be ashamed? For I have no doubt but that I *would* read the book. Is this in any way analogous to the deprived alcoholic drinking down a bottle of shaving lotion?

Other questions. In what way would I read this romance—straight on, or obliquely, as sociology? Would I be deriving more enjoyment from the story, or from the image of myself reading such a book?

Why read it in the first place? Because reading is an end in itself, and because the romance has its place, however ignominious, in the order of the printed word—which is an order unto itself. *Anna Ka-*

renina and *Love's Tender Fury* are more akin to each other than either is to anything in the material sphere.

Psychopathia librorum. I must come clean.

Frequency of immersions, indiscriminacy. I surround myself with the printed word. In my apartment, in my life. It is no accident that I have spent almost one third of my life working in bookstores, exploited and underpaid, and that it was with some reluctance that I changed professions—to become a teacher. When I'm not looking at words I am often generating them myself.

Could it be that the origins of writing are to be found in reading, in the desire to control the source of such pleasurable sensation? Roland Barthes has called that pleasure *jouissance,* thereby identifying its sexual nature.

The world is covered with words, and I go about reading them. The urban surface. Signs, billboards, graffiti. I read and reread the same idiotic slogans on the cereal box morning after morning. If I require more variety, I study the jam jars, breaking apart and recomposing the letters in the lists of ingredients.

Whence this constant impulse to disturb the surfaces of words? Anagram itch. While driving, for instance, I play games with highway signs. I read words backward, scramble letters. Listening to words on the car radio is not enough. There is a hunger in the eye itself. Where does it originate? Can it be controlled? Must I scan the spines of books while in an embrace?

I cannot walk past a newsstand without pausing. What am I looking for?

If I have to take a two-hour bus trip, I will spend an hour beforehand trying to figure out exactly what I want to read. A magazine, a short story, poetry? Why don't I just settle back in my seat and think? Actually, I very often end up doing just that. But I need to know that I have something that I want to read—for security. With that knowledge I can give free rein to my thinking. Indeed, in resisting the temptation to open the book I am somehow *sharpening* my thought.

There is also that kind of reading which is just a looking at books. From time to time—I can't say what dictates the impulse—I pull a chair up in front of a section of my library. An expectant tranquility settles over me. I move my eyes slowly, reading the spines, or identifying the title by its color and positioning. Just to see my books, to note their presence, their proximity to other books, fills me with a sense of futurity. "Books," I once noted grandly, "embody the spirit's dream of perpetual youth." What is important at these moments is not the contents of the books, but the idea of their existence. I have not read every one, nor is it likely that I will—but to know that I might! Don Juanism.

Staring in this way at a whole section of my library, I release associations. When I notice *A Sentimental Education,* for instance, I do not think of the plot—I recall a week spent on Corfu, the shady hut where I sat during the long afternoons . . .

A conversation with T.F. We agreed that sheer proximity to books is civilizing. We spoke, only half-jokingly, of emanations.

Compulsiveness. Exhaustiveness. I have a mania for finishing, even if a book is uninteresting. Not that I always do—but if I abandon a book I reproach myself, my slackness of will.

When I have to stop reading for any reason, I try to get to a round number—page 250, or 400. Substitute closure.

The pleasure taken in finishing, in being able to put a mental tick-mark beside the title. In younger days especially, but even now, the obsessive checking of lists of OTHER AVAILABLE TITLES printed at the back of Vintage and Anchor paperbacks. *The Decline and Fall of the Roman Empire, The Essays of Montaigne* . . . No matter how much I read, I always felt that according to some standard—that of the hypothetical intelligence behind those lists—I didn't know anything and never would. I finished with Thomas Mann and looked to see how much I'd gained on my ignorance. But the list seemed to have expanded again. How was it that I had not yet read *The World's Body* by John Crowe Ransom?

The urge to exhaustiveness has always been there. Just now I recall wandering through the stacks of the Birmingham Public Library as a boy. I had no tools for discriminating among the great, the good, the mediocre; I naturally assumed that all books were equal. And with a mathematical precocity that warred bitterly against my desire, I knew that I would not have the time, ever, to read each one.

I would sit at a library table with an enormous stack of books, no longer excited—as I had been while selecting them—but filled with a torpid despair. How many times in my life have I compiled a list of everything that I would have to read in order to be educated? How did those lists change? How is it that I have given up making them—should I consider that a victory or a defeat?

Fetishism. I bring home a book that I know I will consume promptly. The expectation changes the feel of my life for a time. I must prolong the sensation, but not indefinitely. I leave the book in the bag and set it by the armchair. I go into the kitchen and make lunch. I try to keep the book, and the imminent pleasure, out of my thoughts. I dwell on other things, calibrate delays. I make some coffee, clean up. Then finally, coffee in hand, I go back to the armchair. Coffee cup, cigarettes, ashtray: my accouterments. The cigarette is lit, the book comes out of the bag. But there is much ritual to be gone through before I begin reading. I stare at the cover, turn the book over, and inspect the back. If there is a picture of the author, I study that. I read every bit of print on the jacket flaps carefully. I thumb through to assess the thickness. I inspect the title page, the copyright page. I look to the back for an author's note, a bibliography, an index. Then, not yet willing to plunge in, I dabble. I open the book and read a phrase, turn and read another. A word here, a word there.

There is dread about starting, just as, later, there will be dread about finishing. A complex emotion, really. For as much as I want to read, I also want *not* to read. At this moment, in my anticipation, the book is still pure possibility. Any reading will diminish it. With the first word I will plummet from freedom to contingency. A paradox: for the world of the book represents freedom when set alongside the contingency of daily life. I linger between submission and resistance. The first sentence is there like a distant ledge—I have to will myself to jump

and I have to land in just the right way. The transition from the flickerings of thought to the discipline of reading is always abrupt, a forced deceleration.

I read the first sentence over and over, sounding its depth. I read it as many times as I have to. And only when I feel that I "have" it, do I proceed. The physics of reading: how the eye picks up speed, how the prickly word-clusters flatten as the first planes of sense are established.

Readers of novels. I sometimes think that I could, if put to it, pick the real readers of novels out of a crowd. They have a strangeness about the eye, almost as if there were an extra bit of lens on the cornea. I know the look, too: an intimate detachment, a coolness shot through with abstract passion. The glance of a reader shows me a soul with a different orientation to time, an orientation not encountered in the eye of the swinger of clubs, the hobbyist active on his lathe, or the reclining figure with the remote-control apparatus in his hand.

My father: "There's enough to think about with real problems, why add on the problems of make-believe people?" He's right, in a sense. Life is not only sufficient—it exceeds every criterion of sufficiency. Am I lacking? Or is there something that he doesn't know about?

There is reality, and there is reality. I don't believe that there is any involvement with the world I could find that would turn me from the immersions of fiction. I could not give an adequate definition of reality, but I do know that I *feel* most real, most *in the world,* when I can achieve double vision. When I am able, in other words, to compound involvement and detachment. That exquisite blend: to be engrossed in a certain action and to feel, simultaneously, the place of that action within a larger perspective. While reading I register everything in terms of the latter. When I turn from the book, however, I feel my life reestablishing its firm contours. For a short time the terms are in equation: as much as the fiction felt like life, just so does life feel like fiction. I grasp myself from the point of view of an author who is writing the destiny of the character that is me. Illusion or no, the sensation nourishes my soul, which prolongs it as much as it can.

I am reading *Madame Bovary* for the third, maybe fourth, time. I know full well what is going to happen to the poor woman—curiosity cannot be my motivation. Nor, really, am I reading for moral edification, or for a better understanding of the nineteenth-century provincial life. Why, then? I read the book because of what happens to me when I read it, because it makes me feel a certain way about my life.

It allows me to concentrate on aspects of the real that otherwise elude me.

Flaubert, Graham Greene, Henry James, Virginia Woolf, Robertson Davies, Thomas Hardy—each author allows me to experience sensations that I find nowhere else. Each novel is a differently cut and differently tinted lens that I turn upon myself.

Hardy imparts to me a sense of distance and panorama—I see the lives of Jude and Tess as though from an elevation. I observe their doings, partake of their thoughts, but I also see the countryside receding toward the horizon. Even as I follow Hardy's words, I am grasping something about my own life *sub specie aeternitatis.* When I read *To the Lighthouse,* on the other hand, I feel as though I'm looking at the world through an enlarging mechanism. I see Mrs. Ramsay adjusting the delicate ornaments on her mantelpiece, perceive the glint of light on a surface of rubbed brass, and when I turn from the page—no, even before—I'm conscious of my life as a stream of little movements, a slow-motion study of particulars. It seems, when I look up, that the light from my own windows is falling with special intensity on the dusty carpet.

How to account for that extraordinary excitement that sometimes comes over me in the middle of a page? As Henry Miller has written apropos of Blaise Cendrars: "There were times when reading Cendrars . . . that I put the book down in order to wring my hands with joy or despair, with anguish or with desperation."

The inner switch. When I pick up a novel, I do so with the anticipation of surrendering that loathsome self-consciousness that accompanies me through so much of my waking life. And as I begin to read, as I catch myself slipping past the surfaces of the words, away from one measure of time and into another (which, as duration, is actually without measure), a powerful agitation overtakes me. It is not because I care, really, whether Laura marries Nick—although I must, in a sense, in order to keep reading—it is because as I read about Laura and Nick, about the psychological and emotional intricacies of their relationship, my psyche begins its own strange oscillations. I'm reading about *them,* and paying close attention, but at the same time I'm reprocessing, in split-second bursts, my own history, the events of my own relationships. This is something different from identification. Identification requires a loss of critical distance; this process depends upon maintaining it. I live through episodes from my own life from the point of view of another mind, the author's. I see myself from a remove that I cannot claim when I just close my eyes and think back. When I try to do that I'm too much present—I cannot prevent the director's shaping reflex.

How much do the glimmers of memory triggered while reading a book resemble the contents of involuntary memory as defined by Proust?

This remembering and reprocessing explains why cinema, no matter how sophisticated its registry of psychological process, cannot replace the novel. For when we watch film we are forced to keep pace with the screen event. We cannot stop or hover; we cannot perform those essential pauses, or step back in order to confirm a sensation. The fictional immersion, like the cinematic, belongs to the realm of duration, but only when reading can we experience those exalting collisions between time as sequence (daily life) and time as duration. I look up: I am staring dumbfounded at the plant by the window while still quick with Emma's anxious fear.

Where am I when I'm reading? How can it be that I am more present in Emma's attic than in my own chair? And when I consider that that attic perhaps never really existed, except in Flaubert's mind . . .

A possibility: that I read, finally, just to have that hovering between states. Midway between the novel and the realities of the quotidian lies a horizon and a vanishing point. There the sense of contingency disappears.

Madame Bovary. I reread and cherish this book because it allows me, while I'm reading it, and for a period after I have put it aside, to perceive my life not as a random sequence of events, or an accident, but as a destiny.

I never tire of stories because I never tire of envisioning my own life as a story. I am not so much avid for the plot as for the leverage of distance that it gives me.

My mother has a bottomless fund of anecdotes. "It was an interesting story," she says. "They were very happily married—at least everybody thought so—and they had a beautiful child, a son. But then, for some reason, nobody knows why, he began to drink. And after that things started to fall apart. . . ." The simplest of accounts would kindle me. Why? The story is not *that* interesting, especially when presented without detail or narrative tension. No, I would get excited because the telling put me in the presence of another time-frame. So long as I could actively contemplate life as an illusory condensation of events, I was removed from my imprisoning moment-to-moment awareness.

> The novel is significant . . . not because it presents someone else's fate to us, perhaps didactically, but because this stranger's fate by virtue of the flame which consumes it yields us the warmth which we never draw from our own fate. What draws the reader to the novel is the hope of warming his shivering life with the death he reads about.
>
> —Walter Benjamin

I read about Emma. I see her moving to her doom. At the same time, I am, in a sense, inside Emma, seeing life as it presents itself to her. Her actions are not tainted by the foreknowledge of doom. The tension between perspectives is almost unbearable. Why do I seek it out? Because for once I can be both God—as Flaubert likened the author to God—and creation. I carry the awareness off the page. Am I, too, struggling along in the world of short views, projecting my dreams upon an opaque future, utterly oblivious to the larger pattern already inscribed in my deeds? To call God a novelist and our lives fictions suggests either (*a*) that what we perceive as time is complete in Him as knowledge, or (*b*) that He is creating at every instant, in full command of His enormous inspiration.

One thing that has always been clear to me is that my agitation while reading has more to do with the mystery of my own being than it does with the particular velocity of any character.

Dread about finishing. Diminishment, the return to a fixed contour. I have participated as possibility is artfully narrowed into a fate. I carry that narrowing sensation back into my own life.

Authors, too, must face this termination. I notice how often they take leave of their characters before the last chapter. Time is suddenly compressed, years are made to pass: estrangement tactics. As if the novelist were letting his creations grow away slowly into the lives that he has made possible for them.

George Steiner has lamented that our age is leaving behind the habits of the book. He blames distraction, the loss of private time, and competing media. Why does the idea afflict me with such sadness? After all, people should be able to do what they want. I will always have *my* books; it is not likely that libraries will soon disappear. It must be that for me books are not just objects or means to ends—they are the symbol, and incarnation, of the life of the spirit. I fear that reverie and introspection and ideals of discrimination will gradually vanish from the culture. I fear that linguistic sophistication (and density, and difficulty), and with it our access to the real complexity of the inner life, are being pushed to the side by the simplistic and standardized idiocies of the television idiom. The real fear is that this is the fate of the race in larger evolutionary terms—that the ideals of the Enlightenment were tested, like a tentative morphological feature, and are being discarded; that *Homo sapiens* is deciding, collectively, to rid itself of sapience, because there is no utility in pondering why it exists or where it is headed; that evolution will prove, in terms of the Enlightenment ideal, the very opposite. This is a reader's nightmare. It haunts me whenever I walk through a suburban mall or turn on the television set. I look to my books for reassurance. Sometimes I feel not so much reassured as nearly extinct.

Rereading

Not long after I'd agreed to pull together some thoughts about rereading, I came upon this quotation from Nabokov: "You cannot read a novel, you can only re-read it." Never one to ignore the beck of serendipity, I scribbled the words down; I trusted that they would magnetize the particles needed for a little *feuilleton*. But as that formulation began to radiate its spokes of energy, I found myself more irritated than intrigued. I had the same chafing sensation I'd had in grade school when the wag in the next seat passed me a note that read, "This sentence is false."

I knew what Nabokov meant, of course—that there is no real appreciation without closer focus, that literature does not kiss on the first date, and so on. But I had other problems with his declaration. One was strictly logical: how can we use the word "rereading" unless "reading" already means something? Whether or not we understand a work of literature the first time through, we are nonetheless doing something by moving our eyes back and forth. That's obvious, though, and I'm sure Nabokov knew quite well he was being provocative. The other difficulty, a more serious one, has to do with the implications of the idea. For what he is saying is that there is no living, only remembering. That may have been true for Nabokov (read his *Speak Memory*), but I don't believe it's binding on the rest of us. I would sooner hold, with Heraclitus, that it's always a different river and always a different I stepping into it. In which case, clearly, the proposition would be reversed: you cannot reread a novel, you can only read it.

I can think of a number of reasons for going back to a novel. If it was difficult to get through the first time—as with *Ulysses* or *Molloy*—we may return with a desire for mastery. If, on the other hand, our first experience was one of delight, or discovery, we may try to recoup some of those same sensations. Often we recall not so much the contents of a novel as our reactions to it. "I really loved that book," we might say in all honesty and yet be unable to tell our interlocutor the first thing about it. Then, invariably, there are the select novels we consider our own. We pride ourselves on knowing them well; when we pick them up again, it's for self-confirmation. They are where we store our fantasies and ambitions; we have dreamed our secret lives into them. Opening to the first page is like biting into a honeycomb.

That may be wishful thinking on my part. I know that going back to a novel, even a favorite, can be like running into an old lover on the street: the flat plane of the present gets a hole punched through it. Indeed, the book can be even more disconcerting than the lover. For we know that flesh succumbs to gravity, and we can deflect the true horror of time's passing with a simple reversal: "How you've changed. . . ." But words are supposed to stand still. Were these the people we read about, suffered with? Or did some archfiend come in the night and rearrange the scenes? Soon enough we have to admit it: *we* have changed.

What a perplexing thing! The same letters, the same words and sentences, but everything means differently. When I read *The Great Gatsby* in high school, for instance, I enclosed Jay Gatsby in a soft mist. His love for Daisy Buchanan was noble and rare, and it redeemed any character flaws he might have had. Yet when I reread the book a few years back, I was shocked to see what a pathetically deluded creature he was. Naturally, I prided myself on having picked up a thing or two about human nature. At the same time, though, I found I missed the fellow I had known. Both of them, in fact—Gatsby with his dream of love, and myself in all my susceptible innocence.

As we pass our eyes over rows and rows of words, the situations and sensations that they denote arouse in us a persuasive phantom reality. This mysterious semblance is only in part the author's creation. He marshals his sentences to create one particular world; we elicit from them quite another. We modify landscapes with images from our own experience; we thrust tics and attributes upon characters in order to pull them into the desired shape. When we return to a book, we encounter more than just the author's words—we simultaneously tour the picturesque ruins of our former selves.

We discover, too, how fickle and selective is our gaze. Rushing along to discover whether Alphonse would marry Giselle, we took no notice of Cedric's remarkable yellow waistcoat. The second time through, however, when we know damned well that the lovers will triumph, we find ourselves blinking with delight at the canary brightness of the cloth. Background and foreground are determined only in part by the author, whatever his skills; our own attention pattern decides the rest. Neither can we control what we notice and what we slight. We read and reread with the same irreproducible singularity with which we live and remember. To paraphrase Wallace Stevens: two people talking about one book are two people talking about two books. . . .

Memory compresses impressions, at times to the verge of invisibility. When we finish a novel, we don't retain the whole sequence in our minds. We fold the events and the resolution together into a kind of magician's handkerchief. A conversation or recollection may prompt us to unfold a particular episode for reinspection. But it is not the episode that we originally read, even if we are gifted with perfect recall. For hindsight—our knowledge of how it all came out—has already played its tricks with the passage. Looking back on a novel, or rereading it, is, in this sense, analogous to looking back on events from our own past. With this difference: in the novel the facts are all in and only interpretations remain; in our own lives, however, future events may yet rearrange the past. Closure comes for us, if at all, with the last exhalation.

The subtlest and most potent pleasures of rereading derive from this strange correspondence between written narrative and the narrative that we fashion of our own lives. When we read a novel for the first time, we are paralleling—though in a very compressed way—our own processing of experience. We expect, to be sure, that the novel will have a dramatically satisfying shape. But do we finally hope for anything less with regard to our own lives? Events, unforeseen combinations, and decisions stream toward us out of the diminishing sheaves of type, as if out of the obscurity of the future. We recognize this; we hypostatize the unread pages so that they become, in effect, the future. We could, it's true, skip quickly forward to find out how everything works out. But unless we are perverse, we resist the temptation. It is far more interesting to savor the coming events under the illusory aspect of free choice. Maybe the doomed lovers will find happiness; maybe Gatsby will win Daisy. We pit ourselves against the already determined unknown, and the tension of our will imparts to the words a special electricity.

But then what about rereading? Wouldn't we have to say that reading—finding out—discharges the electricity once and for all? With the ordinary narrative (a run-of-the-mill mystery novel, say), it clearly does. With any novel substantial enough to support a rereading, however, the tension just manifests itself differently.

Reading takes place in the order of free choice, rereading in the order of destiny. As we would probably act differently if we could relive certain parts of our lives, so do we read differently when we know the fates of the characters. The second time around, our desires are set into play against our knowing. The sensations are entirely different: I can still hope that Gatsby will get Daisy, but now I suffer his every move with the certainty that he will not. He becomes another man. In my original reading I felt congruous with him—at least in the sense that I knew no more of the future than he did. Now, of necessity, I am in the superior position. I can only pity his illusion of free choice. He can do nothing that will not lead him to the pistol and the swimming pool. Rereading flatters me by allowing me the vantage of a god, or at least of an author.

Looking at my own shelves, I see only two kinds of novels: those that I mean to read and those I mean to reread. Future and past, you might say. But that wouldn't be quite right. In his essay "Writers and Daydreaming," Freud wrote that the memory of an experience in which a wish was fulfilled "creates a situation relating to the future which represents the fulfillment of the wish." To me that means that when I look at the books I've read and kept—kept because they have in some way fulfilled a desire—I am in fact projecting myself into the future.

I was going to end by saying: tell me what you reread and I'll tell you who you are. Then I changed it to: tell me what you reread and I'll tell you who you'd like to be. But now I'm wondering whether the two are so different. Couldn't we say: you are what you'd like to be? Or is the logic of that simply too Nabokovian?

The Leaning Umbrella: A Reflection on Flaubert

Though I'm probably as jealous as the next writer of the awards and honors bestowed upon my fellows, I have never really coveted anyone else's style or subject—there are limits. Recently, however, I came across an advertisement for a book entitled *The Perpetual Orgy: Flaubert and "Madame Bovary"* (1986) by the Peruvian novelist Mario Vargas Llosa. It was billed as the record of Vargas Llosa's lifelong passion for the novel and its eponymous heroine, a work of celebratory investigation. It was as if I had been in love all these years without knowing it—my realization came with the announcement of betrothal. At that moment, I felt that I had never wanted anything more than to write that book.

I read *The Perpetual Orgy* in a single gulp. I simultaneously hoped that Vargas Llosa would say everything I'd felt and thought about *Madame Bovary,* and that it would miss the mark completely. It turned out to be a case of both and neither. The book was brimming with insights and exclamations; Vargas Llosa pointed out a hundred things that I had never noticed. On the other hand, he neglected to explore some of the facets of *Bovary* that have haunted me most: how Flaubert revealed Emma's destiny as the interaction of character and circumstance—she *willed* her end—or how much the crystalline perfection of the novel's design was rooted in hatred. Observations that Vargas Llosa made in lowercase, I would have capitalized, while certain of his other points seemed marginal to me. Still, it was an admirable labor of love, and Vargas Llosa deserves the gratitude of Flaubert lovers everywhere. These few added reflections are just my way of soothing a galvanized nerve.

Madame Bovary is more than just a supremely crafted novel or a harrowing narrative of a fate unfolding. It is, if I may adopt the fashionable phraseology, fiction in its purest state of fictionality. Unlike certain contemporary texts, however, which remind the reader of their status through the various kinds of authorial subversion (I'm thinking of self-consuming artifacts like Calvino's *If on a Winter's Night a Traveler* and Fowles's *The French Lieutenant's Woman*), Flaubert achieves this effect through the sheer perfection of design. Every scene, every sentence, every *word* has been set into place with tweezer precision; there is not a superfluous syllable in the book. The author's ideal was the creation of a self-sustaining fictional world, one that would be functional down to the smallest cogwheel. To achieve this, he absented himself entirely: at no point can we say, "This is Flaubert speaking." ("The artist," he wrote in a famous letter, "must be in his work like God . . . everywhere felt, but never seen.") *Madame Bovary* manifests a complete relational integrity. Its elaborate invented world exerts upon the reader the full pressure of necessity; the least of its actions is at once a cause and an effect. Naturalistic illusionism—and fictionality—can be taken no further. After Flaubert, the novel as form could only decline, or change.

Any number of novels, I find, can compel participatory involvement. If the characters and the situation are in the least bit interesting, I have no trouble suspending disbelief and immersing myself. Disbelief seems to *crave* suspension. Too often, however, this illusion of being inside another world has more to do with the reader's desire than with the author's skill. I don't know how many novels I've gone back to, only to find that the mainspring has broken—the language will not come alive again. I realize at those times that I have authored much of my own reading experience.

Madame Bovary is different in this way. No matter how often I return to it, no matter how well or poorly I am disposed toward Emma (I have been taken in by her, I have pitied her, I have reviled her), Flaubert's serene-seeming world is waiting to receive me. I do not have to break my way in with exertions of the imagination. The terrain, the town, the rooms—everything is there, undiminished in its palpability. I feel, then, as if I have been off traveling, that I am returning to a place and a way of life that the intervening years have left intact. This is not to say, of course, that Flaubert has left nothing to the reader's imagination. On the contrary: because the ground has been laid out for us so meticulously, we are that much more free to conjure the fine points for ourselves.

Flaubert's agonies of composition are legendary. In letter after letter, he chronicled his ordeal—the days spent grooming the cadence of a single sentence, the long, depressed *marinades* on the couch in his study . . . To Louise Colet he wrote:

> What a beastly thing prose is! It's never finished; there is always something to do over. A good prose sentence must be like a good line of verse, *unchangeable,* as rhythmic, as sonorous. That at least is my ambition (there is one thing I'm certain of: there's no one who has ever had in mind a more perfect type of prose than I have; but as for the execution, what weaknesses, good Lord, what weaknesses!).

Passages like this have contributed to the popular impression that Flaubert was primarily a stylist, that form and presentation had precedence over content. Preposterous! What Flaubert was after in his struggle for a stylistic absolute was a total elimination of the form-content distinction. He believed, like few writers before or since, in the fundamental correspondence between words and the world; every sensation and material detail had its linguistic equivalent. The triumph of style would be implicitly the triumph of content as well.

But Flaubert's obsession went far beyond the painstaking construction of sentences. Structure, too, was a matter of absolutes. The right disposition of description and incident could create in the reader the illusion of an autonomous reality. The composition of *Madame Bovary* took as long as it did—five years of concentrated daily work—not just because the sentences took that long to write, but because the design was of such intricacy. The least movement of a walk-on character, the dilations and contractions of the time-frame, the subtle associative echoes between scenes—*everything* had to be plotted out in advance. Flaubert hovered over his planning sheets like a demented watchmaker. No matter how intently one scrutinizes the text, it's impossible to see through the artifice of its construction.

I have read the book six times now (I've never gone back to anything else more than once). The first time—it was, I remember, the summer after my sophomore year in college—I was bent upon improving myself. I was delighted to discover that a so-called classic could be so involving. The gusts of Emma's suffering had me spinning like a weathervane. As the end drew near, I begged her creator to intercede on her behalf. When she finally died, I was crushed. But I felt that I knew once and for all about the implacability of fate. My immersion had been emotional: I had picked up nothing of the subplots or the satiric interludes.

Since then, I have reread *Madame Bovary* for pleasure as well as for teaching purposes. Each time I have been startled by the changes I've found. It's almost as if the master himself had been there during my absence, adding, subtracting, altering the way the sunlight strikes the slate roofs, bringing minor characters forward into greater prominence. The world is deeply familiar, as I said, but I see so many things in it differently. Emma's visit to the ball at La Vaubyessard, for example: in my memory the festivities go on and on. My last rereading convinced me that my text had somehow been abridged. And Emma's love affair with Rodolphe: I've added a volume of hesitations and coy exchanges to the scene leading up to her surrender.

My first impulse, quite naturally, was to attribute all inconsistencies to the fallibility of my own memory. But no—the longer I live with the novel, the more certain I am that Flaubert intended this experience for his reader. The whole narrative has been structured to expand in retrospect. Through the considered arrangement of resonating details, through the strategic use of time compressions (Vargas Llosa illuminates these expertly), and, most of all, through the associative play of Emma's own memory, Flaubert secures a self-augmenting afterlife for his episodes. My confusion about the ball illustrates this perfectly. The scene itself was not long. But Flaubert let Emma recall one detail after another in her subsequent reveries. What's more, he had arranged it that she should find, and keep, the vicomte's cigar case; the object acquires for her an almost Proustian density of association. It is inevitable that the scene, in recollection, rises up like one of those intricate ships that fill their bottles at a tug of the string.

Reading through *Madame Bovary* with students has only confirmed my sense of its inexhaustibility. We have ranged back and forth, combing the narrative like a team of detectives. The premise behind the activity is very simple: that Flaubert inserted nothing gratuitously, that every detail has a function that can be traced and explicated. What's interesting is that for all our patient plucking of strands, not one student has vented the familiar complaint—that the process is "nitpicky" or irrelevant. More often, I have felt their awe. It is a revelation to most that prose can hold so much, and that microscopic inspection can produce such a yield. I hate to tell them that Flaubert is a special case, that most novels dissolve like cigar ash under similar scrutiny.

Vargas Llosa's keen excitement sent me back for still another plunge. I don't know whether it was my own state of mind, or whether his observations had influenced me, but this time I was intrigued above all by the novel's spatial depth, its material solidity. Objects seemed held in the grip of gravity, and the air surrounding them was not mere absence—its transparence conveyed a sense of cubic volume. Flaubert, I realized, was possessed of an extraordinary optical sophistication. He staged every perspective and vantage to enhance the reader's illusion of three-dimensionality.

The principle behind this is not unlike that of the stereoscope, where the eye superimposes two differently angled images to create a simulation of spatial depth. Knowing that the reader converts verbal description into discrete mental pictures, Flaubert assembled his narrative in such a way that almost every image would call up the memory of a counterpart. Early on, for instance, as some of the Yonville residents gather at the inn to await the arrival of the new doctor, Flaubert lets it drop that Monsieur le curé is waiting to see whether the Hirondelle might not also be carrying the umbrella that he had left behind at the convent in Ernemont. Caught up in the bustle of the Bovarys' arrival, we put the detail completely out of our thoughts. But then, pages later, as the new arrivals are leaving the inn to go to their home, we get this: ". . . the stable boy, lantern in hand, was waiting to light Monsieur and Madame Bovary home. There were wisps of straw in his red hair, and his left leg was lame. He took Monsieur le curé's umbrella in his other hand, and the company set out."

A mere trifle. We forgot, and now we remember. But with this simple completion of the circuit, Flaubert makes us understand that the world did not disappear while the new Yonvillians ate and chattered by the fire. A leaning umbrella (I picture it so) forces us to fill in a world.

A single instance would not, of course, suffice. Here is another. When she is standing in her attic, clutching Rodolphe's goodbye letter, Emma glances out and sees their neighbor Binet in the window opposite. He is bent over his lathe. Much later, when she is in the throes of desperation, rushing from place to place to beg for money, Madame Tuvache and Madame Caron climb to the latter's attic to spy. From their place they watch Emma open the door and step into Binet's workroom; he is, as ever, at his lathe. There are hundreds, maybe thousands, of similar cross-references in *Madame Bovary,* most of them visual. And every time that we are made to recall an image that we have pushed aside, the impression of an independently existing world is fortified.

I dwell on these aspects of the novel because they have most recently been in my thoughts. Even so, every observation I have made has supplanted innumerable others that I would have liked to have made. On the subject of Emma's boredom, for example, or on the question raised by Walker Percy in one of his essays: why does it exhilarate us to read about another person's despair? Or, or . . . A perpetual orgy, I suppose, is one in which the participants are never sated.

Television: The Medium in the Mass Age

No one who has walked through the excavations at Herculaneum and Pompeii is likely to forget the oppressiveness of the experience, far outweighing its historical fascination or its cachet as future table talk. The dreariness of a George Segal sculpture has been multiplied a thousandfold; the heavy seal of Time has been impressed upon the ordinariness of daily life. We are suddenly able to imagine our lives embalmed at a casual moment. Indeed, I sometimes wonder what hypothetical aliens might find if their craft landed, years hence, somewhere on our shores. I try to imagine their exclamations, their cries of puzzlement, as they go from house to house. I envision through their eyes the petrified, white-washed figures, their arrangement—singly, in groups—some four to eight feet from a prominent upended box. There would be boxes with horns, boxes without. Gender markings? The more enlightened among them would shake their heads. "These are clearly religious objects, domestic shrines. We have found the remains of a very spiritual race."

Television. The truth of it is too much to grasp, too various. Seen synoptically, from an imagined altitude, all these blue lights look like a radiant roe, or a swarm of cells in a tissue culture. But from another place, from the ease of a chair in a room, they seem like nothing much, a breather from the assaults of the day, a few laughs, a shine of fantasy. Both views are true; neither view is true. Who is going to say? And how? Stalk it with language and it cackles at you; formulate a concept and it sprays you with dots. It is as tricky as mercury. You shiver it to pieces and it hugs itself back together. Mercury is apt. If you could do the impossible, if you could contrive some kind of barometric instrument for which television and its contents were a mercury, you would be able to read the spiritual air pressure of a time and place. But in fact you can do little more than play, break it into blobs, stare at their sheen, watch as they hurry back into a single imponderable lump.

At one time, twenty years ago, say, to write about television was a more feasible undertaking. Twenty years ago television had not seeped as deeply into the culture; it was not so co-extensive with the social fabric. There were still free zones, places to stand, Archimedean points from which to work the lever. This is no longer the case. Where television could once be considered apart from reality, as a toy, an "entertainment," it has now greatly expanded its reach and impact: it has become, by way of massive social participation, a significant portion of the reality itself. So much so, in fact, that the interface between society and television can no longer be clearly described. Television programs increasingly compose the content of private lives; shows and situations are discussed as if the personalities and events were real and in the world; the information and opinion purveyed determine, to a large extent, the public perception of historical and political events. To discuss the phenomenon, therefore, with some hope of grasping its essential nature, its quidditas, is to embark on one of those classic fool errands—to quest for fleece. Though in this case the fleece takes the form, in Norman Mailer's words, of "a pullulation of electrons."

Tele-vision. Quite literally "vision at a distance" or "over a distance"; also, the instrument or appliance whereby this is accomplished. When not in use it is a strange enough object, an opaque window fronting a box, the box studded with dials and connected, by way of wire and plug, to the sorcery of an electrical system. Its function, by all accounts, is to provide entertainment and information. Like the automobile and the telephone, it has become nearly indispensable. Like the automobile and the telephone, it is one of our guarantors of equality: anyone can drive anywhere, call anywhere—any American can watch any show.

Television watching, this vast and ramified ritual, this mass phenomenon, is scarcely served by the word "entertainment." It wears the guise of being a relaxant—like softball, dancing, or drinking—but it is so much more, or less, than that. If it were simply entertainment or relaxation that people sought, they would soon be driven to other expedients: the fare is passing poor. No, there is very little correlation between the available entertainment content and the eight hundred or so million man-hours that are put in—every day—in front of two hundred million television sets.

Television represents the "outside world" to the individual. This is one of its services. To own a television is to have a seat in the arena where the world is visually presented. Of course, television is by no means co-extensive with the world, nor do its visual contents in any way encompass the world; but it is part of the nature of the medium to convey this impression subliminally. By simply pressing a button, the viewer makes contact with what is, in his imagination, an international information empire. The assurance is patent that if anything of urgent importance happens anywhere in the world, the information will be promptly conveyed. In this one sense television is no different from the radio. The fact that it is a visual medium, however, greatly magnifies the unconscious impact of this function.

But this is basic, obvious. There is another function that is far more important and worrisome: television acts upon the unconscious of the viewer not as an appliance or a plaything, but as a consciousness. It fosters and encourages the most bizarre sort of identification. The implications are staggering. But before we consider them we must question some of the mechanics of this phenomenon.

The identification is not really attributable to the fact that the medium delivers human voices and images. Those are contents. Prior to contents are the impacts of the form itself, the medium. Consider, first of all, the seamlessness: the impression derived from the absence of holes and gaps, coupled with its electronic nature, coupled further with its insistent uniformity. The visual possibilities of the medium are, potentially speaking, inexhaustible. But what has in fact happened is that the corporation-owned networks have narrowed the range and content of presentation to such an extent that it is impossible to distinguish one channel from another. The idea of channels as separate bands is further negated by constant switching. Not only is the medium seamless, its contents are as well. The result is that they become, for the viewer, different simultaneous utterances by the same entity, and, in the last analysis, one utterance. And this entity, television, thereby takes on the lineaments of consciousness.

This ersatz consciousness is, so far as its contents are concerned, rudimentary enough. It scarcely reflects the complexities of the human mental operation. Its form, however, is unconsciously most persuasive. It depends upon—and itself creates—lack of resistance. There are no obstacles. The visual and auditory materials are ingested directly with no need for translation. They are calculated thus: to resemble reality while being simpler than reality. The fluidity of the medium conditions us to passive absorption. There is nothing to engage the conscious faculty. A broad, one-way "channel" is opened between the medium and the unconscious. As we suspend our supervisory powers the medium sets itself up as a surrogate. It is with our consent that a generally flat, banal configuration of materials is alchemized into a ghostly dimensionality.

What is the nature of the medium that can effect so subtle an interchange? Norman Mailer, in his essay "Of a Small and Modest Malignancy, Wicked and Bristling with Dots" (*Pieces and Pontifications,* 1982), writes:

> Often, when the stations would go off the air and no programs were left to watch, he would still leave the set on. The audio would hum in a tuneless pullulation, and the dots would hiss in an agitation of what forces he did not know. This hiss and the hum would fill the room and then his ears. There was, of course, no clamor—it was nearer to antinoise dancing in eternity with noise. And watching the empty video, he would recognize it was hardly empty. Bands of grey and lighter grey swam across the set, rollovers swept away the dots, and something like sunspots crackled forth.

The primeval echo of the passage is not fortuitous—the gray, tuneless hum represents nothing so much as our idea of undifferentiated consciousness. We know these sputtering voids because we produce something very like them in ourselves. Eyes closed, emptied of thought, hovering near sleep, we fill up with a similar pullulation. This is the primary level of identification: that our consciousness generates images and thoughts—contents—out of an agitated void just as television does. The medium has a psychic likeness. And we project upon that likeness something of our own sense of psychic dimension. It is this dimensionality—which does not actually exist—that welds into a disquieting unity the various differentiated emanations.

Identification and projection, both subliminal, secure a reality status for what is, in essence, a play of illusion. It could even be argued that we attribute a higher reality status to television than we do to life itself. I say this only half in jest. I suspect that there is a certain, by no means small, percentage of chronic viewers in whom the organized materials of television programming have effectively replaced any active, discriminating consciousness they might have once possessed. But can it be that the two—consciousness and television—are similar enough to be interchangeable? Or, to put the question differently, can it be that life as seen on television is effectively interchangeable with life as the individual experiences it? These are by no means idle questions.

It is not television that is conforming to modern life so much as it is modern life that is taking on the hues of the medium. The processes that strip modern experience of uniqueness and resonance, that make possible the shopping mall, the housing project, the uniformity of the suburb, the bland interiors of the workplace—the list could go on and on—these prepare us for television. Since television cannot transmit uniqueness or resonance by its very nature (I will discuss this later with reference to the concept of "aura"), it is admirably suited to mirror modern experience. To television belongs all the persuasiveness of the ordinary. Its flatness, banality, the ambient feel it confers to time, all conform closely to our experience. What is more, it presents us with that experience in distilled and organized shape. We experience ordinariness in condensation; it is more real to us than the ordinariness of our lives. The fact that it is electronically "bedded" impresses upon it the stamp of authority.

Television as consciousness. This impression comes, in part, from a simple, potent illusion: that we perceive the medium as layered, and therefore deep. The illusion is created by constant alternation of contents. The hero is, say, trapped inside a burning building; a sudden—but expected—elision brings us the imagery of a tropic isle, a voice enticing us to sample something unique; another elision brings us the face of our local news anchorman, the pulsing sound of a ticker, a quick-paced summary of the hour's headline. And then we are back in the burning building. The impression is not one of segmentation, but of layering. With our partial suspension of disbelief, we imagine that our hero was battling flames while we were hearing the latest on the border war. The illusion reinforces in yet another way the idea that we are in contact with a complex, superintendent, perhaps even profound entity.

Walter Benjamin was one of the first thinkers to investigate seriously the impacts of technology upon the sphere of art. He did not live to see the invention of television, but the structure of his analysis is such that the subsequent technological advance has not altered it significantly. The ideas about "aura" that he articulated and elaborated in his essay "The Work of Art in the Age of Mechanical Reproduction" (*Illuminations,* 1968) are perfectly applicable to the problem of television.

Briefly, aura can be conceived as the invisible envelope of presence or context that surrounds and, in effect, guarantees the uniqueness and reality of a work of art. It is, by nature, impenetrable and intransmissible. Though Benjamin defines the concept primarily with reference to art, he recognizes its generality. Aura is the essential attribute of any individual, location, situation, or object that has not been compromised by displacement or reproduction. He writes:

> We define the aura . . . as the unique phenomenon of a distance, however close it [the object] may be. If, while resting on a summer afternoon, you follow with your eyes a mountain range on the horizon or a branch which casts its shadow over you, you experience the aura of those mountains, of that branch.

Aura forms, in other words, the basis of subjective experience; it cannot be objectively isolated. To take anything from its natural context is to destroy its aura. Anything stripped of its aura is no longer that thing—its certificate of uniqueness is gone. Insofar as it then presents itself in the guise of the original, it is false.

This fairly simple recognition—though, of course, much ramified by Benjamin's prismatic intelligence—was one of the bases for his critique of modern life, a critique that centered itself upon the disintegration of meaning and the radical disharmony between the individual and his world.

A few sentences later, Benjamin claims:

> Every day the urge grows stronger to get hold of an object at very close range by way of its likeness, its reproduction. Unmistakably, reproduction as offered by picture magazines and newsreels differs from the image as seen by the unarmed eye. Uniqueness and permanence are as closely linked in the latter as are transitoriness and reproducibility in the former. To pry an object from its shell, to destroy its aura, is a mark of a perception whose "sense of the universal equality of things" has increased to such a degree that it extracts it even from a unique object by means of reproduction.

If we consider not just objects, but the fragile, context-bound webbing of all human interchange—which television undertakes to mimic and reproduce—then the concept of aura is immensely useful.

We must take care, however, to avoid the direct substitution of terms. The situation is somewhat more complicated. For television does not set out to reproduce the actual world. Nor, with few exceptions, does it pretend to transmit genuine human interaction in context. No, what television does is to manufacture situations and interactions among created, scripted personalities. What it delivers, therefore, is essentially a caricature of social reality, the simulacra of human exchange. There is no question of aura being destroyed—what is captured by the television cameras has no aura to begin with. Instead, subtly and insidiously, reality, the genuine human interaction, is being steadily sponged, divested of authority. The aura is robbed, not directly, but by proxy. All human exchange—travestied, replicated, absorbed by two hundred million watchers—is progressively, and perhaps permanently, diminished.

Television and aura are incompatible. Anything filmed directly—an animal, a landscape, an embrace—is promptly dispossessed of presence. The image preserves certain accuracies while the essence is flattened out and caricatured. What we receive through the picture tube has the outer lineaments of the actual with none of the pith or savor. The viewer, of course, is not unaware of this. The problem is that after a while—after sufficient exposure—he starts to forget. The more he watches, the more the tension between the thing and its image is vitiated.

Television, I have said, provides a psychic likeness and is received by the unconscious as a consciousness. But it is not a consciousness. It is a hybrid, a collage possessing some of the rudimentary attributes of consciousness. It is utterly bereft of aura. And consciousness without aura, without context or uniqueness, is a monstrosity, a no-presence that matches up with nothing in the natural world. It is something that is not alive that is trying to impersonate life: it is travesty. Possibly Mailer has something like this in mind when he writes:

> So, in those early mornings when television was his only friend, he knew already that he detested his habit. There was not enough to learn from watching TV. Some indispensable pieces of experience were missing. Except it was worse than that. Some-

> thing not in existence was also present, some malignancy to burn against his own malignancy, some onslaught of dots into the full pressure of his own strangled vision.

That "something not in existence" is the Frankenstein of a consciousness pieced together like a quilt from a thousand heteroclite fragments.

To turn on the television set is to make the flight from three dimensions into two. It is an escape, an effort to kill self-reflective consciousness, at least for a time. Two dimensions are easier to reconnoiter in than three. But it is not only while watching that one participates in two-dimensionality. After enough exposure to the medium, the world itself—which we may here define as everything that is *not* television—loses some of its thickness and complexity. The eye of the beholder is altered. Television has the same power of alteration as art, except that it works in the opposite direction. The reality content of the world is diminished rather than augmented. But why? That is, why would consciousness, the supreme distinguishing feature of the species, its evolutionary trademark, wish to obliterate itself? It must, to some extent, be due to the quality of life available to the individual. That life consists, for too many people, of meaningless work and prolonged exposure to the concentrated ordinariness of television. A self-perpetuating tautology sits near the heart of the issue.

Television watching also represents a diffusely enacted participation in ritual. The viewer is, to a certain extent, looking past the content, engaging the form itself, the sentient global mesh that gives the medium much of its authority. This participation is passive and abstract. The viewer interacts with the medium; the medium, in turn, interacts with the whole world of viewers. One makes oneself a part of the circuitry and thereby extends and deepens the circuitry. It is participation in the life of the times—insofar as television watching is itself a significant part of the life of our times. Another tautology. The same impulses that were once discharged actively—in public assembly—are now expressed from the armchair. The medium thus becomes the abstraction of community itself. It is a touchstone, a point of reference. A common mental property attains a powerful pseudoreality through cross-referencing. The coffee break ritual—"Did you see *Dynasty* last night?"—is not so much an expression of interest in the show as it is an act of self-substantiation.

Most discussions and analyses of the effects of television occupy themselves with the contents of programming. I would contend that the effects of the medium itself, the fact of it, its form, the structure through which the contents are presented, are of far greater importance. It is the medium that forges the connection with the unconscious, enables the contents to pass directly by all conscious monitoring. It is the form that gradually conditions the psyche of the viewer.

Television establishes a path of least resistance, visually, psychologically—indeed, it *is* that path. It is a prism that refracts the rays of attentiveness. The attention faculty itself is gradually altered. For one thing, new time-expectancies are created. The viewer becomes accustomed not only to thirty- and sixty-minute units, but to mini-units as well, two- and three-minute blocks of commercial interruption coming every five to seven minutes. The effects of this are not easily gauged, except in the realm of television viewing. Here we find that people come to expect—and need—sidetracking every few minutes. Uninterrupted programming generates anxiety and boredom. The fact is that the commercial interruptions are a welcome distraction from the banality of most programming. Night after night, month after month, the mind is made to be a shuttlecock. How can we believe that this leaves its focus and tenacity unimpaired?

In the same way, the structure of programming promotes the idea of resolvability. The container shapes the content, and not vice versa. Thus, every thirty minutes there has to be a wrap-up, a conclusion. Can it be that the constant repetition of this expectation does not begin to affect the viewer's psyche? That it cannot be proven to do so is no assurance. There are other questions. For example: if television does function as a surrogate consciousness, does this in any way undermine the viewer's existential base, his awareness of himself as a creature suffering time? No one will disagree with the assertion that television makes time more palatable. But what does it mean that time is made more palatable? What painful encounters with the voids in the self are thereby short-circuited?

We cannot very well pursue these questions without bringing will into the discussion. Will, the capacity or power whereby the self consciously acts upon itself. It is will that we call upon in order to persevere in an action, to endure difficulty without relinquishing our intention. Any movement against the natural grain of a situation requires some amount of will. But what are the effects upon the will of prolonged passivity, of putting the self repeatedly into a state of suspended animation, of replacing obstacles by a path of least resistance? Is the faculty of will analogous to a muscle—does it atrophy from lack of use? If it is, then the whole issue of television is tremendously important. For the world will not change its nature to conform to the laws of television. If the will is indeed eroded by television watching, then what is affected is the public as well as private domain. The obvious consequence is political passivity, a passivity that readily translates into susceptibility to power. Nature abhors a vacuum; so does the social sphere. Where there is passivity there will flourish, in some form, the will to power. This is not to say that watching television is paving the way for the demagogue. It is to say, however, that the arena of impact may be larger than we at first imagine.

I have avoided almost entirely the discussion of the contents of television. This is not to say that the contents are negligible. They are not. But I don't believe that their effects can be properly taken into account until certain features of the medium have been examined. Secondly—and this is a more elusive reason—I believe that the contents cannot be discussed independently. They are too much influenced and shaped by the nature of the medium. For this reason a substantial amount of what is "on" television exists below the threshold of language. It is too diffuse, too ambient, too random. It generates a liquid near-emptiness that defies words or concepts.

This randomness is an attribute of the medium more than of the contents. It is a direct consequence of the inability of the electron tube to transmit aura. There is a permanent shortage of legitimate material, of visual elements that will effectively "play." The contents, therefore, are always inadequate to the container; they cannot fill it up enough. What happens as a result is that there are, cumulatively speaking, long minutes of visual vacuum—eternal-seeming car-chase sequences, desolate facial pans, etc. Visual Muzak. A network must fill up all of its allotted time, daily, weekly, yearly. There is not enough quality to go around. What little there is must be diluted into the solution of available time. Television maneuvers, therefore, in a field of extremely narrow options. And the options grow fewer as repetition exhausts the basic repertoire of scenarios. Networks are forced to use the same formulaic high-tension sequences over and over. The stock sitcom imbroglio has not changed from the times of Terence. There is no possibility for visual beauty—nothing beautiful has ever survived passage through the electron tube. For beauty is the apotheosis of aura—it dies running the electronic gauntlet. Instead, there is ambience—not "ambiance"—dead time in which the viewer is brought face to face with the medium itself, its gray, crackling, fundamentally alien presentness.

The case of John Hinckley, Jr., invites a few observations on television content. We are informed that the would-be assassin was a misfit and a loner—the usual epithets—and that prior to his attempt on the president's life he put in hundreds of hours in motels across the country watching game shows, soap operas, and crime shows. Now, I would not dare to be so simplistic as to assert any actual causal connection. Hinckley did not become the kind of person he was by watching television—if he had there would be fifty million Hinckleys in the streets. No, he watched as much television as he did because he was the kind of person he was. The question that emerges is whether or not there was some small but vital area of overlap, some way in which watching exacerbated something in his psyche and rendered certain previously passive traits volatile.

In any case, the issue raised—as murky as it is important—is that of the impact of television, form and content, upon the unconscious. Not just the unconscious of John Hinckley, Jr., but of millions of children and adolescents who have not yet integrated the unconscious into their ego structures. The more hours put in before the pullulating tube, the fewer are the hours spent in contact with the stubborn grain of the world. In other words, the materials absorbed into the unconscious include proportionately more illusion. The unformed, atomized ego structure absorbs the form, the violence, the caricature of relations, and shapes itself to those in the way that it should be shaping itself to actual experience. Again, consider the extreme case—Hinckley. He turned to fantasies of violence, I would argue, not because he had been made violent, but because he did not comprehend what violence really is. Shooting the president was a garish fantasy that took up obvious, available imagery without any understanding of its real nature. Not only is the will subject to erosion, the reality sense is as well.

It has been argued that television, along with certain other developments in modern technology—computerization, information processing—is opening the way for a new social evolution, that the time-honored view of the self—as a solitary, suffering being—is giving way to another. Maybe there is a new socially integrated species of "mass man" waiting in the wings. If so, this passive acceptance of circuity, this collective participation in suspended animation, is to be regarded as highly advantageous.

If this turns out to be the case, I, for one, would surround the word "evolution" with a thicket of quotation marks.

I don't believe that transformations like this take place without profound upheaval. I hold with the Freudian model enough to think that repressed instincts return in altered form. The species is not yet at a point where the instincts have atrophied entirely. I pray that it is not one of the secret offices of television to ensure that atrophy.

I come back, finally, to my epiphanic moments on neighborhood streets, to my shock at seeing so many separate patches of blue light. I cannot shake the feeling that these form in their aggregate some new terrestrial constellation. Like all constellations, this one will have to be named and charted. And we will have to determine whether its occult influences are finally benign or not. I would be surprised if they were.

An Open Invitation to Extraterrestrials

I've thought about the matter a great deal, and I'm now convinced that one of the few things that could still save our literature, not to mention the deeper life of culture at large, would be evidence—preferably in the form of direct contact—that there is other sentient life in the universe. What else, really, could replenish the sense of mystery that has been leached out of our lives? It is the absence of *that* that has made most everything our artists venture seem inconsequential, vague, and of aluminum lightness. Or is it just midsummer pressing upon my sensorium?

Every newspaper columnist with pretensions to thought has at one time or another dilated on "the greatest single event" or "the most profound transformation" affecting mankind in our age, advancing claims on behalf of the Holocaust, the microchip, the moon landing, and so on. I'm not about to belittle any of these candidates, but it may just be that the claimants are blinded to the most newsworthy story of all. I'm referring to the wholesale alteration—or deformation—of consciousness, individual and collective, by the media: television, radio, print and photo journalism. So thoroughly (and insidiously) has the metastasis taken place, so utterly saturated are we by the various emanations, that it is impossible to step to one side to see it for what it is. At best, we can try to realize the momentousness of the change. We can consult the memories of our oldest citizens, ask them what life felt like when the airwaves were still empty. "We didn't know so much back then," they say. "Things were slower." And it is astonishing, isn't it, that a few of our countrymen were walking about before the invention of the car and the cathode-ray tube? A person living in 1900 was as close to the civilization in the Tigris-Euphrates as he was to life in modern L.A.

Life changed on every front, at every level. We know that. The media boom was just one development. But it was, and is, the catalytic one. It fashioned of the myriad changes a picture, or idea, of change and injected it into the culture. Where it now lives. For the first time in history people feel that they are living inside a larger kind of "now," a "now" that they are sharing with people whom they have never set eyes on. And this feeling is not shaped by direct contact with experience, by things as they are; it is entirely a product of things as they are *presented.* Of media. What started out as a tool, a combination package of public service/commercial entertainment, has slipped out of individual control and has taken on a life of its own. Now the image in the mirror moves and the body follows.

When I talk about the "wholesale alteration" of our consciousness, I'm not referring so much to the effects upon us of the contents, or "messages," of the media as to the changes worked by the process itself. *That,* said the sage of Toronto, is the message. The frightening thing is that there is no way to gauge what the deluge of secondhand, or "mediated," information and imagery is doing to us. Certainly we are different during exposure—more passive, distracted, impatient, skittish—than otherwise. But now the statisticians tell us that the vast majority of our countrymen have no "otherwise." They are "mediated" (a clever contraction of "media radiated"?) from the first hum of the radio alarm to the last strains of the late-night laugh track. When the car radio goes off, the Muzak in the shopping mall takes over. This collective immersion will not be without consequences, we can be sure of that. Here follow just a few speculative stabs:

1. The media, in the aggregate, are at every second plundering what someone aptly called the stock of available reality. They are, quite simply, demystifying the world. There is no mountain fastness or tropical sanctum (and certainly no indigenous, "primitive" culture) that has not been visited and revisited by the camera crew, the reporter with his notebook, and the stooges with their microphones and sound recorders. There is no mass murderer or creative genius whose secrets have not been exhumed and briskly summarized by one interviewer or another. Though no one has spelled it out for us in so many words, we are grasping the fact that our habitat, the world, is finite and knowable—its wonders have all been catalogued and we are already watching them on reruns, doing our best not to doze off. Of course, it is a superficial kind of "knowing," but the point is that the violation of all possible surfaces has ripped away from everything the sense of uniqueness, the aura. And everyone knows that once we have glanced at the headlines we are much less interested in the fine print. Looming before us is the prospect of a cosmic boredom, a yawn big enough to swallow the universe.
2. Having entrenched themselves, having made themselves entirely indispensable (can we imagine a world without them?), the media realize—that is, their executive brokers realize—that the serpent is eating its own tail. For the media's continued existence depends completely on their success at holding the attention of the populace. To do this they must be either useful or interesting. Unfortunately for the media—and, ultimately, the race—the second term has supplanted the first. So great is the fear of boredom—indeed, is there anything, apart from illness and death (the ultimate condition of boredom, its apotheosis)

that we fear more?—that every last quantum of ingenuity must be exerted in order to outdistance it. News and information alone will no longer hold the mass audience. The appetite for sensation, for the giddy pacing that suggests that *at last something interesting is really happening,* has forced newscasters and publishers to keep one eye fixed on the salability of their "product." (Events as products—property—think of it!)

Where entertainment is concerned, naturally, this has always been the case; and it would have been true in Rome, too, had there been two rival Colossea. The public will unfailingly go for the latest, fastest, least taxing, most immediately stimulating thing. Images and words, words and images. What can be done with them to make the thing—whatever it is—seem new and fresh? Nothing is new under the sun; subjects are only so many. But the "idea men" work through the night to find ways to make the ones we have *seem* new.

3. How? By raiding the word hoard, pumping the residues out of language, plundering the arts. They string together adjectives until they fizz like soda in the brainpan. No proportion need be recognized between the thing presented and the words used to present it. Inflate, expand, enlarge—do anything you like, so long as it captures the attention. And where there is so much competition for attention, where so many channels and stations and magazines vie for the same dollars, acceleration must set in. Things cannot merely seem new every so often, they must seem so every second, or else Mr. Listener-Watcher-Consumer will turn elsewhere with his precious attention (and checkbook). The Nielsen ratings are a thermometer thrust in the mouth of a dying animal—the devouring disease is boredom.
4. Acceleration of word combinations and images erodes the already-threatened attention span, diminishes further the capacity for interest. This may not have been scientifically proven, but one would have to be a cretin not to know it. The race is on. Which will be exhausted first, the repertoire of possibilities, or the psyche of the consumer? Andy Warhol's pronouncement—that everyone, in the future, will be famous for fifteen min-

> utes—is more prophetic than nonsensical. The fame won't be doled out because of merit, however—it will be because the celebrity machine will soon have used up its celebrities and will start looking elsewhere: at you, at me. Start combing your hair!

I'm getting carried away now by apocalyptic fantasy, sure. But these tendencies *do* exist, they are affecting our lives in ways that we cannot even guess at, and you can be sure that nobody is going to come on TV to confirm it for you. Can I prove it? No. There are no facts, no data. Only intuition. And intuition bids me to glance briefly at a not unrelated subject, at that (to me) terrifying cultural phenomenon known as postmodernism.

Do not get taken in by the fashionable sound of that appellation. It is not the "latest thing," the evolutionary advance upon modernism. So far as the arts are concerned, it is the *last* thing. The postmodern sensibility—and I'll characterize it in a moment—represents, in effect, the death of style. By "style" I mean those forms of expression that are seen to characterize a period, and that represent, to their proponents and to the public, something uniquely new, a movement away from the past. Postmodernism is frightening because it is the logical culmination of the processes I have been discussing. It vindicates me, and for once I'd rather not be vindicated. For what it signifies is that the idea of futurity, of progress—the basis for all of our notions of an avant-garde—is defunct; that styles are not advances, but merely shapes on a revolving wheel, and that the wheel has begun to revolve so quickly that all styles look like one.

Postmodernism goes walking into the chronological future backward. It proposes that from now on the new can only be generated out of combinations of the old, that there is no more new, that history is a rummage sale of effects, that Dr. Frankenstein was right: it *is* possible to bring to life something stitched together from various cadavers. Postmodern fiction (all the arts are infected, but I will restrict myself to one) loots among genres, refurbishing with ironic self-consciousness the documentary, the Western, the pulp, the thriller, the historical novel, the fantasy, etc. Leading practitioners include, among others, Burroughs, Doctorow, Oates, Coover, Barthelme, Sorrentino, Connell,

DeLillo, Barth, Fowles, Calvino, Eco . . . Of course, not everybody writing at present is a postmodernist. Thank God! But the tendency is very conspicuous, and is symptomatic of our deeper distress. A great many of our leading artists are throwing up their hands, are saying by way of their aesthetic choices that there is no more unknown from which to draw new resources. The high seriousness that characterized modernism has been replaced by a wink and a tongue in the cheek. One cannot play mix-and-match with the past without donning the ironic mask. And one cannot come up with a product that is not ultimately trivial.

This may be, as they say, *for real.* In our zealous, unthinking consumption of mediated images and words, in that quest for novel sensation that Americans of recent generations have taken as their birthright, we may have used up the unknown—that is to say, the future. The possibility of nuclear incineration aside, what can we now look for? New diseases and new cures; ecological panic; improvements in computer systems; growing population, longer lives, a gradually diminishing quality of life . . . This sounds so pessimistic. Why is it that I can't in all honesty look forward to collective spiritual transformation, or to the appearance of wondrous new works of art and literature?

Because neither, in my view, can come into being where there is no sense of mystery and no significant inner orientation toward the future. Both have been lost, and, ponder as I might, I cannot see how we can regain them. The two potential solutions are so unlikely as to strain the credulity. One: that the media conglomerates would get together for their own SALT talks, with the plan of giving over their holdings piece by piece, dismantling their receivers and transmitters and telecommunications systems until the world was finally restored to a pre-Marconi silence, with nothing more than the hometown newspaper for information. The second, a mere fantasy (shared by Spielberg, et al.), is the one I mentioned at the outset. If we could, through some extraordinary feat of technology, make contact with extraterrestrial life . . . It would be an event more significant than the discovery of America. In a flash the night sky would be charged with possibility, with the unknown, with futurity. Leaders and working stiffs alike would quicken with expectancy. And literature, dear literature . . .

Some Notes Concerning the Impossibility of Literary Biography

He shrugs. "It's stinking dead, the research line;
Just let me put this bastard on the skids,
I'll get a couple semesters leave
To work on Protest Theater."

—*Philip Larkin, "Posterity"*

"Impossibility" may be a little strong, granted. But I wanted something that would convey from the outset what has become increasingly obvious to me: that no other genre offers to its critic so many unresolvable questions about knowing. *Knowing* in the epistemological sense (though is there, ultimately, any other sense possible?). Even the long-suffering discipline of historiography looks solid in comparison. But you would never guess this from reading. Literary biography still tries to pass itself off as what the poststructuralist theoreticians call "a natural sign"—it does not own up to its problematic status.

Many of the points I will raise can be applied to biography in general, and should be. But literary biography is biography with an exponent in front of it. For it involves writer B putting into words the narrative of writer X, who in one way or another has already put the elements of his experience into words. The enterprise is rooted in a mysterious redundancy. B is vying with X in a way that the biographer of a statesman or sports hero never would. By engulfing in language the life of X, he appears to engulf, and somehow supersede, the testimony that is the work itself. A dangerous illusion. For X is the most centripetal of creatures. His importance to the world lies in his ability to express his subjective vision; he is its sole proprietor and witness. While B can assemble information from many fronts, he can never get closer to that vision, that interior life, than the words of X permit. We too readily forget that all other information (X lived here, studied there; he feared lightning, was fond of animals) is ancillary.

X is born, lives, writes, and dies. B is drawn through an interest in the writings to find out about the life. He gathers what facts he can and converts them into a narrative. His biography then goes onto the shelf alongside the works of X. There is now a continuum of language; the all-important distinction between the life and the work has, in appearance at least, been leveled. And with the passing of years, life and work tend increasingly to be regarded as two compatible texts. Everything exists, said Mallarmé, to end up in a book.

This is not the life, these are words about the life. A narrative can be mastered, a life cannot.

The writer works with the materials of his own experience. He attempts to lift them out of the chemical bath of subjectivity and to set them before the world. The biographer discovers what he can about that experience, the outer husk of it, and he puts it before us that we may better understand the writer. On the most superficial level, we confront warring texts. But in truth they are of very different orders. B goes back over the raw materials that X has processed and transformed. He sees the life as it appears before—or after—it has fulfilled its function. All too often he forgets that the only real biography of a creator is to be found in the function itself.

Even if B has amassed every possible circumstantial detail, he has nothing until he finds the key. What drove X to language? What underlay his need to shape experience and sensation into aesthetic forms? If B cannot produce a convincing explanation, his material remains inert. If he can, then he has a hypothesis. But just that.

B's most vexing problem is, of course, the gulf that exists between the objective and subjective statuses of events. There is a hierarchy of convention, a generic kind of extrapolation, that is temptingly easy to rely upon. An achievement is seen as more important than a dream of achievement; a family death weighs more than the death of a neighbor, or a pet. But we all recognize what variations our inmost self is capable of: the unattainable love of adolescence may have molded the core far more than the successful courtships of later years, the death of a classmate brought the fearful mystery of mortality closer than any subsequent loss. . . . The magnitude of an event is determined by the degree of subjective response and nothing else. The literary biographer must be prepared to tear down all familiar coordinates and to improvise new ones according to his intuitions. He should remind himself at all times that he probably does not know what really mattered to X, that X, like everyone else, found it necessary to conceal from the world the ways that his responses deviated from what he believed was the norm.

Is there such a thing as a unified self, a single subject, *a* life as opposed to half a hundred *lives*? The word "biography" means, etymologically, "the line of the life." And, indeed, birth and death are the two determining points. But what if the subject, X, did not feel himself as an integrated, continuous being? The very need to write may have arisen out of an irresistible pressure for self-integration. What about the impression of unity and purpose, singleness of vision, manifested in his words? Is *that* his real life? Was it not to that unity that he sacrificed his happiness, his sanity, his chances for love? Once again, B faces an impossible task. He must trace and explain the divergence between the aesthetic order on the page and the contingent chaos of the life.

The life—this may be the grandest fallacy of all. How shall we define it? Is it the sum of events befalling X? Does X have to generate a coherent explanation of these, at least to himself, before he is entitled to an identity? Does X in any sense *own* his life, serve as its sovereign master, or does he just experience one version, one interpretation, of it? Is there something that we could finally call *the truth* about X's life? Or are there only different interpretations of circumstance, his own among them?

These questions bring to mind the debate that was once so hotly joined by literary theorists. Is the reader/critic constrained by the author's intention in creating a work, or are literary texts untethered in the public domain and open to every possible interpretation? If I find in *King Lear* a parable of happiness, who will say that I am wrong? Stanley Fish and his cohorts made some ingenious arguments on behalf of interpretive license, maintaining that the author's intention was unknowable and, therefore, could not be binding. The reasoning, subtler than what I suggest, can be readily adapted to the matter of biography. Simply: if we do not have direct access to the inner life of the subject—which we do not—then nothing can tie us to any one interpretation. For that matter, who is to say that the subject's own interpretation is privileged? We know enough about the mechanics of repression and unconscious motivation to argue that X may be as deluded in his version as B is in his.

Where, then, is the true picture to be found? *Is* there such a picture that can be abstracted from the complex totality of a life lived from one moment to the next? Or is the only complete map of any terrain the terrain itself?

The biographer flatters himself that by amassing testimony from various sources he comes closer to an objective understanding of his subject. But what he really holds is a fabric woven together from the subjective accounts of others. Is there any reason why he should trust this more? After all, he is engaged in turning a life into a text, and he is to some extent interpreting that life as if it were a text. What would he think of a "reading" of a novel that tried to bring together every available interpretation? He would probably see the juxtaposed views as parts of a self-canceling equation.

Just imagine: X's wife recalls that her late husband was a kind, loving, selfless individual. His editor and longtime friend concedes that he was a monster of self-absorption and was often suspicious to the point of paranoia. A mistress appears. For fifteen years, she says, he was an ardent and inventive lover. Adding these three accounts together does not necessarily give us a better picture of X. We might conclude that he was one way with his wife, another way with editor and friend, and still another when in the arms of his mistress—a many-sided individual. It is likely, though, that we would see some need to modify all accounts. Unless we understood more—much more—about wife, editor, and mistress, and about the nature of their relationships with X, we would not be able to extract very much insight from their versions. And almost instantly the project becomes unwieldy. For every relationship has to be examined as a specific interaction of temperaments and histories. Circumstances become a trail of crumbs leading us further back into the past. The ultimate—impossible—biography is the more or less exhaustive history of the world as it is refracted through the experience of one individual. Every worthy biographer has, I'm sure, goggled at this notion at one time or another.

Axiom: there is no understanding of the life without an understanding of the childhood. I would even go so far as to say that every person lives two separate lives: the child's and the adult's. The former unfolds in the realm of duration, of organic, undivided time, and it decisively shapes the latter. The change from childhood to adulthood, however, is a change of kind, not degree. The immersion in duration time yields painfully to the perception of time as succession. The self-containment of those early years is never regained. It haunts all of us, but no one more than the artist. His whole effort, the work, can be seen as an attempt to repudiate linear time.

Invariably, though, the biographer applies to the duration phenomenon the measuring instruments of time as succession. He lays what bits of information he has gleaned alongside the relative abundance from adult years. The portrait that emerges is not only skewed—its values are completely reversed.

The problem is in part the paucity of evidence and in part the biographer's own failure of imagination. Like any adult, he has forgotten what childhood is: a dense plasma compounded of fantasies, fears, jealousies, fevers, secrets, and ritual incantations. He no longer remembers the expansive thrill of reading or the charge that accrued to words and sounds. His position is hopeless. There is no access to that preserve of feelings and sensations. Indeed, they are so evanescent in their nature that the subject himself could barely have called them up. Though they forced out the peculiar and unalterable lines of character, they were taken up into the becoming and all but vanished.

There is no biography without death. Only then is the subject's experience released from the potential transformations of futurity. Only with the whole in view can the parts be set into relation. Death turns chaos into narrative. More accurately: death makes possible the illusion of narrative.

The narrative temptation is not the biographer's alone. Most of us, I suspect, look upon our lives through some such lens. We speak of fate, of destiny; we are seldom at a loss when an interesting stranger says, "Tell me your story." The danger should be obvious. Storytelling obeys ancient aesthetic principles: recalcitrant details are shorn away in the interest of tension and symmetry; condensations and displacements are routine. The story gains in interest as the actuality of the way things really happened recedes.

But could we not say that the story finally encompasses a deeper truth than the unsculpted presentation of facts, that the truth may ultimately have more to do with narrative coherence than with documentary evidence? Facts are just themselves; interpretation is the path to meaning and truth. And what is an interpretation, after all, but a story? If I told you everything about X, B might say, you would have nothing but a welter of details. Any one of us might say the same thing: if I told you everything about how it happened, I would never finish telling.

B must decide before writing whether the knowledge that he has of X justifies his considering that life as a destiny. That is, as a meaningful sequence that had to happen as it did, and that was perceived by the subject as constituting a narrative. If B believes that X saw his life thus, then he must at every point endeavor to compare his sense of the story with the sense that X may have had. If he has no such belief, on the other hand, he has to be very careful not to succumb to the narrative fallacy. He has to admit that instead of a narrative he can only present a kind of itemized accounting of the life. Only the brashest biographer would venture to call the life of X a *story* if X himself had no such conception of it.

The retroactive fallacy. Knowing how X's life came out, and looking back upon the life in the light of that knowledge, B puts himself in a godlike position. As Moritz Heimann wrote: "A man who dies at thirty-five is at every moment of his life a man who dies at thirty-five." To his biographer, we might add—not to himself. B looks at X's life as through a transparency. X, however, only knew his life as it was set against an opaque, unknowable future. How can the two perspectives be squared? They cannot. B can no more see X's life as he saw it than X can grasp his life out of the futurity granted to B. This absolute opposition of perspectives is what underwrites the biographer's enterprise and excuses, for the reader, its inevitable falsification. We do not want the illusion of life through the eyes of X—we are saddled with enough unknowing of our own. What we want is the illusion of life as seen by a god. Part of the pleasure of reading biography is our fantasied transposition of the biographer's detached vantage to our own experience. What would my doings look like in the eyes of a future researcher?

Since B knows the outcome—the time, place, and manner of X's death—and since he commands a view of the whole of X's life, it follows that he will tend to interpret his materials accordingly. If we watch a movie the second time through, we want to warn the hero: don't go there, watch out for that woman! But we know, like the personified Death in Maugham's fable, that the master has an appointment that very evening in Samarra. By living after X, B has stolen an enormous advantage over him, no matter how great X's legacy has proved to be. A temporal delusion. As B writes, he should imagine *him*self the subject of another's biography. Or, even more to the point, he should consider that every breath he draws might be his last.

* * *

All problems of interpretation ultimately lead us into the treacherous swamps of *meaning*. When we read a text, for example, we try to distinguish between what it means for us and what the author may have intended it to mean. The two may be very different. But how can we ever be sure? Even if the author has publicly stated his intent, a margin of uncertainty remains. He might have been utterly oblivious himself to the patterns created by the pressure of unconscious forces. Meaning, it would appear, cannot be tied neatly to acts of conscious intention.

Reader-response theorists have sought to clarify the situation by setting *meaning* against *signification,* where the former consists in the author's conscious *and* unconscious intention, and the latter refers to whatever interpretations the reader elicits from the work. Not surprisingly, the complexities are compounded when it is a life, not a text, that is being examined.

What is the *meaning* of a life? Is this a question that B should answer before he begins writing, or is the writing itself an attempt to answer? Does every biography bear as its implicit subtitle: *The Meaning of the Life of X*?

My own sense from the biographies that I have read is that all ontological questions are strictly avoided. "This is biography, not philosophy," B might righteously proclaim. Though when backed to the wall, he would perhaps concede: "Of course X's life had meaning! Why else would I bother with it?" As to what that meaning might involve, however, it very likely has more to do with the thoughts and emotions aroused in B than with any essence intrinsic to the life of X.

My point is this: that it is entirely possible for a biographer to write a "life" abounding in discovered significances that never once takes up the question of what that life might have felt like, or meant to, the subject. The reason is obvious enough. Any such wrestling with meaning would immediately install B in the midst of the messiest of philosophical debates: how do we know other lives?

We do not.

And what about the meaning of meaning? Another tangle. It seems that past a point we cannot say what anything means objectively—for objectivity dissolves into a billowing veil of subjectivity. There is no *out there* that is not in the last analysis an *in here*. The edifice of public, social life is founded upon an ever present but concealed intersubjectivity. We can only report upon our own reactions; meaning is finally a matter of private psychic sensation. If anyone asks me the meaning of my life, I can only answer: the meaning of my life is the way that my life feels to me. I *am* my meaning.

This is impossibly diffuse, I realize that. But the diffusion has everything to do with the biographer's undertaking and the resulting product. B cannot know the meaning of X's life. He can only guess at the conditions of that life and explore its significance to himself and others. But this does not mean that he should stop hammering at the barrier. As much as possible, a biography ought to incorporate the impossibility of knowing into its presentation, much as the scientist factors in the falsification inevitable in any staged laboratory experiment. In giving us the life of X, B should constantly remind us that this is *not* the life of X.

Is there an optimum perch in time from which to view the subject? The availability of documents and personal testimony obviously counts for a great deal, but there is also such a thing as having too much material. Time has a way of winnowing superfluities and allowing dominant lines to emerge. But once again, we must be careful not to confuse meaning and significance. As the subject's life recedes in time from the biographer, there is less and less chance that he will be able to catch hold of the subtle traces of self; these survive, if at all, in the reminiscence and anecdote of the eyewitness—in distorted form, of course. What removal in time can confer is a more comprehensive picture of the significance that X had for others, as a craftsman, legend, or maker of visions. And this, properly speaking, is not a part of the line of the life. It is the line of the afterlife. With every passing year, barring the discovery of new information, the biography of X is bound to be less about X and more about the impression that he left in the larger culture.

In the same way, the spirit of the times—the *Zeitgeist*—that all-important and extraordinarily elusive medium in which a life is lived, cannot be resuscitated through research. Documents and period detail are not enough. B must somehow recover the collectively shared impression of a particular historical moment. Unless he participated in that moment himself, he will misconstrue it. If he looks from a great enough temporal distance, he may forget that such a spirit even existed. Or, worse yet, he may unconsciously project the spirit of his own times back upon the past.

There is a way in which biography—the genre—can be seen as a paradigm for our own ideal of self-knowledge, or self-recuperation. It presents, however illusorily, a view of an individual's experience from outside of time—outside of *his* time, that is. In this view, isolated gestures are related to a contained whole. This synoptic vantage is the very thing that we move toward asymptotically, never attaining it, in our own lives. If only there were an interval after death during which we could study the final design! Biography is, for this reason, intrinsically compelling. We may be bored by the substance of X's life, but the perspective itself is exalting.

Unfortunately, the biography is doomed to distort more than it illuminates. Falsification is the price that scope exacts. I see no way around it. I have only to imagine a diligent scholar conjuring with the facts available about my life. I do not doubt for a second but that he would get it all wrong. The fine points, the subtle emphases: the unrecoverable circumstances and reactions are the very ones that would tell the real tale.

Still, the reader who never knew X will probably feel that the information has given him insight, brought him somehow closer. He accepts what he is given and takes the liberty of bodying forth the life in his imagination. No one will contradict him in this. But the person who knew X—and the reaction probably intensifies with the degree of familiarity—will likely feel only the divergences. I have talked with a number of people, for instance, who knew Robert Lowell. They have all asserted that Ian Hamilton's biography, well documented as it is, conveys nothing of the warmheartedness or conversational brilliance of the man they knew. As I had never met the poet, I was able to suspend disbelief as I read. I freely fashioned an image for myself—I now fear that it is a false one.

Works calling themselves revisionist have been appearing in every historical field in the last few decades. Their intent, it appears, is to undo some of the damages wrought by ideologically rooted histories of an earlier time. What's more, since the late nineteenth century there has been an active and ongoing interrogation of the epistemology of historiography. I see nothing of the kind among the myriad practitioners of biography, though it would seem that every supporting premise is in need of thorough reexamination. Could it be that biographers all suspect the truth and fear to face it: that lives cannot be recovered, understood, or narrated? That the entire enterprise rests upon a foundation of illusion and fallacy?

Selective Bibliography

Part I

Robert Musil: To this day we lack a readily available edition of Musil's three-volume masterpiece, *The Man Without Qualities.* Many better bookstores stock the Picador edition imported from England. *Five Women* (issued also as *Tonka and Other Stories*) and *Young Törless* are easily found, and Continuum has published *Selected Writings* by Musil as Volume 72 of its German Library. (This collection contains a beautiful translation of "The Blackbird," possibly Musil's most haunting story.)

First U.S. Editions

The Man Without Qualities, Vol. I, trans. E. Wilkins and E. Kaiser. New York: Coward-McCann, 1953.

Young Törless, trans. E. Wilkins and E. Kaiser. New York: Pantheon, 1955.

Five Women, trans. E. Wilkins and E. Kaiser. New York: Delacorte, 1966.

Selected Writings of Robert Musil, ed. Burton Pike. New York: Continuum, 1986.

Robert Walser: The sublime quirks and crochets of Walser's prose can be found in his novel, *Jacob von Gunten,* his *Selected Stories,* and Mark Harman's *Robert Walser Rediscovered.* This last miscellany includes comments on Walser's work by contemporaries like Franz Kafka, Robert Musil, and Walter Benjamin.

First U.S. Editions

Jacob von Gunten, trans. Christopher Middleton. Austin, Tex.: University of Texas Press, 1969.

Selected Stories, trans. Christopher Middleton et al. New York: Farrar, Straus & Giroux, 1982.

Robert Walser Rediscovered, ed. Mark Harman. Hanover, N.H.: University Press of New England, 1985.

Joseph Roth: Overlook Press is performing a great service for readers by restoring Roth's work to print. Issued thus far:

Flight Without End, trans. David LeVay. New York: Overlook, 1977.

The Silent Prophet, trans. David LeVay. New York: Overlook, 1980.

Job, trans. Dorothy Thompson. New York: Overlook, 1982.

The Radetzky March, trans. Eva Tucker. New York: Overlook, 1983.

The Emperor's Tomb, trans. John Hoare. New York: Overlook, 1984.

Confessions of a Murderer, trans. Desmond Vesey. New York: Overlook, 1985.

Hotel Savoy, trans. John Hoare. New York: Overlook, 1986.

Max Frisch: Most of Frisch's important fiction has been translated. Also available are *Sketchbook, 1946–1949,* and *Sketchbook, 1966–1971.*

First U.S. Editions

I'm Not Stiller, trans. Michael Bullock. New York: Knopf, 1958.

Homo Faber, trans. Michael Bullock. New York: Random House, 1959.

A Wilderness of Mirrors (later reissued as *Gantenbein*), trans. Michael Bullock. New York: Random House, 1966.

Sketchbook, 1966–1971, trans. Geoffrey Skelton. New York: Harcourt Brace Jovanovich, 1974.

Montauk, trans. Geoffrey Skelton. New York: Harcourt Brace Jovanovich, 1977.

Man in the Holocene, trans. Geoffrey Skelton. New York: Harcourt Brace Jovanovich, 1979.

Bluebeard, trans. Geoffrey Skelton. New York: Harcourt Brace Jovanovich, 1983.

Gregor von Rezzori: Rezzori's charming story-cycle, *Memoirs of an Anti-Semite,* and his novel, *The Death of My Brother Abel,* are both available in paperback from Penguin.

First U.S. Editions
Memoirs of an Anti-Semite, no translator listed. New York: Viking, 1981.
The Death of My Brother Abel, trans. Joachim Neugroschel. New York: Viking, 1985.

Heinrich Böll: Any bookstore will have some of Böll's novels and story collections. Leila Vennewitz deserves great credit for translating all of the works cited.

First U.S. Editions
Billiards at Half-Past Nine. New York: McGraw-Hill, 1962.
Absent Without Leave. New York: McGraw-Hill, 1965.
The Clown. New York: McGraw-Hill, 1965.
18 Stories. New York: McGraw-Hill, 1966.
Irish Journal. New York: McGraw-Hill, 1967.
End of a Mission. New York: McGraw-Hill, 1968.
Children Are Civilians, Too. New York: McGraw-Hill, 1970.
Group Portrait with Lady. New York: McGraw-Hill, 1973.
The Lost Honor of Katharina Blum. New York: McGraw-Hill, 1975.
The Bread of Those Early Years. New York: McGraw-Hill, 1976.
Missing Persons and Other Essays. New York: McGraw-Hill, 1977.
And Never Said a Word. New York: McGraw-Hill, 1978.
The Safety Net. New York: Knopf, 1982.
What's to Become of the Boy? New York: Knopf, 1984.
A Soldier's Legacy. New York: Knopf, 1985.
The Stories of Heinrich Böll. New York: Knopf, 1986.

Thomas Bernhard: It is surprising to find the work of a writer as dark and difficult as Bernhard available in attractively packaged trade editions. *Concrete, Correction, Gargoyles, Gathering Evidence: A Memoir,* and *The Lime Works* are all currently in print. There is no easy access to this monomaniacal stylist; *Concrete* is the shortest of his novels and is quite representative.

First U.S. Editions
Gargoyles, trans. Richard and Clara Winston. New York: Knopf, 1970.
The Lime Works, trans. Sophie Wilkins. New York: Knopf, 1973.
Correction, trans. Sophie Wilkins. New York: Knopf, 1979.
Concrete, trans. David McLintock. New York: Knopf, 1984.
Gathering Evidence: A Memoir, trans. David McLintock. New York: Knopf, 1986.

Peter Schneider: Though only *The Wall Jumper* has appeared to date, Schneider has published several thematically related essays in *Harper's* magazine.

First U.S. Edition
The Wall Jumper, trans. Leigh Hafrey. New York: Pantheon, 1983.

Eva Demski: *Dead Alive* is the first work by this young novelist to have been translated into English.

First U.S. Edition
Dead Alive, trans. Jan van Heurck. New York: Harper & Row, 1986.

Part II

Osip Mandelstam: Mandelstam's place as one of the great poets of the Russian language is secure. The reader can discover some sense of his volatile density from the many published translations (Clarence Brown's *Mandelstam* is an invaluable guidebook). Mandelstam's contribution as a prose stylist, however, has yet to be assessed. *The Noise of Time* has been reissued as a paperback, and *Osip Mandelstam: Selected Essays* is available in hardcover. *Mandelstam: The Complete Critical Prose and Letters* is no longer in print, but most libraries will have it. Nadezhda Mandelstam's two volumes of memoirs, *Hope Against Hope* and *Hope Abandoned,* should be required reading for anyone interested in literature in our century.

First U.S. Editions
The Prose of Osip Mandelstam, trans. Clarence Brown. Princeton, N.J.: Princeton University Press, 1965.
Hope Against Hope, by Nadezhda Mandelstam, trans. Max Hayward. New York: Atheneum, 1970.
Mandelstam, by Clarence Brown. New York: Cambridge University Press, 1973.
Hope Abandoned, by Nadezhda Mandelstam, trans. Max Hayward. New York: Atheneum, 1974.
Osip Mandelstam: Selected Essays, trans. Sidney Monas. Austin, Tex.: University of Texas Press, 1977.
Mandelstam: The Complete Critical Prose and Letters, trans. Jane Gary Harris and Constance Link. Ann Arbor, Mich.: Ardis, 1979.

Joseph Brodsky: Brodsky has published two collections of poetry in English, *A Part of Speech* and *Selected Poems.* A third, *Homage to Urania,* is scheduled. In addition to the essays in *Less than One,* the reader is referred to a lengthy interview with the poet in *The Paris Review* no. 83.

First U.S. Editions
Selected Poems, trans. George Kline. New York: Harper & Row, 1973.
A Part of Speech, various translators. New York: Farrar, Straus & Giroux, 1977.
Less than One, New York: Farrar, Straus & Giroux, 1986.

Part III

Blaise Cendrars: Works by Cendrars are hard to find, and those presently listed as in print are not his most important. New Directions used to publish a *Selected Writings* that provided a good sampling of the poetry and several suggestive prose excerpts. Cendrars's most compelling prose is to be found in the three autobiographical works: *The Astonished Man, Planus,* and *Lice* (available from Peter Owen, London). *Gold, Moravagine,* and *A Night in the Forest* are obtainable, as is Monique Chefdor's edition of *Complete Postcards from the Americas: Poems of Road and Sea.* Jay Bochner has written *Blaise Cendrars: Discovery and Re-creation,* which has useful biographical information and some wonderful photographs. And Marjorie Perloff's *The Futurist Moment* does an excellent job of placing Cendrars where he belongs: at the center of the avant-garde turmoil of the early decades of the century.

First U.S. Editions

Sutter's Gold (reissued as *Gold*), trans. Henry Stuart. New York: Harper & Brothers, 1926.

Selected Writings of Blaise Cendrars, ed. Walter Albert. New York: New Directions, 1966.

Moravagine, trans. Alan Brown. New York: Doubleday, 1970.

Complete Postcards from the Americas: Poems of Road and Sea, trans. Monique Chefdor. Berkeley, Calif.: University of California Press, 1976.

A Night in the Forest, trans. Margaret Kidder Ewing. Columbia, Mo.: University of Missouri Press, 1985.

The Futurist Moment by Marjorie Perloff. Chicago: University of Chicago Press, 1986.

Foreign Editions

To the End of the World, trans. Alan Brown. London: Peter Owen, 1966.

The Astonished Man, trans. Nina Rootes. London: Peter Owen, 1970.

Planus, trans. Nina Rootes. London: Peter Owen, 1972.

Lice, trans. Nina Rootes. London: Peter Owen, 1973.

Blaise Cendrars: Discovery and Re-creation, by Jay Bochner. Toronto: University of Toronto Press, 1978.

Marguerite Yourcenar: Yourcenar's two masterpieces, *The Abyss* and *Hadrian's Memoirs,* were both translated by her longtime companion, Grace Frick. But nothing by Yourcenar is minor or trivial.

First U.S. Editions

Hadrian's Memoirs, trans. Grace Frick. New York: Farrar, Straus & Young, 1955.

Coup de Grâce, trans. Grace Frick. Farrar, Straus & Cudahy, 1957.

The Abyss, trans. Grace Frick. New York: Farrar, Straus & Giroux, 1976.

Fires, trans. Dori Katz. New York: Farrar, Straus & Giroux, 1981.

A Coin in Nine Hands, trans. Dori Katz. New York: Farrar, Straus & Giroux, 1982.

Alexis, trans. Walter Kaiser. New York: Farrar, Straus & Giroux, 1984.

The Dark Brain of Piranesi, trans. Richard Howard. New York: Farrar, Straus & Giroux, 1984.
With Open Eyes: Conversations With Matthieu Galey, trans. Arthur Goldhammer. Boston: Beacon, 1984.
Oriental Tales, trans. Alberto Manguel. New York: Farrar, Straus & Giroux, 1985.
Mishima: A Vision of the Void, trans. Alberto Manguel. New York: Farrar, Straus & Giroux, 1986.
Two Lives and a Dream, trans. Walter Kaiser. New York: Farrar, Straus & Giroux, 1987.

Marguerite Duras: The international success of *The Lover* has set off an avalanche of reissues and new translations—Duras is suddenly everywhere. Any list is bound to be inaccurate, but here are the titles currently available.

First U.S. Editions
The Sea Wall, trans. Herma Briffault. New York: Farrar, Straus & Giroux, 1952.
Hiroshima Mon Amour, trans. Richard Seaver. New York: Grove, 1961.
Four Novels, trans. Richard Seaver and others. New York: Grove, 1965.
The Ravishing of Lol Stein, trans. Richard Seaver. New York: Grove, 1966.
The Sailor From Gibraltar, trans. Barbara Bray. New York: Grove, 1967.
Destroy, She Said, trans. Barbara Bray. New York: Grove, 1970.
India Song, trans. Barbara Bray. New York: Grove, 1976.
Whole Days in the Trees, trans. Anita Barrows. New York: Riverrun, 1984.
The Little Horses of Tarquinia, trans. Peter Du Berg. Riverrun, 1985.
The Lover, trans. Barbara Bray. New York: Random House, 1985.
The Malady of Death, trans. Barbara Bray. New York: Grove, 1986.
Outside, trans. Arthur Goldhammer. Boston: Beacon, 1986.
The War: A Memoir, trans. Barbara Bray. New York: Pantheon, 1986.

Michel Tournier: With the exception of *Gemini,* which was never issued in paperback and is out of print at present, the reader should have no trouble obtaining Tournier.

First U.S. Editions
Friday, or, The Other Island, trans. Norman Denny. New York: Doubleday, 1969.
The Ogre, trans. Barbara Bray. New York: Doubleday, 1972.
Gemini, trans. Anne Carter. New York: Doubleday, 1981.
The Four Wise Men, trans. Ralph Manheim. New York: Doubleday, 1982.
The Fetishist, trans. Barbara Wright. New York: Doubleday, 1984.

Primo Levi: Since giving up his career as a chemist in order to write, Levi has produced books at a prodigious rate. Translators are just beginning to catch up. Five works have been issued in the last few years.

First U.S. Editions
The Periodic Table, trans. Raymond Rosenthal. New York: Schocken, 1984.
If Not Now, When?, trans. William Weaver. New York: Summit, 1985.
Moments of Reprieve, trans. Ruth Feldman. New York: Summit, 1986.
The Monkey's Wrench, trans. William Weaver. New York: Summit, 1986.
Survival in Auschwitz/The Reawakening, trans. Stuart Woolf. New York: Summit, 1986.

Umberto Eco: Apart from his international bestseller, *The Name of the Rose* (and the *Postscript to "The Name of the Rose"*), Eco's principal publications are academic. A collection of occasional essays, *Travels in Hyper-Reality,* may be of some interest to the general reader.

First U.S. Editions
A Theory of Semiotics, various translators. Bloomington, Ind.: Indiana University Press, 1976.
The Role of the Reader, various translators. Bloomington, Ind.: Indiana University Press, 1979.
The Name of the Rose, trans. William Weaver. New York: Harcourt Brace Jovanovich, 1983.
Postscript to "The Name of the Rose," trans. William Weaver. New York: Harcourt Brace Jovanovich, 1984.
Semiotics and the Philosophy of Language, various translators. Bloomington, Ind.: Indiana University Press, 1984.
Art and Beauty in the Middle Ages, trans. Hugh Bredin. New Haven, Conn.: Yale University Press, 1986.
Travels in Hyper-Reality, trans. William Weaver. New York: Harcourt Brace Jovanovich, 1986.

Malcolm Lowry: Lowry's magnum opus is, of course, *Under the Volcano.* None of his other works approach that novel in scope or execution. His story collection, *Hear Us O Lord from Heaven Thy Dwelling Place,* is well worth reading. But only the true Lowry aficionado will search out *Dark as the Grave Wherein My Friend Is Laid, Lunar Caustic, Malcolm Lowry: Psalms and Songs* (a miscellany), *October Ferry to Gabriola, Selected Letters of Malcolm Lowry,* or *Selected Poems of Malcolm Lowry.* Douglas Day's biography, *Malcolm Lowry,* is highly recommended.

First U.S. Editions
Under the Volcano. New York: Reynal & Hitchcock, 1947.
Hear Us O Lord from Heaven Thy Dwelling Place. Philadelphia: Lippincott, 1961.
Selected Poems of Malcolm Lowry. San Francisco: City Lights, 1962.
Ultramarine. Philadelphia: Lippincott, 1962.
Selected Letters of Malcolm Lowry. Philadelphia: Lippincott, 1965.
Dark as the Grave Wherein My Friend Is Laid. New York: NAL, 1968.

October Ferry to Gabriola. New York: World, 1970.
Malcolm Lowry: A Biography, by Douglas Day. New York: Oxford University Press, 1973.
Lunar Caustic. Salem, N.H.: Cape, 1975.
Malcolm Lowry: Psalms and Songs. New York: NAL, 1975.

Lars Gustafsson: Gustafsson is very prolific in his native Swedish. Four of his books have thus far been translated, the best of which is *The Death of a Beekeeper.*

First U.S. Editions

The Death of a Beekeeper, trans. Janet K. Swaffar and Guntram Weber. New York: New Directions, 1981.
The Tennis Players, trans. Yvonne Sandstroem. New York: New Directions, 1983.
Sigismund, trans. John Weinstock. New York: New Directions, 1985.
Stories of Happy People, trans. Yvonne Sandstroem and John Weinstock. New York: New Directions, 1986.

V. S. Naipaul: Naipaul's *oeuvre* is immense; no part of it is negligible.

First U.S. Editions—Fiction

The Mystic Masseur. New York: Vanguard, 1959.
The Suffrage of Elvira, in *Three Novels.* New York: Knopf, 1982.
Miguel Street. New York: Vanguard, 1960.
A House for Mr. Biswas. New York: McGraw-Hill, 1961.
Mr. Stone and the Knights Companion. New York: Macmillan, 1963.
A Flag on the Island. New York: Macmillan, 1967.
The Mimic Men. New York: Macmillan, 1967.
In a Free State. New York: Knopf, 1971.
Guerrillas. New York: Knopf, 1975.
A Bend in the River. New York: Knopf, 1979.
The Enigma of Arrival. New York: Knopf, 1987.

Nonfiction

The Middle Passage. New York: Macmillan, 1963.
An Area of Darkness. New York: Macmillan, 1965.
The Loss of El Dorado. New York: Knopf, 1970.
The Overcrowded Barracoon. New York: Knopf, 1972.
India: A Wounded Civilization. New York: Knopf, 1977.
The Return of Eva Perón. New York: Knopf, 1980.
Among the Believers. New York: Knopf, 1981.
Finding the Center. New York: Knopf, 1984.

Derek Walcott: Walcott has recently culled from among his many volumes of poetry a substantial *Collected Poems*—anyone who cares about poetry should own it.

First U.S. Editions

Selected Poems. New York: Farrar, Straus & Giroux, 1964.

The Gulf. New York: Farrar, Straus & Giroux, 1970.

Another Life. New York: Farrar, Straus & Giroux, 1973.

Sea Grapes. New York: Farrar, Straus & Giroux, 1976.

The Star-Apple Kingdom. New York: Farrar, Straus & Giroux, 1979.

The Fortunate Traveller. New York: Farrar, Straus & Giroux, 1981.

Midsummer. New York: Farrar, Straus & Giroux, 1984.

Collected Poems, 1948–1984. New York: Farrar, Straus & Giroux, 1986.

Yaakov Shabtai: *Past Continuous* is Shabtai's only work in English translation. I have heard rumors of an untranslated companion volume.

First U.S. Edition

Past Continuous, trans. Dalya Bilu. Philadelphia: Jewish Publication Society, 1985.

Salman Rushdie: Rushdie's three novels are *Grimus, Midnight's Children,* and *Shame. The Jaguar Smile: A Nicaraguan Journey* has just been published.

First U.S. Editions

Grimus. New York: Overlook, 1979.

Midnight's Children. New York: Knopf, 1981.

Shame. New York: Knopf, 1983.

The Jaguar Smile: A Nicaraguan Journey. New York: Viking, 1987.

Jorge Luis Borges: Along with Borges's many translated collections of fiction, he has also written essays—*Other Inquisitions, 1937–1952*—and poetry: *The Gold of the Tigers, In Praise of Darkness,* and *Selected Poems, 1923–1967.*

First U.S. Editions

Ficciones, ed. Anthony Kerrigan. New York: Grove, 1962.

Labyrinths, ed. Donald Yates and James Irby. New York: New Directions, 1964.

Other Inquisitions, 1937–1952, trans. Ruth Simms. New York: New Directions, 1964.

The Aleph and Other Stories, 1933–1969, trans. Norman Thomas di Giovanni. New York: Dutton, 1970.

Selected Poems, 1923–1967, trans. Norman Thomas di Giovanni. New York: Delacorte, 1972.

A Universal History of Infamy, trans. Norman Thomas di Giovanni. New York: Dutton, 1972.

In Praise of Darkness, trans. Norman Thomas di Giovanni. New York: Dutton, 1974.

The Chronicles of Bustos Domecq (with Adolfo Bioy-Casares), trans. Norman Thomas di Giovanni. New York: Dutton, 1976.
The Book of Sand, trans. Norman Thomas di Giovanni. New York: Dutton, 1977.
The Gold of the Tigers, trans. Alastair Reid. New York: Dutton, 1977.
Six Problems for Don Isidro Parodi (with Adolfo Bioy-Casares), trans. Norman Thomas di Giovanni. New York: Dutton, 1981.

Julio Cortázar: Cortázar wrote four highly unorthodox novels—*Hopscotch, A Manual for Manuel, 62: A Model Kit,* and *The Winners*—as well as a number of speculative and mysterious stories. The reader should not overlook the highly sportive short prose of *Around the Day in Eighty Worlds, A Certain Lucas,* and *Cronopios and Famas.*

First U.S. Editions

The Winners, trans. Elaine Kerrigan. New York: Random House, 1965.
Hopscotch, trans. Gregory Rabassa. New York: Random House, 1966.
The End of the Game and Other Stories (later reissued as *Blow-up and Other Stories*), trans. Paul Blackburn. New York: Random House, 1967.
Cronopios and Famas, trans. Paul Blackburn. New York: Random House, 1969.
62: A Model Kit, trans. Gregory Rabassa. New York: Random House, 1972.
All Fires the Fire and Other Stories, trans. Suzanne Jill Levine. New York: Random House, 1973.
A Manual for Manuel, trans. Gregory Rabassa. New York: Random House, 1978.
A Change of Light and Other Stories, trans. Gregory Rabassa. New York: Knopf, 1980.
We Love Glenda So Much and Other Tales, trans. Gregory Rabassa. New York: Knopf, 1983.
A Certain Lucas, trans. Gregory Rabassa. New York: Knopf, 1984.
Around the Day in Eighty Worlds, trans. Thomas Christiansen. Berkeley, Calif.: North Point, 1986.

Part IV

Erich Heller: Though Heller has written studies of individual writers—*Franz Kafka* and *Thomas Mann: The Ironic German*—he is best known for his exploratory essays. Four collections—*The Artist's Journey into the Interior, The Disinherited Mind, In the Age of Prose,* and *The Poet's Self and the Poem*—provide a comprehensive record of Heller's engagement with the important figures in German literature and philosophy.

First U.S. Editions

The Disinherited Mind. Cleveland: Meridian, 1952.
Thomas Mann: The Ironic German. Boston: Little, Brown, 1958.
The Artist's Journey into the Interior. New York: Random House, 1965.
Franz Kafka. New York: Viking, 1974.

The Poet's Self and the Poem. Atlantic Highlands, N.J.: Athlone, 1976.
In the Age of Prose. New York: Cambridge University Press, 1984.

Walter Benjamin: We are presently in the midst of a "Benjamin boom." New studies and exegeses are appearing monthly; translators are at work in libraries all over the world. By the end of the century, readers will probably have access to every stray notation. Perhaps then the larger picture will emerge: of a critic and thinker who strove to fuse philosophical, political, literary, and theological perspectives in order to realize a totalized understanding of his age. Benjamin's unfinished magnum opus, his *Paris, Capital of the Nineteenth Century*—known also as the "Arcades" project—has not yet been translated. The general reader should begin with the essays collected in *Illuminations* and *Reflections* before moving on to *The Origin of German Tragic Drama* and the recently issued *Moscow Diary.*

First U.S. Editions

Illuminations, trans. Harry Zohn. New York: Harcourt, Brace & World, 1968.
The Origin of German Tragic Drama, trans. John Osborne. New York: NLB, 1978.
Reflections, trans. Edmund Jephcott. New York: Harcourt Brace Jovanovich, 1978.
Moscow Diary, trans. Richard Sieburth. Cambridge, Mass.: Harvard University Press, 1986.

Cyril Connolly: Peter Quennell has edited a *Selected Essays of Cyril Connolly.* It does not, alas, convey the full flavor of the man. I recommend beginning with *The Unquiet Grave* (originally published under the pseudonym Palinurus), an idiosyncratic mélange of reflections, quotations, and self-excoriations. If the prose appeals, then continue with *Enemies of Promise,* which contains a wonderful evocation of Connolly's young manhood, and *The Evening Colonnade.* Connolly's novel, *The Rock Pool,* is slight. The recent *Cyril Connolly: Journal and a Memoir* is cluttered with obscure private references and will defeat most readers.

First U.S. Editions

The Rock Pool. New York: Scribners, 1936.
Enemies of Promise. Boston: Little, Brown, 1939.
The Unquiet Grave. New York: Harper Brothers, 1945.
The Condemned Playground. New York: Macmillan, 1946.
Previous Convictions. New York: Harper & Row, 1963.
The Evening Colonnade. Harcourt Brace Jovanovich, 1975.
Selected Essays of Cyril Connolly, ed. Peter Quennell. New York: Persea, 1983.
Cyril Connolly: Journal and a Memoir, ed. David Pryce-Jones. New York: Ticknor & Fields, 1984.

George Steiner: One of Steiner's favorite words is "polymath"—perhaps because it captures his own aspirations so perfectly. A list of his published books, most of them in print(!), all of them provocative, will give some sense of his range.

First U.S. Editions
Tolstoy or Dostoevsky. New York: Knopf, 1959.
The Death of Tragedy. New York: Oxford University Press, 1961.
Anno Domini. New York: Atheneum, 1964.
Language and Silence. New York: Atheneum, 1967.
Extraterritorial. New York: Atheneum, 1971.
In Bluebeard's Castle. New York: Yale University Press, 1971.
After Babel. New York: Oxford University Press, 1975.
Martin Heidegger. New York: Viking, 1978.
On Difficulty. New York: Oxford University Press, 1978.
The Portage to San Christobal of A.H. New York: Simon & Schuster, 1981.
George Steiner: A Reader. New York: Oxford University Press, 1984.
Antigones. New York: Oxford University Press, 1985.

Eugenio Montale: Montale was one of our century's sovereign poets and his compressed allusiveness has been captured in fine translations by Jonathan Galassi, William Arrowsmith, Charles Wright, and others. His virtues as a prose stylist can be discovered in his compendious *The Second Life of Art,* as well as in *Poet in Our Time,* a collage of short meditative pieces, and *The Butterfly of Dinard,* a sequence of fanciful sketches and portraits.

First U.S. Editions
The Butterfly of Dinard, trans. G. Singh. Lexington, Ky.: University Press of Kentucky, 1971.
Poet in Our Time, trans. Alastair Hamilton. New York: Urizen, 1976.
The Second Life of Art, trans. Jonathan Galassi. New York: Ecco, 1982.

Roger Shattuck: Shattuck's interests are resolutely—but never confiningly—French. He has published books on Proust—*Marcel Proust* and *Proust's Binoculars*—as well as *Forbidden Experiment: The Story of the Wild Boy of Aveyron,* and the wide-ranging excursions of *The Banquet Years* and *The Innocent Eye*.

First U.S. Editions
Proust's Binoculars. New York: Knopf, 1963.
The Banquet Years. New York: Random House, 1968.
Forbidden Experiment: The Story of the Wild Boy of Aveyron. New York: Farrar, Straus & Giroux, 1980.
Marcel Proust. Princeton, N.J.: Princeton University Press, 1982.
The Innocent Eye. New York: Farrar, Straus & Giroux, 1984.

Index

About the Author

Sven Birkerts attended Cranbrook School and the University of Michigan. After receiving his B.A. in 1973, he worked for many years as a bookseller in Ann Arbor, Michigan, and Cambridge, Massachusetts. His essays and reviews have appeared in *The New York Review of Books, The Nation, Partisan Review, Ploughshares, Harper's, The Atlantic, The New Republic,* and other publications. He won the 1986 National Book Critics Circle Citation for Excellence in Reviewing. Mr. Birkerts teaches expository writing at Harvard University. He lives in Arlington, Massachusetts, with his wife, Lynn, and their child, Mara.

Nonpareil Books

NONFICTION

Daniel C. Beard
The American Boy's Handybook
448 pages, $10.95

Lina & Adelia Beard
The American Girl's Handybook
480 pages, $10.95

Brendan Behan
Borstal Boy
384 pages, $10.95

Sven Birkerts
An Artificial Wilderness
429 pages, $14.95

Warren Chappell
A Short History of the Printed Word
288 pages, $10.95

Sidney Cox
Indirections
160 pages, $6.95

Benedetto Croce
Aesthetic
544 pages, $12.95

Will Cuppy
The Decline & Fall of Practically Everybody
256 pages, $9.95

Kennedy Fraser
The Fashionable Mind: Reflections on Fashion
320 pages, $10.95

William H. Gass
Fiction & the Figures of Life
304 pages, $11.95

The World Within the Word
352 pages, $11.95

Donald Hall
String Too Short To Be Saved
176 pages, $8.95

Robert Harbison
Eccentric Spaces
192 pages, $10.95

Elizabeth Hardwick
Selected Letters of William James
304 pages, $8.95

Clare Leighton
Where Land Meets Sea: The Enduring Cape Cod
208 pages, $8.95

John Nance
The Gentle Tasaday
480 pages, $12.95

William Maxwell
Ancestors
320 pages, $9.95

Iris Origo
The Merchant of Prato: Francesco di Marco Datini, 1335-1410
448 pages, $14.95

Donald Culross Peattie
An Almanac for Moderns
416 pages, $8.95

George Seferis
Poems
128 pages, $5.95

Maida Silverman
A City Herbal
192 pages, $12.95

Francis Steegmuller
Cocteau
608 pages, $15.95

Claire Sterling
The Masaryk Case: The Murder of Democracy in Czechoslovakia
380 pages, $9.95

Nonpareil Books returns to print books acknowledged as classics. All *Nonpareils* are printed on acid-free paper and produced to the highest standards. They are permanent softcover books designed for use and made to last. For a complete list, please write to David R. Godine, Publisher.

David R. Godine, Publisher
300 Massachusetts Avenue
Boston, Mass. 02115